Texts in Context

Texts in Context

Traditional Hermeneutics in South Asia

Edited by
Jeffrey R. Timm

State University of New York Press

Published by
State University of New York Press, Albany

Printed in the United States of America

For information, address State University of New York
Press, State University Plaza, Albany, N.Y., 12246

Production by Dana Foote
Marketing by Bernadette LaManna

Library of Congress Cataloging in Publication Data

Texts in Context : Traditional Hermeneutics in South Asia / edited by
Jeffrey R. Timm.
p. cm.
Includes bibliographical references.
Includes index.
ISBN 0-7914-0795-0 (alk. paper).—ISBN 0-7914-0796-9 (pbk. : alk. paper)
1. Sacred books—History and criticism. 2. Hermeneutics—Religious aspects. 3. South Asia—Religion. 4. Hinduism—Sacred books—Hermeneutics—History. I. Timm, Jeffrey Richard.
BL71.T48 1992
291.8'2—dc20 90-49428
CIP

10 9 8 7 6 5 4 3 2 1

To Kanchan Mani
and Radha Kahini

Contents

Part II. Traditional Hermeneutics in Other South Asian Religions

Text Abbreviations

AUŚ	Śaṅkara's commentary on the *Aitareya Upaniṣad*
BGR	*Gītābhāṣya*, Rāmānuja's commentary on the *Bhagavad Gītā*
BGŚ	Śaṅkara's commentary on the *Bhagavad Gītā*
BSM	Madhva's commentary on the *Brahma Sūtras*
BSR	*Śrībhāṣya*, Rāmānuja's commentary on the *Brahma Sūtras*
BSŚ	Śaṅkara's commentary on the *Brahma Sūtras*
BTN	*Bhāgavata Tātparya Nirṇaya* of Madhva
BUŚ	Śaṅkara's commentary on the *Bṛhadāraṇyaka Upaniṣad*
CU	*Chāndogya Upaniṣad*
MP	*Mumukṣuppaṭi* of of Piḷḷai Lokācārya, with Maṇavāḷamāmuni's commentary
MU	*Muṇḍaka Upaniṣad*
PMS	*Pūrva Mīmāṁsā Sūtras* of Jaimini
RTS	*Śrīmād Rahasyatrayasāra* of Vedānta Deśika
SMV	*Sumadhvavijaya* of Nārāyaṇa Paṇḍitācārya
ŚVB	*Śrīvācana Bhūṣaṇa* of Piḷḷai Lokācārya, with Maṇavāḷamāmuni's commentary.
TVD	*Tattvārthadīpanibandha* of Vallabha
TVM	*Tiruvāymoḻi*
UMS	*Uttara Mīmāṁsā Sūtras*
VP	*Vākyapadīya* of Bhartṛhari

One

Introduction

Texts in Context

Jeffrey R. Timm

No one today would dismiss the importance of "scripture" as a significant category of understanding in the study of world religions. Exactly what is meant by "scripture," however, is a serious question—not just what should count from any specific theological perspective (although that too is a serious question, as we shall see), but rather what is meant from the standpoint of the academic study of religion. This question is a major subtext of the present volume, which brings together a wide range of scholarship on the diverse sacred-text traditions in South Asia.

By way of introduction two matters must be considered. The first part of this introduction places the present work in context, with a brief overview of recent Western scholarship on "sacred text" in the religious traditions of South Asia. The second part reviews the contents of the volume, chapter by chapter, touching on the major themes considered and approaches taken. Looking carefully at individual instances of hermeneutical reflection by native exegetes, this volume reveals a complex diversity of text traditions: how texts are utilized and understood in their individual hermeneutical contexts. Through this diversity each chapter raises particular issues that resonate elsewhere in the volume. These "harmonic resonances" sounding within and across traditions indicate elaborate, multidimensional family resemblances, to use Wittgenstein's expression, rather than any set of universal characteristics. Thus, the present volume stands as a challenge to any approach to scripture in South Asian traditions asserting a static definition or valorizing any single methodological approach.

Although contemporary scholars have made great progress in learning to recognize and avoid unhelpful reductionisms, the crucial task of assessing the authenticity of inherited presuppositions remains an ongoing concern. What are these inherited presuppositions? A full retrospective analysis is hardly possible in this brief introduction. Suffice it to say that the Western view of sacred text in South Asia was strongly influenced by early scholars like F. Max Müller and Georg Bühler, whose translation and editorial work purported to identify the "Bibles" of the Indian traditions. The presumption at work here was that the Other is like us; the major sacred text of each tradition, once identified, was supposed to function in much the same way the Bible functioned for Christianity (usually understood as European Protestantism). The use of the scholarly category "scripture" in this manner promoted a false essentialism that was unable to stand the test of time. The fact is that the practitioners of South Asian traditions did not, by and large, understand their holy books in a manner analogous to the Christian West, so it is not surprising that this approach to scripture failed to do justice to the text traditions it claimed to reveal.

A corrective to this early approach to Asian sacred text traditions that gained currency after the Second World War emphasized what we might call "basic" religion. Stationing themselves within the discipline of the "history of religions," scholars dissatisfied with the limitations of the "textual" approach to the study of religion shifted the primary focus onto the so-called primitive or archaic forms of religious expression, downplaying the importance of the scriptural and commentarial traditions in favor of uncovering foundational categories and motifs through which they hoped to reveal the universal patterns and qualities of human religious expression. Although distancing itself from the false essentialism of earlier understandings of scripture, this history-of-religions approach often led to a different problem: the procrustean marginalization of scripture and commentary traditions. South Asian religious traditions play host to a wide range of sacred-text genres, utilizing and understanding these text traditions in a variety of ways central to the tradition's self-understanding. How is this textual diversity to be understood? What is the most productive and authentic approach to the dynamic complexity of South Asian sacred text traditions that emerged over four millennia? Today some scholars are grappling with this question from a number of perspectives.

Miriam Levering is a good example of such a scholar. In the introduction of her book *Rethinking Scripture: Essays from a Comparative Perspective*, she writes, "Clearly there are problems with defining the category [scripture or sacred text] by trying to arrive at lists of characterizing features. If instead we attend principally to the dynamics of the relations that people have had with texts, their ways of receiving texts in the context of their religious projects, then the whole matter becomes more hopeful" (p. 11). Levering's work follows this insight in the search for a generic concept of scripture, identifying dynamic polarities and relationships rather than seeking static universal characteristics. The present volume both supports and challenges the major contribution made by *Rethinking Scripture*. Levering's emphasis on scriptural dynamism and relationship is supported throughout the present work; the search for a "generic definition" is not. The approach of traditional hermeneutics would be jeopardized by an *a priori*, wholesale adoption of any framework, despite its dynamism. My overarching concern in the present work is not to develop a generic concept of scripture; rather, it is to allow a multiplicity of hermeneutical traditions to emerge, to enable the voice of the Other—the native exegete—to be heard.

The inspiration for this concern finds expression in a seminal work read by each author involved in this project, and quoted by many: Jonathan Z. Smith's essay, "Sacred Persistence: Toward a Redescription of Canon," in his book *Imagining Religion: From Babylon to Jonestown* (1982). Like Levering, Smith suggests that a history of religions that is exclusively preoccupied with the primitive or the archaic is limited. He claims that such preoccupation has "given the historians of religion license for ultimate acts of imperialism, the removal of all rights to interpretation from the native, and the arrogation of all such rights to themselves" (p. 43). Smith calls for the reassessment of such an approach and "look[s] forward to the day when courses and monographs will exist in both comparative exegesis and comparative theology, comparing not so much conclusions as strategies through which the [native] exegete seeks to interpret and translate his received tradition to his contemporaries" (p. 52). It is this inquiry into the native exegete's strategies of interpretation and translation that I am calling "traditional hermeneutics."

Scholarship over the past ten years has laid the foundation for a serious attempt to apply Smith's program and formulate a meaningful, scholarly presentation of traditional hermeneutical problems and strategies. The last decade has seen a real shift in thinking about the "the holy book." In 1979 the Berkeley Religious Studies Series published Wendy Doniger O'Flaherty's volume *The Critical Study of Sacred Texts.* This volume focuses heavily on Christian text critical work, but it also includes contributions by Roger Corless and Lewis Lancaster, who consider texts in the Asian context by challenging certain presuppositions about the meaning and contour of text traditions in Indian religions. In her introduction to the volume O'Flaherty describes the overarching concern like this: "For surely the ultimate task of the true textual critic is the interpretation and understanding of the *text in its context*" (p. xiii, italics mine). She goes on to describe this task as a "chicken-and-egg" enterprise, her way of referring to the difficulty of entering the hermeneutical circle of an alien text tradition. Such entry is the explicit goal of the present study in traditional hermeneutics.

The well-known work of Wilfred Cantwell Smith has had a profound impact on the study of religion. During the last ten years he has become increasingly concerned with the understandings of scripture in world religions. (I understand he will soon publish a book on this topic.) As director of two related NEH Humanities Summer Seminars, one in 1982 on "Scripture as Form and Content," he has facilitated much scholarly thinking on this topic. Levering's volume is a direct product of the Smith seminars, as is the 1984 publication of Thomas B. Coburn's " 'Scripture' in India: Towards a Typology of the Word in Hindu Life" in the *Journal of the American Academy of Religion.* Coburn offers important insight into fundamental questions of orality and canonicity in the Hindu context, providing the most valuable typology of Hindu sacred texts presently available, but his own final observations suggest the serious limitation of a typological approach. The very concept of "Hindu" is late, and its use can support a misleading reification. As Coburn points out, "The development of the narrowly 'Hindu' phenomena of scripture has often been intertwined with non-'Hindu' matters" (p. 454). It is just this intertwining (further vitiating any straightforward typology) that the present volume seeks to reveal, even while supporting much of what Coburn says about the fluidity of canon and the primacy of the oral.

The centrality of oral tradition, of recitation in its performative, liturgical, ritual, and aesthetic dimensions, cannot be overemphasized in the context of South Asian religion. The central role played by the oral text has been clearly demonstrated in William A. Graham's *Beyond the Written Word: Oral Aspects of Scripture in the History of Religion.* In a brief chapter called "Scripture as Spoken Word: The Indian Paradigm," Graham covers some significant ground by focusing on Vedic and non-Vedic recitation, the latter illustrated by a recent study done on the *mānasa* recitation tradition of modern North Central India. The central role of oral texts in Indian religion is not exhausted by Graham's succinct treatment; several authors in the present volume build upon Graham's seminal work.

Finally, an important contribution to the fuller understanding of scripture in South Asia is found in Harold Coward's *Sacred Word and Sacred Text.* Coward devotes one chapter each to Hinduism, Sikhism, and Buddhism, giving a general overview of these religious traditions through a sustained discussion of oral and written texts, concepts of language, and canonicity. As an introduction to the scriptural traditions of South Asia, these chapters are exemplary in their concern to recognize the real differences that exist between South Asian and Judeo-Christian religious traditions. Coward is careful to qualify all of his generalizations, but as the scholarship of the present volume indicates, even the most sensitive generalizations tend to valorize particular perspectives or hermeneutical moments from within the tradition. (Compare, for example, Coward's observation that in Hinduism "once the full enlightenment experience is achieved, the 'ladder of scripture' is no longer needed" (p. 106) with Vallabha's concept of scriptural realism examined in chapter 8 of the present volume.)

The most recent scholarship on scripture, coupled with J. Z. Smith's urgings to listen to the voice of native exegetical traditions, has shaped each chapter in the present volume. In one manner or another, from the standpoint of varied interests and diverse methodological sensibilities, each author is committed to the the view that traditional hermeneutical perspectives may no longer be ignored if something meaningful is to be said about sacred texts in the South Asian context.

Each contributor is a scholar of religion whose linguistic training and area of current research provides direct access to the scriptural and commentarial traditions of at least one South Asian religion. And, crucial to the concept of this volume, each has explored the special ways in which particular traditions delineate, think about, understand, and utilize their sacred texts. In an important sense each chapter may be viewed as a collaboration with the native exegete, giving voice to our traditional counterparts who themselves engaged in a self-conscious reflection on the sacred words of their own text traditions.

David Carpenter's "Bhartṛhari and the Veda" (chapter 2) begins this study. The central question posed by Carpenter is whether Bhartṛhari understands the *Veda* as a "canonical text." Contrasting this fifth-century grammarian's view of the *Veda* with Western notions of religious canon and text, Carpenter shows that the general Western presuppositions about the nature and goal of a religious hermeneutical enterprise are incommensurable with Bhartṛhari's understanding of the *Veda*. Carpenter writes, "The Veda is understood to be a manifestation of the ultimate Word (*śabda*) that underlies phenomenal existence . . . [and] is more important for what it *is* and what it *does* than for what it 'means' " (pp. 19–20). Carpenter links the dynamic, nonreferential character of the *Veda* directly to Bhartṛhari's philosophy of language, which asserts the ontological primacy of the "verb" over "substance" that has been central in the Western subject-predicate analysis of language. Hermeneutics, for Bhartṛhari, at least in the context of the *Veda*, has little to do with elucidating the meaning of canonical texts for a religious community.

The next two chapters examine the traditional hermeneutics of Śaṅkara (eighth? century C.E.), the founder of one of the most influential schools of Vedānta. Anantanand Rambachan, in his contribution (chapter 3), unfolds the significance of the *Upaniṣads* according to Śaṅkara, situating Advaita Vedānta's hermeneutics in the context of Pūrva Mīmāṁsā's marginalization of the *Upaniṣads* as ancillary to the *Vedas* and not independently authoritative. Śaṅkara rejected this marginalization by presenting philosophical arguments that purport to show the *Upaniṣads* as the logical, adequate, and productive source of knowledge about ultimate reality (*brahman*). In his examination Rambachan shows that philosophical arguments about the nature of *brahman*—often extracted from the hermeneutical context by Western scholars—are employed to help establish the claim of independent Upaniṣadic scriptural authority contra Pūrva Mīmāṁsā.

Taking a slightly different tack to establish the mutuality of philosophical and exegetical concerns in Advaita Vedānta, Francis Clooney (chapter 4) exposes a foundation for this mutuality by focusing on terminology found in the *Brahma Sūtra* differentiating two major approaches to Upaniṣadic texts. The first is ''coherence'' (*samanvaya*), concerned to show that all contested Upaniṣadic passages support the Vedāntic reading of the *Upaniṣads'* overall theme; the second is ''combination'' (*upasaṁhāra*), concerned with the appropriate handling of intratextual multiplicity in the context of meditation. These two approaches to the *Upaniṣads* serve as complementary foci for understanding Advaita Vedānta as an interplay of philosophy and exegesis. According to Clooney, ''by *samanvaya*, the multiplicity of texts is understood to point to a single topic, *brahman;* by *upasaṁhāra*, it is understood how that single topic, *brahman*, can be known through . . . meditation on the multiple texts'' (p. 55). Clooney goes on to show how an increasing reliance on the ritual/exegetical principles of Pūrva Mīmāṁsā (notwithstanding the serious disagreement regarding the authority of the *Upaniṣads* described by Rambachan) inexorably weds Advaita Vedānta's philosophical program with its scriptural context.

The next four chapters continue an investigation of traditional hermeneutics in Vedānta, shifting from Advaita to the devotional schools. Chapters by Patricia Mumme and Vasudha Narayanan provide two very different windows to Śrīvaiṣṇavism, the community associated with Rāmānuja (eleventh century C.E.). For her contribution, Mumme (chapter 5) focuses on the exegesis of a single half-verse, *Bhagavad Gītā* 18:66a, which fueled a major schism of the Śrīvaiṣṇava community. The central issue at stake is whether this scripture enjoins surrender (taking refuge in the Lord) as an independent and superior means of liberation. If so, the established path of devotion is relegated to a provisional and ultimately illusory status to be abandoned with the advent of true surrender. Mumme compares this hermeneutical strategy with the Advaita Vedānta depreciation of devotionalism as provisional to the path of knowledge, and argues that Vedānta Deśika, a major Śrīvaiṣṇava thinker, rejected this understanding in favor of a contextual approach that he believed protected Śrīvaiṣṇavism from the Advaita-like hermeneutic of his rivals.

Considering a completely different dimension of the Śrīvaiṣṇava hermeneutic, Narayanan (chapter 6) examines the development of the oral and written commentarial tradition based on the *Tiruvāymoḻi*, a Tamil poem written by Nammāḻvār, a poet-saint of the ninth century C.E. Piḷḷān's commentary on the *Tiruvāymoḻi* written in the eleventh century—the first commentary ever composed on a vernacular religious work—utilized a hybrid language that blended Sanskrit with Tamil. This commentarial medium itself stood as a challenge to Sanskritic exclusivity. From the start, commentaries on the *Tiruvāymoḻi* provided an avenue for innovation, challenging social and religious norms through both the form and the content of the commentarial genre. In her examination of this commentarial tradition, Narayanan reveals that the conscious decision to *write* commentaries must be understood in the context of a soteriological valorization of oral commentary, the salvific efficacy grounded in a process of transmitting sacred teachings orally from teacher to disciple that continues up to today.

The basis of commentarial authority is an issue taken up in Daniel Sheridan's chapter on Madhva's interpretation of scripture (chapter 7). By considering the contemporaneous biography of Madhva (thirteenth century C.E.), the *Sumadhvavijaya* written by Paṇḍitācārya, alongside Madhva's own writings, Sheridan argues that genealogical claims, such as the presentation of Madhva as the incarnation (*avatārā*) of Vāyu, should not be dismissed as "dispensable, mythological overlay." Coming to grips with the interpretation of sacred texts, as well as the composition of commentaries, may not be detached from the biographical and theological context that explains the commentator's interpretive authority. In the case of Madhva this authority stems from his encounter with Vyāsa, the legendary seer who is responsible for the compilation of the Vedas, as well as the composition of the *Mahāpurāṇas* and other foundational religious texts. According to the *Sumadhvavijaya*, Vyāsa is Madhva's guru and Vyāsa is the *avatar* of Viṣṇu. These claims are crucial for establishing Madhva's preeminent hermeneutical authority. Understanding the centrality of the Vyāsa–Madhva relationship enables us, according to Sheridan, to recognize Madhva not as a philosopher burdened with mythic accretions, but as a theological interpreter and commentator whose mind—according to the tradition's self-understanding—is informed directly by the mind of God.

In the final consideration of the Vedāntic context, Jeffrey Timm (chapter 8) examines Vallabha's view of scripture. Vallabha, the fifteenth-century founder of an influential form of devotional Vedānta in North India, engaged in sophisticated arguments about the nature of scripture while maintaining the absolute primacy of scriptural revelation over all other means to knowledge. His hermeneutic melds together a fundamentalism that serves to exclude views that conflict with his designated canon, with a contextualism that affirms God as the author of all teachings. The apparent contradiction between the fundamentalist and contextualist approaches is resolved through a consideration of the ontological foundation of his theology, which explores the "logic" of his hermeneutic of scriptural realism.

Bringing the first part of this volume to a close is Madhu Wangu's consideration (chapter 9) of the social and political forces shaping the emergence of a new text tradition in Jammu-Kashmir during the nineteenth century. Dogri Rajputs, the rulers of Jammu for centuries, extended their control over Kashmir in the mid-nineteenth century, bringing political and social stability to a previously tempestuous region. The political integration of two states that were religiously, ethnically, and geographically distinct was facilitated by the emergence of new text traditions that reflected a deliberate infusion of the Dogri Rāma cult into the pantheon of Kashmiri Tantric Śaiva deities. Illustrating the way scriptural text traditions emerge and evolve in response to unique patterns of political and social circumstances, Wangu describes and analyzes the *Śrī Śrī Mahārajñī Pradhurbhāva* written to extol the splendor of the Kashmiri goddess Khīr Bhavāni, to establish Khīr Bhavāni's association with Rāma, and to influence the political and religious loyalties of the Dogri rulers' Śaivite subjects.

Shifting the focus to the non-Hindu South Asian religions, the second part of this volume includes five chapters considering traditional hermeneutics in Jain, Buddhist, Islamic, and Sikh traditions. John Cort's examination (chapter 10) of Jain scripture in a performative context begins by developing a distinction between two notions of canon, which he calls "Canon-near" and "Canon-far," interpretive categories distinguishing the locus of primacy and authority in a given scripture. By presenting three instances of contemporary Jain understandings of their own scripture—recitation of the *Kalpa Sūtra,* "scripture worship," and the relative-authority of religious texts—Cort exposes the nineteenth-century error of first-generation Western scholars of Jainism who assumed the preeminence of Biblical-style canon (Canon-far) and seized on a single fixed Jain canon in the form of the forty-five Āgamas. Instead, Cort reveals the existence of multiple, contextual interpretations of scripture and canon in the contemporary Jain understanding.

Frank Hoffman's contribution (chapter 11) to this volume considers the implications of recognizing the importance of the oral "text" in the Pali Buddhist tradition. Deviating somewhat from the program of presenting a moment of traditional hermeneutics, Hoffman reviews some of the latest scholarship on orality in general and on Buddhist hermeneutics in particular. As a philosopher, he is keen to maintain the centrality of a contemporary philosophical engagement with Buddhism, yet his analysis of the written text as only one sort of text breaks down a pervasive and misleading dichotomy between elite (textual) traditions and popular (oral) traditions operating in much contemporary Western scholarship.

The second Buddhist contribution is José Cabezón's study (chapter 12) of Vasubandhu's text, the *Vyākhyāyukti*, a self-conscious effort to justify the authenticity of early Mahāyāna Sūtras. When these Sūtras first appeared, they were not accepted by many in the Buddhist community; hence, commentators like Vasubandhu developed various hermeneutical strategies in an effort to authenticate these scriptures. In mapping out the various forms that these arguments for authenticity took, Cabezón reveals Vasubandhu's concept of scripture, canon, and authenticity. This Mahāyāna program of defending scripture against outside criticism is rooted in a rejection of the opponent's historical and philological criteria in the determination of canonicity. In place of such criteria Vasubandhu asserts a philosophical principle, "accordance with reality," arguing for an broader intercanonical definition of the Buddha's word that allows for the authenticity of Mahāyāna Sūtras.

Nikky Singh's contribution on Sikh hermeneutics (chapter 13) examines the poetry of Bhāī Vīr Singh, the nineteenth-century interpreter of the *Gurū Granth*. In this chapter Bhāī Vīr Singh's poetic exegesis of Sikhism's most important scripture is examined in the context of the intellectual and cultural ferment of the day.

Finally shifting to the context of Islam in South Asia, Carl Ernst (chapter 14) considers the emergence of a new literary form within the Chishtī Sufi community in the fourteenth century. This new genre, called *malfūẓāt*, was the recording of the oral teachings of the Sufi master. Ernst's detailed description offers insight into the process of a developing text tradition that begins with poet Amīr Ḥasan Sijzī Dihlawī's *Morals of the Heart*, an account of the oral teachings of his master. The immediate popularity of this work as an exposition of Sufi teachings led to a number of imitative efforts, and eventually to the establishment of a *malfūẓat* genre and rivalries among texts for canonical status in the community. In his analysis, Ernst takes up the question of the "inauthentic" *malfūẓat*, texts shown to be fabrications on the basis of Western textual criticism, but that have been generally accepted by the Chishtī community as authentic.

By now the perceptive reader will have recognized that this volume, or the approach of traditional hermeneutics itself for that matter, is not about to neatly synthesize such diversity to provide "useful" definitions of scripture, sacred text, canon, orality, and so on. Each contributor to this volume provides a window onto how texts are used and understood in the context of a single South Asian religious community. Unlike the blind men in the parable about the elephant, even after sharing our individual discoveries we may be no closer to answering, once and for all, the question, "What is scripture *really*?" For this is the wrong question to ask. According to the insight of the traditional hermeneutical approach, any conclusion of this order is more or less problematic, at worst asserting a false essentialism and at best suggesting a typology of universal characteristics that, when misused, becomes a procrustean bed.

Better at this point, at least, take seriously the advice of Wittgenstein that we stop, look, and see. And instead of assuming that there must be something common, we see a whole series of intricate relationships, complex interconnections, similarities of detail and approach between diverse traditions, disparate avenues taken by traditions claiming the same foundational texts, a continuous overlapping and crisscrossing of shared features along with simultaneous discontinuities. This, of course, does not mean that we are limited to nothing more than descriptive analysis, unable to make judgments or come to theoretical conclusions, but it does mean that as we look toward the Other, in our effort to understand, our conclusions must be provisional, our methodological approaches tentative. Anything less is a return to the often unselfconscious exegetical imperialism that has at times marred Western scholarship on South Asian religious traditions.

This book attempts to embody a sensitivity to the Other, giving voice to the Other through representative, in-depth analysis of hermeneutical moments from India's major religious traditions. Such a program depends on a shared belief that much more significant hermeneutical insights may emerge from the traditions themselves than from an appeal to some unifying, extra-traditional, theoretical construct. For this reason the volume repudiates exegetical imperialism and its implicit judgment that traditional exegetes are capable of little more than naive, superficial, or formulaic encounters with their own text traditions. Quite the contrary is the case, as the following chapters will show. Traditional thinkers encountered scripture in a sophisticated process of understanding their inherited text tradition, grappling with issues of canon and creativity, concerns with text and meaning, issues familiar to students of contemporary Western hermeneutics.

Finally a note on method. Approaching the sacred texts of South Asian religions with a sensitivity to traditional hermeneutics is, by necessity, polymethodic. This methodological diversity mirrors the complexity of sacred texts, a category that is fantastically fluid. In each essay the respective author's empathy for the traditional understanding of the text acts as a tether allowing freedom to consider the historical, theological, exegetical, and sociopolitical vistas of South Asia's diverse religious landscape without arrogation of all interpretive authority. Connecting sacred texts with the panorama of religious projects supports Levering's claim that any generalization about scripture—when it is defined as a fixed body of written material carrying normative, prescriptive status for a given religious community—is woefully inadequate. This study of traditional hermeneutics in South Asia reveals a formulation and interpretation of text traditions driven by the entire spectrum of human concerns: soteriological, theological, philosophical, sociopolitical, liturgical, ethical, legal, ontological, epistemological, aesthetic, and nearly every combination thereof.

In a volume of this sort—a collaboration in which a variety of languages play such a central role—the question of consistency poses some difficult choices. In some matters I have chosen to exercise an editor's prerogative, making changes contributing to uniformity and consistency. In no instance did I make such changes at the expense of the authors' meaning, I hope.

To the degree possible I have tried to maintain consistency in the use of italics. This is difficult in the case of the "holy book," which is typically not graced with italics according to current style sheets. Transposing this rule of thumb to the diversity of text traditions and the various valorizations and hierarchies of scripture did not make much sense. In fact, indiscriminately applying such a rule of style may even reflect the sort of false essentialism that this volume is keen to avoid. For the most part I have simply followed the individual author's preferences when it seemed appropriate to override my decision to italicize the titles of all texts. For example, in Carpenter's chapter we see Veda, not *Veda*. This should in no way be taken to imply that the Veda is a sacred text equivalent to the Bible, while the *Bhagavad Gītā*, because it is italicized, is not. Another issue concerns the pluralization of foreign terms (for example, *dharmas, ācāryas*, and so forth). Although technically incorrect, this manner of pluralization seems preferable to any alternative. Finally, the question of transliteration and diacritical marks looms large in a volume of this sort. Here the guideline suggested to authors was this: When in doubt, provide the transliteration and diacritical marks according to the appropriate convention. Since there is no common guide applicable to the diversity of languages employed herein, I left all matters of transliteration up to the individual authors, who are the experts in their respective language areas. The possible inconsistencies between chapters that might result from such an approach seemed preferable to any sort of editorial control I could imagine.

This book is a collaborative effort that has taken shape over two years through panel presentations at the annual meetings of the Association of Asian Studies (1988) and the American Academy of Religion (1988 and 1989), and during a 1988 Harvard NEH Summer Institute, "Teaching Comparative Religion." Many individuals have contributed in different ways, too many to properly acknowledge individually. My job as editor was greatly facilitated by the intelligence and cheerful diligence of each contributor. Two authors require special recognition: José Cabezón, who helped me to formulate the first AAS panel that led to the conception of this book, and Patricia Mumme, who graciously invited me to join a 1988 AAR panel, "Text and Commentary," she had organized. Four of the five papers presented at that latter panel find their latest incarnations in this volume.

Editing a volume of this sort for the first time was a learning experience. Miriam Levering's advice saved me from some early false steps. John Carman was one of the very first people I spoke to about my idea to formulate this book; his words of encouragement along the way did more to carry things forward than he probably imagines. And a special recognition is due Harold Coward, whose contribution to this volume in the form of encouragement and intelligent criticism was invaluable.

Thanks to Francis Kollett and his staff at the Wheaton College Academic Computing Center, the burden of working with a plurality of computer disks was greatly reduced. Typing was provided with accuracy and alacrity by faculty secretary Kathleen Francis; student assistants Elizabeth McGown and Terry Driscoll aided in proofreading.

Finally, I would be remiss if I did not recognize the support of my family, who put up with my absence from home on many days when I should have been away from my desk. Without their love and understanding, this volume would not have taken shape.

References

Coburn, Thomas B.
1984 " 'Scripture' in India: Towards a Typology of the Word in Hindu Life," *Journal of the American Academy of Religion*, 52(3): 435–459.

Coward, Harold
1988 *Sacred Word and Sacred Text: Scripture in World Religions.* Maryknoll, New York: Orbis Books.

Graham, William A.
1987 *Beyond the Written Word: Oral Aspects of Scripture in the History of Religion.* Cambridge: Cambridge University Press.

Levering, Miriam
1989 *Rethinking Scripture: Essays from a Comparative Perspective*. Albany: State University of New York Press.

O'Flaherty, Wendy Doniger
1979 *The Critical Study of Sacred Texts.* Berkeley Religious Studies Series. Berkeley: The Graduate Theological Union.

Smith, Jonathan Z.
1982 *Imagining Religion: From Babylon to Jonestown.* Chicago: The University of Chicago Press.

PART I

Traditional Hermeneutics in "Hinduism"

Two

Bhartṛhari and the Veda

David Carpenter

Introduction

The subject of the present volume of essays is hermeneutics, or more precisely hermeneutics as it has been practiced by scholars belonging to the religious traditions of South Asia. This chapter will consider the thought of the Indian grammarian, and philosopher of language, Bhartṛhari (fifth century C.E.), who may be taken as a representative of the Brahmanical religious tradition that traced its origins back to the Vedas, the "sacred scriptures" of ancient India.[1] It might seem reasonable, therefore, to present what follows as a study of Bhartṛhari's hermeneutics as it applied to the canonical scriptures of ancient India. But is such an approach valid? Is it safe to assume that as a leading intellectual of his day, and as a representative of a normative religious tradition, Bhartṛhari in fact engaged in "hermeneutics" as we understand the term? Are we to assume that he applied his hermeneutics to a textual corpus that he considered to be "canonical"? Did Bhartṛhari in fact correspond to the traditional Western scriptural scholar who sought to plumb the depths of the *Heilige Schrift*?

These are important and potentially fruitful questions. They are particularly appropriate questions at the beginning of a volume that examines the hermeneutical categories of religious traditions of South Asia. Although one may find among these traditions examples of textual exegesis that seem familiar by Western standards, it is perhaps good to begin with a word of caution: it is not at all apparent that the canons of interpretation are everywhere the same. It is indeed possible that the conceptual baggage that Western scholars bring to the study of those whom they take to be their counterparts in South Asia includes unexamined assumptions about the nature of the hermeneutical task that should themselves become the subject of critical scrutiny. Bhartṛhari's "interpretation" of the Veda provides an interesting case in point. Although he was capable of commenting on the texts of his own grammatical tradition in ways that seem familiar to us, his approach to the Veda consistently frustrates our expectations and calls some of our most basic categories into question. Precisely because of the fundamental questions that it raises, an examination of Bhartṛhari's understanding of the Veda provides a useful point of departure for the critical essays that are to follow.

Perhaps we should begin by recalling what is usually implied in our concept of hermeneutics, when applied in a religious context. In such a context, hermeneutics has traditionally referred to the interpretation of sacred scriptures—the canonical texts of religious communities—with the intent of bringing to light their contemporary significance for that community. Furthermore, this contemporary significance is usually sought at the level of textual meaning: it is the "ideality of the text," its relative independence from the conditions of its composition, that makes the hermeneutical task both possible and necessary.[2] How are the meanings preserved in the scriptural texts, originally intended for an audience in the past, to be made to speak to the concerns of the present? How is the historical distance that separates these texts from their original context to be bridged? This idea of the mediation of historical distance and the contemporary reappropriation of the message or "gospel" of a canonical *text* is central to our understanding of the hermeneutical project. We would do well, however, to exercise caution when attempting to apply it to a different culture. In particular, I believe that we must be careful in our use of such key categories as "text," "canon," and "scripture," not to mention the idea of hermeneutics itself.

I do not intend to address the question the appropriateness of the category of "scripture" when applied to Veda. This is a problem that has received a considerable amount of attention already.[3] Here I would like to focus on the two closely related concepts of "text" and "canon," both of which I believe are presupposed by the notion of "scripture." Does Bhartṛhari understand the Veda as in some sense a "canonical text"? And if he does, in what does this canonicity and textuality consist, and how does it affect his understanding of the task of interpretation?

I. The Veda as a "Text"

The first step in examining Bhartṛhari's understanding of the Veda as a "text" is to establish clearly what is meant by the term *text*. Two different senses seem possible, one rather general and the other more specific. Most simply, a text is a discourse that has been given written form, and in this sense even a composition that was in origin oral, such as a hymn from the

Ṛg Veda, may become a text. But the philosopher Paul Ricoeur, who has made a major contribution to our understanding of the interpretation of texts and who may serve as our guide here, has argued that while a text may be viewed simply as discourse fixed in writing, in the strict sense it is actually something more than this. Strictly speaking, a text is not a mere written transcription of a prior oral discourse. Writing rather stands at the origin of the text. It "intercepts" the very intention to speak at its origin, and consequently the written text is the direct "inscription" of this intention. "The emancipation of writing," Ricoeur says, "which places the latter at the site of speech, is the birth of the text" (1981, 147). Ricoeur goes on to say that the emancipation of the text from the site of speech "entails a veritable upheaval in the relations between language and the world" (p. 147). In particular, the referential function of discourse is transformed. Unlike living speech, which draws its meaning from its immediate context, from its reference to the present situation, written discourse is set free from any specific context. The referential function of the discourse is thus suspended "outside" the world of the actual, and it is this suspension of reference that makes interpretation of the text both possible and necessary (p. 148). I believe that it is the text in this second, more specific, sense of the word that is presupposed in most discussions of hermeneutics.[4]

Now, precisely the concept of a text in this second, specific sense is absent from Bhartṛhari's understanding of the Veda. This has important implications for any discussion of Bhartṛhari's "hermeneutics," at least as applied to the Veda. For if Bhartṛhari did not view the Veda as a text in the sense normally presupposed in such discussions, then it seems unlikely that he would have felt the need to "interpret" it in the same way that Karl Barth, for instance, felt the need to interpret St. Paul's letter to the Romans. How then *did* Bhartṛhari view the interpretation of the Veda? If for him the Veda is not a text in this sense, then what *is* it? Fortunately, Bhartṛhari addresses this question directly.

In the *Brahmakāṇḍa*, or "Book on Brahman," that makes up the first part of his major work, the *Vākyapadīya* (VP), or "Treatise on Sentences and Words," Bhartṛhari describes the Veda as the "imitative resemblance" (*anukāra*) of *brahman*, the absolute reality.[5] He describes this absolute reality in turn as *śabdatattva*, the "word-principle."[6] The Veda is understood to be a manifestation of the ultimate Word (*śabda*) that underlies phenomenal existence. It is important to note, however, that here *śabda* refers to sound or speech, rather than to the Greek *logos*. For Bhartṛhari the Veda is first and foremost a cosmic reality, the sonic manifestation of the ultimate ground of reality within the world of time and space. This phenomenal manifestation takes the form of powerful speech, the *mantras* and ritual injunctions employed in the Vedic sacrificial rites. The purpose of this

Vedic speech is to enjoin actions and to bring about transformations in the ontological status of those who employ it properly in the right ritual context. Consequently, for Bhartṛhari, as for many of his co-religionists, the Veda is more important for what it *is* and what it *does* than for what it "means." It is first and foremost a reality of sacred power. Vedic speech is thus not primarily referential.[7] It does not express an individual author's intentionality, but rather makes manifest the objective structures (known collectively as *dharma*) through which the world of time and space is related back to its ultimate ground. It does this not by describing these structures, but by bringing them into existence through the injunctive power intrinsic to the sacred speech. In the redaction of this sacred speech in written form, there is thus no question of "suspending" or "interrupting" its referential function, as described by Ricoeur. Such redaction is not an act of authorship, but merely one of systematization and preservation. To interpret the Veda is accordingly not to discover its meaning. It is rather to show how the different injunctions contained in the text enjoin a consistent set of rites.

It was of course the school of Mīmāṁsā that set for itself the task of interpreting the Veda in this sense. Mīmāṁsā viewed the Veda primarily as a collection of ritual injunctions. These injunctions derived their unity from the rites they enjoined. Mīmāṁsā's exegetical principles were geared to providing for an unambiguous and consistent application of the Vedic injunctions as the authoritative norm for the Vedic sacrifical cult. As a grammarian, Bhartṛhari agreed with much of the Mīmāṁsā method of interpretation. References to the technical terms of Mīmāṁsā exegesis are fairly numerous in his work.[8] Perhaps the clearest indication of Bhartṛhari's sympathy for the Mīmāṁsā position (as well as his move beyond it) comes in his discussion of an attempt to interpret the true "meaning" of the Veda in a sense that is somewhat similar to the Western notion of interpreting a text. I have in mind here the interpretation of the Veda offered by Advaita Vedānta, which claimed to find in the Vedic texts, specifically the *Upaniṣads*, a clear doctrine concerning the nature of ultimate reality. Bhartṛhari's attitude toward such attempts to interpret the "meaning" of the Veda is revealing. His position becomes clear in a brief passage that comes near the beginning of the *Brahmakāṇḍa*:

> The doctrines of the monists and the dualists, which have been variously received, are based upon those of [the Veda's] passages which have the form of [merely] commendatory remarks [intended to encourage one in the performance of one's duty]; [these doctrines] are born of [their authors'] own opinions. The true purity is also expressed there, the truth contained in [only] one word; connected with the syllable *Oṃ*, it is compatible with all doctrines.[9]

In the first of these two verses, Bhartṛhari uses the term *arthavāda*, which I have translated as "commendatory remarks." This term derives from the ritualist milieu and refers to those noninjunctive descriptive or "referential" statements in the Vedic texts that have no direct ritual significance: they do not enjoin ritual activity. In the Mīmāṁsā school they are explained as significant only inasmuch as they encourage one in the performance of the ritual. They thus have a practical significance, even if a derived one. While not strictly speaking "meaningless," they do not provide any information about a permanent reality such as *brahman*.[10] In the verse just quoted Bhartṛhari clearly shows his affinity with the Mīmāṁsā position. Many doctrines (*pravāda*) have been elaborated on the basis of these *arthavādas*, whether by monists or by dualists. All such conflicting doctrines have, according to Bhartṛhari, been born of the mental constructions or imaginings (*vikalpas*) of their authors. Their claim to refer to ultimate reality is unfounded. In contrast to such doctrinal positions, but also in contrast to the strictly ritualist interpretation of the Mīmāṁsā, Bhartṛhari finds the heart of Vedic revelation, the "true purity," to be that knowledge (*vidyā*) that is connected with *praṇava*, namely the sacred syllable *Oṃ*, an important symbol of the Veda as sacred speech. In contrast to mutually exclusive doctrinal positions, this knowledge is *sarvavādāvirodhinā*, literally, "not opposing any doctrine." As Bhartṛhari elsewhere makes abundantly clear, this knowledge is the knowledge of the word-principle itself, which, in the expressed form of the divine speech of the Veda, as *brahman's anukāra*, is subject matter of Bhartṛhari's chosen discipline, the *vedāṅga* or auxiliary Vedic science of *vyākaraṇa*, grammar. Thus if there is a "message" contained in the language of the Veda that must be interpreted, it lies not in the overt meaning of its propositions or its narratives. Rather it lies in what the language *enjoins*, as ritual actions, and most importantly from Bhartṛhari's point of view, in the language itself, as the "imitation" of *brahman*.

It is the Vedic language itself that most interests Bhartṛhari as a grammarian. I would argue that, for Bhartṛhari, in an important sense, to interpret the Veda is to understand that its language, precisely *as* language, is the self-manifestation of the word-principle. This understanding is gained not by attending to what language says, to its content, but to what it is, to its form, precisely as language. This can be made clear by a brief examination of some of the central ideas of his grammatical thought.

Bhartṛhari teaches that the sole genuine unit of language is the sentence, not the word. People do not utter words, they utter sentences. And they utter these not because they wish to refer to things, but because they wish to do things. Language is intended to mediate action, and this means that the heart of language is the sentence centered on the verb. Nouns and the objects they name are merely accessories of the action expressed by the verb.

This emphasis on the dynamic "verbal" character of language means that his understanding of the nature of language is most apparent in his analysis of the sentence rather than in his analysis of individual words. In fact, Bhartṛhari analyzes the sentence into a dynamic relational structure composed of what he calls *kārakas*, literally, "doers." These *kārakas* correspond, at the level of language, to Bhartṛhari's more general ontology of the *śaktis*, the "powers" or "capacities" of *brahman* that underlie the manifest universe, according to which the world is a dynamic matrix of potencies that are continually being actualized in action. It is only through the mediation of language at the level of the sentence that the world's dynamic potential becomes actual, since only the sentence transcends the level of static, named "substances" in order to present them as *sādhanas*, "means" for the accomplishment of action.[11] In the light of Bhartṛhari's ontology, according to which it is precisely the act—the actualization of the *śakti* of *brahman*—that is ultimately real, we may say that language, through its dynamic *kāraka* structure, discloses a truth about the world inaccessible to the naive immediacy of sense perception, focused on separate entities, and to the inferential reasoning based upon such perception, what Bhartṛhari called "dry reasoning" (*śuṣkas tarkaḥ*).[12]

Bhartṛhari develops his theory of the *kārakas* at some length in the *Sādhanasamuddeśa*, or "Discussion of Means," located in the third book of the VP. There he explains that the entire world, as it is presented by language, is divided up into that which is *sādhya*, or to be accomplished, and that which is *sādhana*, or the means for accomplishing something. Whatever language presents as being *sādhya* is an action (*kriyā*). Everything else is subordinated to this action as a *sādhana* or means for its actualization. In the sentence, what is *sādhya*, namely the action to be performed, is expressed by the verb, while the various *sādhanas* required for the action are expressed by nouns. Verbs and nouns are never found in an isolated state, however, as mere "words." Such words are only abstractions. In fact, verbs and nouns are always found in an inflected state, always provided with a suffix or declensional ending (a *pratyāya* or *vibhakti*) that integrates them into the single relational whole of the sentence. Only the whole is real, since only in the relational whole are the potentials of the verbal and nominal stems actualized in a single unit capable of expressing an action.

The conjugational and declensional endings are thus the key morphological features that display the intrinsic relational structure of the language. This relational structure itself, which is expressed by but not identical with these morphological features, is represented by the system of the *kārakas*, of which there are six: *kartṛ* (agent),[13] *karma* (object), *karaṇa* (instrument), *saṁpradāna* (recipient), *apādāna* (origin, point of departure), and *adhikaraṇa* (locus). These relations may be expressed in many different ways at the morphological level, but however expressed, they provide the fundamental structure of the sentence. The sentence with this *kāraka* structure in turn provides for the ordered expression of the myriad *śaktis* that compose our world in the form of discrete actions. Although the *śaktis* seem innumerable, they can be subsumed under the structure of the six *kārakas*, which Bhartṛhari actually refers to as six *śaktis* (VP 3.7.35), and these six, in turn, ultimately express only the one *śakti*, the dynamism of the word-principle as ontological ground of the phenomenal world.

It is interesting, indeed crucial, to note that Bhartṛhari's understanding of the sentence as a structure of *kāraka* relations stands in marked contrast to classical Western views. Beginning with Aristotle's *De Interpretatione*, Western thinkers have been prone to accept a subject-predicate analysis of the sentence or proposition, along with the table of substance-related categories associated with it. Sentences or propositions are intended primarily to connect subjects with predicates. Like texts, language is viewed as primarily descriptive or referential. The comparison with Bhartṛhari is illuminating. The sentence is not interpreted as a subject-object proposition, and it is not associated with a table of categories focused on substance. To the contrary, Bhartṛhari's table of categories is the system of the *kārakas*, the set of ideal relations that together characterize action rather than substance. The sentence is focused on the mediation of action, not on predication.

The ordered relations that are made known by specifically Vedic sentences are known collectively as *dharma*, and it is the chief function of the Veda to reveal them. What is most interesting about Bhartṛhari's view of the Veda is that Vedic speech, as a type of formally correct activity, is itself a form of *dharma*, because as a form of activity it too makes manifest the dynamic, ontological structure of the world, the self-manifestation of the word-principle. And to use this language properly, to speak correctly, is to perform *dharma* just as surely as if one were to perform a Vedic sacrifice. This dharmic character inheres in the structure of the language itself, and not merely in the injunctions and *arthavādas* that are expressed in that language.

Given this understanding of Vedic language as effectively a form of action, it is fairly clear that Bhartṛhari did not view the Veda as a text in the specific sense specified by Ricoeur. Nor is the Mīmāṁsā understanding of the Veda as a collection of ritual injunctions sufficient for Bhartṛhari. Rather for him, the Veda is first and foremost the "perfected" (*saṁskṛta*) speech acts that are the temporal manifestation of the word-principle itself. But this leads to the question: Exactly which speech acts count as

Vedic? In other words, did Bhartṛhari recognize a "canonical" collection of such utterances?

II. Veda as Canon

What does this understanding of the Veda as a form of action, as a form of *dharma*, imply for an understanding of the Veda as canon? Again, we must begin with a brief consideration of what we mean by the word *canon*. The word itself derives from the Greek word for measuring rod and thus at its most basic refers to some kind of measure, a rule or standard, and by extension, to that which conforms to this standard. Thus the standard involved here could be understood as a criterion for the selection of texts as canonical, or, as routinely happens, the measured—the selected texts—could themselves become the measure, the canon, as referring to a delimited corpus of texts in its capacity as an authoritative or normative guide for a community. In either case a canon is understood as a standard of measure, whether what is measured is a collection of texts or the beliefs and practices of a community.

In order to understand how the notion of canon applies in Bhartṛhari's case, I believe that it is important to stay close to the original idea of canon as norm or standard. For clearly the Veda does function as such a standard: it defines *dharma*, the correct and religiously meritorious action. But difficulties develop when one attempts to extend this notion of a canonical standard to the Veda as text, in parallel with what happens in the West.

In principle, the fact that the Veda is not a text in the specific sense discussed above need not rule out the possibility of a Vedic canon defined as a list of texts, if "text" here refers simply to a written document. But even in this more general sense it is difficult to speak of the Veda as a canonical text, for even when the Veda finally came to be written down (and this may have happened quite early), there was no definitive redaction of "the" Veda, but rather a host of Vedas deriving from different family and ritual traditions. What was "canonical" in this process were the actions that the texts enjoined, not the texts themselves. The "canon" was in a real sense more social than textual. It was also closely connected with ritual. The earliest organization of these texts into the three *saṁhītas*, or "collections," reflected the structure of the Vedic ritual, and it was the redactors of the most ritually oriented of these collections, the *Yajur Saṁhīta*, who eventually produced a relatively coherent Veda, in the sense of a well-ordered series of texts that were intended to form a systematic whole.[14] But even in the case of the *Yajur Veda* we do not have "the" canonical Veda, but only one Veda among several, not to mention the fact that there are multiple recensions of the *Yajur Veda* itself. Thus, although there were individual collections of Vedic texts that functioned authoritatively within specific groups, there has never been a single Veda, in the concrete, textual sense, that functioned in this way for all those who recognize the Veda's authority.

Traditional attempts to delimit the Veda in the textual sense have in fact tended to be quite formal. Within the school of Mīmāṁsā, the Veda was defined as consisting of *mantras* and *brāhmaṇas*, referring to the two major genres present within the different Vedic collections. Veda was also equated with *śruti*, literally "hearing" and referring to what has been heard, that is, revealed, and contrasted with *smṛti*, literally "memory," referring to traditional texts of lesser authority. Such criteria provide a standard for limitation on a formal level but hardly provide for the definition of a canon in the more usual, material sense of a specific body of texts. The Vedic canon in this strictly material and textual sense remained quite fluid, a fact that has been frequently noted.[15]

This lack of firm textuality meant that canonicity in regard to the Veda had an irreducible practical and social component. The Veda was not a text that was intended to have an existence independent of the community that employed it. Originally something was part of the canonical Veda simply because the right people—the members of respected Brahmanical families—had recognized and used it as such. And the fact that the Veda never attained a single definitive form as a closed textual corpus made it easier for it to become, in a later age, a largely symbolic source for the legitimation of current practice among the *śiṣṭas*, the learned Brahmans who were the chief religious authorities in Brahmanical society.

This becomes quite clear in Bhartṛhari, who nowhere discusses the Veda as a specific set of texts, nor discusses the extent of these texts, yet makes explicit appeal to the normativity of the Veda as regards current linguistic practice. For Bhartṛhari, the canonicity of the Veda lies primarily in the fact that it is the ultimate source for the norms of correct, or "dharmic," speech. It is the ideal standard of *dharma* that is presupposed by current usage. In the sixth verse of the *Brahmakāṇḍa* Bhartṛhari addresses this question of the normativity of the Veda, which he locates at the level of its language: "There are many paths to [the Veda's] divisions; [yet] it is the accessory in one rite. The fixity of the powers of its utterances is seen in its branches."[16] Here he recognizes the many distinct redactions of the Veda but insists on its ritual unity. All Vedic utterances serve to define a common action: the performance of the sacrifice (or, more generally, the performance of *dharma*). Most importantly, all Vedic utterances are said to be possessed of *yataśaktitvaṃ*, literally the character of having a fixed or restricted power (*śakti*). This restriction is found in the individual branches of the Veda, that is, within the individual ritual schools. The actual "text" of the Veda may differ from branch to branch, but within any given branch the Vedic utterances have a fixed form. The Veda, through the ritual restrictions, or *niyamas*, that it places on speech, is the normative or canonical source of *dharma*.

We have already discussed the importance of the Veda as a source of *dharma*. For Bhartṛhari, the Vedic "auxiliary science" (vedāṅga) of grammar that he practiced was intended to preserve the *dharma* in the form of correct speech. This association of the Vedic *niyamas* with the *niyamas* taught by the grammarians goes back at least as far as the grammarian Kātyāyana, who mentions the parallel:

> In the use of words that are applied to their objects on the basis of the world (i.e., in the ordinary use of language), restrictions [are introduced] by the science [of grammar] for the sake of *dharma*, as is done both in ordinary language and in the language of Vedic revelation.[17] (Keilhorn,1.8.3)

The Veda, and by extension the auxiliary science of grammar and the various treatises on *dharma* that depended on it, serves to establish correct and meritorious linguistic usage, and in this sense serves as a norm or canon. Bhartṛhari refers to this explicitly, making it clear that the normative or restrictive principle (*niyama*) here concerns proper action rather than meaning:

> The correct forms of words, which are means for attaining merit (*dharma*), are established by the learned on the basis of tradition. Incorrect words, although no different from correct words in their capacity to convey meaning, are of an opposite character [as regards merit].[18]

Correct words, "dharmic" words, are made known through the restrictions, or *niyamas*, that are in turn made known through Vedic revelation, *śruti*. Or, as Bhartṛhari says repeatedly, *niyamārthā punaḥ śrutiḥ*, "explicit mention [of a specific form of speech, whether in the Veda or in grammatical *śāstra*], is for the sake of establishing a restriction."[19] For Bhartṛhari canonicity resides in this notion of restriction, which serves as a criterion for correct or meritorious action (*dharma*), for "orthopraxis" rather than "orthodoxy." Normativity lies in the Veda's language per se, in the correctness of its form more than in its content. It is the formal perfection of Vedic speech, and of the dharmic actions mediated by it, that constitutes the canonical standard represented by the Veda. The object of this standard remains action itself, whether the overt physical action of ritual sacrifice or the action of correct speech modeled on the Vedic norms. It is not a standard applied to texts *qua* texts.

This highly formal and "pragmatic" notion of canonicity served Bhartṛhari and his co-religionists well. By his time, the time of the Guptas, the central content of the Veda, the elaborate *śrauta* sacrificial system that was at its heart, had become largely irrelevant in the increasingly devotional spirit of the classical Hinduism. A "material" canon would have proved more a burden than a source of guidance. But as a formal ideal that could be realized in speech, even in the absence of the prescribed sacrifices, the *Veda* could—and did—continue to function as a kind of canon in the life of orthoprax Hindus. It was "interpreted" and "reinterpreted" through their continued efforts to lead a life of *dharma*, a life conformed to a Vedic ideal of formal perfection, a life of *saṁskāra*. So central was this notion of the Veda as a norm for dharmic action, rather than as a specific corpus of texts, that the later Mīmāṁsaka thinker Kumārila would argue that if dharmic actions are described in the texts of the tradition (*smṛti*) that are nowhere mentioned in the extant Vedic texts, then one must infer that Vedic texts ordaining such actions previously existed but have now been lost.[20] Here the canonicity of the act reigns supreme over the canonicity of the text.

III. Conclusion: Bhartṛhari and Hermeneutics

When it comes to hermeneutics as commonly understood among Western scholars, we could say that Bhartṛhari in a sense stands Paul Ricoeur on his head. Whereas Ricoeur has argued that the textual model of interpretation can be extended to cover meaningful action,[21] Bhartṛhari would argue quite the reverse, in the case of the Veda at least: the text must itself be understood on the model of action. It would be misleading, however, to generalize on the basis of what has been said in this chapter and conclude that Bhartṛhari has nothing to teach us about hermeneutics. This is true for at least two reasons. First of all, it would require overlooking the fact that Bhartṛhari did in fact write commentaries that were intended to clarify the meaning of texts written by individually known authors. In addition to a commentary on Patañjali's *Mahābhāṣya*, Bhartṛhari also wrote a commentary, or *vṛtti*, on his own *Vākyapadīya*. A study of either of these commentaries would undoubtedly present us with a much more familiar picture, one more in keeping with our Western expectations. But the fact that these expectations are frustrated in the case of the Veda is significant. It points to an aspect of the Brahmanical religious tradition that cannot be well understood through an uncritical use of our own text- and meaning-oriented categories. For those who have preserved it over the centuries, the Veda is a source of sacred power more than a source of religious meaning. And it is a source of power that overflows the textual boundaries of specific Vedic texts to make itself felt wherever the divine speech is uttered. It is a reality to be appropriated through a long and tedious process of memorization and recitation. More than through reading and reflection, one appropriates the Veda through embodiment: one does not "understand" the Veda, one enacts it; and ideally one *becomes* it.

This leads to the second reason why we should be slow to speak of Bhartṛhari's ignorance of hermeneutics in regard to the Veda. We have to do here more with canonical actions than with canonical texts. To the extent that interpretation here deals with texts, these texts themselves are concerned primarily with the mediation of actions rather than meanings. But this need not imply that such texts are not the proper subjects of a hermeneutic. It may well be the case that Western theories of interpretation can be enriched by what at first appears to be their contradiction. Has not one of the leading lights of Western hermeneutical theory, Hans-Georg Gadamer, asserted that *all* interpretation is application, and suggested that we may achieve some of our deepest insights into the nature of hermeneutics by studying the methods of legal interpretation, where the question of practical application is paramount?[22] I suspect that Bhartṛhari would agree. For him, text and canon are inseparable from the conditions of their practical employment; apart from this context they have no meaning (or no use!). The analogue in the West for much of what we find in the Brahmanical traditions of India may well be the interpretation of canon law rather than the interpretation of canonical scriptures. And beyond speaking of canonical law (that is, *dharma* and its extensions), it may prove helpful to speak of "canonical persons" as well. Here, too, I believe there is a clear analogue in the West: the canonization of saints. In an important sense the Brahmanical counterpart of the canonized saint is the *śiṣṭa*, the learned Brahman who has internalized, "become," the Veda through committing it to memory and acting in accord with its *dharma*. Those are the true "hermeneuts" of the Veda, who make it actual in their speech and their actions and thereby apply its norms to the changing demands of everyday life. Interpretation here is a practical affair that one accomplishes as much with one's body as with one's mind. I believe that such a view of the hermeneutical task merits our serious consideration. In an intellectual environment where it is not unusual to speak of an "absolute" text understood in isolation from the practical conditions of its production and transmission, perhaps there is something yet to be learned from someone like Bhartṛhari, who insists on the practical import of living speech and its living embodiments.

Notes

1. To present Bhartṛhari as such a representative figure is not without its problems. What I have referred to as the "Brahmanical religious tradition" was a complex of distinct and often competing traditions, holding divergent positions on the very questions to be examined here—namely the status of the Veda and the manner of its interpretation. Even though all agreed in attributing an authoritative status to the Veda, in practice this meant different things to different people. Nevertheless, Bhartṛhari's thought holds a special significance. As a grammarian he belonged to one of the most prestigious intellectual traditions of his day, developing directly out of the ancient Vedic tradition, and he seems to have had a conscious interest in preserving some of the most fundamental aspects of that tradition within the greatly altered conditions of post-Vedic, Gupta India.

2. For a more detailed discussion of this understanding of the hermeneutical project, see Ricoeur 1973.

3. The limitations of the notion of scripture when applied to the Vedic tradition have been noted frequently. See, for instance, Thomas Coburn, " 'Scripture' in India: Toward a Typology of the Word in Hindu Life," *Journal of the American Academy of Religion* 52 (1984): 435–59, reprinted in Levering 1989 (pp. 102–28); and Graham 1987 (especially chapter 6, "Scripture as Spoken Word: The Indian Paradigm"). For a good discussion of some of the problems involved in placing *too* much emphasis on the orality of the Veda, see Goody 1987, chapter 4, "Oral Composition and Oral Transmission: The Case of Veda."

4. I do not wish to imply that there is a single, monolithic model of Western hermeneutics that is always and everywhere the same, and which could be opposed to an equally monolithic Eastern or Indian model. However, I do believe that the view of textual interpretation presented here as "Western" has been dominant at least since the time of Schleiermacher.

5. *prāptyupāyo 'nukāraṣ ca tasya vedo maharṣibhiḥ / eko 'py anekavartmeva samāmnātaḥ pṛthak pṛthak //* (*Vākyapadīya* [hereafter VP] 1.5).

6. *anādinidhanaṃ brahma śabdatattvam yad akṣaram /* (VP 1.1 a–b).

7. Wade Wheelock has described the function of Vedic speech as "situational" and contrasted this with the "informational" function of language. See his illuminating essay, "The Problem of Ritual Language: From Information to Situation," *Journal of the American Academy of Religion* 50 (1982): 49–71.

8. See for instance the *vṛtti* on VP 1.151–52 and the lengthy discussion of Mīmāṁsā exegetical principles at VP 2.77–88. See also V. A. Ramaswami Sastri, "Bhartṛhari as a Mīmāṁsaka," *Bulletin of the Deccan College Research Institute* 14 (1952):1–15; and V. Swaminathan, "Bhartṛhari and Mīmāṁsā," *Proceedings of the All-India Oriental Conference* (Bhubaneshwar, 1959):309–17.

9. *tasyārthavādarūpāṇi niśritāḥ svavikalpajāḥ / ekatvināṃ dvaitināṃ ca pravādā bahudhāgatāḥ // satyā viśuddhis tatroktā vidyaivaikapadāgamā / yuktā praṇavarūpeṇa sarvavādāvirodhinā //* (VP 1.8–9).

10. The Mimāṁsā attitude is well summarized by John Taber, with specific reference to the Mīmāṁsā position on *mantras*: "While the Mīmāṁsaka employs the thesis that all language is expressive to argue that mantras are meaningful, we should have no illusions about where he is going with this argument. He is not hoping to restore the literal or symbolic significance of the Veda. Indeed, he is doing nearly the opposite, reducing the text to a series of mere references." See his "Are Mantras Speech Acts? The Mīmāṁsā Point of View," in Alper 1989 (p. 159).

11. Language is capable of this feat because it does not exist in the mode of an object, but rather is endowed with a "secondary" or "metaphorical" (*aupacārika*) mode of being. See VP 3.3.39–51 for Bhartṛhari's discussion of this concept.

12. Bhartṛhari warns that this type of dry reasoning (*śuṣkas tarkaḥ*) is destructive of tradition and ultimately groundless. See VP 1.153 *vṛtti: śabdaśaktirūpāparigṛhītas tu sādharmyavaidharmyamātrānusārī sarvāgamopaghātahetutvād anibandhanaḥ śuṣkas tarka ity ucyate //*.

13. Note that here Bhartṛhari refers to the *agent* of the sentence, rather than to the *subject*.

14. For a more detailed examination of these developments, see Louis Renou, *Les Écoles Védiques et la Formation du Véda* (Paris: Imprimerie Nationale, 1947).

15. See, for instance, the remarks of Gerhard Oberhammer, "Überlieferungsstruktur and Offenbarung: Aufriss einer Reflexion des Phänomens im Hinduismus," in *Überlieferungsstruktur und Offenbarung*, by Gerhard Oberhammer and Hans Waldenfels (Vienna: Institut für Indologie der Universität Wien, 1980), 15–36.

16. *bhedānāṃ bahumārgatvaṃ karmaṇy ekatra cāṅgatā / śabdānāṃ yataśaktitvaṃ tasya śākhāsu dṛṣyate //* (VP 1.6).

17. Quoted by Patañjali, in his *Mahābhāṣya* 1.8.3: *lokato'rthaprayukte śabdaprayoge śāstreṇa dharmaniyamaḥ / yathā laukikavaidikeṣû //* See Keilhorn 1880–1885.

18. *śiṣṭbhya āgamāt siddhāḥ sādhavo dharmasādhanam / arthapratyāyanābhede viparītās tv asādhavaḥ //* (VP 1.27). See also VP 3.3.30.

19. VP 2.244. See also VP 3.1.89, 3.14.432, and 2.416.

20. See Kumārila Bhaṭṭa, *Tantravārttika*, edited by Gaṅgādhara Śastrī, Benares: Benares Sanskrit Series, No. 5:75.

21. See his article "The Model of the Text: Meaningful Action Considered as a Text" in Ricoeur 1981.

22. See Gadamer 1975, pp. 289–305, "The exemplary significance of legal hermeneutics."

References

Alper, Harvey P.
1989 *Mantra*. Albany: State University of New York Press.

Gadamer, Hans-Georg
1975 *Truth and Method*. New York: Seabury Press.

Graham, William A.
1987 *Beyond the Written Word: Oral Aspects of Scripture in the History of Religion*. Cambridge: Cambridge University Press.

Goody, Jack
1987 *The Interface Between the Written and the Oral*. Cambridge: Cambridge University Press.

Keilhorn, F., ed.
1880–85 *Mahābhāṣya* (of Patañjali), 3 vols. 1962–72. Reprint. Poona: Bhandarkar Oriental Research Institute.

Levering, Miriam, ed.
1989 *Rethinking Scripture: Essays from a Comparative Perspective*. Albany: State University of New York Press.

Rau, Wilhelm, ed.
1977 *Bhartṛhari's Vākyapadīya*. Wiesbaden: Kommission-verlag Franz Steiner.

Ricoeur, Paul
1973 "The Hermeneutical Function of Distanciation." *Philosophy Today* 17: 129–41.

1981 *Hermeneutics and the Human Sciences*. Edited and translated by John B. Thompson. Cambridge: Cambridge University Press.

Three

Where Words Can Set Free

The Liberating Potency of Vedic Words in the Hermeneutics of Śaṅkara

Anantanand Rambachan

Introduction

The aim of this chapter is to unfold Śaṅkara's understanding of the significance and authority of the *Upaniṣads* as an integral part of the Vedas.[1] This will be done by studying his response to the Pūrva Mīmāṁsā exegesis of the purport of the Vedas. The Pūrva Mīmāṁsā contention that the *Upaniṣads* have no independent purpose but are merely an appendage to the main body of injunctive text was a formidable challenge to Śaṅkara.[2] He saw the *Upaniṣads* as having an autonomous function in the revelation of *brahman* (ultimate reality). It was necessary, therefore, for Śaṅkara to develop a comprehensive view of the authority of Vedas in which the special significance of the *Upaniṣads* could be preserved. It will be obvious that Śaṅkara's recourse to the Vedas was neither adventitious nor merely an attempt to align his views with a traditional authority. Liberation (*mokṣa*) and its attainment, in Śaṅkara, cannot be understood apart from his conception of the nature and operation of a valid source of knowledge (*pramāṇa*) and his affirmation that the Vedas constitute such a source. For Śaṅkara, unlike Bhartṛhari, described in chapter 2 of this volume, it is the capacity of the Vedic words to reveal valid knowledge that constitutes their significance and purpose.

This study is divided into six sections. We begin with a brief summary of the Pūrva Mīmāṁsā arguments. This will be followed by an examination of Śaṅkara's rationale for the Upaniṣads as a logical source of knowledge about *brahman*, as an adequate source of knowledge about *brahman*, and as a fruitful source of knowledge about *brahman*. We will then consider the sixfold criteria (*ṣadliṅga*) employed by Śaṅkara for determining the intent of the *Upaniṣads* and conclude with an overview of the relationship between the *Upaniṣads* and the other sections of the Vedas.

I. Pūrva Mīmāṁsā Exegesis of the Vedas

The Pūrva Mīmāṁsā exegesis, in so far as it is relevant to Śaṅkara, contends that the Vedas have their purport only in the inculcation of *dharma*.[3] The latter is defined by Jaimini as "that which, being desirable, is indicated by Vedic injunctions" (*Pūrva Mīmāṁsā Sūtras* [hereafter PMS] 1.1.2). On the basis of this view, Pūrva Mīmāṁsā argues that only injunctions (*vidhi*) inculcating the performance of acceptable acts and prohibitions (*niṣedha*) instituting restraint from acts opposed to *dharma* are direct and independent in authority (PMS 1.2.1). The authority of all other texts is indirect and dependent for their meaningfulness on a connection with the injunctions. They are not viewed as having any independent end in themselves. Many Vedic texts, for example, including the sentences of the *Upaniṣads* (*vedānta-vākyas*) are seen as having their purpose only in praising what has been enjoined in the injunctions[4] (PMS 1.2.7). Pūrva Mīmāṁsā argues that if such sentences are taken by themselves, they are absolutely meaningless, because they neither impel us to activity nor restrain us from prohibited actions.[5] According to Pūrva Mīmāṁsā, the *Upaniṣads* are merely an appendage to the main body of injunctive statements. The utility of the *Upaniṣads* lies only in praising the prescribed action or in providing some useful information, such as knowledge of the deity or agent for performance of a particular rite. Statements about already existent entities are without fruit, for they neither prompt the performance of *dharma* nor the avoidance of *adharma*. Against the independent authority of the *Upaniṣads*, Pūrva Mīmāṁsā contends that knowledge about already accomplished things, such as *brahman*, is obtainable from other sources of knowledge (*pramāṇas*). The knowledge of *dharma* and *adharma*, however, is not otherwise obtainable.[6]

This Pūrva Mīmāṁsā exegesis is obviously incompatible with Śaṅkara's justification of the role of the Vedas. It is irreconcilable with his view that the *Upaniṣads* are an independent means of knowledge (*pramāṇa*) for *brahman*. He attempts, therefore, to establish that the *Upaniṣads* are not subservient to any other texts in the Vedas, but have an independent concern and authority in the revelation of *brahman*.

II. The Upaniṣads *as a Logical Source of Knowledge about* Brahman

Śaṅkara seeks to refute the Mīmāṁsā proposition that if the words of the Vedas are understood to signify already existing things, they become redundant. While agreeing that most existent things are knowable through ordinary sources of knowledge, Śaṅkara contends that *brahman* is unique.

According to Śaṅkara, the two categories of knowledge inaccessible to all other *pramāṇas* and attainable exclusively through the Vedas are *dharma* and *brahman* (Śaṅkara's *Brahma Sūtra Bhāṣya* [hereafter BSŚ] 2.1.6).[7] Śaṅkara is in agreement with Mīmāṁsā exegetes about the Vedas as a source of knowledge for *dharma*. We are afforded a clear statement of Śaṅkara's view on the knowledge of *dharma* in BSŚ 3.1.25. Here he is responding to the objector's claim that the slaying of animals in sacrifices might be responsible for the soul's birth as a plant. He answers that the knowledge of merit (*dharma*) and demerit (*adharma*) is derived solely from the scripture. From the Vedas alone we can know which acts are meritorious and which are not. The reason is that these are supersensuous realities beyond the capacity of the senses. In addition to this, *dharma* and *adharma* vary with time and place. An act that may be approved under certain circumstances may not be sanctioned with a change of these factors. It is impossible therefore, to learn of *dharma* from any other source.[8]

Śaṅkara, however, differs from the Mīmāṁsā exegete in claiming that the revelation of *dharma* does not exhaust the authoritative subject matter of the Vedas. The knowledge of *dharma* is derived from the first sections of the Vedas, which deal with ritual action (that is, the *karmakāṇḍa*). The final sections of the Vedas (referred to variously as *jñānakāṇḍa, vedānta-vākyas, upaniṣad*) have an entirely different purpose in the revelation of the knowledge of *brahman*.

The cornerstone of Śaṅkara's case for the *Upaniṣads* as the valid means of knowing *brahman* is based upon the very nature of *brahman*; a source of knowledge in the form of words (*śabda*) is the only logical means. What gives Śaṅkara's argument its force is the logical interdependence he tries to demonstrate between the appropriateness of the *pramāṇa* and the nature of the entity to be known. The relationship here is between *brahman* as the entity to be known and *śabda* as the means of knowledge.

The case for the *Upaniṣads* consists of showing why this knowledge cannot be attained through the other ways of knowing, and this Śaṅkara does at every available opportunity in his commentaries. He is tireless in explaining the incompetence of sense perception to apprehend *brahman*. He refuses to accept the notion that *brahman*, because it is an existent entity, must be the object of other sources of valid knowledge. Each sense organ is naturally capable grasping and revealing a quality that is appropriate to its own nature. Sound, sensation, form, taste, and scent are their respective spheres of functioning. *Brahman*, however, remains unapproachable through any of these because of its uniqueness (BSŚ 1.1.2). *Brahman* has neither sound, touch, form, taste, or smell. It is without qualities (*nirguṇa*) and is therefore outside the domain of the sense organs. *Brahman* is limitless and nondual; to be an object of sense knowledge to be finite and delimited, to be one object among many objects. A *brahman* that is sense-apprehended is, in the view of Śaṅkara, a contradiction. Śaṅkara refutes the allegation that there is any contradiction in the *Bhagavad Gītā*'s denial of *brahman* as both *sat* (existent) and *asat* (nonexistent) by interpreting these terms with reference to the nonavailability of *brahman* as an object of sense knowledge.

> Objection: Every state of consciousness involves either the consciousness of existence or that of nonexistence. Such being the case, the Knowable should be comprehended either by a state of consciousness accompanied with the consciousness of existence or by a state of consciousness accompanied with the consciousness of nonexistence.
>
> Answer: No; for being beyond the reach of the senses, it is not an object of consciousness accompanied with the idea of either (existence or nonexistence). That thing, indeed, that which can be perceived by the senses, such as a pot, can be an object of consciousness accompanied with the idea of nonexistence. Since, on the other hand, the Knowable is beyond the reach of the senses and such can be known solely through that instrument of knowledge that is called Śabda, . . . and is therefore not said to be "sat" or "asat". (BGŚ 13:12).

In addition to the inherent limitations of the sense organs, there is the impossibility of objectifying *brahman*. The process of empirical knowledge involves a distinction between subject and object, the knower and the known. We know things by making them objects or our awareness, and in this way they are available for scrutiny and analysis. Knowledge of an object presupposes the subject, the knower. *Brahman*, however is the eternal subject. As awareness (*caitanya*), it illumines everything—and the entire universe, including mind, body, and sense organs, as its object. The unchanging knower can never be made an object of knowledge. It is absurd to conceive of the subject as an object, for in its absence there is no subject to know the subject is an object (BUŚ 2.4.14). Nor is it possible to circumvent this by positing that *brahman* can be both subject and object. By nature, the subject and object are entirely opposed, the former being sentient and the latter inert, and such contradictory qualities cannot be posited of the same entity (BSŚ, introduction). No division of any kind can be made in the case of *brahman* (AUŚ 2.1).

If perception is inappropriate for furnishing us with the knowledge of *brahman*, are any of the other four *pramāṇas* (inference, comparison, postulation, and noncognition) more competent? Śaṅkara's view is that these sources are more or less dependent on perception for their data and can have no access to areas from which it is debarred. Inferential knowledge, for example, is derived from a knowledge of the invariable relation between a thing inferred and the ground from which the inference is made. *Brahman*, however is not invariably related to any apprehensible or differentiating qualities that can form the ground of inference (BSŚ 2.1.6). It is impossible, therefore, to infer the existence of *brahman*.

III. The Upaniṣads *as an Adequate Source of Knowledge about* Brahman

There is another important and complementary dimension of Śaṅkara's rationale for the *Upaniṣads*. Given the nature of *brahman* and the fact that the fundamental human spiritual problem is one of ignorance (*avidyā*), the knowledge derived from the words of these texts can be an adequate solution.

The case for the adequacy of the *Upaniṣads* is founded on the argument that the words of these texts are not required to produce *brahman* or to demonstrate its existence. There are several important and interesting discussions in Śaṅkara's commentaries that are relevant to this issue. In his introduction to the BSŚ, an objection is raised against the superimposition argument. The objector's view is that superimposition is possible only on something that is available for sense perception. In the mistaken apprehension of a rope for a snake, for example, at least the outline of the rope is seen. How can anything, however, be superimposed on *brahman* that is not an object of the senses? Śaṅkara's reply is to suggest that even though *brahman*, as the self (*ātman*), is not an object of perception, it is not entirely unknown, and wrong attribution is possible.

> The self is not absolutely beyond apprehension, because it is apprehended as the content of the concept ''I'', and because the Self, opposed to the non-Self, is well known in the world as an immediately perceived (i.e., self-revealing entity). (BSŚ introduction)

Elsewhere, the objector asks whether *brahman* is known or unknown (BSŚ 1.1.1). The point of query here is that if, on the one hand, *brahman* is known, then there is no need for a means of knowledge or an inquiry to ascertain its nature. If, on the other hand, *brahman* is unknown (that is, not even the object of a desire to know), then it cannot become the subject for any kind of inquiry. Śaṅkara denies that *brahman* is completely unknown.

> Besides, the existence of *brahman* is well known from the fact of Its being the Self of all; for everyone feels that his Self exists and he never feels, "I do not exist." Had there been no general recognition of the existence of the Self, everyone would have felt, "I do not exist." And that Self is *brahman*. (BSŚ 1.1.1)

If *brahman* is thus known, is not an inquiry into the words of the *Upaniṣads* redundant? Śaṅkara's response is to suggest that the knowledge we possess of *brahman* is of a general nature only (*sāmānya jñāna*). There is a lack of specific knowledge (*viśeṣa jñāna*), and this makes superimposition possible. In fact, wrong attribution or superimposition occurs only where knowledge is of a general nature and lacks specificity. In the case of *brahman*, that "I exist" and "I know" are self-revelatory. Upon this existence (*sat*) and awareness (*cit*), the limited qualities of the body, sense organs, and mind are superimposed, and *brahman* is taken to be finite and mortal.

Clearly, from Śaṅkara's standpoint, the problem does not involve the knowledge of an entirely unknown, unrevealed, or remote *brahman*. It is one of incomplete and erroneous knowledge of an ever-available and self-manifesting entity. The function of the words of the *Upaniṣads*, in this context, lies primarily in the negation of attributes imposed through *avidyā* on *brahman*. The *Upaniṣads* do not reveal an unknown being (BGŚ 18:50). One of the important reasons for emphasizing the immediate availability of *brahman* and clarifying the nature of the ignorance pertaining to it is that it establishes the possibility of the words of the *Upaniṣads* giving rise to direct and immediate knowledge. The challenge is not one of creating anything new, but of understanding what is always available. Śaṅkara clearly accepts that the knowledge derived through words (*śabda*) is not an end in itself if the object about which we are informed is not yet in existence or not immediately available. If the object is available but misapprehended, like *brahman*, correct knowledge through the words of a valid source (that is, the *Upaniṣads*) is adequate.

> The attainment of the Self cannot be, as in the case of things other than It, the obtaining of something not obtained before, for here there is no difference between the person attaining and the object attained. Where the Self has to obtain something other than Itself, the Self is the attainer and the non-Self is the object attained. This, not being already attained, is separated by acts such as producing,

> and is to be attained by the initiation of a particular action with the help of auxiliaries. And the attainment of something new is transitory, being due to desire and action that are themselves the product of a false notion, like the birth of a son etc. in a dream. But this Self is the very opposite of that. By the very fact of Its being the Self, It is not separated by acts such as producing. But although it is always attained, It is separated by ignorance only. (BUŚ 1.4.7)

IV. The Upaniṣads *as a Fruitful Source of Knowledge about* Brahman

One of the principal contentions of the Pūrva Mīmāṁsā school, as we have seen, is that only the injunctions of the Vedas impelling us into activity or restraining us from prohibited actions are direct and independent in authority. All other sentences derive their meaningfulness from a connection with the injunctions. Sentences of the *Upaniṣads* are redundant if they merely reveal already existing things and do not subserve the injunctions.

Śaṅkara does not accept that sentences cannot have a factual referent or significance.[9] He points out that even though a sentence might have its ultimate purport in initiating some activity, it does not thereby cease to communicate valid factual information. Even as a person traveling to some destination perceives the existence of leaves and grass at the side of the road, a statement might have its aim in activity, but its factual content is not thereby invalidated (BSŚ 1.3.33). In response to the Mīmāṁsā exaltation of injunctions, Śaṅkara points out that injunctions are valid not simply because they are injunctions, but because they are revealed in an authoritative *pramāṇa* (BUŚ 1.3.1).

Replying to the claim that mere factual statements that neither persuade us into activity nor dissuade us from it are fruitless, Śaṅkara asserts that

> the test of the authority or otherwise of a passage is not whether it states a fact or an action, but its capacity to generate certain and fruitful knowledge. A passage that has this is authoritative and one that lacks it is not. (BUŚ 1.4.7)

He never tires of continuously affirming the independent fruitfulness of the *Upaniṣads* sentences. Even as a simple statement of fact, "This is a rope, not a snake" is fruitful in removing the fear occasioned by the error of taking a rope for a snake. The *Upaniṣads*, by helping us to distinguish the self from the nonself, release us from the sorrow of taking ourselves to be incomplete and finite beings (BSŚ 1.1.4).

> Is or is not certain and fruitful knowledge generated by passages setting forth the nature of the Self, and if so, how can they lose their authority? Do you not see the result of knowledge in the removal of the evils which are the root of transmigration, such as ignorance, grief, delusion and fear? Or do you not hear those hundreds of Upaniṣadic texts such as "Then what delusion and what grief can there be for one who sees unity?" (*Iśā Upaniṣad* 7; BUŚ 1.4.7)

Śaṅkara also points to the transformed life of the knower of *brahman* as further evidence of the fruitfulness of knowledge gained through the words of the *Upaniṣads*.

> For one who has realised the state of the unity of the Self and Brahman, it cannot be proved that his mundane life continues just as before; for this contradicts the knowledge of the unity of Brahman and the Self arising from the Vedas which are a valid means of knowledge. From noticing the fact that a man can have sorrow, fear, etc. as a result of identifying himself with the body etc., it does not follow that this very man will have sorrow etc., contingent on false ignorance, even when his self-identification with the body etc., ceases after realization of the unity of Brahman and the Self, arising from the Vedas which are a valid source of knowledge. (BSŚ 1.1.4)

Śaṅkara often repeats the contention, supported by numerous scriptural references, that for the prepared and qualified aspirant, the fruit of spiritual knowledge (liberation, or *mokṣa*) is simultaneous with the gain of that knowledge. He is emphatic in his denial of the necessity for any intervening action between the two.[10] In fact, from the standpoint of Śaṅkara, it is not even accurate to say that liberation is the fruit or effect of knowledge (*jñāna*). Liberation, being identical with *brahman*, is ever accomplished and eternal. The function of knowledge revealed in the *Upaniṣads* lies in the removal of obstacles. The relationship, says Śaṅkara, is comparable to that obtaining between standing and singing, where no other action intervenes (BSŚ 1.1.4).

V. The Sixfold Criteria for Determining the Purport of Scripture

Śaṅkara's case for the independent authority of the *Upaniṣads* is not only dependent upon the general kinds of arguments that we have so far examined. From a hermeneutical point of view, the most important basis for his position is his contention that by right correlation (*samanvaya*), it can be demonstrated that the sentences of the *Upaniṣads* have their purport (*tātparya*) only in the revelation of *brahman*.

> Besides, when the words in the Upaniṣadic sentences became fully ascertained as but revealing the nature of Brahman, it is not proper to fancy some other meaning; for that will result in rejecting something established by the Vedas and accepting some other thing not intended by them.(BSŚ 1.1.4)

In order to discover the purport of any scriptural passage, Advaita Vedānta makes use of the sixfold criteria (*ṣaḍliṅga*) formulated by Pūrva Mīmāṁsā exegetes.[11] These very important exegetical canons are as follows:

1. *Upakramopasaṁhāra* (the beginning and the end). This refers to the presentation of the subject matter at the beginning as well as at the end of any particular section of the scriptural text. A unity of the initial and concluding passages is considered to be a good indication of the intention of the text. For example, *Chāndogya Upaniṣad* (hereafter CU) 6.2.1 begins with the text, "In the beginning, my dear, this was being only, One without a second." The section ends: "All this is identical with That; That is the Self; That Thou Art, O Śvetaketu" (6.16.3).

2. *Abhyāsa* (repetition). The purport of the text is also suggested by the frequent repetition of a theme in the course of a discussion. In CU 6 the sentence "That Thou Art" (*tat tvam asi*) is repeated nine times.

3. *Apūrva* (novelty). The idea here is that if the subject under discussion is knowable through other *pramāṇas*, it cannot be the purport of the scripture. As a *pramāṇa*, the main function of the Vedas is to inform us of things that are inaccessible through any other means of knowledge. *Brahman* is considered unknowable through any means but the Vedas.

4. *Phala* (fruit). The purport of a passage is also indicated by the clear mention of an independent result. The fruitfulness of the sentences of the *Upaniṣads*, as we have seen, is an argument to which Śaṅkara returns again and again. CU 6.14.2 mentions liberation (*mokṣa*) as the fruit of the knowledge of *brahman* (*brahmajñāna*). In other words, if a particular passage mentions its own independent result, such a passage cannot be seen as being merely subservient to some other parts of the text. A distinct result is a good indication of a different purport.

5. *Arthavāda* (commendation). This is the praise of the subject matter in the course of the discussion. "Have you ever asked for that instruction by which one hears what has not been heard, one thinks what has not been thought, one knows what has not been known?" CU 6.1.3 is seen as a praise of *brahmajñāna*.

6. *Upapatti* (demonstration). This indicates the use of arguments to suggest the reasonableness of the subject presented. CU 6.1.4–6 uses a variety of illustrations to demonstrate the nondifference of cause and effect and to explain *brahman* as the material cause of the universe.

Advaita contends that by the application of the *ṣaḍliṅga,* it can be proved that the sentences of the *Upaniṣads* are not ancillary to other texts but have an independent purport in revealing *brahman*.

VI. Conclusion: The Relationship between Jñānakāṇḍa *and* Karmakāṇḍa

Having highlighted Śaṅkara's arguments for the autonomy of the *Upaniṣads* and the liberating potency of its words, we can now conclude by summing up his conception of the subject matter and purport of the Vedas as a whole. In Śaṅkara's view, the passages dealing with ritual action (*karmakāṇḍa*) inform us of approved means for attaining desirable but yet unaccomplished ends.[12] The *Upaniṣads* (jñānakāṇḍa), on the other hand, inform us of an already available *brahman*.[13] These two sections are clearly distinguishable in four ways (BSŚ 1.1.1.).

1. *Viṣaya* (subject matter). *Karmakāṇḍa* is, as we have seen, concerned with the revelation of *dharma*, while the *jñānakāṇḍa* has *brahman* as its subject.
2. *Adhikārī* (qualified aspirant). The aspirant, seeking the ends prescribed in the *karmakāṇḍa, is one who has not yet grown to understand the limitations of any result achieved by karman*. The aspirant of the *jñānkāṇḍa*, however, has appreciated the noneternity of *karman*-accomplished ends and seeks a limitless end (MU 1.2.12).
3. *Phala* (result). The *karmakāṇḍa* has wordly prosperity and heavenly enjoyment as its result. The aim of the *jñānakāṇḍa* is spiritual liberation (*mokṣa*).
4. *Sambandha* (connection). The information revealed in the *karmakaṇḍa* informs us of ends not yet in existence. The actualization of these ends depends upon being effected by appropriate action. Knowing is not an end in itself. The *jñānakāṇḍa*, however, reveals an already existent *brahman*. The knowledge of *brahman* (*brahmajñāna*) is an end in itself, affirming the connection between a revealed object and a means of revelation. *Jñānakāṇḍa* fufills itself in its informative role, while *karmakāṇḍa* impels us into activity.

Śaṅkara makes frequent reference in his commentaries to the criticism that the nondual *brahman* of the *jñānakāṇḍa* renders invalid the entire *karmakāṇḍa* with its dualistic presuppositions. His general response is that the Vedas are realistic and practical in their awareness of the human condition and provide solutions that are appropriate to human needs and demands. The Vedas do not instruct us at birth about the duality or unity of existence and then about ritual actions or *brahman*. In fact, adds Śaṅkara, the notion of duality does not have to be instructed. It is initially accepted as naturally true by all. Scripture, recognizing this and recognizing as well the multifarious desires in us, prescribes through the *karmakāṇḍa* appropriate rites for securing these ends (BUŚ 5.1.1.). In doing this the Vedas do not comment on the reality or falsity of these actions. Scripture simply instructs in accordance with capacity, since to exercise forceful restraint is impossible.

> People have innumerable desires and various defects, such as attachment. Therefore, they are lured by the attachment to external objects, and the scriptures are powerless to hold them back; nor can they persuade those who are naturally adverse to external objects to go after them. But the scriptures do this much that they point out what leads to good and what to evil; thereby indicating the particular relations that subsist between ends and means; just as a lamp, for instance, helps to reveal forms in the dark. But the scriptures neither hinder nor direct a person by force, as if he were a slave. We see how people disobey even the scriptures because of an excess of attachment. Therefore, according to the varying tendencies of people, the scriptures variously teach the particular relations that subsist between ends and means. (BUŚ 2.1.20)

When one finally appreciates the limited nature of results achieved through *karman* and seeks an unlimited end, the Vedas stand ready to impart *brahmajñāna*. For such a person the validity of duality, presupposed in the *karmakāṇḍa* is negated. Therefore, Śaṅkara concludes, the texts that teach the unity of *brahman* are not antagonistic to those enjoining ritual action, nor do the ritual texts deprive the *Upaniṣads* of authority. Each is authoritative in its own sphere (BUŚ 2.1.20).

In responding to Pūrva Mīmāṁsā's interpretation of the nature and scope of Vedic authority, Śaṅkara offers a rationale that goes beyond the mere dogmatic assertion of scriptural authority. His response raises issues relating to the authority and nature of scripture that provide a promising basis for dialogue with other traditions. The issues highlighted in this chapter—concerns about the logical necessity for a scripture, its fruitfulness, the criteria for determining its purport, the challenge of reconciling divergent subject matter within a single corpus—these are all matters of contemporary concern.

Notes

1. The Vedas are collectively referred to as the *śruti* (that which is heard). This term suggests the oral transmission of knowledge in a succession of teachers and students. It has been suggested that the reason for the oral transmission was the absence of written script at the time when the Vedas were composed. It appears, however, that even long after writing was introduced, there was a clear preference for the oral transmission of scripture, and religious learning through the written word was looked down upon. Vedic words had to be handed down exactly as they had been heard, and correct sounds and pronunciation became all important. See Cenker, 1980.

2. Advaita Vedānta epistemology borrows a great deal from the Pūrva Mīmāṁsā school. The word *mīmāṁsā* means inquiry, and this system undertakes a systematic analysis of the first (pūrva) sections of the Vedas, the *mantras* (hymns in praise of various deities), the *brahmanas* (guide books for the performance of sacrifices), and the *āraṇyakas* (philosophical interpretations of the sacrifices). Vedānta is referred to as *uttara mīmāṁsā* because its concern is with the last (*uttara*) sections of the texts, the *Upaniṣads*.

3. The word *dharma* in this context indicates any action, ritualistic or otherwise that results in the production of merit (*puṇya*) and leads to enjoyment in this or other worlds.

4. A sentence that subserves an injunction by praising the act or its result is termed an *arthavāda*.

5. For example, it is argued that a sentence such as *Vāyu is a swift deity* is purposeless by itself. When, however, it is seen in relation to the injunction, "One who wants prosperity should touch a goat relating to Vāyu," it serves as a praise of the deity and a recommendation of the ritual.

6. The argument here is that *dharma* is not amenable to any other *pramāṇa* because it has no tangible or external form. It also has to be brought into existence by prescribed acts. Vedic injunctions are the only source of its knowledge. We should remind ourselves that Śaṅkara accepts the Vedas as a *pramāṇa* for *dharma*. The word *pramā* is generally used to designate a true cognition. The special source of a particular *pramā* is termed *pramāṇa*. A *pramāṇa*, therefore, is a cause of valid knowledge. In producing knowledge, this cause plays an active and unique role.

7. It is again important to note the specific sense in which Śaṅkara is using the concepts of *dharma* and *adharma*. They indicate merit (*puṇya*) and demerit (pāpa) accruing particularly from the performance or nonper-

formance of recommended ritual action. Actions are understood as having a twofold result: seen (*dṛṣṭa*) and unseen (*adṛṣṭa*). Śaṅkara's argument is that the unique relation between any action and its result can be known only from the Vedas.

8. Mīmāṁsā is in full agreement with Śaṅkara on this point, even though it does not agree that the *Vedas* are also a *pramāṇa* for *brahman*.

9. There is a linguistic dimension to the Mīmāṁsā argument that the central concern of the *Vedas* is the initiation of activity through injunctive statements. They hold the view that in all sentences, words derive their meanings only from their relationships with the verb, and all usage is thus meant for instituting action. A factual statement, therefore, is never an end in itself, but has its reference in some activity. See PMS 1.1.25.

10. It should be emphasized here that in Śaṅkara view, knowledge itself, once it has emerged, requires no accessories for giving rise to liberation (*mokṣa*). Its emergence, however, is dependent upon various factors, including a transformation of intellect, will, and emotion. The qualified aspirant is one endowed with *sādhana-catuṣṭaya*, a group of four qualities considered indispensable for knowledge of *brahman*. These are as follows: (1) *viveka* (discrimination), (2) vairāgya (nonattachment), (3) *śamādisadhanasampatti* (the six accomplishments beginning with *śama*), and (4) *mumukṣutvam* (desire for liberation). See BSS 1.1.1.

11. For good definitions of the sixfold criteria, see Sadānanda's *Vedāntasāra*. There is little information on Sadānanda (ca 1450 C.E.). It is not known whether he wrote any work other than the *Vedāntasāra*. The text itself systematically presents the main doctrines of Advaita Vedānta

12. The desirable ends attainable by adopting the means prescribed in the *karmakaṇḍa* and sometimes classified as *dharma*, *artha* (wealth), and *kāma* (pleasure). These three are referred to as *pravṛtti dharma* (the way of works).

13. The *Upaniṣads* are also referred to as *jñānakāṇḍa* (section dealing with knowledge). The end here is *mokṣa*, also referred to as *nivṛtti dharma* (the way of renunciation). The sections treating ritual action and those dealing with the knowledge of *brahman* do not necessarily occur in different places in the text.

Abbreviations for Primary Texts Cited

AUŚ — Śaṅkara's commentary on the *Aitareya Upaniṣads* in *Eight Upaniṣads* with the Commentary of Śaṅkarācārya, 2d ed.,

	volume two. Translated by Swami Gambhirananda. Calcutta: Advaita Ashrama, 1966.
BGŚ	*The Bhagavadgītā: With the Commentary of Śaṅkarācārya*. Translated by A. M. Sastry. Madras: Samata Books, 1977.
BSŚ	*The Brahma-sūtra Bhāṣya of Śaṅkarācārya*. 3d ed. Translated by Swami Gambhirananda. Calcutta: Advaita Ashrama, 1977.
BUŚ	*The Bṛhadāraṅyaka Upaniṣad: With the Commentary of Śaṅkarācārya*. 5th ed. Translated by Swami Madhavananda. Calcutta: Advaita Ashrama, 1975.
CU	*The Chāndogya Upaniṣad with the Commentary of Śaṅkara*. Translated by Ganganatha Jha. Poona: Oriental Book Agency, 1942.
MU	*Muṇḍaka Upaniṣad* in *Eight Upaniṣads: With the Commentary of Śaṅkarācārya*, 2d ed., volume two. Translated by Swami Gambhirananda. Calcutta: Advaita Ashrama, 1966.
PMS	*The Pūrva Mīmāṁsā-sūtras of Jaimini: With an Original Commentary in English*. Translated by Ganganatha Jha. Varanasi: Bharatiya, 1979.

References

Cenker, William
1980 "The Pandit: The Embodiment of Oral Tradition." *Journal of Dharma* 5: 237–51.

Nikhilananda, Swami, trans.
1974 *Vedāntasāra or the Essence of Vedānta of Sadānanda Yogindra*. 6th ed. Calcutta: Advaita Ashrama.

Four

Binding the Text

Vedānta as Philosophy and Commentary

Francis X. Clooney, S.J.

Introduction

Let us first review what we are talking about when we speak of "Vedānta." India's Vedānta is comprised of a group of orthodox schools of thought that developed from textual and practical roots reaching back into the classical *Upanṣads* of the seventh to third centuries B.C.E., and that gained articulated form as a series of interpretations of the *Uttara Mīmāṁsā Sūtras* of Bādarāyaṇa, a fifth-century text that sought to regularize, and explain definitively, the *Upaniṣads.*

If, as Anantanand Rambachan showed us in the previous chapter, the development of the Vedānta from its Mīmāmsā roots was a very complex, multilevel enterprise, the modern reception of the Vedānta has been equally complex. From the time of Paul Deussen (1973 [1883]) in the last century, it has been noticed that this Vedānta is both a *philosophy* that inquires into the ultimate nature of reality and makes claims about it, and a *system of commentary* that strives to read revealed texts faithfully and then to "read" reality out of the texts.[1] But for reasons that have to do more with the tastes and expectations of nineteenth-century Europeans than with the proper nature of Vedānta itself, the acknowledgment that Vedānta is both philosophical and commentarial has usually been followed by almost exclusive attention to its philosophical side. The standard works in Indian philosophy recount the metaphysical, cosmological, and epistemological tenets of Vedānta, while having little to say about the bulk of the commentaries in which those tenets are imbedded. Some modern scholars, such as Eliot Deutsch (1969), have made this extraction their explicit project, and have sifted through Śaṅkara's great commentary on the basic *Uttara Mīmāṁsā*

Sūtras (henceforth UMS) of Bādarāyaṇa, his other works, and some later Vedānta works in order to retrieve the partially concealed philosophical nuggets. Some scholars, such as Murty (1974) and Halbfass (1983), have called out attention to the importance of the exegetical side of Vedānta, while perhaps only P. M. Modi (1956) has studied in detail the exegetical portions of the text.

I wish to suggest that we understand Vedānta properly only when we understand it as a conscious intersection between the philosophical and commentarial projects, and not as one or the other alone. Rambachan has already demonstrated for us the way in which Advaita Vedānta had to articulate new philosophical positions to support its focus on a new body of texts (the *Upaniṣads*) and its defense of the new themes and goals implied by that material. To complete our understanding of the competing roles of philosophy and exegesis in Advaita Vedānta, we must first engage in the further corrective project of gaining a clearer sense of the neglected commentarial side of Vedānta and its exegetical mode of thinking, thereby showing how the exigencies of exegesis and commentary are not only replaced by the philosophical Vedānta, but frame, instigate, and focus that philosophical development. My hope is that the following reflections will help to establish a framework in which the much larger project of a full retrieval can occur, and so provide us with a more adequate apprehension of the hermeneutical categories at work within the Vedānta, as an exegesis *of* texts and a philosophy responsive *to* texts.

I will first say something about the *Upaniṣads* as the source of the twofold Vedānta and about Bādarāyaṇa's treatment of them in the UMS; in the succeeding sections I will show how the philosophical and commentarial strands developed in Śaṅkara's *advaita* (nondualist) tradition.[2]

I. Vedānta as a Response to the Upaniṣads' *Multiple Modes of Signification*

According to the *Upaniṣads*, *brahman* is the highest reality and reference point for all meaning, and ultimately for salvation as well. Vedānta is both a speculative system that thinks about *brahman* as simply pointed out or announced *by* texts, and an exegetical system that discovers *brahman in* the text. To understand why this is so, one must begin by noting that the *Upaniṣads* themselves, those ritual-mystical-philosophical texts that are the primary sources of Vedānta,[3] invite a variety of uses. They first of all point out the possibility of traveling a path toward *brahman*, and are signs of what lies beyond themselves, encouragements toward the attainment of a goal for which one ultimately needs a *guru* and not a text. On this level, the *Upaniṣads* can be thought to reveal the *truth* of *brahman*, informing us of a reality that may, for most, remain unknown until the text tells us about it, but that, after it has been pointed out, is to be known by other means, apart from texts.

The texts can also be thought to have an inherent, enduring value, as the indispensable and never to be superseded locus of knowledge about *brahman*, the unique textuality of salvation—perhaps even the "verbal body" of *brahman*. To know the texts and become involved in their discourse is what constitutes knowledge; it is to know a "grammar of *brahman*," which one practices through hearing—or reading—and interiorizing the text.

The *Upaniṣads* abound in instances of passages that allow for multiple determinations as to how they relate to the knowledge they communicate. For example, the well-known dialogue between Uddālaka and his son Śvetaketu in *Chāndogya* 6 reports the variety of techniques by which Uddālaka helped his son to pass beyond a merely notional knowledge of the Vedas to a personally realized apprehension of *brahman*: he asked questions, made his son abstain from food for a time, used "props" such as saltwater and mustard seed, and so on. The account can be read as indicative of a process that requires some parallel encounter with a guru if it is to be effective. Or, when Uddālaka repeatedly concludes with the words "that thou art" (*tat tvam asi*) and thereby shows his son that "he" is the eternal self, this remarkable teaching might be thought to be detachable from the text as a new and very important "revelation," to be mediated on apart from the rest of the text. This is the possibility that led the later Vedānta to focus on several "great sayings" (*mahāvākya*) as the true essence of all the *Upaniṣads*. Finally, one might take the entirety of *Chāndogya* 6 as a sacred text for meditation, to be read and mastered thoroughly as a whole, not to be replaced by an activity, relationship, or main point. The *Chāndogya Upaniṣad* itself, in its discursive richness and ambiguity, is the means to salvation.

Although Advaita Vedānta does not definitively choose among these options regarding how to read Chāndogya 6, it is fair to say that the second and third together constitute the "object" of the Vedānta inquiry as it is textually preserved for us; they respectively prompt its tendencies toward philosophy and toward "permanent" exegesis. To generalize, we can say that Advaita Vedānta is a *philosophy* insofar as it stresses the role of the *Upaniṣads* as indicative of a reality beyond them, and that it is an *exegesis* insofar as it treats the *Upaniṣads* as the location where *brahman* is to be known and "read." The interplay of these two tendencies, not either alone, shows us the full texture of Vedānta; but to understand the interplay, we need to understand them distinctly.

Bādarāyaṇa's UMS shows how the two approaches began to take shape, and why. In its four *adhyāyas* (books, sections) it sorts out the content of the *Upaniṣads* into a set of statements about *brahman*, primarily in UMS 1, with UMS 2 as its adjunct, and into a set of texts used in meditation, in UMS 3, with UMS 4 as its adjunct.[4] What happens here can be traced by attention to two concepts: *samanvaya* as the search, undertaken particularly in UMS 1, for the single, primary meaning of the *Upaniṣads*, and *upasaṁhāra* as the search, undertaken particularly in UMS 3.3, for the rules governing the use of the varied, multiple *Upaniṣads* in a process of mediation that focuses on *brahman* as the ultimate, extratextual reality. In the next two sections of this essay I will consider these concepts in detail, as the sources of Advaita Vedānta as philosophy and permanent commentary.

II. The Roots of Vedānta as Philosophy in UMS 1: The Principle of Samanvaya

The main project of *Adhyāya* 1 is the demonstration of *samanvaya,* "coherence," in order to show that *brahman* is the primary and coherently described key topic of all the *Upaniṣads*. Śaṅkara explains the general point of *samanvaya* in his comment on 1.1.4:

> That all-knowing, all-powerful Brahman, which is the cause of the origin, subsistence, and dissolution of the world, is known from the Vedānta-part of Scripture. How? Because in all the Vedānta-texts the sentences construe in so far as they have for their purport, as they intimate that matter (viz., Brahman).[5]

In response to claims of the Sāṁkhya and other systems that the *Upaniṣads* do not, or do not uniformly, point to *brahman* as the absolute, highest reality, the Vedānta subjects all the contested texts to careful scrutiny in order to show their true topic.

Samanvaya structures the consideration in UMS 1 of various problematic *Upaniṣad* texts, taken up in a sequential order that was, to my knowledge, first noted by Deussen (1973, 121–22.) For example, the following *Chāndogya* texts are considered in the following UMS *adhikaraṇas* (topical sections): *Chāndogya* 1.6.6 [UMS 1.1.20–21]; 1.9.1 [1.1.22]; 1.11.5 [1.1.23]; 3.13.7 [1.1.24–27]; 3.14.1 [1.2.1–8]; 4.15.1 [1.2.13–17]; 5.11–24 [1.2.24–32]; 7.23 [1.3.8–9]; 8.1.1 [1.3.14–18]; 8.12.3 [1.3.19–21; 1.3.40]; 8.14 [1.3.41].

UMS 1.2.1–14, a section comprised of four *adhikaraṇas*, adequately exemplifies the kinds of problem noted and solved in the Vedānta analysis. In each *adhikaraṇa*, the adversary (*pūrvapakṣin*) suggests that the text is inappropriate to *brahman* as known from other texts:

> 1–8: Is it *brahman* or the human self which is described in *Chāndogya* 3.14.2, where it says that "Mind is his stuff, living

(breathing) is his body, light his form, resolution his truth, his self is infinity . . ." etc.? How could *brahman* be connected with "mind," "breathing" etc.?[6]

9–10: Is it *brahman* (or fire, or the human self) which is meant in the *Kāṭha* 1.2.25, where it says, "The Brahmana [*brahman*] and warrior [*kṣatram*] both are consumed by Him, as if they were His food, seasoned or steeped in the sauce of death; who would find Him who is such a one?" How could *brahman* be thought to enjoy and eat as do beings in *Saṁsāra*?

11–12: The next section of the *Kāṭha*, 1.3.1, says, "The two, the drinkers of the requital of works, high above in the yonder world, they enter into the cavity or the cavern . . ." *Brahman* has just been referred to in *Kāṭha* 1.2.25 and might be considered one of the two drinkers, but how can *brahman* be localized as "drinking" and "entering a cave"?

13–14: *Chāndogya* 4.15.1 says, "The man whom one sees in the eye is the Ātman . . . He is the immortal one, the fearless one, he is Brahman." Is it *brahman*, or the human self, which is thus placed in the eye—and how could *brahman* be thus localized?

In each case, reasons (too lengthy and complex to reproduce here) are given to show that the cited Upaniṣadic text, when understood properly in its context, does indeed refer to *brahman*. None of these texts, nor any other text, promises salvation by meditation on realities other than *brahman*.

Even if the demonstration of *samanvaya* is the specific, limited goal of UMS 1, a secondary but very significant effect was the regularization of the *Upaniṣads*, the homogenization of their explorations and stories and experiments into an informative "metadiscourse" about *brahman*. Bādarāyaṇa's analysis allows for and encourages the digestion of the *Upaniṣads* into the "best of the *Upaniṣads*," a clear and usable body of information about an existent reality. Once it is understood that the extratextual *brahman* is the uniform and coherently described topic of the *Upaniṣads*, there is a strong tendency to abstract from them that single meaning, and thereafter to use the texts merely as initial occasions or starting points for an ever more independent consideration of *brahman*. This shift to knowledge about *brahman*, extrapolated from the texts as their meaning, is at the source of Vedānta as philosophy.

Two additional factors contribute to the formation of the philosophical strand of Vedānta: the decontextualized (mis)use of the *nirguṇa*/*saguṇa* distinction, and the apologetic necessity.

First, the distinction between *brahman* as *saguṇa* (describable by various textual qualifications, *guṇas*) and *brahman* as *nirguṇa* (beyond these qualifications) was originally (as explained in 3.2.11ff.) a distinction in service of the project of meditation as a meaningful and efficacious enterprise that begins with texts and yet is not imprisoned in language. If Śaṅkara's *Advaita* school insisted that *brahman* was "really" *nirguṇa*, this was to prevent the reduction of *brahman* to a merely available, known object about which many things can be said by any well-read, learned person; to know *brahman* and hence to be liberated is not merely to know a great deal about *brahman*, about its *guṇas*. So too, if *brahman* were merely *saguṇa*, known only as it is knowable in meditation, one would never finish meditating and never get beyond the stubborn plurality of texts; the potential fruitfulness of meditation on *saguṇa brahman* requires, in *Advaita* Vedānta, the declaration that *brahman* is ultimately *nirguṇa*, "beyond the text." Conversely, the achieved realization of *brahman* as *nirguṇa* is itself not just one more thing to be known about *brahman*; it is a realization located at the culmination of an active process of "realizing" the *saguṇa* texts (even if in *Advaita* it cannot be the effect of that process).

This performative balance between the *nirguṇa* and *saguṇa* was liable to distortion when considered in abstraction. When attention to *brahman* "as it really is" became detached from meditation and its exigencies, the study of *nirguṇa brahman* gradually took on a life of its own; it became the subject of philosophical defenses and explanations that reached beyond what was said in the texts, and the differentiation of the two kinds of language of *brahman* became a separation. The distinction between the *nirguṇa* and the *saguṇa* was hypostatized as a higher truth; the *saguṇa* was confined to the level of ignorance and "merely popular" religion, while the *nirguṇa* became the property of the philosophers.[7]

Second, the universal claims made by Vedānta required it to engage in apologetics, to say something about and to other, differing systems of thought. The UMS 2 is Vedānta's effort to establish the reasonability of the positions developed out of *Upaniṣadic* sources, to argue that Vedānta's positions not only are scripturally correct, but also are more reasonable than the alternatives. In UMS 2.2, this requires the serial critique of major heterodox positions,[8] each in the series being a little less wrong than the one prior to it: Sāṁkhya (2.2.1–10), Vaiśeṣika (11–17), Buddhism in its Sarvāstivāda (18–27), Vijñānavāda (28–31), and Śunyavāda (32) schools, Jainism (33–36), Pāśupata (Śaiva) theism (37–41) and Pāñcarātra (Vaiṣṇava) theism (42–45). Even here there is no reliance on pure reason, since it is possible to show, I believe, that the Vedāntins rely largely on a scriptural framing of the world even when they seek to argue without presuming it.[9] Nevertheless, the argumentation has a life of its own and invites development in the ongoing debate with those heterdox systems, in the context of which the scriptural warrants recede ever more distantly into the background.

We can couple with this development in UMS 2 the characteristic effort to establish at the beginning of a commentary all the prerequisites to a proper and unobstructed reading of the text to follow; hence a great deal of metadiscourse flourishes at the beginning of UMS 1.1. The commentaries on UMS 1.1.1–4, the so-called *Catuḥsūtrī* (Four Sūtras), approximated freestanding works able to be read independently of the rest of any given commentary.

These developments, together with the effect of the defense of *samanvaya*, established the basis for Vedānta as a philosophy. Later on, of course, there were works more explicitly and independently philosophical. Treatises such as the *Upadeśasāhasrī, Vedānta Paribhāṣa,* and *Vivekacūḍāmaṇi* develop the "philosophical" side of the Vedānta, often in part according to the canons of the logical schools of Nyāya, Buddhist, and other systems of thought. It is these texts that have most often provided the basis for modern reworkings of Vedānta as a philosophy.

III. The Roots of Vedānta as Commentary in UMS 3.3: The Principle of Upasaṁhāra

However prominent its philosophical discourse became, Vedānta has always remained a strongly commentarial tradition. I wish now to trace this development, and to show how Vedānta built into its inquiry certain principles that made exegesis of primary and secondary tests a permanent feature of all Vedānta inquiry.

If the search for *samanvaya* encourages attention to what the *Upaniṣads* say, as distinct from how they say it, a different principle and different result characterize the other large exegetical *pāda* (chapter), UMS 3.3. There, the goal is the explication of *upasaṁhāra* (combination), the strategy by which different Upaniṣadic texts can be selectively and partially combined by the meditator.

Upasaṁhāra is proposed in 3.3.1–5, where it is explained that one can and must construct an intricate balance between two facts: *brahman* is an extratextual reality, and *brahman* is, for now at least, only textually accessible. *Upasaṁhāra*, modeled on the resultant principle of a Mīmāṁsā debate in which rules were spelled out as to how ritual performers could "borrow" details of ritual performance from the texts of other schools, suggests that extratextuality of *brahman* partially modifies our reading of the texts of various schools without rendering that reading superfluous. The questions include: How are texts to be used in conjunction with one another? How, by implication, are meanings related to tests? and How, finally, is *brahman*, which is extratextual, to be known from texts while at the same time influencing the reading of those texts? UMS 3.3 asks *how* texts mean, and how they form a context for one another; its goal is not a philosophical knowledge of *brahman*, but a refined set of rules by which one engages in a permanent act of "reading" *brahman* in the text.[10]

The practical question underlying *upasaṁhāra* can be illustrated as follows. If *brahman* is in one text referred to as "existent," in a second as "desiring the good," and in a third as "in the heart," can a person meditating on one of three such texts introduce into meditation the other two qualifications—and can the meditator be selective and introduce just one of those other two? Vācaspati Miśra explains, in his comment on 3.3.11, that one must allow the possibility of such borrowing and of selective borrowing, since if *brahman* exists, it is not possible to keep redefining its nature from text to text; certain important qualifications—*brahman* is, is powerful, is unlimited, and so on—pertain everywhere, regardless of where they are first mentioned. Yet as the context implies (and as is stated somewhat belatedly at 3.3.58), the various texts do really count, and one cannot simply conflate them all into one theoretical account. Hence, one has to read correctly and with discrimination. Some qualifications, such as "existence", can be applied everywhere; others, such as "in the heart," apply only in the meditation where mentioned. One has to acquire facility in judging what to borrow and what not to borrow.

If we recall the sequential order of texts examined in UMS 1, it is striking to note that no such sequence appears in UMS 3.3 (Deussen 1973, 43–44). The *pāda* is structured not according to texts presented in the order in which they are found in the *Upaniṣads*, but by the logic of a series of refinements and limitations of the basic notion of *upasaṁhāra*. The following three *adhikaraṇas*, as I summarize them according to the insights of a number of the commentaries, illustrate the main lines of the *pāda*.[11]

3.3.11: Is there a principle by which some qualifications attributed to *brahman* in one or another text can be recalled and introduced during a meditation on any given text, even though other qualifications will not be so recalled and introduced? Qualifications that delimit the nature of *brahman* as it is in itself must be distinguished from those that "form" it for this or that meditation. The former, and not the latter, can be transferred from text to text.[12]

3.3.33 When certain limitations are denied—*brahman* is not dirty, not measurable, not perishable, and so forth—can these too be applied everywhere without the meditator ending up with an infinite list of qualifications that do not apply to *brahman*? The correct rule is still the one given in 3.3.11: unless the negative qualifications are purely contextual, the meditator (who must judge from past familiarity with text and meditation whether or not this is the case) can apply them elsewhere; but there is no reason to introduce every conceivable negation.

3.3.39 A statement from one meditation can be introduced into another, even if it is mixed description, some parts of it pertaining to *saguṇa brahman*, others to *nirguṇa brahman*. This is so even if a few parts do not fit the new context that itself is primarily *nirguṇa* or *saguṇa*, such that most of the parts of the other statement fit it, but not all. One can read a text, determine its major points, and use it appropriately, and still downplay the parts that are there for some secondary, supporting reason and not as primary to the meditation.

The process of *upasaṁhāra* does not conclude that *brahman* can be thought about in general, under a composite form constructed by harmonizing all Upaniṣadic texts. Rather, it presumes an irreducible, ongoing act of reading, remembering, and combining texts, in which the extratextual and full nature of *brahman* modifies how we read texts with their many distinctions. In a sense, *upasaṁhāra* is the complement to *samanvaya*: by *samanvaya*, the multiplicity of texts is understood to point to a single topic, *brahman*; by *upasaṁhāra*, it is understood how that single topic, *brahman*, can be known through intelligent and discriminating meditation on the multiple texts. It is this latter insistence on meditation that keeps the knowledge of *brahman* within Vedānta's orthodox horizon.

Attention to the textual, exegetical component of knowledge of *brahman* is neither simply the residue of an older tradition nor a secondary, unreflective aspect of Vedānta. Quite the contrary: through an *increasing* use of the older principles of the Pūrva Mīmāṁsā ritual/exegetical system, Vedānta makes possible and necessary a continuing attention to texts as the proper context for its philosophical thinking. How this is so requires a more lengthy treatment than is possible here, and I will restrict myself to four comments on the way in which the commentarial component of Vedānta is maintained and becomes more and not less explicit as Vedānta develops: (1) the reliance on *intratextual rules* for the ascertainment of meaning; (2) the identification of *case-based rules* (*nyāya*); (3) *performance-oriented interpretation* in which all meaning is purpose, intending the performance of meditational knowledge; and (4) *expanded contextuality* and the interpretation of the *Upaniṣads* and the UMS.

IV. Reliance on Intratextual Rules

The Mīmāṁsakas articulated rules according to which the grammatical and literary connections of a text provide all the information needed for the interpretation of the text. Grammar, literary structure, and context are the adequate keys to meaning. This effort to articulate rules by which texts will be the guides to their own interpretation presupposes a refusal to depend on the author's intention, or the nature of the object of reference, as the primary guides for the fixing of meaning.

The doctrine of *apauruṣeyatva*—the Veda has expositors, but no authors (*puruṣa*)—reflected the Mīmāṁsā school's desire to show that the Vedic complex of sacrifice and text was not dependent on any transitory and self-motivated agents and things; external reference to impermanent realities threatened ultimately to undercut the posited eternity and permanence of the sacred text itself. The system had to be nonreferential, meaningful in itself, and expressive of that meaning, in order to be protected from a changing and unpredictable world.

Vedānta follows the Mīmāṁsā lead and develops ways of explaining texts without appealing to an author's intention, even though in Vedānta the doctrine seems to be an imitative one, introduced to maintain the Mīmāṁsā notion of independent authority and thus to enhance the status of the *Upaniṣads*. The *Upaniṣads* themselves do not require any such doctrine, and Bādarāyaṇa's text itself could lend itself to the idea that the *Upaniṣads* communicate various authors' intentions and point to a reality beyond the text. In any case, by this adoption Vedānta too became increasingly dependent on the text itself as the self-referential source for the rules of its own interpretation. The project of the interpretation of the *Upaniṣads* via the UMS became increasingly the project of elaborating meaning as discoverable strictly in the words, sentences, and contexts themselves. Like the Mīmāṁsakas, the Advaitic commentators at every turn "restrain" extratextual reference within the overarching frame of the text, which is not replaced by knowledge, even if the object of knowledge remains "outside the text."[13]

V. The Identification of Case-based Rules

One of the primary supports of this stubborn adherence to the text itself is the process of explaining primarily through the examination of textual cases by which rules are identified, tested, modified, and related to one another by metarules, etc. Like jurisprudence, Mīmāṁsā/Vedānta interpretation proceeds by cases and the accumulation of precedents (Clooney, *Thinking Ritually,* 1990, chapter 2). Some of the rules are highly articulated. For instance, the Mīmāṁsā identifies two sets of six textual *pramāṇas* (means of sure knowledge) as important tools of the articulation of meaning in the text. Vedānta accepted these sets of rules, and only with great care made modifications and explanations to fit the new specifications of the Upaniṣadic material. Every Vedānta text requires that we attend to the working of these rules in it.[14]

Less defined that these two sets, but of great importance, are the continuous efforts in every *adhikaraṇa* to discover rules, or to refine and limit already known rules, to deal with specific problems. As already noted, both *samanvaya* and *upasaṁhāra* are specified through the examination of a series of contested situations in which the general principle as thus far stated is tested, clarified, expanded, and limited in an ever more nuanced body of rules (*nyāyas*), and the first and third *adhyāyas* abound in rule making and stretching.

An example drawn from 3.3 will illustrate the nature of the process of inquiry and refinement. The commentaries regularly introduce, either to use in solving difficult cases, or to modify, or even to refuse to use (for certain reasons that can thereby be noticed), Mīmāṁsā rules that themselves had been articulated in some particular problematic context. To illustrate this, the following are three among the Mīmāṁsā rules introduced in order to clarify the limits of *upasaṁhāra in UMS* 3.3.1–5.

1. The *Pūrva Mīmāṁsā Sūtras* (henceforth PMS) 2.4.8–33 give us the rule that it is proper to borrow ritual details from the texts of other schools, by *upasaṁhāra*, even if those schools are truly different, and even if not every element of every text should be thus introduced. So too, meditators can borrow from the meditation texts of other schools (first enunciated by Bādarāyaṇa).

2. A rule enunciated in PMS 10.5.34–41 tells us that an apparently possible introduction of a ritual detail at an ectypal rite is overruled when there is a text that explicitly connects the detail with the archetypal rite;[15] for the allocation of details depends on the text. But by contrast, when texts about *brahman* are at issue, the decision about where to introduce any given qualification is not limited by what is explicitly stated, because the meditator is able to recognize where the details appropriately belong (even if it is not so stated). (That is, because *brahman* is not constituted solely by the text, the Vedāntin may make judgments about the use of texts that go beyond what the texts state) (Ānandagiri).

3. The "Gṛhamedhīya-rite rule," enunciated in PMS 10.7.24, indicates that in a ritual setting where it is understood that all the details of a new rite might be borrowed from another rite that is its archetype, the actual mention of only a few of those potentially borrowed details is meant to tell us that the mentioned details alone are to be borrowed and that the remaining, unmentioned details are *not* allowed. One might want to apply this in the Vedānta setting, and claim that if one meditation text mentions

certain of the qualities found in another, but not all, then all the unmentioned qualifications are excluded. But, the Vedāntin replies, the Gṛhamedhīya-rite rule is not adequate regarding texts about *brahman*, since these texts are not related to one another in the archetypal-ectypal pattern according to which rites are connected (Vācaspati).

Although such rules often reflect a commonsense viewpoint on how to read correctly, they are also, as we can see here, obstinately complex because permanently contextual: they remain imbedded in ritual and meditational detail, and one can use them in a wider set of contexts only after becoming familiar with the original specific instances involved.

Training in Vedānta is not simply the accumulation of more and more information to hold in the mind, nor is it only an abstract knowledge. Rather, it is also about knowing the rules of the text, rules that embody strategies for reading and thinking and that, as such, govern further practical acts of reading and interpreting. Because these strategies are performative, they permanently resist transformation into (mere) knowledge about *brahman*; because they are strategies rooted in examples, they resist abstraction. This is a refined sort of knowledge, but it does not tend toward the philosophical; it entails a "metareasoning" that is able to step back from the details in reflection upon them, while yet remaining irreducibly dependent on those details.[16]

VI. Performance-oriented Interpretation

Again following the Mīmāṁsā lead, Vedānta presupposes that text and performance—meditational or sacrificial—imply, reflect, and instigate one another. The *Upaniṣads* were understood to operate analogously to the ritual texts, and the rules worked out in Mīmāṁsā for the harmonization of texts about rituals were likewise accepted as governing how meditation and its texts relate. The texts used in meditation—in UMS 3, and then by extension in UMS 1—function analogously to how the ritual texts function regarding action, its results, and performers, etc.; both sets of texts intend and structure action and have meanings that can be determined by asking about their usefulness. Vedānta shared the view that the sacred texts are practical texts, and held that the *Upaniṣads* were meant to help the meditator attain liberation.

In general, meaning and purpose converge. Therefore, readings that give texts a clearer and more useful purpose are always preferable, and apparently useless or merely obscure statements are not allowed to remain so. Much exegetical energy goes into ascertaining potential levels of usefulness for obscure texts, so as to be able thereby to discern right interpretation accordingly. For example, when *Chāndogya* 3.14.2, as cited at UMS 1.2.1–8, says that "mind is his stuff, living (breathing) is his body, light his form, resolution his truth, his self is infinity . . . ," Prakāśātman, in his *Śārīrakanyāyasaṁgraha*, argues that the series of descriptive qualifications points best to *brahman*, since the multiple qualifications would be superfluous regarding the human self, which is already known from ordinary experience and which would therefore require the mention of only one of its characteristics to define it. Lest the text be considered verbose, it should be understood to apply to *brahman*, which is not otherwise known. So too, he argues, even if there are textual reasons to think that the human self is the topic of the section, since we know that meditation on *brahman* is more useful—efficacious toward liberation—than meditation on the human self, an interpretation that identifies *brahman* as the topic is to be preferred.

This kind of calculation helps to preclude the transformation of interpretation into a detached, speculative understanding of the *Upaniṣads*. The questions "What for?" and "So what?" are always prominent. Not only must the texts continue to be attended to, but they must also be interpreted so as to continue to be usable for spiritual advancement.[17]

VII. Expanded Contextuality

Finally, there is what I tentatively call "expanded contextuality." As the Vedānta commentarial tradition grows, the core Upaniṣadic body of texts to be interpreted is supplemented by each successive layer of commentary as itself in need of commentary. The UMS are established as a coherent text (which in turn is partially intertexted with the PMS) that needs to be read as a whole, alongside the *Upaniṣads*, and understood as more than a series of *ad hoc* comments on the *Upaniṣads*. It too has a logic and completeness of its own, which must be highlighted.

So too, the Vedānta tradition began early on to treat Śaṅkara's commentary on the UMS as a text with its own dynamic, which then had to be interpreted and related back to the UMS and then to the *Upaniṣads*. The increasing volume of material requiring commentary affected both the mode of commentary, as more sophisticated and refined rules had to be articulated, and the content of commentary, as the *Upaniṣads* and later texts had now to be read in the light of the UMS version of them, Śaṅkara's basic viewpoint about them and the UMS, the juxtaposed and then interwoven PMS, and its sources and implied rules, etc. The "fate" of the *Upaniṣads* and their doctrine of *brahman* was to be ever more complexly mediated through this web of text and tradition.

An important and characteristic sign of this expanding commentarial process was the ideal of and search for *saṁgati* as the connectedness of the commented-on text. This is a search founded on the belief that even an apparently *ad hoc*, problem-solving investigation follows a logic not determined simply by the demands of the set of successive problematic texts requiring comment. The "original" text is relocated, as "pretextual" to the commentary now being commented on; it is now to be read only through the logic of that commentary and its necessary order.

Bādarāyaṇa himself may have been the first to establish this broader and more complex textuality, by his conscious appropriation and imitation of the PMS.[18] And although Śaṅkara for the most part attended directly to the *Upaniṣads* through the UMS as a neutral lens, and usually simply deferred to Bādarāyaṇa's viewpoint without treating the UMS as itself a work requiring interpretation, he occasionally discovered in the UMS an integrative, organizing role helping to structure the reading of the *Upaniṣads*, and drew attention to the fact of *saṁgati*.

For instance, although 1.1–3 seems to be simply a straightforward treatment of Upaniṣadic texts in sequence, and is best taken as having no more intricate arrangement than that, the *pādas* were explained by Śaṅkara as more complexly arranged, according to how texts are able to express *brahman*. As he explains at 1.2.1, 1.1 dealt with texts with straightforward meanings, and 1.2–3 with texts whose meanings are ambiguous. The later Vedānta commentators developed this sense of a larger structure more fully. Thus, Amalānanda further differentiates 1.2 from 1.3 by offering (at 1.2.1) this explanation:

> In the first *pāda* those statements which contain clear indications of *brahman* are the topic, in the second and third *pāda*, those which lack such clear indications. These two *pādas* are in general further differentiated by having as their respective topics *brahman* with specifications (*saviśeṣa*) and *brahman* without specifications (*nirviśeṣa*), and by dealing, respectively, with the etymological meanings (*yoga*) and conventional meanings (*rūḍha*) of words.

The explanation of the *saṁgati* between the individual *adhikaraṇas* was also a primary task for the commentators. To illustrate their reasoning by reference to a now familiar locus, the following summarizes the three most notable explanations of the *saṁgati* connecting the first *adhikaraṇas* of 1.2.

1. The *saṁgati* between 1.2.9–10 and 1.2.1–8: It was shown in 1.2.1–8 that *brahman* is not a mere enjoyer of material things; so it seems to follow, says the adversary, that the "eater of *brahman* and *kṣatram*" (*Kāṭha* 1.2.25) referred to in 9–10 could not be *brahman*. This line of reasoning (though in error) establishes the continuity (cf. Amalānanda).

2. The *saṁgati* between 1.2.11–12 and 1.2.9–10: 9–10 dealt with *Kāṭha* 1.2.25, and here (11–12) we simply take up the next part of the *Upaniṣad*, *Kāṭha* 1.3.1 (Govindānanda).

3. The saṁgati between 1.2.13–14 and 1.2.11–12: We learned in the previous section (11–12) that the opening of a text is usually determinative of the topic of what follows. So too here (13–14): The opening—"the man whom one sees in the eye . . ." (*Chāndogya* 4.15.1)—is privileged, and so *brahman* cannot be the topic, the adversary says, since it cannot be seen (Govindānanda).

These proposed connections are often slender threads, or merely apparent connections wrongly posed by the adversary. Occasionally they are unconvincing, and occasionally the commentators do not venture to suggest any at all. Yet the idea that there is *saṁgati* is crucial, since it shows that the UMS, like the *Upaniṣads*, is understood to be a coherent text in which every element has its purpose, and is a text to be read and interpreted along with the *Upaniṣads*.[19]

While the search for the *saṁgati* of the UMS as a text need not in itself deflect or defer a proper understanding of the *Upaniṣads*, which remain the ultimate textual object of commentary, this procedure effects a continuing enlargement of the frame of meaning in which the older texts are to be read, philosophical arguments are to be made, etc. Although the Indian tradition on the whole has not asked about the background and redaction of texts, and therefore has not raised the question of "history" in critique of philosophy and related notions of truth, meaning, etc., the determination of *saṁgati* (along with the articulation of *nyāyas*, in a ritual/meditative performative framework) has served to subject philosophical thinking to a rigorous critique of another sort, a permanent contextualization that resists the move toward abstract, idealized knowledge.[20]

VIII. Conclusion

The preceding remarks on the philosophical and commentarial tendencies in Advaita Vedānta, as traced back to the *Upaniṣads* and discovered in the procedures of *samanvaya* and *upasaṁhāra* regarding the *Upaniṣads*, point up the complexity of the Vedānta project and its irreducibility to either a strictly philosophical system or a system of open-ended, contentless commentary. It is permanently about the reading and use of texts, *and* about *brahman* as an extratextual reality communicated through texts, without either the text or the reality being thereby rendered superfluous. Since modern scholarship has stressed the philosophical merits of Advaita

Vedānta, it has been necessary to indicate how in practice and its articulated methodology Vedānta consciously refused to move away from its texts and the concomitant commentarial and meditational procedures.

Whatever distinctions one makes between the philosophical and commentarial sides of the Vedānta texts, one therefore has to understand them together, as distinct but separately insufficient modes of discourse. Advaita Vedānta lies in the creative tension of the two modes of explanation, not apart from it. Neither the *Upaniṣads* nor the UMS invite a sharp distinction between content and use; nor was it Bādarāyaṇa's intention to force a cleavage between the content of the texts and their mode of expression.

To read the *Upaniṣads* through Vedāntin eyes, and to read the UMS and Śaṅkara's *Bhāṣya* and the later commentaries as a true series of wider contexts, is to read back and forth, from text to increasingly (though never completely) independent reasoning to text again, from commentary to philosophy and back again. It is to see how exegesis continually brought about a rereading of philosophical discussions on a more textual basis, and how philosophy established new, right readings of the texts.

Finally, a few comments regarding ourselves. Our study of the texts of non-Western cultures is of course mediated through the concerns and values of the modern and postmodern West, and we must therefore be attentive to two biases that are likely to distort our reading of Vedānta. On the one hand, it has been our cultural preference from at least the time of the Enlightenment to take the philosophical more seriously than the commentarial, and this is a preference that encodes into modern scholarship a whole set of more basic attitudes toward thinking, speaking and writing, truth, experience, originality, and creativity. The insistence of Advaita Vedānta on the importance of the Upaniṣadic texts as a privileged canon that constructs the frame in which inquiry of all sorts is to proceed is something we may tend to overlook, to explain away as a culture-specific residue. We may even try to reject it under the guise of attention to selected parts of the Advaita system, such as the notion of *nirguṇa brahman*, despite the fact that the Advaita Vedāntins managed to adhere both to that notion and to the practice of vigorous commentary.

As Michel Foucault (1973, especially 78ff.) has shown, we have much to learn about our contemporary discourse of knowledge and inquiry just from the simple fact of the distance we experience from the commentarial worldview. As Smith (1982), Lindbeck (1984), Derrida (1982), and others have indicated, attention to and appreciation of the reading of texts, religious or otherwise, assigns us a task with enormous implications in regard to both detail and larger priorities. An engagement in these "postmodern" issues is prerequisite to the proper study of Vedānta in a "post-Indological" age in which the set categories of philosophy and philology have broken down.

On the other hand, however, the same postmodern agenda favors a thoroughly open-ended view of text and commentary, in which meaning is only a series of provisional, deferred, and deflected interpretations, readings. As I have suggested elsewhere (Clooney 1987, 680–82), if the Mīmāṁsā-Vedānta tradition intriguingly invites comparison with deconstructionist thought, it does so with the provisos that the boundaries of one's body of texts can be meaningfully fixed, that there is an extratextual reality that serves as a reference point by which to critique wrong readings of texts, and that, finally, one can eventually finish reading and attain liberation.

While this permanently commentarial side of Vedānta is of course not exempt from some of the same criticisms pointed at traditional religious thought in the West, it is also not exactly the same as that thought. It partially intersects with current retrievals of text and interpretation, is akin to deconstructionism, and then, at the same time, shares much with older, pre-Enlightenment notions of text and commentary. It deserves, then, a careful and fresh reading, so as to sort out how it relates to the whole spectrum of Western ideas, premodern, modern, and postmodern.

The project before the contemporary student of Vedānta in a comparative context is therefore a complex one requiring many skills and areas of attention. Nevertheless, I suggest, it is the genius and enduring value of the Vedānta system that a careful study of the UMS and its commentaries, in the entirety of that tradition's rich variety and not selectively, remains our best guide to an encounter with the contemporary agenda: reading Vedānta compels us to read our modern world carefully, and differently.

Notes

1. Throughout I use words such as *philosophy, exegesis, commentary,* and *theology* in a nontechnical manner, to help distinguish in a preliminary and provisional fashion the two major aspects of Vedānta. I do not intend to reduce exegesis to a nonphilosophical way of thinking (or nonthinking), nor to claim that philosophy is necessarily independent of the acceptance of a canon of texts, religious or otherwise. For further development of my understanding of these terms, see Clooney (''Vedānta, Commentary, and the Theological Component,'' 1990).

2. I limit my remarks exclusively to the school of Śaṅkara (eighth century), since he sets the questions and project even for those later Vedāntins (e.g., Rāmānuja [eleventh century], Madhva [thirteenth], and Vallabha [sixteenth]) who disagree with him. In my analyses I will refer also to these later *Advaita* thinkers who wrote commentaries on Śaṅkara's *Bhāṣya* on the

Uttara Mīmāṁsa Sūtras (UMS): Ānandagiri (late eighth century), Vācaspati Miśra (ninth), Amalānanda (thirteenth), Govindānanda (sixteenth), and Appaya Dīkṣita (sixteenth); I will also refer to Prakāśātman (tenth), who wrote the *Śarīrakanyāyasaṁgraha*, a treatise that succinctly identifies the rules of interpretation (*nyāya*) used by Śaṅkara and other early commentators. Of these, only Śaṅkara's commentary has been translated. For the rest, I have used the editions mentioned in the bibliography for this essay.

3. For an overview of these *Upaniṣads* as relevant to Vedānta, see Nakamura 1983.

4. UMS 2, to which I will refer below, intends primarily a defense of *Advaita* Vedānta's views against those who do not accept the authority of the *Upaniṣads*; UMS 4 focuses on the actual practice and results of meditation.

5. As translated by Thibaut (1962, 1:22).

6. Here and throughout I use Deussen's 1980 translation.

7. This sketch of the origins and distortions of the *nirguṇa/saguṇa* distinction is here presented as a hypothesis; its documentation is for now an unfinished part of my ongoing study of the UMS and *Advaita* Vedānta.

8. Thus setting the model for the later and more well-known *Sarvadarśanasaṁgraha* of Madhavācārya, which arranges fifteen systems on the basis of their distance from the *Advaita* position.

9. On the theological, scriptural basis for the *Advaita* "philosophical" position on theodicy, as spelled out in UMS 2.2; see Clooney 1989.

10. The third *adhyāya* in general is a reflection on the presuppositions of meditation, including the order of the world (3.1), the nature of human self and *brahman* (3.2), and the nature of the mediating person as "orthodox" (3.4).

11. Here I follow Appaya Dīkṣita's comments on 3.3.1. Modi, who is interested more in retrieving Bādarāyaṇa's system than in Śaṅkara's version of it, offers a different and important explanation of the structure of the *pāda*.

12. Vācaspati distinguishes between qualifications that attest to *brahman*'s basic nature—being, truth, bliss, etc.—and those that do pertain, but only as posited in the specific context: "being that toward which all blessings go," or "whose desires are true." The former belong everywhere, the latter only where introduced. Appaya Dīkṣita adds the point, significant for the Advaita Vedāntins, that even the first set of basic qualifications are more of the nature of boundary setting than essence describing.

13. On the notion of *apauruṣeyatva* and the uses of it in Mīmāṁsā and Vedānta, see Clooney 1987. On the effort to interpret a text through itself (and its contexts), see Lindbeck on "intratextuality" (1984, 113–24).

14. The two sets of rules are described in the *Pūrva Mīmāṁsā Sūtras* (PMS), the basic Mīmāṁsā text, equivalent in stature to Bādarāyaṇa's UMS, and probably the model for it. The first, listed in PMS 3.3.14 and described thereafter, provides six ways of determining the meaning of a text, each less persuasive than the one listed before it: What is explicitly said (*śruti*); what is implied by what is said (*liṅga*); what can be construed from syntactical units such as sentences (*vākya*); how two parts of a text can be linked as a context, to fill out their meaning (*prakaraṇa*); what can be estimated based on the proximity or order of ideas in a text (*sthāna, krama*); and what can be learned from names analyzed etymologically (*samākhyā*). The second group is given in PMS 5.1 and is used for determining the order of the performance of ritual actions; here too, each in the list is less persuasive than the one listed before it: what is explicitly said (*śtruti*), the respective purpose of the actions (*artha*), the order of the actions in the text (*pāṭha*), priority of place in the original context (*sthāna*), the respective importance of the actions involved (*mukhya*), and preference for actions begun first (*pravṛtti*). For a reasonably succinct summary of both sets, see *Āpadeva's Mīmāṁsā Nyāya Prakāśa*, nn. 68–181 and 199–224, respectively, in Edgerton's translation. See also Clooney ("Vedānta," 1990) on rules in Vedānta, and on PMS 3.3.14 in particular.

15. For the sake of descriptive economy, the Mīmāṁsakas conceived of more complex rites as ectypal derivations from simpler rites, their archetypes; only a few differences in detail are required to distinguish the former from the latter.

16. Prakāśātman's *Śārīrakanyāyasaṁgraha* brings this process of the use and refinement and amplification of Mīmāṁsā rules to its perfection. For each *adhikaraṇa* in the UMS, he introduces and assesses the rules appropriate to the context.

17. I have recently explored this ritual/pragmatic side of Vedānta exegesis in a paper entitled "India's Vedānta as a Theology of Practice," presented in April 1989 at the meeting of the Boston Theological Society.

18. I have not been convinced by efforts either to see the PMS and UMS as a single text or to see them as contemporary. The UMS makes best sense as a later, nuanced limitation of the PMS. For the view that they were originally possibly one text, see Parpola 1981.

19. There are in the Mīmāṁsā and Vedānta further refinements of the kinds of *saṁgati* between *adhikaraṇas*: for example, a side question merely occasioned by the preceding *adhikaraṇa*, the effort to pose an example that is directly counter to the previous one, etc.

20. This contextual limitation of philosophical thinking is partially mirrored in deconstructionism's textual (and also not primarily historical) ''margination'' of philosophy. See Derrida 1982.

References

Clooney, Francis X.

1987 ''Why the Veda has No Author: Language as Ritual in Early Mīmāṁsā and Post-Modern Theology.'' *Journal of the American Academy of Religion* 55: 659–84.

1989 ''Evil, Divine Omnipotence, and Human Freedom: Vedānta's Theology of Karma.'' *Journal of Religion* 69: 530–48.

1990 *Thinking Ritually: Rediscovering the Pūrva Mīmāṁsā of Jaimini*. De Nobili Research Series, vol. 17. Vienna: De Nobili Research Library.

1990 ''Vedānta, Commentary, and the Theological Component of Cross-Cultural Study.'' In *Towards a Comparative Philosophy of Religions*, edited by F. Reynolds and D. Tracy, 287–314. Albany: State University of New York Press.

Derrida, Jacques

1982 ''Tympan.'' In *Margins of Philosophy*, translated by A. Bass, ix–xxix. Chicago: University of Chicago Press.

Deussen, Paul

1973 *The System of the Vedānta*. Translated by Charles Johnston 1883. Reprint. New York: Dover

1980 *Sixty Upaniṣads of the Veda*. 2 vols. Translated by V. Bedekar and G. Palsule. 1897. Reprint. Delhi: Motilal Banarsidass.

Deutsch, Eliot
1969 *Advaita Vedānta: A Philosophical Reconstruction*. Honolulu: East-West Center Press.

Edgerton, Franklin, trans.
1929 *Mīmāṁsā Nyāya Prakāśa*. New Haven: Yale University Press.

Foucault, Michel
1973 *The Order of Things*. A translation of Les Mots et Les Choses. 1966. New York: Vintage Books.

Halbfass, Wilhelm
1983 *Human Reason and Vedic Revelation in the Philosophy of Śaṅkara*. Studies in Kumārila and Śaṅkara. Studien zur Indologie und Iranistik, vol. 9. Reinbeck: Verlag für Orientalistische Fachpublikation.

Joshi, K. L., ed.
1981 *Brahma Sūtra Śaṅkara Bhāṣya*, with the Bhāmatī of Vācaspati Miśra, the *Vedāntakalpataru* of Amalānanda and the *Kalpataruparimala* of Appaya Dīkṣita. 2 vols. Parimala Sanskrit Series, no. 1. Ahmedabad: Parimal.

Lindbeck, G.
1984 *The Nature of Doctrine: Religion and Theology in a Postliberal Age*. Philadelphia: Westminster Press.

Modi, P. M.
1956 *A Critique of the Brahmasūtra* (III.2.11–IV). 2 vols. Baroda: Author.

Murty, S.
1974 *Revelation and Reason in Advaita Vedānta*. Delhi: Motilal Banarsidass.

Nakamura, H.
1983 *A History of the Early Vedānta School*. Part 1. Translated by T. Leggett, et al. Delhi: Motilal Banarsidass.

Parpola, A.
1981 "On the Formation of the Mīmāṁsā and the Problems concerning Jaimini." *Wiener Zeitschrift für die Kunde Sudasiens* 25: 145–77.

Prakāśātman
1939 *Śārīrakanyāyasaṁgraha*. Madras: University of Madras.

Shastri, J. L., ed.
1980 *Brahmasūtra-Śāṅkarabhāṣyam* of Bādarāyaṇa with the *Bhāṣyaratnaprabhā* of Govindānanda, the *Bhāmatī* of Vācaspati Miśra and the *Nyāya-Nirṇaya* of Anandagiri. Delhi: Motilal Banarsidass.

Smith, Jonathan Z.
1982 "Sacred Persistence." In *Imagining Religion: From Babylon to Jonestown*. Chicago: University of Chicago, Press.

Thibaut, George
1962 *The Vedānta Sūtras of Bādarāyaṇa*. 2 vols. Sacred Books of the East, nos. 34 and 38. 1890–96. Reprint. New York: Dover.

Five

Haunted by Śaṅkara's Ghost

The Śrīvaiṣṇava Interpretation of Bhagavad Gītā *18:66*

Patricia Y. Mumme

sarvadharmān parityajya / mām ekaṁ śaraṇaṁ vraja
ahaṁ tvā sarvapāpebhyo / mokṣayiṣyāmi mā sucaḥ

Having relinquished all dharmas, resort to me alone as refuge. I will save you from all sins; do not fear.

—*Bhagavad Gītā* 18:66

Introduction: Metaphysics and Interpretive Strategies

It is remarkable how metaphysics in Indian thought are so tightly bound to interpretive strategies. The views of reality seen in the various schools are driven by specific strategies of scriptural interpretation. In fact, metaphysical categories are often mirror images of interpretive strategies. Mīmāṁsā's reputed atheism follows from its axiom that injunction to action is the essential meaning of scripture. Śaṅkara's two levels of reality, the ultimately real *brahman* and the provisionally real realm of *māyā* or *avidyā,* is supported by his appeal to two levels of truth in scripture. Rāmānuja's Viśiṣṭādvaita metaphysics hinge on his use of the notion of the inseparability of quality and qualified (*apṛthaksiddhibhāva*) in scriptural interpretation. At the heart of all three systems we find a major interpretive strategy that not only helps them find and utilize scripture to support their positions, but perhaps more importantly, allows them to tackle scriptural passages that seem contrary to their metaphysics and to convert them to supporting passages. Mīmāṁsā's hermeneutic allows it to cast aside all references to the existence of God or gods. Śaṅkara's device of the "two levels of truth" takes care of passages that suggest reality is more than one, or that something other than knowledge of the one *brahman* leads to liberation (*mokṣa*) from the ceaseless rounds of rebirth and redeath. Rāmānuja's use of the close—yet not identical—relationship between substance and attribute allows him to handle both the Upaniṣadic passages that imply difference between the world and *brahman* as well as those passages that claim nondifference without threat to his metaphysics. It seems that success in Indian philosophy demands at least one good interpretive device that can defuse the major scriptural passages that run counter to the views one is attempting to put forth. This imaginative creativity in devising interpretive strategies allows for the diversity of Indian metaphysical systems that claim to be rooted in the scriptural authority of the Veda and the later *śāstra*.

However, far more has been written on the metaphysics of Indian philosophical systems than on the interpretive strategies that make them possible. It may be a Western bias to assume that a metaphysical system is the goal of philosophy, and that scriptural interpretation is secondary or merely instrumental. From an Indian perspective, an orthodox metaphysical system may be only a by-product of a proper hermeneutical approach to scripture. It is certainly true that creative philosophical systems in Indian thought cannot gain the stamp of orthodoxy without equally creative interpretive approaches to scripture. The question of which has priority in the mind of the traditional Indian philosopher—hermeneutics or metaphysics—is probably unanswerable. Nevertheless, Western Indologists need to divert some attention from the metaphysical carts in Indian thought in order to give closer scrutiny to the hermeneutical horses that may be driving them.

Certainly that is the approach of this volume; for this reason, the present effort deals only secondarily with the doctrinal dispute that began to arise in the late thirteenth century between two Śrīvaiṣṇava subsects—the Teṉkalai, or southern school, and Vaṭakalai, or northern school—over the relationship between the path of devotion (*bhaktiyoga*) and surrender to the Lord (*prapatti*).[1] This chapter examines two very different interpretive strategies developed in Śrīvaiṣṇava commentaries on a single verse of the *Bhagavad Gītā*, called the *Caramaśloka*, where the issue of this relationship arises.[2] Historically and doctrinally, the Śrīvaiṣṇava tradition follows the philosophy of Viśiṣṭādvaita Vedānta, wholeheartedly rejecting Śaṅkara's monism. Though the later Śrīvaiṣṇava *ācāryas*[3] of the Teṉkalai and Vaṭakalai subsects developed and modified the views of the founding *ācāryas* from the thirteenth to fifteenth centuries, both schools continued to affirm adamantly the philosophy of Rāmānuja and to eschew that of Śaṅkara. However, when approaching the Teṉkalai-Vaṭakalai dispute in terms of their interpretive strategies, rather than in terms of their metaphysical doctrines, we find that commentarial literature in the Teṉkalai school uses some interpretive strategies very similar to those used in Śaṅkara's Advaita Vedānta. This, we shall see, does have a pronounced effect on Teṉkalai doctrine, and makes for a counterreaction in the Vaṭakalai school's strategies and doctrines.

I. Background: Śaṅkara, Yāmuna, and Rāmānuja on the Caramaśloka

In the first line of *Bhagavad Gītā* 18:66, Kṛṣṇa says, "*sarvadharmān parityajya, mām ekaṁ śaraṇam vraja*—Having relinquished all dharmas, resort to me alone as a refuge." But what *dharmas* are intended? What does it mean to relinquish them? What does it mean to resort to Kṛṣṇa? It will be helpful to first review the Advaitin interpretation of Śaṅkara (ninth century C.E.?) and to compare it to the rival interpretation of Yāmuna and Rāmānuja (eleventh and early twelfth centuries C.E.), the founders of both Viśiṣṭādvaita Vedānta philosophy and the Śrīvaiṣṇava religious tradition.

Śaṅkara's commentary on the *Bhagavad Gītā* (BGŚ) makes liberal use of his "two levels of truth" strategy. Śaṅkara claims that agency (*kartṛtva*), like individuality, is an *upādhi*, or limiting adjunct of the self (*ātman*)—only provisionally real for those under the influence of ignorance; thus the ability to act is not part of the soul's essential nature. On the highest level of truth, the true self is pure consciousness, identical with *brahman*, the self of all, and to realize this is liberation. Śaṅkara assumes that one who has reached sufficient self-understanding to know that the self is not an agent will abandon all action and devote himself to the higher knowledge of the *ātman*. Thus the path of action (*karmayoga*) as outlined in scripture is for the ignorant; the wise must relinquish it in favor of the path of knowledge (*jñānayoga*) (BGŚ 508). To get the *Bhagavad Gītā* to conform to this doctrine, Śaṅkara interprets passages enjoining action or works of devotion as applying to the lower or conventional level of truth (*vyavahārikā*) in which the soul, under the influence of ignorance (*avidyā*), is assumed to be an agent. (Most of Dharmaśāstra, according to Śaṅkara's reasoning, also falls into this category.) Such passages in the *Bhagavad Gītā* he clearly distinguishes from those that deal with the higher truth of renunciation and self-knowledge (*paramārthikā*).[4]

For Śaṅkara, *Bhagavad Gītā* 18:66 is in the category of verses teaching the higher truth. Here Kṛṣṇa addresses Arjuna as an *ātmajñānaniṣṭhā*, one who has realized the true nature of the self as a nonagent and has thus risen above the path of action. The first *pāda*,[5] "Having relinquished all dharmas" (*sarvadharmān parityajya*), enjoins Arjuna to completely renounce all actions, both those required and those prohibited. Then, "Resort to me alone as refuge" (*mām ekaṁ śaraṇam vraja*) enjoins him to turn to the path of knowledge (*jñānayoga*) by telling him to understand the one *brahman* (*īśvara*) to be the sole reality, the self of all, identical with Arjuna's own self. So Śaṅkara claims the first *pāda* enjoins giving up action and the second enjoins a kind of knowledge or understanding, not action (BGŚ 499).

Both Yāmuna, in his brief "Gītārthasaṅgraha," and Rāmānuja, in his *Gītābhāṣya*, reject Śaṅkara's notion that agency is only a superficial, limiting attribute (*upādhi*) of the self and, concomitantly, reject his view that here the *Bhagavad Gītā* is enjoining outright abandonment of action. The Viśiṣṭādvaitins claim that the soul is genuinely an agent, though that agency is dependent on the Lord.[6] Action per se is not incompatible with the soul's true nature; it is selfish attachment to action and its fruits that runs counter to the soul's dependence on the Lord. In interpreting *Bhagavad Gītā* 18:66, they take "*sarvadharmān parityajya*" as enjoining the pure renunciation (*sāttvikatyāga*) explained earlier in chapter 18—that one should continue to perform required duties, but relinquish all attachment to agency, results, and ownership of these actions.[7] The whole point of the *Bhagavad Gītā*, as the Viśiṣṭādvaitins see it, is to show that performance of scripturally enjoined action is not an obstruction to liberation (*mokṣa*) when done without attachment; such action can in fact lead to liberation when done with devotion to the Lord. So, after first enjoining one to give up these attachments to required duties even while continuing to perform them (*sarvadharmān parityajya*), Kṛṣṇa then says to seek only him as a refuge (*mām ekaṁ śaraṇam vraja*). This second *pāda* they take as enjoining an attitude of surrender, devotion, and subservience, telling one to think of the Lord alone as the agent, object, goal, and means (*upāya*) to reach liberation. Taken as a whole, these two *pādas* enjoin *bhaktiyoga*, the path of devotion, along with its ancillary (*aṅga*) *karmayoga;* that is, performance of duties in loving devotion to the Lord and without personal attachment.[8]

It is important to notice that Śaṅkara and the Viśiṣṭādvaitins disagree fundamentally on whether the first *pāda* enjoins relinquishing action or performing action. However, they agree that both *pādas* enjoin something. The latter *pāda* they agree enjoins a mental act, a special kind of knowledge or attitude, though they differ on its contents.

Rāmānuja also offers an alternative interpretation in his commentary, which supposes that this *śloka* addresses Arjuna's grief at his sins that prevent him from beginning the path of devotion (*bhaktiyoga*). Here Rāmānuja is willing to take the phrase "having relinquished" (*parityajya*) as enjoining actual abandonment of action, but only if the meaning of "all dharmas" (*sarvadharmān*) is limited to the expiatory rites (*prāyaścitta*) needed to remove obstacles to beginning *bhaktiyoga*. In this interpretation, the verb in the first *pāda* (*parityajya*) enjoins giving up these expiations; the verb in the second *pāda* (*vraja*) enjoins surrender to the Lord, who will then himself become the means for removing the obstructing sins, standing in for the expiatory rites. Rāmānuja doesn't clarify whether this surrender is a mental attitude or a ritual performance, but there is no doubt that, as in his first interpretation, the means to liberation being taught is the path of devotion (*bhaktiyoga*), which includes loving performance of duties, not the path of knowledge (*jñānayoga*), which (according to Śaṅkara) demands the renunciation of all activity.[9]

II. Later Śrīvaiṣṇava Interpretations: Enjoining Independent Prapatti

New developments in the interpretation of the *Caramaśloka* surface among Rāmānuja's followers in the thirteenth century. By this time the Śrīvaiṣṇava tradition had come to recognize *prapatti* or *śaraṇāgati*—surrendering to or taking refuge in the Lord—as a separate means to liberation, distinct from the path of devotion (*bhaktiyoga*). Earlier, both Rāmānuja and Yāmuna had taken 18:66 to enjoin surrender to the Lord (*prapatti*) as an ancillary to *bhaktiyoga*, which involves loving performance of all obligatory Vedic ritual activity (*karma*). These later *ācāryas* agree that taking refuge in the Lord is an essential aspect of *bhaktiyoga*, but they also see surrender to the Lord (*prapatti*) as an independent means that does not demand concomitant performance of Vedic ritual activity; thus, unlike *bhaktiyoga*, *prapatti* is not restricted to twice-born males who are qualified to perform Vedic rituals. Taking refuge in the Lord is open to those of all castes and genders, young and old.

By the twelfth century, *prapatti* seems to have been ritualized into a formal initiation ceremony that involved utterance of three sacred *mantras*, or secret formulas (*rahasya*)—one of which is *Bhagavad Gītā* 18:66. By the thirteenth century, *rahasya* commentaries on the esoteric meaning of the three mantras become the main vehicle for explicating Śrīvaiṣṇava soteriology. These texts are written in a vernacular Sanskritized Tamil (Maṇipravāḷa)[10] that was accessible to members of the community who could not study Sanskrit. In these *rahasya* commentaries the later Śrīvaiṣṇava *ācāryas* interpret the *Caramaśloka* to enjoin independent surrender to the Lord (*prapatti*) that is open to all. But this poses a problem: how to account for the fact that the written works of their illustrious founding *ācāryas*—Yāmuna and

Rāmānuja—never took 18:66 to teach *prapatti* apart from *bhaktiyoga?* Not surprisingly, they appeal to the notion of "secret doctrine," certainly an interpretive strategy with wide currency in Indian thought. They claim that Yāmuna and Rāmānuja knew *prapatti* to be the secret meaning of the *Caramaśloka,* but did not reveal this meaning in their Vedāntic works, since these were aimed at a twice-born audience who would be qualified for *bhaktiyoga,* the Vedic path of devotion. However, these later *ācāryas* claim, independent *prapatti* was the means to salvation that Yāmuna and Rāmānuja themselves practiced, elucidated in their poetic works, and taught to their disciples as the secret meaning of the *Caramaśloka.*[11] This strategy allows the later Śrīvaiṣṇava *ācāryas*—both Vaṭakalai and Teṉkalai—to ignore the earlier commentaries of Yāmuna and Rāmānuja on 18:66 as irrelevant when the *Caramaśloka* is taken as enjoining independent *prapatti.* Thus Rāmānuja's and Yāmuna's interpretations are never cited in *rahasya* commentaries on the *Caramaśloka.*

However, the later *ācāryas* still needed to answer the more ticklish question of how to understand the relationship between independent *prapatti* and the *bhaktiyoga* that Rāmānuja and Yāmuna explicated. That issue must be faced squarely in expounding the first line of the *Caramaśloka*—"Having relinquished all dharmas, resort to me alone as refuge." For if the second *pāda* now enjoins independent *prapatti,* then the first *pāda* must refer to actually relinquishing all other means to liberation—including *bhaktiyoga.* Otherwise, what is enjoined in the second *pāda* would not be independent *prapatti,* but surrender to the Lord as an ancillary of *bhaktiyoga.* Why and under what conditions should one employ independent *prapatti* over *bhaktiyoga?* Is one means better than the other? Or are the two meant for different people? If so, for whom? Why would Kṛṣṇa tell Arjuna to abandon the paths of devotion and action he has so carefully explained in the previous chapters? Why would so many scriptures—and Yāmuna and Rāmānuja themselves—teach the path of devotion if surrender to the Lord (*prapatti*) is preferred? Creative interpretive strategies are needed to circumvent the problems these questions pose. The Śrīvaiṣṇava *ācāryas* rise to the occasion, but we find that the Teṉkalai school in Śrīraṅgam develops a very different strategy for answering these questions than their Vaṭakalai colleagues further north in Kāñchī.

III. The Teṉkalai "Advaitin" Strategy

Periyavāccāṉ Piḷḷai (1167–1262 C.E.), Piḷḷai Lokācārya (1205–1311 C.E.), and Maṇavāḷamāmuni (1370–1443 C.E.)—the founding *ācāryas* of the Teṉkalai school—all wrote *rahasya* commentaries in Tamil Maṇipravāḷa that interpret the *Caramaśloka.*[12] Though all claim to be following the tradition of Yāmuna and Rāmānuja, Periyavāccāṉ Piḷḷai, in his *Parantarahasya,* goes so far as to bring up both of Rāmānuja's interpretations of the *Caramaśloka* (without mentioning their author) and refute them.[13] In the *Mumukṣuppaṭi* (MP), Piḷḷai Lokācārya and his commentator Maṇavāḷamāmuni merely ignore the "Gītārthasaṅgraha" and *Gītābhāṣya* because, unlike Yāmuna and Rāmānuja, they understand themselves to be explaining the *Caramaśloka*'s secret meaning—that surrender to the Lord (*prapatti*) is an independent path to liberation open to all. However, it is surprising that in defiance of the best efforts of Rāmānuja to distance his tradition from that of the Advaitins, these Teṉkalai *ācāryas* end up using a remarkably Advaita-like strategy in articulating the relationship between *bhaktiyoga,* the path of devotion, and *prapatti,* or surrender to the Lord. In fact, this strategy brings their interpretation of 18:66 rather close to that of Śaṅkara in many respects (dangerously close, according to Vedānta Deśika of the Vaṭakalai school, as we will see).

Piḷḷai Lokācārya and Maṇavāḷamāmuni employ a "two levels of truth" strategy, making the bold claim that *bhaktiyoga* and *prapatti* are means to liberation for those who have lesser and greater knowledge of the self, respectively. Those who are not fully aware of the soul's utter dependence on the Lord are attached to action, thinking they have to do something to achieve liberation. For those people the Lord enjoined *bhaktiyoga,* which involves devoted performance of ritual actions according to the Vedic texts, as explicated by Yāmuna and Rāmānuja. But those who have realized their dependence on the Lord know that it is improper for them to do anything to save themselves. Therefore they give up all such means to salvation and merely rely on the Lord to save them.

Piḷḷai Lokācārya takes the word *dharmān* to refer to all the other duties that are enjoined as means to liberation—the paths of action, knowledge, and devotion (*karma-, jñāna-,* and *bhaktiyoga*)—along with their ancillaries; but he claims these are here only "called *dharmas* because of the confused notion of Arjuna" (MP 198). They are not really duties or means enjoined on one who seeks liberation but are actually impediments to salvation (MP 200, 203). Thus Maṇavāḷamāmuni calls them "illusory means" (*ābhāsamāṉa upāya*) that must be abandoned as obstacles to liberation (MP 203–4).[14] Eventually, the Teṉkalai *ācāryas* claim, those following *bhaktiyoga* and the like must come to realize their inherent dependence on the Lord, give up all efforts to save themselves, and surrender to the Lord alone as means to liberation (MP 203–4). Maṇavāḷamāmuni explains:

> One who has entered the last stage of life (*āśrama*) [as a *sannyāsin*] relinquishes the duties (*dharma*) of the previous stages; it is

> the same for one who has gained this measure of ripened knowledge, such that he employs only [the Lord himself] (*siddhopāya*), realizing that these other means are contrary to the soul's true nature. There will be no fault if he gives up these other means. (MP 268–69)

Piḷḷai Lokācārya doesn't hesitate to use a very Advaitin analogy to illustrate this: "Like those who have conceived mother-of-pearl to be silver . . . we have attributed the notion of 'means' (*upāya*) to things which are not means" (MP 200).[15] But when we fully realize the soul's dependent nature, we will see that they are not true means to *mokṣa* at all. One who has reached this self-understanding is enjoined in the first *pāda* of the *Caramaśloka* to give up all such efforts (*sarva dharmān parityajya*) and merely surrender to the Lord alone (*mām ekaṁ śaraṇam vraja*) as one's means of salvation.

The Teṉkalai *ācāryas* clearly insist that outright relinquishing of other duties is what is being enjoined in "sarvadharmān parityajya." They claim the gerund form, *parityajya* (having relinquished), is a *vidhi,* or commandment (MP 202), to give up these apparent or illusory means that are contrary to the soul's true nature. Thus, in the *Caramaśloka*'s first line, Kṛṣṇa first orders Arjuna to relinquish all other means of liberation and then orders him to recognize the Lord as the true means (*upāya*).

Notice the striking parallels between the Teṉkalai interpretation and that of Śaṅkara. Both agree that the first *pāda* is a commandment to renounce duties (*dharma*) outright—to not do them (MP 202). Both work from a presumption that there are two levels of truth, lower and higher, that are correlated with two kinds of means (*upāya*) for liberation. The lower means are predicated on a misunderstanding of the soul's true nature and must be given up once that higher understanding is realized. Both use the shell–silver analogy to illustrate this misunderstanding. *Prapatti*'s relation to the paths of action and devotion (*karmayoga, bhaktiyoga*) for the Teṉkalai, is directly analogous to *jñānayoga*'s relation to the paths of action and devotion for Śaṅkara. Both would agree that there is only one true means to liberation—surrender to the Lord for the Teṉkalai, knowledge of the one *ātman/brahman* for Śaṅkara—and that the other provisional or illusory means ultimately must be abandoned once a certain level of understanding is reached.

For the Teṉkalai as well as for Śaṅkara, the lower means are inferior because they demand action and self-effort. Śaṅkara had claimed that all forms of activity must be given up to reach liberation, because activity—agency—is not truly part of soul's nature, but only a superficial, limiting adjunct (*upādhi*). Rāmānuja's *Śrībhāṣya* on the *Brahma Sūtras* (BSR) had refuted this view, arguing that the soul (*ātman*) has to be considered the agent, or else scriptural injunctions to act are meaningless (BSR 2.3.33–40). Though the Teṉkalai *ācāryas* do not deny Rāmānuja's Viśiṣṭādvaita doctrine of the soul's inherent agency (*jīvakartṛtva*), they arrive at their position by emphasizing that the soul is a dependent agent, a *śeṣa* of the Lord, as Rāmānuja had also claimed. They see subservience (*śeṣatva*) and dependence (*pāratantrya*) toward the Lord as even more essential to the soul's true nature than its ability to act.[16] For a subservient entity (*śeṣa*), the only proper activity is to serve and glorify the Lord, the *śeṣin*.[17] All self-serving action violates the principle of subservience (*śeṣatva*). It is for this reason that the Teṉkalai *ācāryas* claim that actively performing a means whose aim is one's own liberation is contrary to the soul's essential nature as *śeṣa* and must be relinquished by those who have reached a true understanding of the self (ŚVB 70–77, 115–17; MP 256). Thus the Teṉkalai *ācāryas* take scriptural injunctions regarding means to obtain liberation much like Śaṅkara takes all injunctions to act: they have a provisional validity for those who have not realized the soul's true nature and must be given up when that realization is attained.

The Teṉkalai *ācāryas* are careful to point out that relinquishing action as enjoined in the first *pāda* is not itself an action, and that the command to seek refuge (*śaraṇam vraja*) in the second phrase of the first line is a strictly mental or cognitive phenomenon, not an action (MP 238–39). They even cite a verse from the *Mahābhārata* declaring "*mokṣa* is from knowledge" (*jñānāt mokṣa*) to support their position.[18] (Certainly that is a line that Śaṅkara would like more than would Rāmānuja!) Surrender to the Lord (*prapatti*), as they see it, is only a mental recognition of one's own dependence and the Lord's status as means, not an action and therefore not a means.[19]

IV. Vedānta Deśika's Mīmāṁsā-Dharmaśāstra Strategy

Just like his Teṉkalai counterparts, Vedānta Deśika (1269–1370 C.E.), foremost champion of the Vaṭakalai school, ignores the interpretations of Yāmuna and Rāmānuja when interpreting the *Caramaśloka* as teaching independent surrender. However, his commentaries on the three *rahasyas*, especially in his *Rahasyatrayasāra* (RTS), use a very different interpretive strategy than the Teṉkalai in articulating the relationship between surrender to the Lord (*prapatti*) and the path of devotion (*bhaktiyoga*)—a strategy with ample precedent in Mīmāṁsā and Dharmaśāstra. His main concern is to preserve the legitimacy of both *bhaktiyoga* and *prapatti* and the authoritative scriptures that command them. If one finds a discrepancy in Dharmaśāstra—where passage A says to do a ritual one way and passage B says to do it another—how should they be reconciled? Deśika says that if one looks more closely it will become apparent that the two methods are specified for different circumstances, depending on such factors as the caste or the lifestage (*aśrama*) of the performer, time of day or month, and so on. For instance, Deśika notes that there are many different kinds of purificatory baths prescribed in the scriptures; though equally valid, only one type will be appropriate in any particular circumstance, depending on the health of the participant, availability of water, etc. (RTS 24:715–16). Similarly, he claims that *bhaktiyoga* and *prapatti* are equally valid means to liberation enjoined for two different sets of qualificants: *bhaktiyoga* is for twice-born males with the patience to undergo it, and *prapatti* is for everyone else who lacks one or more of these qualifications (RTS 29:1051).

Deśika supports this view by taking the gerund form of the verb in "having relinquished all *dharmas*" (*sarvadharmān parityajya*) as an *anuvāda*, a statement of prior fact specifying the conditions under which one should choose *prapatti*, rather than as a commandment (*vidhi*). "Having relinquished all *dharmas*" refers to the state of being of one who is not qualified for *bhaktiyoga*. Dharmaśāstra often uses the same format. If scripture states, "Having eaten something forbidden, do such and such as expiation," the gerund form in this case doesn't order one to go out and eat forbidden things and then do the expiation. Instead, such a statement only orders the expiation if one has eaten something forbidden. Deśika points out that Kṛṣṇa himself uses a similar form in *Bhagavad Gītā* 9:33—"Having reached this impermanent and sorrowful world, worship me." The gerund "having reached" functions as a statement of prior fact (*anuvāda*), not as a commandment. Similarly here "having relinquished" (*parityajya*) does not order Arjuna to give up all other paths to liberation. The gerund here only confirms that Arjuna had already given them up because he was not qualified; though he was from a twice-born caste, he was too impatient to bear the delays of *bhaktiyoga* (RTS 29:1036–37). For one in the position of being disqualified for *bhaktiyoga*—because of caste, education, impatience, or whatever—*prapatti* to the Lord as a separate means is enjoined in the second *pāda:* "Resort to me alone as refuge" (*mām ekaṁ śaraṇam vraja*). This is the heart of the *Caramaśloka*'s secret meaning, according to Vedānta Deśika.

Furthermore, in commenting on the second *pāda,* which commands that one seek refuge with the Lord, Deśika emphasizes that the surrender enjoined is not just a mental attitude or form of knowledge but a means to be performed and an action in which the soul's dependent agency operates (RTS 24:696; 29:1100–1). The Teṉkalai position, that no action on the part of the soul is implied in this line, Deśika claims to be inconsistent: "It is certainly seen in the world and in Vedic scriptures that even ceasing from action is a form of activity, and that this can be done for one's own protection" (RTS 29:1045).[20] The Teṉkalai approach is wrongheaded, according to Deśika, because there is no need to posit any contradiction between an individual's subservience (*śeṣatva*) to the Lord and use of his God-given agency to engage in actions enjoined as a means to liberation. "For one who is a dependent *śeṣa*, it is no fault to perform activity for his own protection" (RTS 24:706).[21] Indeed, it is the Lord himself who has commanded in scripture the performance of this activity—in the form of either *prapatti* to the Lord or *bhaktiyoga*—according to the individual's qualification.

Notice here how Deśika's interpretation differs from all the others. His major innovation is that the first *pāda* ("having relinquished all dharmas") is not a command but a statement of prior fact (*anuvāda*) that restricts the applicability of the commandment of independent *prapatti* in the second *pāda*. Furthermore, he maintains that the second *pāda* ("resort to me alone as refuge") enjoins a performance, not merely a mental attitude or way of thinking. Deśika's reading shows some similarity in form to Rāmānuja's second interpretation in taking the first *pāda* to refer to the devotee's lack of qualification. (Grammatically, however, the gerund—"having relinquished"—in the first *pāda* is still an injunction for Rāmānuja, and not a statement of prior fact.)[22] Both interpretations limit the injunction of surrender in the second *pāda* to those disqualified from the path of devotion.

V. Deśika's Critique of the Teṉkalai Quasi-Advaita Hermeneutic

Deśika's criticism of the Teṉkalai interpretation shows that he is reacting against the Advaita-like leanings of the southern school, which he fears will undermine some of the fundamental tenets of Viśiṣṭādvaita that Rāmānuja had tried so hard to establish—the soul's agency, the validity of scriptural injunctions, and the idea that liberation (*mokṣa*) is gained by a path of both knowledge and devoted action, not knowledge alone. One of his major objections to the Advaita school is that by denying the soul's agency, they render all scriptural injunctions of action meaningless or delusory, and relegate all who practice them to an inferior state of knowledge. This is also the core of his objection to the Teṉkalai interpretation of *Bhagavad Gītā* 18:66. He refutes the Teṉkalai abuse of the "*mokṣa* is from knowledge" principle, and their claim that *dharmas* such as *bhaktiyoga* (which demand effort) are not really means, by claiming that their views will end up denying the validity of the scriptural authority just as the Advaitins did (RTS 24:695–98; 29:1111–12). By exaggerating the soul's subservience and dependence, at the expense of the soul's agency, the Te<u>n</u>kalai render all scriptural injunctions regarding means to liberation meaningless or delusory, and imply that all who practice them are ignorant (RTS 24:705–17; 29:1111–12, 1042, 1052). As Deśika sees it, the only way to save the validity of scriptural injunctions of *bhaktiyoga* and its Vedic ancillaries is to affirm that the soul is an agent and that its dependency on the Lord does not preclude actively performing a means enjoined in scripture.

It seems that Śaṅkara's ghost, haunting the southern school's interpretation of *Bhagavad Gītā* 18:66, gave quite a fright to Vedānta Deśika, who felt called to protect Viśiṣṭādvaita philosophy from any potential encroachment from Advaitin scriptural hermeneutics or doctrine. He took it upon himself to refute the Advaita leanings in the Te<u>n</u>kalai explication of 18:66, which implied that the path of devotion and other scripturally enjoined means to liberation are only for those ignorant of the highest truth of the soul's dependent nature. Utilizing a hermeneutic imported from the Dharmaśāstra to support his own interpretation, he tried to explicate the nature of *bhaktiyoga, prapatti,* and the soul, as well as their interrelationships, in ways that would not compromise the validity of scriptural injunctions regarding means to liberation. This interchange between Vedānta Deśika and his Te<u>n</u>kalai counterparts, though it focuses on the grammatical form and meaning of two verbs from a single line of a single *śloka,* cannot be dismissed as a teapot tempest. The different hermeneutical strategies used here gave form and support to some of the basic doctrinal differences between the two schools of Śrīvaiṣṇava *ācāryas,* which led, in turn, to the Te<u>n</u>kalai-Vaṭakalai sectarian schism of the seventeenth and eighteenth centuries.[23]

Notes

1. The Te<u>n</u>kalai (literally, "southern school") of Śrīvaiṣṇava *ācāryas* originated in Srirangam and follows a lineage through Piḷḷai Lokācārya (d. 1311 C.E.) and Maṇavāḷamāmuni (d. 1443 C.E.). The Vaṭakalai (meaning "northern school") originated in Kāñchī and follows a lineage through Vedānta Deśika (d. 1370 C.E.). These two schools probably did not fully separate until the seventeenth or eighteenth century, when rivalry for temple control erupted between the two groups. The theological differences between these two groups, however, is traceable in the writings of the founding *ācāryas* of the thirteenth and fourteenth centuries. See Patricia Y.

Mumme, *The Śrīvaiṣṇava Theological Dispute: Maṇavāḷamāmuni and Vedānta Deśika.* (Madras: New Era Press, 1988). Hereafter, Mumme 1988.

2. Actually, the metaphysical issue hinges on the interpretation of only the first half of the *Caramaśloka, Bhagavad Gītā* 18:66a.

3. The term "*ācārya*" designates the thinkers and teachers of the Śrīvaiṣṇava tradition.

4. Immediately after his gloss of *Bhagavad Gītā* 18:66, Śaṅkara goes into a lengthy exposition of his doctrine that the self is a nonagent and that knowledge alone—not knowledge combined with action—results in liberation (*mokṣa*). Only those who are *sannyāsins,* who have renounced all forms of actions, and who "know that the Self is one and non-agent, who are engaged in the higher devotion of knowledge" are freed from karmic bondage, not those who "are ignorant, who follow the path of works, who are not *sannyāsins*" (BGŚ 509).

5. A *pāda* is quarter verse made of eight syllables. Four *pādas* form one *śloka.*

6. This is explained in Rāmānuja's *Śrībhaṣya,* his commentary on *Brahma Sūtras* 2.3.33–41. See BSR 3:131–41.

7. Yāmuna's gloss of 18:66 in "Gītārthasaṇgraha" 31, though only one *śloka,* makes it clear that he takes this verse to enjoin not cessation from duties, but their performance without attachment:

> *nijakarmādi bhaktyantaṁ kuryātprītyaiva kāritaḥ*
> *upāyatāṁ parityajya nyasyed devetu tāmabhīḥ*
>
> "He should perform everything—from his own duties to *bhakti*—doing them solely out of love; relinquishing the idea that [they are] the means (*upāya*) [for *mokṣa*], he must place [that idea] in God and be rid of fear" (Appendix to BGR, p. 492).

8. Rāmānuja closely follows and elaborates Yāmuna's "Gītārthasaṅgraha":

> Renouncing all dharmas which consist of karmayoga, jñānayoga and bhaktiyoga, which constitute the means for the highest good (of salvation) and which are being performed with great love as My worship according to qualification—(renouncing them all) with the complete renunciation of the sense of agency, possessiveness in works, fruits, and such other things, in the manner taught: (having done so), continuously think of Me as the agent, the object of worship the goal of attainment and the means.

He goes on to clarify that the renunciation here refers to the threefold renunciation explained in 18:4 and 18:9–11 (BGR 474–76).

9. "In order to succeed in starting bhaktiyoga, surrender, finding refuge with Me alone, who am supremely merciful, who am the refuge of all persons . . . and who am the sea of parental solicitude for those dependent on Me" (BGR 476).

10. In the next chapter, Narayanan discusses the form of Maṇipravāḷa used in Śrīvaīṣṇava commentary tradition. See p. 89.

11. Vedānta Deśika expresses this idea in the 24th chapter of RTS; Maṇavāḷamāmuni does so in the introduction to the *Caramaśloka* section (MP 151).

12. Periyavāccāṉ Piḷḷai wrote the earliest extant *rahasya* commentary in Sanskritized Tamil (Maṇipravāḷa), the *Parantarahasya*. Piḷḷai Lokācārya wrote several commentaries on the three *mantras* or *rahasyas*. His most famous is the *Mumukṣuppaṭi*, on which Maṇavāḷamāmuni commented.

13. Periyavāccāṉ Piḷḷai refutes Rāmānuja's second interpretation by claiming that Arjuna had no sins that would demand expiatory rites (p. 43). The idea that *prapatti* is being taught here as an ancillary (*aṅga*) of the paths of action and devotion appears as a view of an opponent and is rejected in his conclusion. Here, Periyavāccāṉ Piḷai claims this *śloka* teaches that all other duties (*dharmas*), along with their accompaniments, must be relinquished in favor of the Lord himself, who becomes the means for liberation instead of them. See *Parantarahasya* of Periyavāccāṉ Piḷai, in *Parantarahasya and Māṇikkamālai*, ed. P. B. Annangaracharya (Kanchi: Granthamala Office, 1949), 43, 55–56. My translation of this work is in progress.

14. The Teṉkalai *ācāryas* do not seem to think the devotional path is entirely ineffective as a means to liberation, since it includes *prapatti* within it. Piḷḷai Lokācārya and Maṇavāḷamāmuni make the analogy that *prapatti* is mixed in with *bhaktiyoga* like medicine is mixed in with milk to make it more palatable. The efforts of following the path of devotion make surrender to the Lord more palatable to those addicted to selfish action. But this weakens the dose, making the cure take longer. That is why the path of devotion is a longer and more arduous means than surrender to the Lord (*Śrīvācana Bhūṣaṇa of Piḷḷai Lokācārya* [ŚVB] 127–28).

15. See Śaṅkara's introduction to his commentary on *Brahma Sūtras* 1.1.1, his *Bṛhadāraṇyaka Upaniṣad Bhāṣya* on 3.5.1, and *Upadeśasāhasrī* 1.2.51 for examples of the analogy of mother-of-pearl (or shell) that is taken by superimposition (*adhyāsa*) to be silver and sublated (*bādhā*) by subsequent knowledge.

16. See MP 56; ŚVB 71. This idea is most clearly explicated in Maṇavāḷamāmuni's commentary on the *Ācārya Hṛdaya* (sūtras 21–24) of A̱ḷakiyamaṇavā̱ḷa Perumāl Nāyaṉār, Piḷḷai Lokācārya's younger brother. Mumme 1988, 50–60.

17. The Teṉkalai *ācāryas* in this context appeal to Rāmānuja's definition of a *śeṣa* in his *Vedārthasaṅgraha* as "that whose essential nature consists solely in being useful to something else by virtue of its intention to contribute some excellence to the other [the *śeṣin*]" (cited by Maṇavāḷamāmuni in his commentary on *Ācārya Hṛdaya* 25). Mumme 1988, 59.

18. In MP 240 both Piḷḷai Lokācārya and Maṇavāḷamāmuni use the phrase "jñānāt mokṣa," which editors have claimed derives from a *śloka* in the Śāntiparva of the *Mahābhārata: "jñānānmokṣo jāyate"*—liberation arises from knowledge. This *śloka* is found in the critical edition by Vishnu S. Sukthankar (Poona: Bhandarkar Oriental Research Institute, 1927–66) at 12.306.84.

19. Here too, the Teṉkalai seem to echo Śaṅkara, who repeatedly makes the claim that knowledge alone—not action—can remove the ignorance responsible for bondage, and that knowing is not an act. Śaṅkara's opponents on this issue seem to be both the Mīmāṁsā school, who claim that liberation is from action, and the Bhedābhedins, who claim that liberation is from knowledge and action combined. See Karl H. Potter, *Encyclopedia of Indian Philosophies: Advaita Vedānta up to Śaṅkara and His Pupils.* (New Delhi: Motilal Banarsidass, 1981), 38–41.

20. *nivṛttiyum vyāpāraviśēṣameṉṉumiṭamum atuvum svarakṣaṇārthamāmeṉṉumiṭamum lokavēdasiddhamiṟē* (RTS 29:1045). Translation is mine.

21. *ākaiyāl śeṣabhutaṉumāyp paratantraṉumāḻna ivaṉukku yathādhikāram svarakṣaṇārthavyāpāram paṇṇak kuṟaiyiḷḷai* (RTS 24:706). Translation is mine.

22. Deśika's subcommentary on the *Gītābhāṣya* calls the gerund "*parityajya*" in Rāmānuja's second interpretation a "kind of injunction" (*vidhicchāya*). See *Bhagavad Gītā* with Rāmānuja's *Bhāṣya* and Vedānta Deśika's *Tātparyacandrikā,* edited by U. T. Viraraghavacharya (Madras: U. T. Viraraghavacharya, 1972), 601.

23. For this phase of the Teṉkalai-Vaṭakalai dispute, see Arjun Appadurai, *Worship and Conflict Under Colonial Rule: A South Indian Case* (Cambridge: Cambridge University Press, 1981).

Abbreviations for Primary Texts Cited

BGR — Rāmānuja. *The Gītābhāṣya of Rāmānuja.* Translated by M. R. Sampatkumaran. Bombay: Ananthacharya Indological Research Institute, 1985. Includes text and translation of Yāmuna's "Gītārthasaṅgraha" in Appendix.

BGŚ — Śaṅkara. *The Bhagavad Gītā with the commentary of Śrī Śaṅkarāchārya.* Translated by Alladi Mahadeva Śastri. Madras: Samata Books, 1977.

BSR — Rāmānuja. *The Vedānta Sūtras with the Śrī-Bhāśya of Rāmānujāchārya.* Translated by M. Rangacharya and M. B. Varadaraja Iyangar, 3 vols. Madras: Educational Publishing Co., 1965.

MP — Piḷḷai Lokācārya. *The Mumukṣuppaṭi of Piḷḷai Lokācārya with Maṇavāḷamāmuni's Commentary.* Translated by Patricia Y. Mumme. Bombay: Ananthacharya Indological Research Institute, 1987. (Citations to this volume indicate *sutra* numbers.)

RTS — Vedānta Deśika. *Śrīmad Rahasyatrayasāra of Vedānta Deśika.* Edited by U. T. Viraraghavacharya. 2 vols. Madras: published by the editor, 1980.

ŚVB — Piḷḷai Lokācārya. *Śrīvācana Bhūṣaṇa of Piḷḷai Lokācārya, with Maṇavāḷamāmuni's Commentary.* Edited by P. Raghava Ramanuja Swami. Madras: R. Rajagopal Naidu, 1936. (Citations to this volume indicate *sutra* numbers.)

Six

Oral and Written Commentary on the *Tiruvāymoḻi*

Vasudha Narayanan

> To interpret . . . is to bring out what is concealed in a given manifestation, to make evident what in the manifestation is not evident to the milieu in which the interpreter's audience lives. . . . To interpret verbal utterance is to bring out what the utterance does not itself reveal to a given audience. What utterance reveals calls for no interpretation.
>
> —Walter Ong[1]

> Revered people say that a commentary clarifies [the original] and teaches us other things as well.
>
> —*The Splendor*[2]

Introduction

The previous chapter considered the philosophical and theological implications of the Śrīvaiṣṇava interpretation of the *Caramaśloka*. The present chapter considers this tradition once again, this time making an inquiry into the nature of commentary and interpretation from a very different hermeneutical moment. But before probing the Śrīvaiṣṇava understanding of the interpretive process, perhaps we should consider briefly what we mean by the word *hermeneutics*.

In his 1969 volume *Hermeneutics: Interpretation Theory in Schleiermacher, Dilthey, Heidegger, and Gadamer,* Richard Palmer explains that the verb *hermeneuein* and the noun *hermeneia,* which are the roots for the word *hermeneutics,* are both connected with the wing-footed messenger-god Hermes. Hermes was associated with the function of transmuting "what is beyond human understanding into a form that human intelligence can grasp" (p. 13). Palmer points out the three directions of meaning of *hermeneuein* and hermeneia in ancient usage. These were (1) to say, or to express aloud in words; (2) to explain; and (3) to translate from one language to another. Thus, "interpretation," or hermeneutics, referred to three rather different matters: an "oral recitation, a reasonable explanation, and a translation from another language" (p. 14). In all three cases, Palmer argues, the foundational "Hermes process" is at work;

> something foreign, strange, separated in time, space or experience is made familiar, present, comprehensible; something requiring representation, explanation, or translation is somehow "brought to understanding"—is interpreted. (p. 14)

Comment and interpretation become necessary when an original statement does not seem self-explanatory. This chapter is a study of interpretation in Hindu literature; specifically, the interpretation of a Tamil poem, the *Tiruvāymoḻi* (abbreviated as TVM). The *Tiruvāymoḻi,* which has 1,102 verses, was composed by Nammāḻvār, a poet-saint who lived in the ninth century C.E. In the eleventh century the Śrvaiṣṇava community of South India introduced the poem into the temple and home liturgies and began to comment on it—initially orally and through the performing arts, and then later in writing. The poem was always recited or sung *orally.* There was a tradition of *explanation,* or commentary, in which several distinctive positions were asserted. Finally, there was a unique kind of *translation* involved: the Tamil poem was said to be equivalent to the Sanskrit Vedas, and this equivalence was portrayed by rendering the meaning of the poem in Sanskrit, Maṇipravāḷa, and a "newer" (and presumably more easily understandable) kind of Tamil.

Through the elaboration of the commentarial tradition on the *Tiruvạymoḻi,* the Śrīvaiṣṇava community affirmed some distinctive positions that defined its identity. These positions included the attribution of equal importance to the Sanskrit and Tamil Vedas, and holding the *Tiruvāymoḻi* to be a text that gave salvific knowledge.

I. The Importance of the Tiruvāymoḻi *and the Commentarial Tradition*

Nāthamuni, who lived around the tenth century C.E., is considered to be the first Śrīvaiṣṇava teacher (*ācārya*). He is said to have recovered the

Tamil poems of Nammāḻvār and eleven other poet-saints (*āḻvārs*) from obscurity, and divided them into passages that could be set to music and verses that could be chanted. The Śrīvaiṣṇava community understood this to be an act that emphasized the equivalency of the poems to the Sanskrit Vedas; *The Splendor* says that just as the legendary sage Śrī Veda Vyāsa divided up the Sanskrit Vedas according to the forms of chants involved,[3] Nāthamuni divided the Tamil poems into music and chant. Nāthamuni is said to have transmitted the proper singing and interpretation of the *Tiruvāymoḻi* to his two nephews, and *The Splendor* specifically mentions that another disciple, Uyyakoṇṭār, was given the task of disseminating the *Tiruvāymoḻi* and the other works of the *āḻvārs* (*The Splendor,* 122, 124).[4] There is epigraphical evidence that the *Tiruvāymoḻi* was chanted in temples at least from 1023 C.E. (Raman 1981, 36), and *The Splendor* tells us that Nāthamuni introduced the *Tiruvāymoḻi* and other Tamil hymns into home and temple liturgies and initiated an annual ten-day "Festival of Recitation" that was accompanied by oral and performing commentaries.

Selections from the *Tiruvāymoḻi* are recited daily at Śrīvaiṣṇava homes and temples. The poem is recited in its entirety at funeral services, ancestral rites, birthdays of saints, and rituals connected with pregnancy, during the investiture of the sacred thread for young boys, and at several temple rituals.[5] A full recitation with verbal and performative commentaries is held during the *adhyayana utsava,* the annual Festival of Recitation.[6]

The *Tiruvāymoḻi* was interpreted either by long commentaries or by short summaries. Chronologically, the long commentaries came first, beginning with the recording of the oral commentaries in the late eleventh to early twelfth centuries. The earliest commentary was written by Tirukkurkai Piraṉ Piḷḷāṉ (late eleventh to early twelfth century). This commentary was called the Āṛāyirappaṭi, or "*Six Thousand paṭi.*" Later commentaries that are considered to be classical by the community are called the "*Nine Thousand paṭi,*" "*Twelve Thousand paṭi,*" "*Twenty-four Thousand paṭi,*" and the "*Thirty-six Thousand paṭi.*" A *paṭi* was a literary unit of 32 syllables. Thus Piḷḷāṉ's commentary has 32 × 6,000 syllables and was numerically modeled on a Sanskrit work of the same length, the *Viṣṇu Purāṇa.* This self-conscious modeling is, of course, significant in the twofold Sanskrit-Tamil tradition.[7]

Starting in the thirteenth century, there were several short summaries, usually in the form of a poem. These poems were either independent pieces or sometimes part of a longer narrative. Independent pieces include Vedānta Deśika's Sanskrit poem *The Gem-Necklace of Reality in the Tamil Upaniṣad (Dramidopaniṣad Tātparya Ratnāvaḷi)* and the Tamil poem *The Hundred Verses on the Tiruvāymoḻi (Tiruvāymoḻi Nūṟṟantāti).* These works have a similar format: Each set of "ten" verses in the *Tiruvāymoḻi* is summarized by one verse in the poem. Each set of ten verses in the *Tiruvāymoḻi* is presented as containing a coherent theme, and the main philosophical idea of those ten verses (as perceived by the interpreting poet) is condensed into a single verse.[8] Thus, in these summaries, there was a "translation" either from Tamil into Sanskrit, or from "older" Tamil into a more current Tamil of that age.

The longer commentaries, on the other hand, were detailed prose interpretations of the original *Tiruvāymoḻi* verses, containing several quotations from Sanskrit scripture. Piḷḷāṉ, the first commentator on the *Tiruvāymoḻi,* elucidated each verse of the *Tiruvāymoḻi,* but frequently wrote a short introduction to each set of ten verses. The comment is not a word-by-word elucidation of the poem (as later commentaries tended to be), but an interpretation of the verse as a whole, with the commentator supplying a context or framework to the verse.

There is only one woman who is known to have written a commentary on the *Tiruvāymoḻi,* but this is rather different in style from the earlier commentaries. This commentary was written by Tirukkōnēri Dāsyai and is a comment only on a hundred verses of the *Tiruvāymoḻi*. She tries to bring in themes from the rest of the *Tiruvāymoḻi* and show how they may be discerned by rearranging the words in the first verse itself.[9]

II. Written and Oral Comment

According to the *The Splendor,* it was during the time of Rāmānuja (1017–1037 C.E.), the most important teacher of the community, that the first commentary on the *Tiruvāymoḻi* was written by his cousin Tirukkurukai Pirāṉ Piḷḷāṉ. The writing of a commentary on the *Tiruvāymoḻi* marks a new epoch in Hindu literature. While commentaries were frequently written in Sanskrit for Sanskrit literary and religious works, the commentarial tradition in Tamil began only about the eighth century.[10] No Hindu religious work in the vernacular had been deemed worthy of a written commentary, although a strong oral tradition on the *Tiruvāymoḻi* had probably existed even before Piḷḷāṉ committed one to writing for the first time.

Piḷḷāṉ's first commentary highlighted and articulated certain ideas that challenge traditional norms of the Hindu culture without rebelling against them. The very fact that he, a Brahmin scholar well versed in Sanskrit, wrote a commentary on a Tamil hymn composed by a person, believed to have been from the "fourth class" (i.e., a *śūdra*), was an unprecedented act. Nammāḻvār was of the Veḷḷāḷa community, which, though high among the non-Brahmin castes, was still considered as "low" from the Brahminical standpoint. The writing of the commentary challenges two claims made by the traditional Hindu society: the consideration of Sanskrit as the exclusive vehicle for revelation and theological communication, and the importance of the hierarchical class system that denied salvific knowledge to the *śūdra*. This latter point is openly refuted by Piḷḷāṉ's assumption that Nammāḻvār is the ideal devotee who is always at the Lord's feet, and whose name, in fact, is synonymous with the Lord's grace. The close connection between Nammāḻvār and divine grace is articulated by a ritual associated in Śrīvaiṣṇava temples. A silver crown engraved with the feet of the Lord is placed on the head of every devotee; the feet symbolize the grace of the Lord, and the crown itself is called "Śaṭhāri," which is a name of Nammāḻvār. The first written reference to this ritual, significantly enough, is in Piḷḷāṉ's commentary.[11]

Piḷḷāṉ wrote his commentary in Maṇipravāḷa, a new hybrid language of communications used in Śrīvaiṣṇava circles. The Tamil of Nammāḻvār was "translated" and explained in a new "situational language." "Maṇipravāḷa" means "gems and corals" or "pearls and corals" and refers to a combination of Sanskrit and Tamil. Unlike other forms of Maṇipravāḷa (Venkatachari 1978, 4–5, 167–171), the Śrīvaiṣṇava variety always retained Tamil grammar and endings, though the sentences were heavily interspersed with Sanskrit words. The language of the commentary itself gave the message effectively, proclaiming the equivalency of the Sanskrit and Tamil languages and literatures. This type of communicating—in speech and writing—flourishes even today in the Śrīvaiṣṇava community.

Why was the commentary committed to writing in the late eleventh century? The oral commentarial tradition must have become popular by the time of Yāmuna (ca. tenth century), who was Rāmānuja's teacher's teacher. His opinions have been preserved in the longer written commentaries on the *Tiruvāymoḻi*.[12] We may speculate about the reasons that prompted Rāmānuja to permit the writing of the first commentary. It is possible that Rāmānuja wanted the opinions of the earlier *ācāryas* to be preserved for posterity, and committing the texts to writing ensured that they would not be forgotten. He may have also believed that the comments and opinions of earlier *ācāryas* would add to the flavor of the community's understanding of the poems. The poems were meant to be relished, enjoyed, and experienced; hearing the anecdotes and earlier interpretations (some of which were at variance with each other) would encourage the listeners to participate in the meaning of the poems without feeling confined to hold on to the interpretation they had just heard.

According to *The Splendor*, there had been an earlier incident in Rāmānuja's life that, we believe, may have led to his decision to record the commentary. Apparently, while learning the meaning of the *Tiruvāymoḻi* from Tirumālai Āṇṭāṉ, Rāmānuja differed from his teacher's interpretation of the verses several times, offering alternate explanations. After Rāmānuja offered a different interpretation for *Tiruvāymoḻi* 2.3.4, Āṇṭāṉ ceased his instruction, saying that these were mischievous explanations, which he had not heard from *his* teacher, Yāmuna.[13] The stalemate was resolved by another disciple of Yāmuna, Tirukkōṭṭiyūr Nampi, who reconciled Āṇṭāṉ and Rāmanuja by proclaiming that he had heard the alternate interpretation from Yāmuna. What is interesting to note is that Rāmānjua's position had to be vindicated by another teacher's recollection of Yāmuna's commentary, and there was no text to check it with.

The Splendor (pp. 199–200) goes on to say that at a later time, Tirumālai Āṇṭāṉ again hesitated at a certain interpretation, but Rāmānuja said that he was a disciple of Yāmuna like the legendary Ekalavya was a disciple of Droṇa; a student who learned from a master in spirit, without actually ever being in his presence. So, even when there was no witness to attest that Rāmānuja's opinion had been stated earlier by Yāmuna, the community assumed that whatever Rāmānuja said would have been said by or at least permitted by Yāmuna. *The Splendor's* account of Rāmānuja's learning the *Tiruvāymoḻi* gives us a glimpse of the transmission of the poem, and at this stage it still seems to have been on the model of a ''private tuition'' and not a public oration to a Śrīvaiṣṇava audience. The commentarial tradition certainly did become that in later years, and we hear of large audiences listening to the *ācārya's* exposition of the Tamil poems.[14]

Rāmānuja's permission to allow the commentary to be written, therefore, may have stemmed from his desire to preserve all possible alternate opinions in writing, so that later generations may know that these opinions, and others, *within reason,* were admissible. Similarly, by not writing the commentary himself, Rāmānuja made sure that the line of commentaries on these hymns that were meant to be ''experienced'' and enjoyed by all would keep growing. Rāmānuja's comments were considered authoritative and would have been held to be the final word on a topic, and it seems probable that the teacher wanted to encourage a chain of commentaries, rather than establish one set of ''correct'' interpretations. The *Tiruvāymoḻi* has inspired a long line of commentaries in which the community relives and reexperiences the emotions of the *āḻvārs.* Sanskrit literature, on the other hand, is perceived as embodying one truth for all time—after Rāmānuja's commentary on the *Bhagavad Gīta* and the *Brahma Sūtras,* no Śrīvaiṣṇava wrote another commentary on them.[15] Usually commentaries preserved the correct interpretations and the right opinions on a text; interestingly enough, the commentaries on the *Tiruvāymoḻi* preserve a diversity of opinions. However, it is important to note that the diversity of the opinions did not at any time involve important theological issues pertaining to the supremacy of Viṣṇu, his auspicious nature, and other doctrines cardinal to the community, but usually reflected the flavor of the teachers' enjoyment of the poem.

Despite the writing of the commentaries, it seems clear that the community was and remains one where the oral comment was primary. It is clear that in the past, not too many people had access to the written commentaries, and interested disciples were always taught the commentary orally. The function of the written commentaries, therefore, was probably to serve as a teacher's guide, inspiring new oral commentaries. The written commentaries seem to have served not so much as firm boundary fences but as elastic parameters.

III. The Question of Authority

The community believed that the *Tiruvāymoḻi* contained sacred knowledge and that only "worthy" souls may receive such instruction, in the form of a commentary. A thirteenth-century commentary gives this process of oral transmission a name; it is called "the way of individual instruction" (*ōrāṇ-vaḻi*).[16] In keeping a close watch on *who* received this information, the community affirmed that while members of all castes and both sexes could hear the commentaries on the *Tiruvāymoḻi* (and thus the belief that the poem is meant for *all* people), a teacher could withhold instruction depending on his perception of the disciple's worthiness. Even the scribe who copied the commentary had to prove himself worthy of the knowledge he had to record: the story of Nañjīyar (a late-twelfth-century teacher) and his scribe-disciple Nampiḷḷai is instructive. This story, as translated here, is recorded in *The Splendor.*

> Nañjīyar, by the grace of [his teacher] Bhaṭṭar composed a commentary on the *Tiruvāymoḻi*. The commentary was the size of the *Śrī Bhāṣya* [Rāmānjua's Sanskrit commentary on the *Brahma Sūtras*]. Holding the manuscript,[17] he asked . . . Is there anyone who can write this [neatly]? His disciples answered "Nampūr Varadarājan̲ from the south bank comes here often; he writes well."
>
> Nañjīyar invited Varadarājan̲ and asked him to write a syllable. . . . Seeing it, [Nañjīyar] thought, "His writing is as beautiful as a pearl, but still, this is a commentary on the *Tiruvāymoḻi* and [now] it is to be written by a stranger. How can I ask him to write it just because his name is sacred? [*Varadarājan̲* is a name of Viṣṇu.] This commentary ought to be written by a specially knowledgeable person." While he was skeptical [about the scribe's worthiness], Varadarājan̲, understanding Nañjīyar's mind said, "Can you not guide me, your servant, and make me acceptable to your heart?" Nañjīyar was overjoyed [at the scribe's humility and perceptiveness] and immediately adopted him [as a disciple], graciously initiated him with the five-fold sacrament [as befits] one

> who had submitted himself to God and taught him the scriptures. . . . He taught the Nine Thousand *paṭi* commentary [on the *Tiruvāymol̲i*] once, fully, to Varadarājan̲ and said, "Write it thus, without deviating from it." He delivered the manuscript to Varadarājan̲'s hands. . . .
>
> When Varadarājan̲ was crossing the Kāveri river, he came to a place where he had to swim for a short distance. He tied the manuscript to his head but as he swam, a wave hit him and swept the book (*grantham*) away. When Varadarājan̲ came to the other bank, he was devastated: "The manuscript is gone! What shall I do?" He procured blank palm leaves that were joined together for writing and wrote down well the meaning that Nañjīyar had graciously [revealed] to him. Because he was a Tamil scholar . . . in some places he brought out a special meaning by using felicitous and majestic words. Having written [the commentary] he gave it to Nañjīyar, who opened up the sacred text and read it. He saw that though his opinions were given, the words were particularly fitting in several places and special meanings had been given. His heart was elated; looking at Varadarājan̲, he said, "This is excellent—but how did it come about?" Varadarājan̲ was frightened and remained silent. Nañjīyar reassured him and said, "Speak the truth!" Varadarĵan̲ told him [what had happened] . . . and concluded "and so . . . the waves made your book sink. I wrote this because you had gone through the whole [text] with me once."
>
> Overjoyed, Nañjīyar . . . realizing his [scribe's] wisdom embraced him and said, "You are our son . . ." Since Nañjīyar had called him "our son" (*nam piḷḷai*), Varadarājan̲ was called Nampiḷḷai after that day. (*The Splendor,* 364–67)

It is clear from the first part of the story that Nañjīyar believed his scribe should understand the material and be initiated to the proper study of the text prior to his reading it and copying it. Reading a commentary on the *Tiruvāymol̲i* (in the process of copying it) was obviously not the correct way of receiving salvific knowledge: the transmission of such knowledge had to be through oral discourse.[18] Because the matter discussed was of utmost importance, the teacher had to ensure that the pupils understood the verses; and as in all oral utterances, meaning was negotiated in the discursive process. In oral discourse, the commentator interpreted himself as he proceeded, shaping his commentary to fit the audience on hand.[19] The second part of the story shows that Nañjīyar was not upset with his scribe upstaging him and highlighting certain meanings: the student's innovation was rewarded.[20]

In the past, students listening to this comment wrote it out, with (occasionally, without) the teacher's permission. *The Splendor* narrates a story connected with Nampiḷḷai (Varadarājan̲'s) life. When he became the next teacher, succeeding Nañjīyar, he gave several oral commentaries on the *Tiruvāymoḻi*. With his permission, one of his students, Periyavāccān̲ Piḷḷai, wrote a commentary that was equivalent in length to the *Rāmāyana*.[21] This commentary was apparently based on the oral discourses that Nampiḷḷai gave to his students. Another disciple, Vaṭakku Tiruvīti Piḷḷai, is said to have heard the commentary during the day and written it out at night, without telling his teacher. Vaṭakku Tiruvīti Piḷḷai gave it to his teacher, Nampiḷḷai, who read it and was happy with it, but said that since the commentary had been written without his permission, it could not be recognized as an authorized work. Nampiḷḷai took the original and locked it away. A disciple who heard about this incident prayed to the Lord that the commentary should be brought to light, and according to *The Splendor,* the Lord at Śrīrangam instructed Nampiḷḷai to *teach* from the new commentary of his disciple. Nampiḷḷai obeyed the Lord, and that commentary became the most famous of all the *Tiruvāymoḻi* commentaries.[22]

A footnote has to be added to this emphasis on oral commentary and strict control over what was committed to writing. While the process of orally transmitting commentary from the teacher to disciple still continues within the community, it is obvious that there has been a major change in attitude in the twentieth century. This is evident in the decision to publish and bring to public attention all the classical medieval commentaries as well as the modern ones. For the first time in Śrīvaiṣṇava history, these sacred matters (*bhagavad viṣayam*) are available (for reading, at any rate) to anyone who chooses to buy the texts; the writing of a commentary on a sacred text and publishing it, knowing that it may well be read by "outsiders" without an authorized person to interpret it, is a phenomenon we encounter in the twentieth century and a distinct break from earlier days. There has been no self-conscious statement made about this change in attitude, and the impact of non-Śrīvaiṣṇavas commenting on sacred matters is an issue still be be assessed.

To summarize: Despite the conscious decision to *write* commentaries, the Śrīvaiṣṇava tradition has a strong oral base and believes that oral interpretation is the only way of communicating a commentary if the purpose is to obtain salvific knowledge. Both oral and written comment share certain features: there is a desire to proclaim the equality of both Tamil and Sanskrit Vedas; an emphasis on cardinal doctrinal positions that defined the Śrīvaiṣṇava community's identity; and the incorporation of large stretches of Rāmānuja's words in the commentary to show correspondence between the *Tiruvāymoḻi* and Rāmānuja's philosophy. The language used in both written and oral commentary is Maṇipravāḷa, and here, the medium itself was the message: a harmonious combination of Tamil and Sanskrit.

IV. The Commentarial Agenda

Commentaries on the *Tiruvāymoḻi* were given to groups of students, and in the process of commenting, the teacher drew from the earlier ones he had studied, but paraphrased them in his own words. Generally, commentaries were written or recorded after a teacher had orally commented upon them several times. Both oral and written commentaries share common features, and in the following pages I shall focus on some of these similarities, looking to the first commentary on the *Tiruvāymoḻi,* written by Piḷḷāṉ, for examples to illustrate the points.

1. The commentarial tradition allows for the elaboration of doctrine and the strengthening the notion of the Dual Vedānta. The language of the *Tiruvāymoḻi* itself can be understood easily; the concept that has to be communicated to the audience is something that was already present in Nāthamuni's incorporation of the hymn in liturgy: that this poem was equivalent to the Sanskrit Veda. One of the principal tasks of the commentarial tradition seems to have been the establishment of this concept. The commentaries are directed to an audience that is familiar with both the Sanskrit Vedas and the Tamil verses. The lengthiest comments occur either when there are issues of doctrinal importance to be proclaimed or where there are parallels in Sanskrit literature; we see important examples in Piḷḷaṉ's comments on *Tiruvāymoḻi* 1.1.7 and 4.10.1. The commentator perceives these verses as (a) proclaiming the relationship between Viṣṇu and the universe as analogous to the relationship between a human soul and the physical body, and (b) the supremacy of Viṣṇu. Here, there are long lists of quotations from Sanskrit Vedas and later literature; the written commentary records and preserves these lists of quotations, thus reiterating the notion of the Dual Vedānta.

2. There is also extensive incorporation of Rāmānuja's formulaic phrases and lines in almost all the long commentaries. This is particularly seen in Piḷḷāṉ's commentary; reading it, one gets the distinct impression that here is a disciple who has listened to his teacher for many years, and one who is eager to show that his commentary is close in spirit to his master's thought. He uses formulaic phrases, especially those describing qualities, auspiciousness, and purity of the Lord, in his paraphrase and condenses Rāmānuja's lengthy discourses into brief theological platforms. In the following example, the commentary on the first verse of the

Tiruvāymoḻi, phrases used both by Rāmānuja and Piḷḷāṉ are given in italics, and details are given in the notes.

Tiruvāymoḻi 1.1.1

Who is he possessing the highest good?
Who is he, who slashes ignorance,
  by graciously bestowing wisdom and love?
Who is he, the commander of the never-tiring[23] immortals?
O my mind!
  Worship his radiant feet
  that destroy all sorrow,
and rise.

Piḷḷāṉ's Six Thousand Paṭi Commentary

The *āḻvār* with his holy soul "experiences" the supreme person as he really is. This is the supreme person who has *transcendent, extraordinary, divine ornaments, weapons, consorts and attendants*[24] and *whose sport is the creation, development, etc. of this universe.*[25] The *āḻvār* speaks as he experiences the love that arises from his being with the Lord. [The *āḻvār* says], "[The Lord] is wholly opposed to all fault, and [is characterized] by the statement 'He who has the bliss a thousand times that of human beings (*Taittrīya Upaniṣad* 2.8.1.).' [The Lord] is an immense ocean of *infinite bliss that is multiplied a thousand fold*[26] and other countless *auspicious attributes.*[27] He who has this bliss and other auspicious attributes, further has that great quality, like gold having a fragrance, of making himself known to me, without reason, such that there is not even a trace (*"whiff"*) *of ignorance.*[28] [He arouses in] me unsurpassed *bhakti* toward his sacred feet. This Lord who has all auspicious attributes shows his generosity to Śeṣa, Garuḍa and other innumerable divine beings who are naturally and wholly without fault and *who have unflickering wisdom.*[29] His flowerlike feet have the inherent nature of dispelling all sorrows of his devotees. Serve these feet at all places, times and conditions [as befits [a] servant and live." Thus speaks [the āḻvār] to his holy soul.

In oral discourses also one frequently encounters the incorporation of formulaic phrases seen in the writings of Rāmānuja. Last year, I recorded a discourse on the life of Nammāḻvār. The orator, in the first five minutes of discourse, used thirteen Sanskrit phrases seen frequently in Rāmānuja's writings and ten from the Tamil poems of the *āḻvārs.*[30]

3. Piḷḷāṉ and later commentators elucidated the verses with categories not intrinsic to the poems but which were borrowed from Sanskrit literature. Such extrinsic categories included *bhakti yoga*, *upāya* and *puruṣakāra*. Where the poem merely hints at a topic, the commentators use formulaic phrases from Sanskrit to explain the idea. Thus, if the poet mentions Śrī (the consort of Viṣṇu) in the verse, the commentators take it as a signal for "divine intercession," as the following example makes clear.

Tiruvāymoḻi 6.10.10

O [Lord] on whose breast
resides the lady of the flower who says:
"I cannot move away from him even for a second!"

Piḷḷāṉ's Six Thousand Paṭi Commentary

> I, your servant, who am without refuge, without any other goal, having the divine Mother *as the mediator*, took refuge at your sacred feet.[31]

A mere mention of Śrī is interpreted as "mediator," and her position as one who intercedes between human being and God is seen to be indicated by this verse. Like Piḷḷāṉ, later commentators also take this verse to be one where the poet formally seeks refuge from the Lord.

5. Variations in opinion and particular incidents connecting the verses with the earlier teachers are narrated to make special points. *The Thirty-six Thousand Paṭi,* the thirteenth-century commentary on the *Tiruvāymoḻi,* records many instances of earlier conversations and discussions on the meaning of a certain word or phrase.

> Empār [Rāmānuja's cousin] would say "The Lord of all, has three kinds of souls as his servants. . . . The liberated souls and the *eternally* liberated ones[32] are blissful and make [the Lord] happy; the bound souls are not blissful, but still make him happy. All [categories of souls form] part of his play." Piḷḷai Tirunaṟaiyūr Aṟaiyar asked Empār: "Why should [Nammāḻvār] who has obtained 'wisdom and love' (*Tiruvāymoḻi* [TVM] 1.1.1) petition 'take me as yours' instead of saying '[the Lord] will do as he pleases'?" Empār replied: "Listen; it is like Śrī saying 'I cannot move away from him even for a second' (TVM 6.10.10), when in fact, she *never* parts from him. She is never reunited with him, because she always resides on his breast. Similarly the *āḻvār* is praying for the pleasure of the goal."[33]

In this conversation, Empār answers a subtle theological question posed by Aṛaiyar: Why is the *āḻvār* actively *asking* me the Lord to do something instead of calmly waiting for the Lord's will to be done? Empār defuses the question by using the analogy of Śrī's inseparability with the Lord, thus implying that the *āḻvār's* request is almost rhetorical one.[34]

Improvisation is allowed but only with the usage of standard phrases and techniques. Sometimes, in earlier commentaries, two or more sequential explanations are given, as in the following example. This is a translation from Periyavāccāṉ Piḷḷai's *Twenty-four Thousand Paṭi* commentary on the TVM, and is his introduction to 2.10.

> Āḷavantār (Yāmuna) would say: [Nammāḻvār] takes refuge with the sacred hill to obtain the goal that he sought in the verse "My father's house. . . ." (TVM 2.9.1.).
>
> While that [explanation] exists, Emperumaṉār [that is, Rāmānuja] would say, The goal desired earlier would have been obtained in heaven when his body [dies]. But the āḻvār does not think [like us]; in his fervor, he says [he wants the goal] "quickly" (TVM 2.9.1) and "without losing time. . . ." (TVM 2.9.2). He wishes to experience the [supreme goal] with his earthly body itself.

In the above example, the commentator first records the interpretation of Yāmuna, who had provided the context for TVM 2.10. But the later teacher Rāmānuja had provided further exegesis, saying that in the following set of verses, Nammāḻvār wants to experience the supreme goal in his earthly body and not wait for heaven. Rāmānuja says that in the previous set of verses, the poet had craved immediate fulfillment for his desires, and this seems to be achieved now. Rāmānuja was only expanding Yāmuna's line of thinking by giving further reasons (from the poetry itself) as to why Nammāḻvār said the ten verses that are being introduced. The commentator who is writing this introduction probably heard these contextual explanations orally from his teacher, Nampiḷḷai, and is using the material from earlier oral tradition as part of his own written introduction.

In the example quoted above, another feature of a commentary is also clearly visible: the commentator tries to connect the verses into a coherent framework and give links to sets of poems. He attempts to provide connections that may not be evident in the poem itself.

In oral commentaries today, while the commentator may be familiar with details of interpretation for all the verses, because of time constraints, and to hold audience interest, he may pause only at those words or lines that he thinks are striking, and introduce some new examples to make the poem seem relevant. In a sense, therefore, the stages of composition and transmission of the commentary were collapsed to one event.[35]

6. In the early commentaries, normative ideas for the ideal "Śrīvaiṣṇava" and the ideal community were forcibly stated. For example, Piḷḷān says in his comment on *Tiruvāymoḻi* 3.5.4;

> He is Śrīdhara ("The supporter of Śrī"); he is so called, because to unite with the Lady Nappiṉṉai, he subjugated the seven bulls. His passion caused his red lips to glow.
>
> What is the use of people being born amidst Śrīvaiṣṇavas if they do not become excited by the wondrous love that is born out of thinking of the [Lord's] passion [for Nappiṉṉai]?

A Śrīvaiṣṇava is exhorted to visibly show his fervor, his joy in contemplating the Lord's qualities. In a later comment, Piḷḷān addresses another issue that he and later commentators believe to be very important: a Śrīvaiṣṇava is told to be the servant of other Śrīvaiṣṇavas.

> This set of ten verses says that the supreme goal is to be the slave of any Śrīvaiṣṇava, *whosoever* he may be, if that Śrīvaiṣṇava has been conquered by and is a slave of the Lord's innumerable qualities. . . . For all those who learn this set of verses, all obstacles that may lie in their path to be a slave (*śeṣa*) of the Lord's devotees will vanish. (*Piḷḷāṉ's Six Thousand Paṭi* 3.7.11)

The *whosoever* is an important caution, a direct statement warning one not to discriminate on basis of caste. An ideal Śrīvaiṣṇava is to be a servant of all other devotees of Viṣṇu, not withstanding caste, social, or financial status.

V. Concluding Remarks

The history of interpretation, both oral and written, for this sacred poem in the Hindu tradition still continues. Nammāḻvār, like the poets described by Socrates in Plato's dialogue the *Ion*, is himself a "messenger of gods" (*hermenes eisin ton theon;* Palmer 1969, 13). Like Hermes, this poet is a "go-between" from God to human being in the Śrīvaiṣṇava community; his enunciation of the poem, his "simply saying . . . or proclaiming is an important act of 'interpretation'" (Palmer 1969, 15). Nammāḻvār is thus an "interpreter" in a primary sense, for before him the words were not yet said. Nammāḻvār asserts in one memorable verse that the Lord speaks through him; in this sense, the poem is taken to be revelation. For the Śrīvaiṣṇava, the "*Tiruvāymoḻi*" (Sacred word of mouth; sacred utterance), then, is an interpretation of the ultimate unspoken truth.

The contemporary commentator who recites these words and then elucidates them in Sanskrit and Tamil is a part of the long hermeneutical tradition that goes back to Nammāḻvār. From Nammāḻvār to the twentieth-century commentator, each tries to express the truth, *utter* it as he or she *sees* it. From their *insight,* words are articulated, and the process of explanation, of making relevant in an understandable language, is set in motion. Seeing the truth and orally expressing it become two interconnected parts of the interpretive process. This uttered word, this spoken word, empowers the written word of the commentator. The written commentaries in tandem with the oral disclosures have fostered the commentarial tradition for several centuries, but within the Śrīvaiṣṇava community, at least, the written forms of explanation have not displaced the oral nature of the hermeneutical process.

Notes

1. Ong 1987, 7–8. I am indebted to Professor Harold Stahmer, University of Florida, for drawing my attention to this article and also to Palmer's book in hermeneutics. Research for this paper was done under a summer stipend from the National Endowment for the Humanities, 1987. Tape recordings of the *Tiruvāymoḻi* and some commentarial narration was done with financial assistance from the Division of Sponsored Research, University of Florida.

2. From a work called *Vādikēcari Kārikai,* quoted in *The Splendor,* a fourteenth-century hagiography, p. 366. The *Guruparampāraprabhāvam-āṛāyirappaṭi,* "The Splendor of the Succession of Teachers, in 6,000 units of 32 syllables," which I refer to as *The Splendor,* was written in a hybrid language of Sanskrit and Tamil (Maṇipravāḷa) around the fourteenth century C.E. by Piṉpaḻakiya Perumāḷ Jīyar. It contains pious accounts of the lives of the *āḻvārs* and early *ācāryas.*

3. The division was into Udātta and Anudātta. Udātta is "high, elevated; acutely accented" and Anudātta is "not elevated or raised, accentless [in chanting]." Meanings taken from Apte's *The Student's Sanskrit-English Dictionary* (1982).

4. The *Kōyil Oḻuku,* which purports to be a chronological account of the Śrīraṅgam temple, states that Nāthamuni established classes in which the *Tiruvāymoḻi* was taught (Hari Rao 1961, 34).

5. Details of the ritual context were kindly provided to me by Śrī Ashtagothram Nallan Chakravarthy Parthsarathy Iyengar, Triplicane, Madras. I

had the opportunity to hear the *Tiruvāymoḻi* during the funeral rites and ancestral ceremonies in 1983. Further information was obtained during visits to Śrī Parthasarathy temple (Triplicane, Madras), the Śrīrangam temple in 1987, and the Nammāḻvār Sanniti (Bangalore) in 1983 and 1985.

6. I will be dealing with the recitation and performative aspects of the *Tiruvāymoḻi* in my book *The Vernacular Veda: Revelation, Recitation, and Ritual* (University of South Carolina Press: forthcoming).

7. The later commentaries are also believed to be as long as certain Sanskrit works. The *O<u>n</u>patināyirappaṭi (The Nine Thousand Paṭi)* was the commentary of Nañjīyar and was rewritten by Nampiḷḷai, who is said to have lost the original work of his teacher. This work is said to be numerically equivalent to the *Śrī Bhāṣya* of Rāmānuja. The *Iṛupatinālāyirappaṭi (The Twenty-four Thousand Paṭi,* written in the thirteenth century by Periyavāccā<u>n</u> Piḷḷai) was said to be as long as the *Rāmāyaṇa,* and the *Īṭu-Muppattāṛayirappaṭi (The Thirty-six Thousand Paṭi)* written by Vaṭakku Tiruvīti Piḷḷai, a contemporary of Periyavāccā<u>n</u> Piḷḷai, was said to be as long as the *Śrutaprakāśika,* the commentary on Rāmānuja's *Śrī Bhāṣya.*

8. Other summaries of the *Tiruvāymoḻi* are contained in the Tamil poem *Nammāḻvār Tiruttāllāṭṭu* (A Lullaby for Nammālvār; probably fourteenth century, according to its editor) and the biographical poem on the *āḻvārs* called *Āḻvārkal vaibhavam* (The Glory of the Āḻvārs). The latter work may have been written around the fifteenth century.

9. Women are allowed to comment on the *Tiruvāymoḻi,* but I have not known anyone to do so. However, I was recently informed about an eighty-year-old woman near Madras who had formally studied both poems of Nammāḻvār and the later commentaries on them, fifteen times under a certain (male) teacher. She is reported to give brilliant oral commentaries on the *Tiruvāymoḻi.*

10. One of the earliest Tamil commentaries was Nakkīrar's commentary on Iṛaya<u>n</u>ār's *Akapporuḷ* written about the eighth century C.E. This work was a commentary on the "secular" love poetry of the classical era. For further details, see Zvelebil 1973, 26. For the commentaries on the Tamil grammar *Tolkāppiyam,* see Zvelebil 1973, 135. Zvelebil discusses the commentarial tradition in Tamil on pp. 247–63.

11. Piḷḷā<u>n</u>, *The Six Thousand Paṭi,* 10.9.10.

12. In the later commentaries on the TVM, (the *Twenty-four Thousand Paṭi* of Periyavāccā<u>n</u> Piḷḷai and the *Thirty-six Thousand Paṭi* of Vaṭakku Tiruvīti Piḷḷai), there are several verses where the special interpretations of

Yāmuna are quoted. There are about thirty-five instances in these two commentaries alone where the opinions of Yāmuna are quoted. These verses are catalogued in Narayanan 1987, 179. Some of these instances are repeated in *The Splendor.*

13. Yāmuna was an important teacher of the Śrīvaiṣṇava tradition and had (according to biographical tradition) summoned Rāmānuja to the temple town of Śrīraṅgam to be his disciple. By the time Rāmānjua came to Śrīraṅgam, Yāmuna had passed away. Later on, Yāmuna's disciples taught Rāmānjua the various texts sacred to the Śrīvaiṣṇava tradition.

14. *The Splendor,* 373. It is said that after an exposition of the *Bhagavad Viṣayam* (Sacred Matters, a term used for commentaries on the *Tiruvāymoḻi*), crowds of Śrīvaiṣṇavas were leaving the teacher Nampiḷḷai's room when a Śrīvaiṣṇava king who was passing by wondered out loud: "Is this a dispersal of Śrīvaiṣṇavas from Nampiḷḷai's audience chamber or Namperumāḷ's (i.e., the Lord at Śrīraṅgam) [worship] chamber?" Note that the reference is to a *Śrīvaiṣṇava* crowd that has the authority to listen to interpretations of the *Tiruvāymoḻi* and *not* a general audience.

15. While the Śrīvaiṣṇavas after Rāmānuja did not comment directly on the *Bhagavad Gītā* or the *Brahma Sūtras,* they commented on Rāmānuja's commentary on these works. Sudarśana Sūri wrote a commentary on the *Śrī Bhāṣya,* which was Rāmānuja's commentary on the *Brahma Sūtras* and Vedānta Deśika wrote a commentary on Rāmānuja's commentary on the *Bhagavad Gītā.* These later commentaries only elucidated and elaborated Rāmānuja's commentaries, which were considered to be the authoritative and only correct interpretation of the Sanskrit works. The *Bhagavad Gītā and the Brahma Sūtras,* therefore, have had only one primary commentary within the Śrīvaiṣṇava community. On the other hand, there have been several direct commentaries in Maṇipravāḷa on the TVM. Most of the Maṇipravāḷa commentaries are directly on the poem, though there are a few that comment on a commentary. The TVM and the other Tamil hymns were probably at the center of so many direct commentaries primarily because they were considered to be *anubhava grantha* or works that could be "experienced" and "enjoyed" directly by the audience.

16. Vaṭakku Tiruvīti Piḷḷai's *Īṭu-Thirty-six Thousand* commentary on *Tiruvāymoḻi* 6.10.4. The *Tamil Lexicon* derives *ōrāṉ* from ōr (one) + an- (Male). Vaḻi is "way"; thus ōraṉ vaḻi is defined as "unbroken lineage from individual to individual." S. Venkataraman (1985, 26), describes *ōrāṉ-vaḻi* as "an unbroken [chain of] transmission from teacher to disciple."

17. I have translated the Tamil word *paṭṭōlai* as "manuscript" for convenience. It literally refers to palm leaves with their ribs removed. The

other meanings of *paṭṭōlai* are "first draft of petition, especially what is written to dictation"; "edict of royal proclamation"; "consolidated statement of ledger accounts"; "lists, catalogs of articles, inventory."

18. Donna Wulff (1983, 152), discussing the transmission of classical music, quotes a South Indian scholar V. Raghavan: "For when a thing is taken from a book, it is like a faggot without fire, but when the guru imparts it he transmits also a part of his power and grace." However, the scribe has evidently moved a long way from his original lowly position that Frits Staal and Cheever Mackenzie Brown have spoken about. For an excellent summary of Staal's position and other arguments detailing the Hindu bias against writing, see Brown's (1986) article "Purāna as Scripture: From Sound to Image of the Holy Word in the Hindu Tradition."

19. Ong (1987, 8) says:

> The world of oral utterance is typically one of discourse, in which utterance gives rise to another, that to still another, and so on. Meaning is negotiated in the discursive process. . . . What I say depends on my conjectures about your state of mind before I begin to speak and about the possible range of your responses. I need conjectural feed back even to formulate my utterance. . . . Oral discourse thus commonly interprets itself as it proceeds. It negotiates meaning out of meaning.

20. Nampiḷḷai became the next formal teacher of the Śrīvaiṣṇava community. He was the scribe—coauthor, according to *The Splendor*—but only Nañjīyar's name is associated with the commentary referred to in this story. Nampiḷḷai's students wrote two commentaries on the *Tiruvāymoḻi.*

21. Periyavāccāṉ Piḷḷai (born 1228 C.E.) also wrote commentaries on all the other hymns of the *āḻvārs.*

22. This is the *Thirty-six Thousand Paṭi* commentary that is frequently referred to as the *Īṭu* or "equivalent [to the original]." *The Splendor,* 391. Relatively speaking, Vaṭakku Tiruvīti Piḷḷai fared well in this incident. *The Splendor* also narrates that one Bhaṭṭar, a disciple of Nampiḷḷai, wrote a commentary that was 100,000 *paṭis,* without his teacher's permission. Nampiḷḷai was angry that the inner meaning of the *Tiruvāymoḻi,* which he had *orally* given, was now committed to *writing* so that the world may read it. He reprimanded the student and said that the meaning cannot be known without going through apprenticeship as a disciple and experiencing the honorable relationship between teacher and disciple. Apparently Nampiḷḷai threw away the commentary and let the termites waste it. *The Splendor,* 390.

23. "*Ayarvu aṟum.*" The word *ayarvu* may be translated as fatigue, forgetfulness, or sorrow. All these meanings are given by Uttamūr Vīrarāghavācāriyar in his commentary on this verse. Uttamūr Vīrarāghavā-

cāriyar, *Nammāḻvār aruḷiceyta Tiruvāymoḻi, prabandha rakṣai,* vol. 1. This phrase is quoted frequently by Piḷḷāṉ and is used to describe the "immortal ones" who serve Viṣṇu.

24. This list is an abbreviated version of Rāmānuja's description of Viṣṇu. See, for instance, "Introduction to *Gīta Bhāṣya,*" in *Rāmānujagranthamāla;* Rāmānuja, *Vedārthasaṁgraha,* edited by van Buitenen, para. 127.

25. *"Nikhila jagad udaya vibhava ādi līlanāy."* Rāmānuja frequently uses this phrase. See "Introduction to *Gītā Bhāṣya,*" in *Rāmānujagranthamāla,* 37; *Vedārtha Saṁgraha* in *Rāmānujagranthamāla* 3.

26. Piḷḷāṉ employs a phrase that Rāmānjua uses in the description of bliss. See Śrī *Bhāṣya* 1.1.13 in *Rāmānujagranthamāla* 87.

27. *"Asaṅkhyeya kalyāṇa guṇa mahodadhi."* Perhaps the most frequently used phrase by Rāmānjua in talking to God. See, for instance, *Gītā Bhāṣya* Introduction: *Vedārtha Saṁgraha* 1, etc.

Later commentaries say that Yāmuna, a Śrīvaiṣṇava teacher who lived a generation before Rāmānuja, used to explain the word *uṭaiyavaṉ* (He who possesses) in the verse with the phrase *anavadhika atiśaya ādisaṅkhyeya kalyāṇa guṇa gaṇa* (having a host of countless, infinite, wonderful auspicious attributes). Both the *Twenty-four Thousand Paṭi* of Periyavāccāṉ Piḷḷai and the *Thirty-six Thousand Paṭi* of Vaṭakku Tiruvīti Piḷḷai quote Yāmuna as the oral authority for this frequently occurring phrase.

28. Another phrase used by Rāmānuja. Rāmānuja uses the phrase "without a 'whiff' (*gandha*) of" when he wants to say "without a trace." See, for instance, *Śrī Bhāṣya* 1.1.21.

29. The phrase "unflickering wisdom" is used by Piḷḷāṉ in later comments (5.3.6 and 10.9.10) as well as by Rāmānuja (*Vedārtha Saṁgraha,* in *Rāmānujagranthamāla* 39).

30. The recording was made in August and September 1988 and was a forty-five minute discourse on the life of Nammāḻvār. The narrator was Sri Saranathan, a Vatakalai Śrīvaiṣṇava priest at Sri Venkateswara Temple, Pittsburgh. This preceded the recitation of the entire *Tiruvāymoḻi.* The narrator only knew that I was interested in listening to the *Tiruvāymoḻi* and had no prior knowledge that I was going to analyze some features of traditional Śrīvaiṣṇava oral discourse. I would consider this overwhelming usage of Rāmānuja's phrases and other lines from *āḻvār* poetry to be typical of almost all traditional oral commentary in the Śrīvaiṣṇava tradition.

31. Partial translation from TVM and *The Six Thousand Commentary* on 6.10.10.

32. The Śrīvaiṣṇava tradition counts three kinds of souls: those who are eternally liberated (i.e., those who have never been born on the earth), those who were once bound to the cycle of life and death, but are now liberated, and finally, those who are now in the realm of life and death.

33. Vaṭakku Tiruvīti Piḷḷai's commentary, *The Thirty-Six Thousand Paṭi* commentary on TVM 2.9.4.

34. This point of whether one can petition the Lord for salvation, or simply wait for him to save us when he so decrees, is one that theologically splits the Śrīvaiṣṇava community in the thirteenth century, and socially a few centuries later.

35. This process is not too far removed from puranic transmission as described by Giorgio Bonazzoli. See his "Composition, Transmission, and Recitation of the Purāṇa-s" (1983), especially pp. 266–67, where he discusses a modern work by a Svamin Tapovanam as one that is written in a puranic style of the *mahātmyās*. Focusing on his formulas, Bonazzoli says:

> These and similar formulas were composed and written by Tapovanam, who was strongly influenced by the purāṇa-s, which he had surely read and heard. It is very improbable that he copied these expressions from the purāṇa-s directly; he most probably had them in his mind and used them because they were fitting his purpose and gave to his composition the flavour of a purāṇic *mahātmyā*. Such formulas formed his luggage of knowledge not because he was a bard but because he was acquainted with purāṇic literature which contained—in a written form—those expressions. . . . Moreover, even his knowledge of the purāṇa-s could have reached him both orally by listening to them and/or through writing by reading. So here, we have an example of mixed influence, oral and written, from which no conclusion can be drawn whether the formulas, used by him were previously written or oral. This modern example is probably similar to what used to happen in the past, at least at the time of the composition of the purāṇic texts we possess now. Thousands of Svāmin Tapovanams must have existed, who composed . . . . collecting matter from previous texts and adding something of their own while keeping the purāṇic style by using the same kinds of purāṇic expression slightly modified according to necessity and personal likings.

References

Aṇṇaṅgārācariyar, P. B.
1949–63 (ed) *Nālāyira tivviyap pirapantam*. Kānci: V. N. Tevanātan.

1975–76 (ed) *Pakavat Viṣayam*. 4 vols. [With Nañjīyar's *Nine Thousand*, Periyavāccān Piḷḷai's *Twenty-four Thousand* and Vaṭakku Tiruvīti Piḷḷai's *"Īṭu" Thirty-Six Thousand* Commentaries.] Kānci: n.p.

1971 *Tiruvāymoḻi*. 10 vols. Kānci: n.p.

Apte, Vaman Shivram
1982 [1890] *The Student's Sanskrit English Dictionary*. New Delhi: Motilal Banarsidass.

Bonazzoli, Giorgio
1983 "Composition, Transmission, and Recitation of the Purāṇa-s. (A Few Remarks)." *Purāṇa* (July): 254–80.

Brown, C. Mackenzie
1986 "Purāṇa as Scripture: From Sound to Image of the Holy Word in the Hindu Tradition." *History of Religions* 261: 68–86.

Carman, John, and Vasudha Narayanan
1989 *The Tamil Veda: Piḷḷāṉ's Interpretation of the Tiruvāymoḻi*. Chicago: University of Chicago Press.

Clooney S. J., Francis X.
1987 "Why the Veda Has No Author: Language as Ritual in Early Mīmāmsa and Post-Modern Theology." *Journal of the American Academy of Religion* 55(4) 659–86.

Goody, Jack
1986 *The Logic of Writing and the Organization of Society*. Cambridge: Cambridge University Press.

Hari Rao, V. N., ed. and trans.
1961 *Kōil Oḷugu: The Chronicle of the Śrīrangam Temple with Historical Notes*. Madras: Rochouse & Sons.

Kōyiloḻuku
1976 Edited by Kiruṣṇasvāmi Ayyaṅkār Svāmi. Tirucci: Śrī Vaiṣṇava Grantha Prakācaṉa Samiti.

Krishnasvami Ayyangar, ed.
1924–30 *Bhagavad Viṣayam,* 10 vols. [With Tirukkurukai Pirāṉ Piḷḷāṉ's *Six Thousand,* Nañjīyar's *Twelve Thousand,* Periyavāccāṉ Piḷḷai's *Twenty-four Thousand* and Vaṭakku Tiruvīti Piḷḷai's "*Īṭu*" *Thirty-six Thousand* Commentaries.] Madras: Nobel Press.

Narayanan, Vasudha
1987 *The Way and the Goal.* Washington: Institute for Vaishnava Studies, and Cambridge, Mass.: Center for the Study for World Religions (Harvard University).

forthcoming *The Vernacular Veda: Revelation, Recitation, and Ritual.* Columbia: University of South Carolina Press.

Ong, Walter
1987 "Text as Interpretation: Mark and After." In *Orality, Aurality, and Biblical Narrative,* vol. 39 of *Semeia,* edited by Lou H. Silberman, 7–26.

Palmer, Richard E.
1969 *Hermeneutics: Interpretation Theory in Schleiermacher, Dilthey, Heidegger, and Gadamer.* Evanston: Northwestern University Press.

Piṉpaḻakiya Perumāḷ Jīyar
1975 *Āṛayirappaṭi Guruparamparāprabhāvam.* Edited by S. Krishnasvami Ayyaṅkār. Tirucci: Puttur Agraharam.

Raman, K. V.
1981 "Divyaprabandha Recital in Vaishnava Temples." In *Professor T. K. Venkataraman's 81st Birthday Commemoration Volume,* edited by S. Nagarajan. Madurai: Madurai Tamilology Publishers.

Rāmānuja
1956 *Rāmānuja's Vedārtha Samgraha.* Edited and translated by J. A. B. Van Buitenen. Poona: Deccan College.

1974 *Śrībhāṣya, Vedārtha Saṁgraha, Gītābhāṣya, Gadya-traya.* In *Rāmānujagranthamāla,* edited by P. B. Annangaracariyar. Kānci: n.p.

Rāmānujan, A. K.
1981 *Hymns for the Drowning. Poems for Viṣṇu by Nammāḻvār.* Princeton: Princeton University Press.

Tirukkurukai Piraṉ Piḷḷāṉ
1924–30 "Āṛāyirappaṭi Vyākkyānam." In *Bhagavad Viṣayam,* edited by Sri S. Krishnasvami Ayyangar, 10 vols. Madras: Nobel Press.

Vedānta Deśika
1974 *Dramidopaniṣad Tātparya Ratnāvaḷi and Sāra.* Translated by R. Rangachari. Madras: Vedānta Deśika Research Society.

Venkatachari, K. K. A.
1978 *The Maṇipravāḷa Literature of the Śrī Vaiṣṇava Ācāryas.* Bombay: Ananthācārya Research Institute.

Venkataraman, S.
1985 *Araiyar Cēvai.* Madras: Tamilputtakalayam.

Wulff, Donna Marie
1983 "On practicing Religiously: Music as Sacred In India." In *Sacred Sounds,* edited by Joyce Irwin. JAAR Thematic Studies 50 (1), 149–72. Chico, Calif.: Scholars Press.

Zvelebil, Kamil
1973 *The Smile of Murugan.* Leiden: E. J. Brill.

Seven

VYĀSA AS MADHVA'S GURU

Biographical Context for a Vedāntic Commentator

Daniel P. Sheridan

> The supreme meaning of all the Scripture is the pre-eminence of Viṣṇu over every other entity.
>
> —Madhva's *Viṣṇu Tattva Nirṇaya* (Raghavachar 1959, 98)

Introduction

The study of traditional hermeneutics in South Asia is an effort to understand religious texts in their indigenous contexts. In the case of the commentarial traditions, this understanding must appreciate the dynamics of the commentator's religious authority. Not just anyone was authorized to comment on sacred texts. In most cases little historical information on such matters is available, but Madhva (1238–1317 C.E.) stands out among the great Hindu *ācāryas* in the extent of historicity that may be attached to his life as known to us.[1] This is because knowledge of that life is based on an almost contemporaneous biography of Madhva by Nārāyaṇa Paṇḍitācārya, the *Sumadhvavijaya*.[2] This biography can be trusted as an outline of Madhva's life and also as an indigenous interpretation of that life written within a decade or two after Madhva's death. In B. N. K. Sharma's view,

> Madhva and his biographer were not far removed in time from each other, the work is able to achieve a far greater measure of

historical accuracy and wealth of contemporary details, than was possible for the authors of Śaṇkara's biographies, who were removed from their subject by more than five to six centuries and are guilty of many anachronisms. (Sharma 1981, 218)

Although there does seem to have been an earlier biography to which Nārāyaṇa refers, his is the earliest extant biography. Nārāyaṇa Paṇḍitācārya was the son of a householder, Trivikrama (c. 1258–1320 C.E.), who was converted by Madhva after an extended polemic with Madhva. This incident figures prominently in the son's *Sumadhvavijaya.* Nārāyaṇa Paṇḍitācārya was thus the son of a man who had at first opposed Madhva and then accepted Madhva as his *guru.* Nārāyaṇa Paṇḍitācārya accepted the claim that Madhva was an *avatāra* of the god Vāyu, the son of Viṣṇu, the Supreme Deity, and of Śrī his consort, and that Madhva had been taught by Vyāsa, an *avatāra* of Viṣṇu himself. What I will argue in this chapter is that these genealogical claims—far from being a dispensable mythological overlay—are the keys that unlock the indigenous significance of Madhva as an interpreter and commentator of scripture.

One of the consequences for the study of Hindu thought of overemphasizing "philosophy" as the paradigmatic category of understanding has been a persistent undervaluation and misunderstanding of the religious and theological elements in a thinker like Madhva. For example, R. G. Bhandarkar wrote cynically: "Probably he [Madhva] would have set aside the *Brahma Sūtras* altogether, but he could not do so, since the work had acquired an uncontested authoritativeness as regards religious truth before his time" (Bhandarkar 1965, 58). Yet Madhva composed four commentaries on the *Brahma Sūtras*! This distortion by reliance on nonindigenous philosophical categories also leads to an underestimation of historical and biographical contexts. As Nicholas B. Dirks laments: "[T]raditional Indian 'historiography,' when referred to at all, is most often characterized as fabulous legend and religious myth, bearing no relation to the past succession of real events" (Dirks 1987, 55). What is characterized as "fable" and "myth" are precisely what for this early biographer of Madhva was the historical basis for Madhva's authority as a commentator who had sure knowledge of God. This "knowledge," so often ignored as "myth," must be taken seriously if we are to understand both Nārāyaṇa Paṇḍitācārya and Madhva. If we take it seriously then we are enabled "to create and configure our own analytic consideration of their past, to help us select relevant events, and then to interpret these events" (Dirks 1987, 59).

Nārāyaṇa Paṇḍitācārya was, in the words of B. N. K. Sharma, an "ardent Mādhva, the fire of religious zeal seems to have burned in his heart with a steady glow and with all the freshness and vigor of recent converts"

(Sharma 1981, 217). Nārÿaṇa Paṇḍitācārya's biography is the primary basis for what we know about Madhva's life. However, the distinct insights "of the fire of religious zeal" that he brings to that life tend to be screened out as hagiographical and mythological embellishments. This is an unfortunate instance of the tendency of contemporary historians to "teach" the past according to what is evidentially allowable or not allowable rather than to learn from the past. That neither Madhva nor Nārāyaṇa Paṇḍitācārya share the contemporary restrictions on what is permissible in religious and historical experience is apparent. Profound religious experiences that lie within the historial realm are narrated in this biography. These experiences assume a "mythic" and historical importance for the biographer, since they are the reason why Madhva is religiously and theologically significant. Further, the text of Nārāyaṇa Paṇḍitācārya's biography provides the context that makes interpretative sense of the affirmations that Madhva makes about himself precisely as an interpreter of authoritative texts. In the study of Hinduism the interpretation of text and commentary should not be detached from biographical and theological context.[3] The juxtaposition of what Nārāyaṇa Paṇḍitācārya affirms about Madhva and of what Madhva affirms about himself provides direct and mutual illumination of the sources of the authority of Madhva as a Vaiṣṇava interpreter of Vendānta and of its texts.

Five themes run through the *Sumadhvavijaya:* (1) the sole independent divinity of Nārāyaṇa/Viṣṇu; (2) Vyāsa's appearance as *avatāra* of Viṣṇu; (3) Madhva's appearance as *avatāra* of Vāyu, the son of Viṣṇu and Śrī, who had also appeared as Hanumān and as Bhīma; (4) Madhva's appearance for the purpose of undoing the commentorial evil wreaked by Śaṅkara, a demonic *avatāra* of Maṇiman who had been killed by Bhīma in the *Mahābhārata;* and (5) the intimate dependence of true and authoritative interpretation of *śruti* and of *smṛti* upon Madhva's *guru,* Vyāsa. These five themes may be reduced to the last, to the single historical fact of mythic importance that, according to Nārāyaṇa Paṇḍitācārya and according to Madhva himself, Vyāsa—the legendary *ṛṣi,* compiler of the Vedas and author of the *Mahāpurāṇas*—was Madhva's *guru.* This identification is central to an understanding of Madhva as an interpreter. It is the indigenous key to the study of Madhva's biography, to the understanding of the commentaries where he interprets texts, to an appreciation of his polemic against Advaita Vedānta, and to an appreciation of his Dvaita theology.

In this chapter we will first discuss Nārāyaṇa Paṇḍitācārya's biography of Madhva, secondly look at Madhva's writings themselves to corroborate the themes derived from Nārāyaṇa Paṇḍitācārya, and thirdly draw conclusions about the biographical context for Madhva's role as a Vaiṣṇava commentator of Vedānta.

I. The Sumadhvavijaya *of* *Nārāyaṇa Paṇḍitācārya*

Nārāyaṇa Paṇḍitācārya, in his first canto of the *Sumadhvavijaya*, condemns Śaṅkara. "They call him the great thief who criticized the vehicle for the collection [of the Vedas], that is, the sun of the collected *Brahma Sūtras* which manifest the whole [of reality] by their very words."[4] Śaṅkara is seen as a closet Buddhist who has beclouded this sun of the *Brahma Sūtras*. The supreme Deity Nārāyaṇa did not wish to incarnate himself in this *kali* age of evil commentaries. Instead he commissioned his son Vāyu to appear as Madhva, addressing him:

> O gracious god, a share of your being adorns the earth in a separate form for the ascertainment of my true qualities, bless our people, whose refuge is pity and who are afflicted and distressed by the search for the path of the Vedānta.[5]

Madhva, also known as Ānandatīrtha, was born in 1238 C.E. of Brahmin parents in the village of Pājaka near Uḍupi in Tuḷunāda, about forty miles north of present-day Mangalore in Karnataka province of India. From the age of six (1244) he studied the Vedas and the Śāstras. At sixteen (1254), he was initiated as a *sannyāsin* into the Tīrtha Order by Acyutaprekṣa, a traditional Advaitin follower of Śaṅkara. Under him, Madhva studied the *Iṣṭasiddhi* of Vimuktātman (fl. 950 C.E.). This study was terminated when Madhva pointed out the invalidity of Vimuktātman's thought, finding thirty-two errors in the work's first verse. Madhva and his *guru* thus had a basic disagreement about the nature of *brahman*.

Acyutaprekṣa once queried Madhva about Madhva's knowledge of variant readings in the *Bhāgavata Purāṇa*. He addressed Madhva: "How do you know what was not read by you in this birth?" To his astonishment, Madhva replied, "All this I knew in my former births."[6] In spite of this the disciple-*guru* relationship of Madhva and Acyutaprekṣa continued. However, it is very significant that Acyutaprekṣa is nowhere in Madhva's writings honored as his *guru* in the customary manner, or even mentioned, for that matter.

Local success in disputation encouraged Madhva, accompanied by Acyutaprekṣa, to undertake a tour of South India of two to three years (1256–1258). Here Madhva learned that others besides himself had proposed alternatives to Śaṅkara's interpretation of the *Brahma Sūtras*. One day an Advaitin challenged him to compose his own *bhāṣya*, since "the exposition of the meaning of the *Brahma Sūtras* greatly exceeds propriety in those who have not composed a *bhāṣya*."[7] This emphasizes that Madhva did not yet have the proper authorization, since he would not write this *bhāṣya* for another eight years.

First, however, on the return to Uḍupi, Madhva composed a *bhāṣya* on the *Bhagavad Gītā* based on his Dvaita, dualist, theology of God's independent relationship to the world and to individual souls. In Uḍupi Madhva assumed the primary role in Acyutaprekṣa's *maṭha*, and in 1265 he asked permission of the man he still recognized as his *guru*, Acyutaprekṣa, to make a pilgrimage north to Badarīkāśrama, Vyāsa's home in the Himalayas. Reaching Badarī, Madhva recited his *Gītā Bhāṣya* before the idol of Nārāyaṇa, which repeatedly responded: "Let it be spoken."[8] He was then invited by Vyāsa to go further into the mountains to Uttara Badarī. Cantos 7 and 8 recount Madhva's visit to Vyāsa's hermitage at Uttara Badarī. Vyāsa is identified as an *avatāra* of Nārāyaṇa/Viṣṇu. Nārāyaṇa Paṇḍitācārya describes Vyāsa's hermitage as if it were Vaikuṇṭha, the abode of Viṣṇu. Many Brahmins and *ṛṣis* were there, including Vyāsa's son Śukācārya. Madhva saw there the Badarī tree on which hung the *Purāṇas* and the *Mahābhārata*. On a platform in the center of the tree sat Vyāsa, "a spotless sea of innumerable qualities, who is indeed entirely Nārāyaṇa himself."[9] From him are born the *Purāṇas*, the *Mahābhārata*, and the *Brahma Sūtras*. Madhva praised Vyāsa by prostrating at his feet. Vyāsa then raised Madhva and embraced him. Thus Viṣṇu embraced his son Vāyu.

Madhva becomes Vyāsa's student.

> He soon heard from Vedavyāsa the excellent meaning of the uncounted series of scriptures, which had been joined together as the collection of the Pāñcarātra, dear to the truthful, then the Sūtras, the beautiful Purāṇas, and the Epics.[10]

Madhva then went to see Vyāsa's other more primary form as Nārāyaṇa at another hermitage further into the mountains. Here he sat between Vyāsa and Nārāyaṇa, hence surrounded by God. Nārāyaṇa told him:

> The interpretation *[bhāṣyam]* of the heart of the Sūtras, dear to the truthful, is obstructed by others who, according to their own desires, spoil the natural meaning of the *śruti* and *smṛti*, which having been corrupted, is set aside. Undo this evil done by the wicked, lead the people back to the auspicious path. O learned one, make an unhesitating interpretation of the *Sūtras* and by grace link the *śruti* and the *smṛti*.[11]

Madhva responded that in the *kali* age there were none with minds suitable enough to hear this knowledge. Nārÿaṇa replied that there are indeed "persons in this world with intellects fit for the divine qualities. By means of the pure rays of light cleanse of their defects these pure persons who lack the good qualities."[12] Nārāyaṇa Paṇḍitācārya poetically comments here: "That pure river of Sarasvatī, for the enjoyment of the worlds, came forth from the mouth of the mountain, and entered the ocean of the great mind of Madhva."[13] Madhva and Vyāsa leave Nārāyaṇa's hermitage. Madhva, "having reached the other hermitage, knowing the mind of the preceptor, influenced by the *guru's* mind, heard everything that should be heard from Kṛṣṇa [Vedavyāsa]."[14] Madhva then left Vyāsa and went down to lower Badarī. Vyāsa followed him by indwelling Madhva's mind, so that Madhva henceforth spoke both with the words that Vyāsa had taught him and from a mind in which Vyāsa indwelled. At lower Badarī (1265 C.E.) he composed the long-awaited, but now authorized and thus authoritative, commentary *(bhāṣya)* on the *Brahma Sūtras* (hereafter BSM).

> He composed the interpretation that teaches the countless true qualities of Vāsudeva, which is very dear to the heart of the god Vyāsa, which is free from all defects on the path, which gives devotion and knowledge, and which gives eternal welfare.[15]

As Madhva dictated, his disciple Satyatīrtha wrote it down. Madhva then concluded his northern tour and returned to Uḍupi, where he taught his *Bhāṣya* to Acyutaprekṣa, who had not previously accepted Madhva's teaching but now did. Acyutaprekṣa, who was originally the *guru,* now became the student of his former disciple, Madhva, whose own authentic *guru* is Vyāsa, the appearance of the supreme deity Nārāyaṇa.

Later Madhva returned to Badarī for a second, longer northern tour (1280–1290). There Vyāsa gave Madhva Vyāsapuṣṭi stones in which Nārāyaṇa and Lakṣmī indwell. He commissioned Madhva to write a commentary on the *Mahābhārata,* in which Madhva had been a chief character in his *avatāra* as Bhīma. Madhva then visited for four months Hastināpura, the capital of the Kauravas, before moving on to Kāśī. At Kāśī, he debated with Advaitins or, as Nārāyaṇa Paṇḍitācārya usually refers to them, the Māyāvādins. One of them said: "This interpretation is associated with authority. It cannot be refuted by our widespread Māyāvāda. It is not without the support of reasoning."[16] Madhva then reached Kurukṣetra, where he found the mace belonging to Bhīma, his previous incarnation.

Nārāyaṇa Paṇḍitācārya in Canto XI poetically describes Vaikuṇṭha, the abode of Nārāyaṇa where dwell the liberated souls:

> Those persons, gods and human beings, who repeat by their own power in words and in mind the doctrine of the interpretation of

the great Ānandatīrtha truly enjoy this liberation by the grace of Mukunda [Nārāyaṇa].[17]

On the return to Uḍupi, Madhva encountered the Advaitins, Padmatīrtha and Puṇḍarika Purī, who wished to refute Madhva:

> Come, hear our lament, our Māyāvāda is ruined. . . . The followers of Bhaṭṭa have fled, the light of Prabhākara has not penetrated there, nor that of the Mahāyānists. It is not proper that we overlook the tongues of fire of the *tattvavāda* [Madhva's teaching about reality] which desires to burn the *māyāvāda* [Śaṅkara's teaching about illusion]. . . . Is this Madhva indeed Vedavyāsa? Is he the appearance of the Veda? Is this body with the gentle smile divine? We have seen him and his compassionate voice cuts the root of the teaching of *māyā* . . . the time of the destruction of our teaching by him is like the water of the end of the world at the time of the destruction of the world.[18]

In reply Madhva expounded the *Ṛg Veda.* Out of frustration Padmatīrtha then stole Madhva's library of authoritatively interpreted texts. The extent of Madhva's familiarity with Hindu scriptures and the extent of his citations from them has always annoyed Advaitins. Later, in the sixteenth century, an attempt was made to discredit Madhva by accusing him of forging many of his citations, the sources of which by then were lost. However, the theft of the library is to no avail. In Nārāyaṇa Paṇḍitācārya's view,

> Nārāyaṇa, in the appearance of Madhva, who has the collection of the Vedas as Sudarśana, the shining True Logic *[brahma tarka]* as the sound of the conch, the shining Purāṇas as the mace, the Ślokas as the Śarṅga bow, the True Sūtras as arrows, the Epics as the famous Nanda sword, he has arrived desiring to overpower the demonic misinterpreters of the scriptures.[19]

Through the intervention of King Jayasiṃha, Madhva's library is restored to one Śaṅkarācārya, Nārāyaṇa Paṇḍitācārya's uncle and Madhva's librarian. The king himself came to meet Madhva at the Viṣṇumangala temple. Together they heard the *Bhāgavata Purāṇa* read by Hṛṣikeśatīrtha. Hṛṣikeśatīrtha will later be commissioned by Madhva to gather all thirty-seven of his writings together into the *Sarva Mūla,* the collected works of Madhva. A palm-leaf copy of this is said to be extant and to be the basis of the Akhila Bharata edition (Govindacharya). Madhva then publicly taught the meaning of the *Purāṇas.* Here is probably Nārāyaṇa Paṇḍitācārya's indirect reference to Madhva's composition of the *Bhāgavata Tātparya*

Nirṇaya on the *Bhāgavata Purāṇa*. In fact it seems that one of the organizing principles of Nārāyaṇa Paṇḍitācārya's *Sumadhvavijaya* is the sequence of Madhva's writings, all of which are mentioned directly or indirectly.

At this reading of the *Bhāgavata Purāṇa* Madhva met Trivikrama, an Advaitin householder, the father of Nārÿaṇa Paṇḍitācārya. Śaṅkarācārya, his brother and Madhva's librarian, gave him Madhva's *Brahma Sūtra Bhāṣya* to read. He then listened to Madhva's public exposition of the Upaniṣads. Incidentally, Nārāyaṇa Paṇḍitācārya describes here the manner of Madhva's teaching. Madhva first worshiped Nārÿaṇa, following which there was a public reading, then an exposition of the text. Finally, Trivikrama listened to Madhva's own exposition of his BSM, which proved the superior reality of Viṣṇu with citations from the Vedas, with reasoning, and with citations from the *smṛtis*. In Madhva's view Viṣṇu has infinite attributes, is omniscient, and is the eternal sustainer of the coeternal universe. The world itself needs the creative will of a self-dependent being in order to exist. The Vedas support the inferential argument that God is not the material cause of the world. In the polemic, Nārāyaṇa Paṇḍitācārya has Madhva refute Nirīśvara Sāṃkhya, Seśvara Sāṃkhya, Cārvāka, Bhāṭṭa, and Prabhākara Mīmāṁsa, Bhāskara Vedānta, Vaiśeṣika, the Tārkika logicians, Mādhyamika, Māyāvāda, Śunyavāda, the latter two being equated, and finally the *sphoṭa* theory of grammar. Trivikrama tried to respond point by point for fifteen days. Finally Trivikrama acquiesed and surrendered his resistant will: "May the service of your lotus feet be given to me."[20] In response Madhva ordered Trivikrama to write the *Tattva Pradīpa,* the first commentary on Madhva's *Brahma Sūtra Bhāṣya.* After Trivikrama panegyrized all the works of Madhva, according to his son Nārāyaṇa Paṇḍitācārya, he asked Madhva to write his crowning and final work, the *Anuvyākhyāna,* an extended commentary on the *Brahma Sūtras.* This is a different kind of work from Madhva's other witings. It is an extended verse exposition of Madhva's views in relation to the *Brahma Sūtras* rather than the interpretative mosaic of citations that Madhva usually produced. In Nārāyaṇa Paṇḍitācārya's words, the *Anuvyākhyāna* "is a nectar to the good, a lightning flash to the darkeness of the Māyāvādins, and a mountain against fraud from the pride of disputants."[21]

Nārāyaṇa Paṇḍitācārya, without mentioning the disappearance or death of Madhva (1317), concludes the *Sumadhvavijaya* with the praise of Madhva by the gods who claim Madhva as their *guru:*

> "Praise to the Lord of every living being, you came for prosperity of those who have saluted you. Praise to Lord Hanumān, dear to Rāma, who has the quality of *guru*. Praise to the mighty Bhīma, beloved of Bhagavān Kṛṣṇa. Praise to Lord Madhva."[22]

II. The Writings of Madhva

Thus far we have looked at Nārāyaṇa Paṇḍitācārya's view of Madhva's relationship as disciple to his *guru*, Vyāsa, the appearance or form of Nārāyaṇa/Viṣṇu, that is, God. For Nārāyaṇa Paṇḍitācārya, the authority of Madhva as commentator and teacher is based on that discipleship. Although Nārāyaṇa Paṇḍitācārya wrote the *Sumadhvavijaya* as a *mahākāvya*, utilizing the *kāvya* stylistic devices and embellishments of the fourteenth century, there is a historical core to his presentation of the life of Madhva that is corroborated by an investigation of those passages in Madhva's own writings where Madhva refers to himself. Madhva refers frequently to the fact that Vyāsa was his own *guru*, and that Madhva himself was the third *avatāra* of Vāyu after Hanumān and Bhīma.[23]

Acyutaprekṣa, the *guru* who initiated Madhva, was a *sannyāsin* member of the Tīrtha order of Śaṅkarite *sādhus* that was centered in Dvārakā and, according to legend, had been founded by Śaṅkara. The first Tīrtha *jagadguru* was Hastamalaka, who was said to have visited Uḍupi. The Brahmins from whom Madhva was descended were probably of the Smārta Bhāgavata *saṃpradāya*, revering both Hari and Hara, Viṣṇu and Śiva. They were by tradition both Advaitin and devotees of these forms of *brahman*. Uḍupi was in a region originally Śaiva, so that the Bhāgavata *saṃpradāya* with its dual worship served a transitional function in a local shift to Vaiṣṇavism. This transition was then accelerated by Madhva. Madhva was thus rooted in local tradition as a Brahmin whose family had a Bhāgavata *saṃpradāya* loyalty and as a young man who had become a *sannyāsin* in the Tīrtha Advaitin order (Farquhar 1920, 235–236). Yet he brought about a radical transformation of the former, and a revolution in the latter. His espousal of a profound *dvaita*, dualism, between God and the world, and between God and the individual selves, which is rooted in Vaiṣṇava Vedānta, is an innovation or, seen from within Madhva's tradition, a restoration. This restoration is based, if we can trust Nārāyaṇa Paṇḍitācārya, on an experience of personal conversion and encounter with Nārāyaṇa in the form of Vyāsa. Further, Madhva clearly distinguished Viṣṇu, the supreme God, from Śiva, a dependent god.

Indicative of this transformation of the local tradition is the fact that nowhere in Madhva's writings does he give obeisance to Acyutaprekṣa as his own personal *guru*, nor does he refer to Acyutaprekṣa's *guru* lineage. Instead we find from his first works to his last that Madhva says that Nārāyaṇa/Viṣṇu, appearing under the form of Vyāsa, was his *guru* and that his works of interpretation were inspired and commissioned by Vyāsa out of compassion for a world whose vision of God-Viṣṇu was obscured by the demonic interpretations of Māyāvāda.

For example, in the BSM:

> In the age of *dvāpara,* knowledge became everywhere disturbed, and Brahmā, Rudra, and the other gods having prayed for its correct declaration, Bhagavān Nārāyaṇa appeared as Vyāsa . . . for the purpose of making this known, he divided the Vedas into four parts for the purpose of making them manifest . . . and for the sake of correct explanation of their meaning, he composed the *Brahma Sūtras.*[24]

Madhva concludes his BSM by referring to Viṣṇu (= Vyāsa) and to the appearance of Vāyu:

> Praise be to Viṣṇu who is perfect in all qualities, knowledge, joy, etc., who is my *guru,* always and in every way most dear to me. Of Vāyu whose three divine forms are spoken of in the words of the Vedas, whose is the great splendor of a god, bestowed and thus visible—this Vāyu, whose first appearance is as the bearer of the word to Rāma [Hanumān]; the second, the "destroyer" [Bhīma]; the third Madhva by whom indeed this *Bhāṣya* is produced showing the supremacy of Hari.[25]

According to Nārāyaṇa Paṇḍitācārya, this BSM was written immediately after Madhva's personal encounter and retreat with Vyāsa. The *Bhāṣya* itself seems to be based on personal experience and conviction. Further, the authority that the *Bhāṣya* asserts is based on the personal encounter of Madhva with Viṣṇu. The worthiness of Madhva to encounter Vyāsa is based on Madhva's conviction that he is indeed the appearance of Vāyu. According to the *Sumadhvavijaya,* Madhva's BSM supersedes the *Bhāṣyas* of twenty-one other interpreters, including Bhāskara and Rāmānuja, but especially Śaṅkara, an evil *avatāra* of Maṇiman who had been vanquished in the *dvāpara* age by Madhva's earlier *avatāra* as Bhīma. Madhva's own words in the introduction and conclusion to his BSM, in his *Bhāṣyas* on the *Chāndogya* and the *Bṛhadāraṇyaka Upaniṣads,* and in his other works, and the words of the poetic narrative of Nārāyaṇa Paṇḍitācārya, coincide in identifying Madhva's *guru* as Nārāyaṇa/Viṣṇu (= Vyāsa) and in identifying Madhva as Vāyu.

In the *Bhāgavata Tātparya Nirṇaya,* a commentary on the *Bhāgavata Purāṇa,* Madhva begins:

> He on account of whom there are the origin, maintenance, and destruction, and also the regulation, knowledge, obscurance, bondage, and liberation; who ensouls Śrī, Brahmā, Rudra, etc., the gods, men, sky, lord, and the enemy; by Viṣṇu these are made distinct

> and pervaded; he is the receptacle of divisible qualities, lacks all defects, is full of job and imperishable, he is the excellent *guru*, I consider him great.[26]

Although Vyāsa as the appearance of Nārāyaṇa/Viṣṇu is not directly mentioned here, that may be because the age in which the events of the *Bhāgavata Purāṇa* take place are in the *dvāpara* age, while Madhva encounters Vyāsa in the *kali* age.

At the end of his life, in his final work, the *Anuvyākhyāna*, a second extended commentary in verse on the *Brahma Sūtras*, Madhva begins:

> Moved by devotion for that Being whose only body is the plenitude of perfections, for the immaculate God supremely attainable through the totality of the sacred words, for the cause from whom all this has originated, whose excellences render him worthy of adoration, for the being most dear to me, Nārāyaṇa—I prostrate myself before him. I worship in sincerity the source of the Śāstras, the *guru* of universal *gurus*, and particularly my own, and proceed, myself, to explain the knowledge called the supreme, in sequence. Entreated by the gods headed by Viriñci [Brahmā] and Bhava [Śiva], Hari [Nārāyaṇa] manifested himself as the sage Vyāsa, and produced the unsurpassed Śāstra, known as the supreme knowledge. Bādarāyaṇa [Vedavyāsa], the *guru* of *gurus*, the origin of the Śāstras—from him arose the norm of sacred knowledge, for the sake of such beings as the gods. The harmony between speaker, the listener, and the conditions of their dialogue make for reliability. Hence because of its reliable pronouncements, its basis in *śruti*, and its foundation in reasoning—we see, concentrated in one, the great triple authority of the *Brahma Sūtras*, an authority that is elsewhere dispersed. Hence, nothing is known which is so consummately the norm of knowledge. I have written a commentary on this before, but I write this one for greater clarity.[27]

III. Nārāyaṇa Paṇḍitācārya's Context for Madhva's Text

Five conclusions may be drawn from the juxtaposition of Nārāyaṇa Paṇḍitācārya's *Sumadhvavijaya* and the passages of Madhva's own writings in which he refers to himself. First, Nārāyaṇa Paṇḍitācārya in his biography of Madhva has united a theology of the transcendence of God and of the condescension of that God to appear at Badarī as Vyāsa to Madhva. The authority of God is the authority with which Madhva spoke and wrote. This claim is confirmed in Madhva's writings. Even Madhva's visit to Badarī is mentioned in his *Mahābhārata Tātparya Nirṇaya.*

Second, Madhva in his writings uses dozens of *smṛti* works, ostensibly written by Vyāsa, to support his interpretation of the Vedas, the *Bhagavad Gītā,* and the *Brahma Sūtras.* He uses Vyāsa to interpret Vyāsa. By both maintaining that the Vedas are authorless and that Nārāyaṇa/Vyāsa is responsible for their form, Madhva avoids the oddness of a theory of a transcendent God disconnected from the eternal Vedas. The Vedas, like everything else, are dependent on God but are materially different from God's being. The Vedas, since they are eternally dependent on God's will, are different from God in an eternal manner. The will of God, however, determines their form and their utility from age to age. The Vedas, both the *karmakāṇḍa* and the *jñānakāṇḍa,* are informed by the mind and intelligence of God, and thus their eternal meaning and import is dependent upon a knowledge that may only be derived from God. For an understanding of the Vedas, one must have God for a *guru,* or someone who has God for a *guru.* This is all the more so for the noneternal *smṛti* texts that have God in the form of Vyāsa as their author; here one must have contact with the mind of the author. Madhva's view that *smṛti* texts have as their purpose the ascertainment of the meaning of the Vedas is clearly exemplified by Madhva's own practice of citation of *smṛti* to clarify the meaning of the Vedas. If Vyāsa is the arranger and collector of the Vedas, and the author of the *smṛtis,* then their meanings must be consonant and not at odds with one another. This presumption informs all of Madhva's writings (Siauve 1957).

Third, unlike the Māyāvāda view, which seems to distinguish the figure Vyāsa from the figure Bādarāyaṇa, Madhva identifies the figures of Vyāsa, Bādarāyaṇa, and Kṛṣṇa Dvaipāyana. Vyāsa appears in the *Mahābhārata* and in many of the *Purāṇas* as a figure related to Brahmā (Sullivan 1987). The further elevation of this figure to the status of equality with the supreme deity is original, so far as I can tell, with Madhva. It is a peculiarity and necessity of Madhva's theology of difference between God and all other realities, both material and intelligent, that the true appearance of God must be equal to God in reality. A corollary of this is that all *avatāras* of God are equally real. There are no "part" manifestations of God for Madhva.

Fourth, there is also, however, for Madhva a second level at which an *avatāra* may appear—that is, as the appearance of a dependent intelligent being such as a god or a human being. Both gods and human beings are intelligent dependent beings who differ only in degree. Thus Madhva can be the *avatāra* of a god who is separated from God, Nārāyaṇa/Viṣṇu, by an abyss as wide as the difference between an infinite self-dependent being like Nārāyaṇa and a finite dependent being like Vāyu. What exactly is the significance of the filiation of Vāyu is not immediately clear. No claim is being made that Madhva is God. He is only the appearance of a god, an intelligent being like human beings. There is as much difference between Vāyu/Madhva and Nārÿaṇa as between any other intelligent being and Nārāyaṇa.

Finally, Nārÿaṇa Paṇḍitācārya's *Sumadhvavijaya* in its historicity, corroborated in many details by Madhva's own writings, allows us to read Madhva not as a philosopher but as a theological interpreter and commentator who stands in the moment of immediate witness of that about which he teaches. His experience is equal to that of a witness of God. His mind is informed by the mind of God. This is what gives him his authority as an interpreter of *śruti* and *smṛti*. The claims about this status as witness in Madhva's own writings, as well as the claims about Madhva's experiences in Nārāyaṇa Paṇḍitācārya's, are not mythological trimmings, accomodations to popular religion, or literary embellishments, but the heart of the matter for an assessment of the meaning of Madhva's life and work both for the fourteenth century and the twentieth. Madhva was commissioned by Nārāyaṇa/Vyāsa to establish the truth, to refute the erroneous and demonic interpretations of the school of Māyāvāda, and to teach what Nārāyaṇa/Vyāsa had taught. Madhva's claimed status as an *avatāra* of Vāyu and as a student of Vyāsa is in a very real way the "text," and Nārāyaṇa Paṇḍitācārya's narrative of Madhva's life is the "context." This "text" and this "context" are the measures for a constructive reading of Madhva's work as an authoritative interpreter of Vedāntic texts such as the *Brahma Sūtras*, the *Bhagavad Gītā*, the *Mahābhārata*, the Upaniṣads, and the *Bhāgavata Purāṇa*. Thus the key to understanding Madhva's hermeneutical authority is his status as disciple to his *guru* Vyāsa, who is none other than God-Viṣṇu, the collector and the author of the Scriptures.

Notes

1. For a discussion of the dates of Madhva's birth and death, see Sharma (1981, 77–79).

2. For a revived interest in Hindu hagiographical biographies, see Granoff (1985, 459–67).

3. Even a historian as sympathetic to Madhva as B. N. K. Sharma is reluctant to give theological themes priority in the study of Madhva. He understands Madhva as a philosopher whose work can stand on its own, philosophically, without support from authoritative texts:

> While . . . the foundations of his theistic system and its general main outlines are well supported by the extant literature of the Vedic and Post-

> Vedic periods, its logical and philosophical superstructure is built upon independent philosophical cogitation and analysis of concepts and can bear examination independently of textual authority. The appeal to texts occurs only in respect of purely theological issues and interpretations of disputed texts. (Sharma 1981, 86).

Such says more about the prejudices of the twentieth century than those of the thirteenth.

4. *yadbrahmasūtrotkarabhāskaraṃ ca prakāśayantaṃ sakalaṃ svagobhiḥ / acūcudvedasamūhavāhaṃ tato mahātaskaramenamāhuḥ // Sumadhvavijaya* (SMV 1.52). Translation from this text is my own, based upon Rau 1982.

5. *vedāṃtamārgaparimārgaṇadīnadūnā daiviḥ prajā viśaraṇāḥ karuṇāpadaṃ nah. / ānandayeḥ sumukha bhūṣitamūmabhāgo rūpāṃtareṇa mama sadguṇanirṇayena //* (SMV 2.3).

6. *atra janmani na yatpaṭhitaṃ te jaitra bhāti kathamityamunokte / pūrvajanmasu hi veda puredaṃ sarvamityamitabuddhiruvāca //* (SMV 4.53).

7. *aprāṃśunūtnopapadādhivāsajaḥ sa saṅkaro vairaparāyaṇaḥ punaḥ / asūyayoce'tra mahānatikramaḥ sūtrārthavādo'kṛtabhāṣyakeṣviti //* (SMV 5.38).

8. *tena tatpravacane vihite'laṃ śuśruvuḥ praśayitā api śiṣyāḥ / ucyatāmiti muhuḥ sa pṛthivyāsphālanaṃ padamaho hariṇoktam //* (SMV 6.41).

9. *agaṇeyaguṇārṇavo'malaḥ sa hi nārāyaṇa eṣa kevalam / vidhinānusṛtaṃ parāśarātsuṣuve satyavatī kilātra yam //* (SMV 7.18).

10. *itihāsasundarapurāṇasūtrasatpriyapañcarātranijabhāvasaṃyutam / aśṛṇodanantahṛdanantato'cirātparamārthamapyagaṇitāgamāvaleḥ //* (SMV 8.4).

11. *apidhāya sūtrahṛdayaṃ satāṃ pryaṃ prabidhāya bhāṣyamadhunā nijecchayā / aparaiḥ śrutismṛtinijārthadūṣkaiḥ surtarām tirobhavati saṃvidāhatā // apanetumenamanayaṃ kṛtaṃ khalaiḥ pratinetumātmajanatāṃ śubhāṃ gatim / kuru sūtrabhāṣyamavilambitaṃ vrajeḥ sumatena yojaya kaveḥ śrutismṛtīḥ /* (SMV 8.45–46).

12. *iti taṃ bruvāṇamayamabravīdvibhurbhuvi saṃti saumya puruṣāḥ guṇocitāḥ / vimalānmaṇīniva guṇojjñitānimān dayayā viśodhaya viśuddhagogaṇaiḥ //* (SMV 8.50).

13. *iti sā mahīdharamukhādviniḥsṛtā jagatāṃ sukhāya viśadā sarasvatī / dvijarājagoviṣayatātipūritaṃ praviveśa madhvapṛthubuddhivāridhim //* (SMV 8.52).

14. *āśramāṃtaramavāpya kṛṣṇataḥ śrāvyameṣa sakalaṃ ca śuśruvān / cittavṛttimanuvṛttimān guroḥ sādhvavetya gamanonmukho 'bhavat //* (SMV 9.2).

15. *vyāsadevahṛdayātivallabhaṃ vāsudevamagaṇeyasadguṇam / sādhayatsakaladoṣavarjita jñānabhaktidamanantasaukhyadam //* (SMV 9.8).

16. *samānayā yānamāsa māyayā tatayāyamā / nayāsanā nāsā yā na yātanālalanā tayā //* (SMV 10.48).

17. *mahānandatīrthasya ye bhāṣyabhāvaṃ mano vagbhirāvartayante svaśaktyā / surādyānarāntā mukundaprasādādimaṃ mokṣameti bhajante sadeti //* (SMV 11.79).

18. *jñāniśreṣṭhaśreṣṭhavijñānivarge nairguṇyasthe sāmprataṃnāthabhūtaḥ / ākrandaṃ me hanta śruṇvantu so'yam hā hā māyāvāda utsādameti // bhraṣṭā bhāṭṭā na prabhākṛtprabhābhūttrastā māhāyānikādyāśca yatra / durgaṃ māyāvādasatraṃ didhakṣurnopekṣyā nastatvavādāgnijihvā // . . . ve- davyāsonveṣa vedo nu mūrto divyā mūrtiryasya sā susmitasya / taddraṣṭṛṇāṃ ceti vāṇīkṛpāṇī nūnaṃ māyāpakṣamūlaṃ chinatti // . . . vāhutryena hyetaduktvā khalu drāgete viśvaṃ prāpnuvanti prakāmam / asminnasmaddarśanapāyakāle yadvallokāpāyakāle layāpaḥ //* (SMV 12.7, 8, 12, 16).

19. *vedaprātasudarśanaḥ parilasattarkākhyaśaṅkhadhvaniḥ vibhrājiṣṇupurāṇasaṃhatigadaḥślokaidhaśārṅgānvitaḥ / satsūtreṣvitihāsanandakacaṇo madhvākhyanārāyaṇaḥ prāpto vo nijivṛkṣayā dravata he māyāvidevadviṣah //* (SMV 12.53.)

20. *padapadmarajodāsyaṃ dhruvaṃ me dīyatāmiti //* (SMV 15.70b).

21. *ityarthito vyadhānmadhvaḥ so'nuvyākhyāṃ satāṃ sudhām / durvādigarvādripaviṃ māyidhvāṃtaravidyutim //* (SMV 15.88).

22. *namaste prāneśa praṇatavibhavāyāvanimagāḥ namaḥ svāmin rāmapriyatama hanūman guruguṇa / namastubhyaṃ bhīma prabalatama kṛṣṇeṣṭa bhagavān namaḥ śrīmanmadhva pradiśa sadṛśaṃ no jaya jaya //* (SMV 16.57).

23. For an affirmative judgment that these passsages are authentic to Madhva and are not later interpolations, see Siauve (1968, 5).

24. *dvāpare sarvatra jñāna ākulībhūte tannirṇayāya brahmarudrendrādibhirarthito bhagavān nārāyaṇo vyāsatvenāvatatāra / atheṣṭāniṣṭaprāptiparihārecchūnāṃ tadyogamavijānatāṃ tajjñāpanārthaṃ vedasutsannaṃ vyañjayaṃścaturdhā vyabhajat / caturviṃśatidhaikaśatadhā sahasradhā dvādaśadahā ca / tadarthanirṇayāya brahmasūtrāṇi cakāra / (Brahma Sūtra Bhāṣya* [BSM], Govindacharya 1.1). Translation adapted from Rau, (1904;3).

25. *yasya trīṇyuditāni vedavacane rūpāṇi divyānyalaṃ baṭ tad darśatamitthameva nihitaṃ devasya bhargo mahat / vāyo rāmavaconayaṃ prathamakaṃ pṛkṣo dvitīyaṃ vapurmadhvo yattu tṛtīyametadamunā bhāṣyaṃ kṛtaṃ keśave // jñānānandādibhiḥ sarvairguṇaiḥ pūrṇāya viṣṇave namo'stu gurave nityaṃ sarvathā'tipriyāya me /* (BSM, Govindacharya 1.229; Rau 1904, 294).

26. *sṛṣṭisthityapyayehāniyatidṛśitamobandhamokṣāśca yasmādasya śrībrahmarudraprabhṛtisuranaradyvīśaśatrvātmakasya / viṣṇorvyastāḥ samastāḥ sakalaguṇanidhiḥ sarvadoṣavyapetaḥ pūrṇānando'vyayo yo gururapi paramaścintaye taṃ mahāntam // (Bhāgavata Tātparya Nirṇaya* [BTN], Govindacharya 3.1). Translations my own.

27. *nārāyaṇaṃ nikhilapūrṇaguṇaikadehaṃ nirdoṣamāpyatamamapyakhilaiḥ suvākyaiḥ / asyodbhavādidamaśeṣavisesato'pi vandyaṃ sadā pryatamaṃ mama sannamāmi //1// tameva śāstraprabhavaṃ praṇamya jagadgurūṇāṃ gurumañjasaiva / viśeṣato me paramkhyavidyāvyākhyāṃ karomyanvapicāhameva //2// prādurbhūto harirvyāso viriñcabhavapūrvakaiḥ / arthitaḥ parividyākhyaṃ cakre śāstramanuttamam //3// gururgurūṇāṃ prabhavaḥ śāstrāṇāṃ bādarāyaṇaḥ / yatastaduditaṃ mānamajādibhyastadarthataḥ //4// vaktṛśrotṛprasaktīnāṃ yadāptiranukūlatā / āptavākyatayā tena śrutimūlatayā tathā //5// yuktimūlatayā caiva prāmāṇyaṃ trividhaṃ mahat / dṛṣyate brahmasūtrāṇāmekadhā'nyatra sarvaśaḥ //6// ato naitādṛśaṃ kiñcit pramāṇatamamiśyate / svayaṃ kṛtā'pi tadvyākhyā kriyate sphaṣṭatārthataḥ //7// (Anuvyākhyāna on the Brahma Sūtras* 1.1.1, Govindacharya 1.1–2; translation adapted from Pereira 1976, 124–25).

References

Bhandarkar, R. G.
1965 *Vaiṣṇavism, Śaivism, and Minor Religious Systems.* Varanasi: Indological Book House.

Dirks, Nicholas B.
1987 *The Hollow Crown: Ethnohistory of an Indian Kingdom.* New York: Cambridge University Press.

Farquhar, J. N.
1984 *An Outline of the Religious Literature of India.* 1920. Reprint. Delhi: Motilal Banarsidass.

Govindacharya, Bannaje
1969–80 *Sarvamūla Granthāḥ*. Five volumes. Bangalore: Akhila Bharata Madhwa Mahamandana.

Granoff, Phyllis
1985 "Scholars and Wonder-Workers: Some Remarks on the Role of the Supernatural in Philosophical Contests in Vedānta Hagiographies." *Journal of the American Oriental Society* 150: 459–67.

Pereira, Jose
1976 *Hindu Theology: A Reader.* New York: Doubleday.

Raghavachar, S. S.
1959 *English Translation of Śrīmad Viṣṇu-Tattva-Vinirṇaya of Śrī Madhvāchārya.* Mangalore: Sri Ramakrishna Ashrama.

Rau, D. R. Vasudeva
1982 *Nārāyaṇa Paṇḍitācārya's Sumadhva Vijaya.* Visakhapatnam: Srimananda Tirtha.

Rau, S. Subha
1904 *The Vedānta Sūtras with the Commentary by Śrī Madhwācārya.* Madras: Thompson & Co.

Sharma, B. N. K.
1981 *History of the Dvaita School of Vedānta and Its Literature.* Delhi: Motilal Banarsidass.

Siauve, Suzanne
1957 *La Voie vers la Connaissance de Dieu (Brahma-Jijñāsā) selon l'Anuvyākhyāna de Madhva.* Pondichery: Institut Français D'Indologie.

1968 *La Doctrine de Madhva: Dvaita Vedānta.* Pondichéry: Institut Français D'Indologie.

Sullivan, Bruce M.
1987 "Vyāsa, Author of the *Mahābhārata.*" Mimeographed for the conference "The *Mahābhārata:* Interpretation and Performance," UCLA.

Eight

Scriptural Realism in Pure Nondualistic Vedānta

Jeffrey R. Timm

Introduction

The last twenty years have witnessed a growing sophistication in Western scholarship on Indian thought. It has become increasingly clear that any serious claim to understand and to adequately represent a particular school of Indian religious and philosophical thought must be textually grounded. The text must be taken seriously, not just as a purveyor of thought, but as intimately and inexorably connected with that thought.

Today the requirement of textual sensitivity becomes immediately apparent in even a casual review of scholarship on those schools in Hinduism collectively designated as "Vedānta." This has not always been the case. In fact, the shift that has occurred over the period of only one generation of scholarship is nothing short of remarkable. In 1969 Eliot Deutsch presented his work *Advaita Vedānta: A Philosophical Reconstruction*. Why was this work a reconstruction? Because, as Deutsch points out in his introduction, although Vedānta is as much a product of scriptural exegesis as it is a philosophical analysis, his book would focus exclusively on the latter. Twenty years ago the argument was compelling.

> The exegetical dimension of Vedānta is . . . of very little interest to Western students of philosophy. We do not accept the authority of the Veda (or, for the most part, the authority of any other scripture); consequently, we are not concerned whether one system or another best interprets certain obscure passages in it. (p. 5)

The question, of course, was never whether or not Western scholars could accept the authority of the *Veda*. The question was whether or not something akin to a Bultmannian demythologization could be invoked to isolate ''kerygmatic'' philosophical issues from the exegetical concerns that traditional thinkers had with the text.

Deutsch's own reassessment of the question seems to support the assertion that even if such a demythologization is possible, something crucial may be lost. In an article written twenty years after *Advaita Vedānta,* marking not only a shift in his own thinking but the maturation of a field as well, he writes that

> Something important and essential is lost when we study (and teach) philosophy—as has unfortunately become typical in many contemporary analytic circles—as if it were made up of a series or set of alternative arguments, ideas, or isms capable of being abstracted from the concrete forms in which these arguments, ideas, and theories were presented and shaped. (Deutsch 1988, 166)

Speaking of comparative philosophy, he goes on to argue that both text and context must be taken seriously, and that the very notion ''text'' must be appreciated contextually.

This effort includes not just a ''primary'' scriptural canon; the myriad commentaries, subcommentaries, glosses, and so on must be taken seriously because they ''form, hermeneutically, integral parts of a continuing text'' (Deutsch 1988, 170). Getting close to the immense collection of commentarial literature in even a single school of Vedānta is a daunting task. Good translations (or any translations at all) remain the exception, not the rule. Thus, the effort to achieve authentic insight into Indian thought must be, by necessity, collaborative. But not only must scholars collaborate with each other as contemporaries who possess the necessary linguistic access and who have mastered a small piece of a much larger puzzle, they must also begin to collaborate more fully with the historical, traditional thinkers themselves who creatively appropriated scriptural authority, who embraced the text, coaxing meaning from it to find meaning in life, and who left their reflections for us to explore.

The present volume embodies just such a dual collaboration. The previous five chapters have considered various dimensions of Advaita, Viśiṣṭādvaita, and Dvaita traditional hermeneutics. This chapter concludes the exploration of Vedānta with an examination of the Śuddhādvaita, or pure nondualistic Vedānta, by considering the traditional hermeneutics of a fifteenth-century Vaiṣṇava theologian who founded what continues to be a highly influential religious community in northwestern India: Vallabhācārya or Vallabha (1479–1531 C.E.).

Vallabha's appearance on the religious horizon of his day helped bring devotional Hinduism to its zenith. He was a *bhakti* philosopher *par excel-*

lence and consequently, like Madhva, a staunch opponent to Advaita Vedānta. This opposition was rooted in more than sectarian rivalry for religious authority; it had to do with what he saw as the very foundation of salvation, the authority of revealed scripture. One of the primary articles of all Hindu religious debate was the epistemological status of scriptural revelation, *śabda-pramāṇa,* beginning with the *Veda.* Conversant with the variety of hermeneutical positions, both Vedāntic and extra-Vedāntic, and using Advaita Vedānta as a foil, Vallabha developed his theological hermeneutic, which he called *śuddhādvaita* or pure nondualism (Timm 1988). Purified nondualism challenged Advaita Vedānta to abandon the cosmic dualism it affirms when it calls the world an illusion and describes ultimate reality as unqualified *(nirguṇa brahman).* In the contemporary context Vallabha remains a standing challange to modern neo-Vedāntic descriptions of Hinduism as a syncretic, all-embracing, "everything for everybody" culminating in the silence of relationless Being, a view of Hinduism encountered all too often in college textbooks and in popular understanding. According to Vallabha the affirmation of a silent God is anathema, for it fails to take seriously God's speaking to the world in the form of scriptural revelation, or *śruti.* On the importance of scriptural revelation he would agree, both in tone and in substance, with the sixteenth-century Madhvite who wrote,

> One who is afflicted with a mania producing conviction in an inextinguishable "Great Illusion," who moreover declares, while posturing as one grounded on the Scriptures, a belief in the world's depravity *based on* the depraved condition of the all-assisting Scriptures, kills his own mother! I believe that he gets amusement by bringing harm to everyone. (Betty 1978, 17)

For Vallabha, as well, scriptural revelation is "all-assisting," the very foundation for any effort to understand the nature of reality, and to achieve salvation. But instead of leading to a metaphysical dualism, as it did for Madhva, the epistemological priority accorded scripture leads Vallabha to a quite different view of God, the world, and the relationship between the two.

This chapter, then, begins by examining Vallabha's view of canonical scripture, the preeminence of *śabda-pramāṇa,* revealed scripture as the basis for all knowledge about God. Such a view of scripture could perhaps be called "fundamentalist," but Vallabha does not end with a narrow, exclusivist fundamentalism. Instead, honest to the holistic ontology of his *advaitic* theology, Vallabha melds the fundamentalist temper with an affirmation of pluralism. In this way he escapes the negative consequences of both exclusivism and relativism, formulating a hermeneutic of scriptural realism honest to the words of God (Yadav 1980).

Evidence supporting this assessment may be found by considering how he employs scripture throughout his voluminous writings, but it is in his work, the *Tattvārthadīpanibandha* (hereafter TVD), especially the first section, which he calls *Śāstrārtha,* along with its accompanying commentary, *Prakāśa,* where he presents his definitive statement on the nature and interpretation of scriptural revelation. A consideration of this work will elucidate Vallabha's hermeneutic of scriptural realism. Three related issues must be explored: (1) *śabda-pramāṇa* and its relation to other *pramāṇa,* (2) the hierarchical structure of revealed scripture, and (3) the ontological foundation of scriptural realism.

I. Śabda-pramāṇa *and Its Relation to Other* Pramāṇa

Knowledge of reality is directly related to the primary soteriological objective of Indian thought, the achievement of liberation from a ceaseless round of birth, death, and rebirth called *saṁsāra,* but the various schools have not always agreed about the nature of knowledge, or the appropriate means to this knowledge. Diverse theories give conflicting answers to questions about the object of knowledge *(prameya),* the means to knowledge *(pramāṇa),* and knowledge itself *(pramā).* This diversity has been considered elsewhere (e.g., Chatterjee 1950) and need not be reviewed here. One school, however, must be mentioned. That school is, of course, Nyāya.

The Nyāya theory of knowledge was, in part, a response to the Buddhist Naiyāyika claim that a means to knowledge, like perception or inference, is possible only within the context of a creative faculty of mind. Basing its theory of knowledge on an ontology of empirical realism, Nyāya argued that knowledge must depend on what really exists in the world (Bijalwan 1977). And conversely, knowledge aims at placing the really existent objects of the world in some sort of coherent scheme. According to Nyāya the way to achieve knowledge is fourfold: perception, inference, comparison, and verbal testimony.

As a Vedāntin, Vallabha accepts each of these; however, his acceptance is provisional. Even though he would agree with Nyāya's assertion that the objects in the world are real, his concept of *prameya*—the object of knowledge—leads him beyond Nyāya's empirical realism. True to his Vaiṣṇava roots, Vallabha insists that, in the final analysis, there is only one object of knowledge. All knowledge in one way or another is knowledge of that One, nondual, ultimate reality variously referred to as *brahman, paramātman, bhagavan,* and Kṛṣṇa. In fact Vallabha often uses the term *prameya*—the object of knowledge—as a synonym for ultimate reality. For instance he says,

> Bhagavan incarnated for the sake of liberating everyone; therefore, even in the absence of individual qualification, the result will be achieved through the strength of the object of knowledge *(prameyabalena)*.[1]

and similarly,

> If there is an accomplishment of these [five aspects of the path of devotion] through the strength of the object of knowledge, let it be so; but not otherwise.[2]

This use of the word *prameya* points to the fact that for Vallabha the "object of knowledge" is not something passive, out in the world, waiting to be known; it is the power through which God expresses salvific compassion. Through the "strength of the object of knowledge" *(prameyabalena)* knowledge arises, not through some intermediary. Even when secondary means are present, like the five aspects of the devotional path (knowledge of scripture, worship with love, renunciation, detachment, and yoga), their success depends on the will of the efficient cause—God. According to Vallabha, Nyāya's view of *pramāṇa* is useful for worldly thinking, but this thinking has little utility in the quest for knowledge about God.

> Indeed, *brahman* alone is the support of all. . . . This quality, actually inhering in the cause *[brahman]*, appears in the world. That this is not [established] by any sort of ordinary reasoning, on account of *brahman's* property of being "unknowable," is stated: "He is not known through reasoning."[3]

This is where Nyāya goes astray. God's nature—embracing the coincidence of all qualities—transcends the ken of reason, because the foundation of reason—the principle of noncontradiction—is inapplicable. Consequently Vallabha rejects any attempt to establish a "rational theology." How, then, is God to be known?

According to Puruṣottama (a seventeenth-century commentator in the Vallabha tradition), knowledge about God, which he calls "eternal knowledge" *(nitya jñāna)*, has four dimensions (Dasgupta 1975, 4:336). The first is knowledge of God's essential nature, which is the essence of liberation. This is knowledge not as objective certainty, but as "self-knowledge"; that is, the individual soul's immediate experience of God as immanent. In other words, the soul has knowledge of God as its divine self. Vallabha identifies God's essential nature with the quality of bliss, and describes liberation as the manifestation of this bliss aspect within the soul.[4] The second dimension of eternal knowledge, according to Puruṣottama, is knowledge of God's great and noble qualities. Unlike the preceding knowledge of God as self, here God is known as creator, the divine Other. Scripture expresses God's glory by describing the extent and greatness of God's many creations. The purpose of this knowledge is the establishment of God's worship by the devotees. Vallabha puts the matter like this:

> The purpose behind the various statements about creation is stated:
> In one manner or another God's glory is described everywhere.
> [This is done] only for the sake of the establishment of worship.
> [The statements] "That thou art," etc., are the same.[5]

Here Vallabha is not only explaining the proper connotation of statements about creation, he is explicitly rejecting an Advaita Vedānta technique of elevating, and taking out of context, specific scriptural statements—the so-called *mahāvākya*—that support the Advaita metaphysical position.

The third dimension of eternal knowledge described by Puruṣottama is the manifestation of the *Veda* at the beginning of creation. Vallabha, himself, explains that the *Veda* is, quite simply, God in another form.

> [*Bhagavan* assumes a form] like the fivefold fire sacrifice and so on. He [manifests] in the form of the means: space, time, substance, the sacrificer, and the *mantra* [in the form of the] threefold [*Veda*] consisting of *mantra, brahmana,* and *upaniṣad.*[6]

Veda, as scriptural revelation, is special because it embodies the three epistemological categories. First, it is a form of divine knowledge *(pramā),* one of the dimensions of eternal knowledge described by Puruṣottoma. Second, the *Veda* is equivalent to an object of knowledge *(prameya);* regarded as a form assumed by God, it shares the status of ultimate reality as the divine object of knowledge. Third, the *Veda* as *śabda-pramāṇa* is a means to valid knowledge.[7] The embodiment of *praymeya, pramā,* and *pramāṇa* in the *Veda* points to the foundational status of the third dimension of eternal knowledge, knowledge of God as scriptural revelation.

To these three dimensions of eternal knowledge (God as Self, God as Other, and God as scriptural revelation in the form of the *Veda*) Vallabha adds a fourth; knowledge of God as creation itself. This form of eternal knowledge reveals the pure nondualism of God and the world. In the opening verse of the TVD, Vallabha says,

> Adoration to *bhagavan,* to him, to Kṛṣṇa whose deeds are wonderful; he delights freely, [he] who is the world [and] from whom [it arises], through formal and conceptual diversity.[8]

This fourth dimension of eternal knowledge is crucial, for it explains the ontological foundation of the world and ultimately provides the basis for divine revelation that occurs in, and through, the world. Through the unending diveristy of forms and concepts arising in the world, God is revealed.

These four aspects of eternal knowledge act together in Vallabha's theology, making the connection between being and knowing, between the world as ontological revelation and scripture as epistemological revelation. It is this connection that drives Vallabha's hermeneutic. But before turning to the relationship between epistemology and ontology, Vallabha's understanding of canon and scriptural authority must be considered.

II. The Hierarchical Structure of Revealed Scripture

Human understanding of God is dependent on God's will to be known.[9] It is only through God's will and compassion toward the world that such knowledge arises at all. This compassion is given its widest scope through redemptive revelation, *śabda-pramāṇa* in the form of divine scripture and teachings. According to Vallabha, *śabda-pramāṇa* is the only "self-validating means to knowledge."[10] God can reveal the knowledge of divine essential nature—thereby affecting the liberation of the individual soul—whenever, wherever, and to whomever God chooses. In keeping with the linguistic structure of human experience, and for the purpose of facilitating liberation, God employs the revelatory words forming *śabda-pramāṇa*. By self-definition, God's words are crucial.

Vallabha not only affirms the seriousness of God's words in general, he also designates the four primary collections of sacred scripture that provide the basis for all eternal knowledge: *Veda, Bhagavad Gītā, Brahma Sūtras,* and *Bhāgavata Purāṇa.*[11] These four form the canonical hierarchy of *śabda-pramāṇa* in which "the latter ones are proclaimed to remove doubts arising about the earlier ones."[12] When a "unity of sense" *(ekavākyatā)* among these scriptures is achieved—when the understanding arises that every statement in every scripture shares one common meaning—then knowledge of God results.[13] Other texts may be accepted as authentic teachings only to the extent that they do not contradict this canon. Vallabha makes it clear when he says,

> Whatever does not contradict them is a means to valid knowledge and not otherwise. Whatever contradicts them has no authority in any way whatsoever.[14]

Following this rule of noncontradiction, Vallabha includes the following texts: *Dharma Śāstra (The Laws of Manu), Rāmāyaṇa, Mahābhārata,* and *Pāñcarātra.*

> Only this purport—[expressed] by means of all the sentences of the *Veda,* the *Rāmāyaṇas* supported by the *Mahābhārata,* by the *Pāñcarātras,* and by the words of other *śāstra* in concert with the real *sūtra*—is continually ascertained, with compassion, by the Lord alone.[15]

By affirming only views about God and the world based on a "unity of sense" emerging from the primary scriptures, Vallabha confirms *śabda-pramāṇa* as the only valid basis for theology. Discursive reasoning is always subordinate; any attempt to elevate reason above divine revelation, any effort to establish a "natural theology," leads to error and delusion. Ignoring this subordination of reason has drastic existential ramifications. Rationalizing scriptural revelation amounts to subordinating the words of God to the finite human mind, and by opposing the literal sense of scriptural revelation in this way a person remains trapped in *saṁsāra.*

> This alone is the great delusion, this is the deception: that the wise, intent on studying the *śāstra* and performing their duties, do not worship Kṛṣṇa. Living under the influence of *karma,* being born in this world again and again will be their only destiny.[16]

By opposing the literal meaning of scripture, by denigrating the preeminence of *śabda-pramāṇa,* delusive teachings like Vaiṣeśika, Nyāya, and Advaita Vedānta are established that possess the capacity of leading people away from the truth. Vallabha says,

> For the purpose of spreading delusion, they established the various views like Vaiśeṣika, Nyāya, Māyāvāda (Advaita Vedānta), and so on. Their seductive words are instruments of delusion.[17]

The distinction Vallabha makes between scriptural means to liberative knowledge and seductive words of erroneous teachings promoting bondage to *saṁsāra* could not be more striking. At this point his epistemology is exclusivist, formalist, and dualist: only a literal appreciation of *śabda-pramāṇa* provides the means to eternal knowledge and counteracts the effects of the delusive words of erroneous teachings. But in the context of pure nondualism, how and why do these erroneous teachings arise in the first place?

This question is sharpened by Vallabha's harsh, even ironic, evaluation of alternative views like Advaita Vedānta, teachings that he believes are based on an inappropriate understanding or faulty interpretation of *śabda-pramāṇa.* Advaita Vedānta's own answer to this question made an appeal to beginningless ignorance *(avidyā)* as the ultimate cause of error and bondage to *saṁsāra.* This opened it to Rāmānuja's charge that ignorance was an extra-*advaitic* category, thereby undermining its claim to nonduality (Thibaut 1976, 102–19). Vallabha's answer to this question takes him on a very different tack. Appealing to Purāṇic evidence, he explains that the origin of erroneous teachings is none other than God.

> But now (in the *kali* Age), the Lord incarnates as the Buddha; the gods under his control, taking birth among Brahmins, create confusion with various doctrines.[18]

In a radical reversal of Advaita Vedānta's claim that error stems from a principle of beginningless ignorance, Vallabha asserts that God *(bhagavan)* himself authorizes the production of erroneous teachings, which in turn promotes the spread of ignorance. But why does God cause this to happen? In order to answer this question Vallabha turns to the *Vahara Purāṇa* where Bhagavan says,

> And you, Oh Rudra! Oh Strong Arms! Have the delusive śāstras composed, make the lies and half-truths appear. Make yourself visible and conceal me.[19]

The purpose of God's command, which results in the spread of delusive teachings, is further explained in the Lord's speech to Śiva in the *Padma Purāṇa,* quoted by Vallabha: "Through your counterfeit teachings make the world turn away from me; hide me so that creation may arise again and again."[20]

God arranges for the production of delusive teachings because they are necessary to keep creation in proper balance so that it may "rise again and again." But because such subtle and divinely inspired delusive teachings are in the world, even the devotee who possesses spiritual readiness, who should be worshiping the Lord, is led away from God. For this reason, says Vallabha, he composes the TVD and points to the consequences of making the wrong choice, the danger of opposing the true meaning of the genuine teaching; at the same time he ascribes both genuine and counterfeit teachings to the same nondualistic source.

Despite the nondualistic source of all teachings, Vallabha often negatively evaluates those viewpoints he consider erroneous. He describes, for example, the Advaita Vedānta assessment of devotionalism, saying,

> In this way they teach even the path of divine love as a part of knowledge, and they say that devotion is to be done until the advent of knowledge. They say that the object of devotion is a subjective fabrication.[21]

Elevating the path of knowledge above the path of devotion and then reducing the Lord as a useful device for traversing the subordinate path is not only erroneous; according to Vallabha's reading of *śabda-pramāṇa,* it is positively harmful. From a soteriological perspective, the Advaita Vedānta perspective is dangerous because it denigrates God's primacy in the human quest for liberation, thereby assuring the soul's continual rebirth in *saṁsāra*. From a philosophical perspective, Advaita Vedānta is inherently self-contradictory.

> According to the view of Advaita Vedānta, Kṛṣṇa is not considered *brahman* due to his existence in the world; but they say *brahman*'s essential nature is being-consciousness-bliss. On account of absence of proof, in their own view, they proclaim this state of affairs by following the path of devotion. This should be understood. They accept truth established by a logic opposed to their own position.[22]

Advaita Vedānta subordinates Kṛṣṇa to *brahman* because Kṛṣṇa is qualified by his existence in the world; while at the same time it describes the nature of *brahman* based on a scriptural authority, which is qualified by *its* existence in the world. Following a logic consistent with its own position on Kṛṣṇa would reduce Advaita Vedānta to silence on the nature of *brahman*. Vallabha is here voicing the same objection as the Madhvite who, a century later, accused the Advaitin of being like the man who kills his own mother. Appealing to the authority of scriptural revelation, Advaita Vedānta is asserting a metaphysical position that undermines the possibility of that very authority.

Nevertheless, Vallabha does not categorically reject the path of knowledge. But even when it is pursued in conjunction with devotion to Kṛṣṇa, the path of knowledge is not free of risk, because the devotee may encounter the delusive interpretations and erroneous teachings that will impede the achievement of liberation.

> By following the path of devotion, people who accept different views, but worship and teach consistently [with the path of devotion], are not rejected. But impeded by their variable behavior, they never achieve the final result.[23]

Due to individual ignorance a person may be persuaded to accept notions about God compromising the path of devotion. According to Vallabha there are many systems of thought promoting such compromise: dangerous, erroneous teachings based on either an inappropriate interpretation of *śabdapramāṇa* or else a complete disregard for the fourfold scriptural norm.

Despite the negative assessment of views like Advaita Vedānta, Vallabha confirms that the final goal is attainable even on a nondevotional path. However, liberation achieved by following the path of knowledge cannot compare to the experience enjoyed by the Lord's devotees who follow the path of devotion. Vallabha makes this distinction clear.

> Those who have entered into the bliss of *brahman* experience it only through the self, because their senses and so on have been dissolved. But the devotees experience it in a special way: through all their senses, mind, and self as well. Consequently, [experience of] the *brahman* state is excelled in the home life of the devotee.[24]

His own commentary on this passage explains that "free devotees," like the *gopis* who enjoyed intimacy with Kṛṣṇa, experience the bliss of God through every form, every aspect life. In this way, the ordinary family responsibilities in the life of the householder become a medium for the richest experience of bliss by the grace of God. This elevation of the householder stage of life is one of Vallabha's most significant contributions to the religious scene of his day (Timm 1991). "The path of devotion is superior," says Vallabha, because "on the path of knowledge the senses and the power of action are fruitless."[25]

Although Vallabha does not reject the path of knowledge, he clearly subordinates it. By describing knowledge as an aid in the establishment of true devotion, he reverses the Advaita Vedānta claim that devotion is only a means of a higher path.

> Having prescribed knowledge of His nature, having stated the goal of this knowledge, it is established that the goal [is achieved] only when *bhagavan* is revealed. For the sake of such revealment, service with love is described.[26]

At the same time he affirms knowledge as an important aspect of the spiritual quest: there is no one greater than the person who has first followed the path of knowledge and then proceeds to serve and to worship Kṛṣṇa.

> He is great who, having first followed the path of knowledge and achieved knowledge, gives up his dependence on that [path] and is prepared [to act] for the purpose of Kṛṣṇa's service.[27]

Vallabha establishes a scriptural basis for differentiating authentic from erroneous teachings; he rejects some teachings as promoting delusion by showing their contradiction with, or divergence from, *śabda-pramāṇa*. However, in the midst of this concern Vallabha suggests a second explanation of divergence from the fourfold scriptural norm that seems to compromise the fundamentalism of this exclusivist hermeneutical stance. This apparent compromise first appears in his approach to problems of contradiction between fourfold canon and the supplementary texts he would like to designate as *śabda-pramāṇa*. Vallabha first asserts the canonical authority of the fourfold scriptural norm over texts like *Dharma Śāstra.*

> *Manu [Dharma Śāstra]* has authority only through noncontradiction with these [four primary sources of scriptural revelation] . . . *Manu* is means to valid knowledge only when it does not contradict the *Veda.*[28]

But in his commentary on the very next verse of the TVD, he challenges this assertion. Vallabha brings the dilemma into full relief by quoting the *Veda,* which says, "Whatever *Manu* has stated is a remedy."[29] The problem, simply put, is this: *Dharma Śāstra* may sometimes contradict *śabda-pramāṇa,* yet *śabda-pramāṇa* confers authority upon the *Dharma Śāstra.*

On the one hand, how can the *Dharma Śāstra* be accepted with certainty as a means to knowledge, when it sometimes deviates from the fourfold scriptural norm? On the other hand, how can the *Dharma Śāstra* be rejected when it is explicitly authorized by the *Veda?* Like Vedānta Deśika's approach to the *bhakti-prapatti* dilemma (see chapter 5), Vallabha appeals to context. First, he explains, the word *dharma* has two meanings: (1) "having the property of being prescribed by the *Veda,*" and (2) "having the property of performing duties."[30] The *Dharma Śāstra,* he reasons, follows the second meaning, describing the minutiae of regulations and duties controlling social life. The *Veda,* as Puruṣottama's subsequent analysis of eternal knowledge indicates, is a text of a different order; it provides the genuine means to liberation. Therefore, any conflict between the two can be defused by appealing to the contexts in which individual statements are made. Vallabha explains this with an analogy that takes things one step further. Moving beyond a concern with *Dharma Śāstra,* he broadens this contextualist approach, saying,

> Just as mutually contradictory sentences in tradition texts *(smṛti)* are harmonized by the commentators of those texts, so too, even mutually contradictory conclusions are noncontradictory when they are considered from their respective contexts, like Vaiṣṇava, Smārta, etc.[31]

Here Vallabha is clearly suggesting that the truth of a statement is dependent upon the context in which the statement is made. Conflicting statements—made from different points of view—may appear contradictory when in fact they are not. By the logic of this hermeneutical stratagy, a pluralism of views may be affirmed, each meaningful in its own context. Even Advaita Vedānta, Buddhism, or views of modern Western philosophy unanticipated by Vallabha have their truth to offer. Like the cows watched over by the young cowherd Kṛṣṇa, some teachings wander far from him, but they remain his despite their distance. This, of course, stands over and against the earlier fundamentalist claim that whatever contradicts the fourfold scriptural norm has no authority whatsoever. By itself the contextualist claim could open the floodgates of relativism; taken together with the earlier exclusivist stance, it becomes even more problematic, for it appears to reduce Vallabha's hermeneutic to self-contradiction.

III. The Ontological Foundation of Scriptural Realism

Vallabha has a good reason for affirming both fundamentalism and contextualism, and presenting a hemeneutic that, at first glance, may appear self-contradictory. Despite its nonduality, or perhaps it would be better to say because of its *pure* nonduality, Vallabha's theology affirms a distinction between the devotee and the Lord, a fundamentalist requirement for any form of devotional expression. This ontological distinction has its epistemological counterpart.

> Having [earlier] explained what is acceptable as *pramāṇa* prior to the advent of complete knowledge, [now consider what is acceptable as] *pramāṇa* after [the advent of complete knowledge].[32]

This distinction between the two modes of acceptable *pramāṇa* holds the key. Prior to the advent of perfect knowledge about the nature of God and the world, a devotee of the Lord must rely on the absolute authority of the sanctioned fourfold scriptural norm. But once eternal knowledge is achieved, the situation becomes radically altered. Vallabha says,

> Or, [due to the fact that God is made manifest] through the inseparability of words and objects—characteristic of all forms—all [scriptural sentences] are a means to valid knowledge; insofar as their mutually contradictory aspects can be given up.[33]

In other words, all scriptures, all sentences, all words become recognized as the means for eternal knowledge because one realizes that God becomes manifest through all linguistic forms. From this perspective the capacity of words to express truth becomes universalized, no longer limited to a specific sectarian tradition or a designated collection of canonical literature.

Basing his hermeneutic upon the ontological insights emerging from scripture, Vallabha is claiming that the power of words to convey truth becomes universalized at the highest level of knowledge. By appealing to God as the coincidence of opposites, Vallabha absolutizes the contextualist approach. In the final analysis there is only one context: God. All words have their final denotative locus in God, who is the ultimate and, in the final analysis, the only object of knowledge. Thus Vallabha's hermeneutic of scriptural realism comes full circle.

This circle is not vicious; Vallabha has not simply ended up from where he started. The reaffirmation of absolutism shifts the fundamentalist tone of the hermeneutic into a new key. This shift is revealed in God's paradoxical relationship to all metaphysical thinking. Each and every metaphysical theory, because it is relative to human reasoning, is unable to capture the reality of God. According to Vallabha,

> He, who alone is the abiding inner reality [of things] everywhere, is not touched by them. That, which He manifests by having entered into it as His body, does not know Him as such. [For] Him, who goes along with the various theories, all theories are unsuitable.[34]

No human mental construct is able to capture God, nor will any "megatheory" ever resolve theoretical pluralism. But because each and every theory is a partial explanation of God emphasizing particular statements in scripture or describing particular qualities, God is associated with all theories. The various theories, ideologies, philosophies, and worldviews can never be rendered compatible. This incompatibility, however, reflects the very nature of God as the ground of contradictory qualities and mutually exclusive forms, and it stands as a testimony to God's greatness, not a philosophical problem to be resolved by human ingenuity. Vallabha's God is a God who is greater than the human capacity for rational understanding. So he says,

> Only He—in whom mutually contradictory qualities are observed—is great. And those two qualities [which are mutually exclusive] are both real; otherwise, being like an actor [who plays a fictional role by taking on characteristics contradicting his actual nature], His majesty is not proved. Therefore, [there should be] no exclusion of either of the two [mutually exclusive qualities] by means of reasoning.[35]

Given God's nature as the ground of mutually exclusive qualities, and viewed from the perspective of enlightenment all metaphysical systems, all doctrinal schemes, all scriptural traditions—not to mention art, poetry, literature, drama, dance, music—may become means to knowledge about God. The achievement of eternal knowledge reveals that God speaks through all words, all forms.

The power of Vallabha's hermeneutic of scriptural realism is generated by a tension between the fundamentalist, "either/or" model presupposing an objectivist epistemology, and the pluralist, "both/and" model at work in a contextualist theory of knowledge. Vallabha rejects the view of Advaita Vedānta, which claims that diverse forms, ideas, scriptures, and so on have only a provisional reality, that difference is ultimately swallowed up in the experience of God's absolute nonduality. For Vallabha, God speaks to humanity through diversity, and any suggestion that the diversity through which God speaks is unimportant arises from a foolhardy human arrogance. For this reason Vallabha warns against trivializing the Word of God in any way; how we can hope to know God without a deep appreciation of what God has spoken? It is through this appreciation that the devotee is guided toward enlightenment.

From the perspective of eternal knowledge, everything in creation is recognized as God, the ultimate meaning of all words, the foundation for all relationships expressed grammatically through the seven Sanskrit case-endings.[36] Again, quoting a Purāṇic source, Vallabha writes,

> Wherever, by whom, from whom, of whom, to whom, as whatever, whenever—all this is *bhagavan* directly as matter, person, and Lord.[37]

By an ontological "speech act," God becomes matter, person, and Lord. Thus, Vallabha explains, "*bhagavan,* Himself, is present within every effect [which corresponds to] the meaning of a word."[38] The created universe is God's speaking, an autobiography of the transcendent Lord; but it is important to remember that within this ontological, autobiographical speech act there is another kind of speaking. In the words of redemptive, scriptural revelation God provides *śabda-pramāṇa,* the authoritative means to eternal knowledge, the means to liberation.

IV. Conclusion

This chapter has considered the hermeneutical stance of one important Vaiṣṇava thinker from the fifteenth century. Vallabhācārya's *Tattvārthadīpa-nibandha* provides the basis for describing his perspective of "scriptural realism." Several important issues have been considered. First, Vallabha's understanding of *śabda-pramāṇa* was compared with the views of Nyāya and Advaita Vedānta. This reveals Vallabha as much more than a simple man of devotional piety. At the same time, his willingness to engage in sophisticated philosophical argumentation is balanced by his insistence on the primacy of scriptural revelation over all other means to knowledge, including rationality. Second, by looking at Vallabha's designation of scriptural canon—the primary and secondary literature that provides authentic teaching—two complementary facets of his hermeneutical stance were exposed. On the one hand he adopts a fundamentalism that serves to exclude, and to label as erroneous, any teaching that conflicts with the fourfold canonical scripture. On the other hand he asserts a contextualist logic that affirms God as the author of all teachings. Finally, the apparent contradiction between fundamentalist exclusivism and contextualist relativism is resolved by considering the ontological foundation of scriptural realism. Remaining honest to the logic of pure nondualism, Vallabha affirms the reality of God, of the world, and of the relation between the two. Thus, unlike the Advaitin "who kills his own mother," Vallabha's ontology provides the foundation for taking seriously the salvific words God has provided as the means to eternal knowledge.

This study may be an interesting exercise in "hermeneutical archeology." It certainly illustrates Vallabha's concern with canon and its exegesis, a category of human religious expression that has been described as "the most characteristic, persistent, and obsessive religious activity" (Smith 1982, 43). But does Vallabha have anything to say to us today? I think he does. Vallabha's hermeneutical theology, as I have shown, is based upon a creative melding of the fundamentalist embrace of scriptural authority and the affirmation of religious pluralism. Today such matters have taken on new urgency. In an increasingly pluralistic world, the role and scope of authority, in whatever form, becomes a crucial and complex concern. It matters little that, as Deutsch pointed out twenty years ago, "we do not accept the authority of the Veda (or for the most part the authority of any other scripture)" (Deutsch 1969, 5) because the ideologies, religions, psychologies, philosophies, and shared presuppositions that variously function as our "canon" today—as pluralistic as these may be—are often no less authoritative for us than Vallabha's were for him. For this reason, Vallabha's traditional hermeneutic, although emerging in a medieval Indian historical/cultural milieu, may suggest a viable strategy in our day-to-day efforts to reconcile the diverse and often conflicting claims made on our allegiance.

Notes

1. *avtīrṇo bhagavān sarvamuktyarthamiti prameyabalenaiva phaliṣyatītisvādhikārābhāve'pi tataḥ phalaṁ bhaviṣyatītyarthaḥ / Prakāśa on* TVD 19. From Vallabha's *Tattvārthadīpanibandhaḥ (saprakāśa)*. 2d ed., vol. 1, edited by Gosvāmi Śyām Manohar; Kolhāpur Maharashtra: Vaibhava Cooperative Society, 1981. All translations from this text are mine; numbers refer to verses in the *Śāstrārthaḥ* section.

2. *prameyabalena teṣāṁ siddhirbhavati ced bhavatu, nānyathetyarthaḥ // Prakāśa* on TVD 103.

3. *brahmaiva hi sarvādhāram / yathā bhūmiḥ sahajaviruddhānāmapi mūṣkādijīvānām / kārṇagatadharmaḥ pṛthivyāṁ bhāsate / viśeṣeṇa laukikayuktiratra nāsti, tadagamyatvādityāha yuktyagocaramiti // Prakāśa* on TVD 71.

4. *ānandāṁśaprakāśāddhi brahmabhāvo bhaviṣyati /* TVD 36a.

5. *anekadhā sṛṣṭikathanasya prayojanamāha—yathākathāñcinmāhātmyaṁ tasya sarvatra varṇyate / bhajanasyaiva siddhyarthaṁ tattvamasyādikaṁ tathā // Prakāśa and* TVD 41.

6. *agnihotrādipañcātmakaḥ / tatsādhanadeśakāladavyakartṛ mantrātmakaḥ / trividhamantrabrāhmaṇopniṣadātmakaḥ / Prakāśa* and TVD 43.

7. *laukikaṁ hi lokyuktyā'vagamyate / brahma tu vaidikam / vedapratipaditārthabodho na śabdas ādhāraṇavidhyayā bhavati // Prakāśa* on TVD 62b.

8. *namo bhagavate tasmai kṛṣṇāyādbhutakarmaṇe / rūpnāmavibhedena jagat krīḍati yo yataḥ //* TVD 1.

9. *indriyāṇāṁ tu sāmarthyādadṛśyaṁ svecchayā tu tat //* TVD 72b. *tadanugrahatadicchābhyāṁ dṛk paraṁ hariṁ spṛśedityarthaḥ / Prakāśa* on TVD 75.

10. *tatsvataḥsiddhapramāṇabhāvaṁ pramāṇam / Prakāśa* on TVD 7.

11. *vedāḥ śrīkṛṣṇavākyāni vyāsasūtrāṇi caiva hi / samādhibhāṣā vyāsasya pramāṇaṁ taccatuṣṭayam //* TVD 7.

12. *uttataṁ pūrasaṁdehavārakaṁ parikīrtitam //* TVD 8a.

13. *etaccatuṣṭayamekavākyatāpannaṁ pramājanakamityarthaḥ // Prakāśa* on TVD 7.

14. *aviruddhaṁ tu yattvasya pramāṇaṁ tacca nānyathā / etadviruddhaṁ yatsarvaṁ na tanmānaṁ kathañcana //* TVD 8bc.

15. *artho'yameva nikhilairapi vedavākyai rāmāyaṇaiḥ sahitabhāratapañcarātraiḥ / anyaiśca śāstravacanaiḥ saha tattvasūtrairnirṇīyate sahṛdayaṁ hariṇā sadaiva //* TVD 104.

16. *ayameva mahāmoho hīdameva pratāraṇam // yatkṛṣṇaṁ na bhajet prājñaḥ śāstrābhyās aparaḥ kṛtī // teṣāṁ karmavaśānāṁ hi bhava eva phaliṣayti //* TVD 16.

17. *mohanārthaṁ nānāmatāni kurvanti, kāṇādanyāyamāyāvādādirūpāṇi / vākpeśalatvānmohanarūpatvam //* *Prakāśa* on TVD 15.

18. *buddhāvatāre tvadhunā harau tadvaśagāḥ surāḥ / nānāmatāni vipreṣu bhūtva kurvanti mohanam //* TVD 15ab.

19. *tvañca rudra mahābāho mohaśāstrāṇi kāraya / atathayāni vitathyāni darśayasva mahābhuja / prakāśaṁ kuru cātmānamaprakāśaṁ ca māṁ kuru / Prakāśa* on TVD 15.

20. *svāgamaiḥ kalpitaistvañca janānmadvimukhān kuru / māñca gopaya yena syātsṛṣṭireṣottarottarā / Prakāśa* on TVD 15.

21. *tathā bhaktimārgamapi jñānaśeṣtayopadiśanti, jñānaparyantaṁ ca tatkaraṇamityāhuḥ / bhāvanākalpitatvaṁ viṣayasyā'huḥ / Prakāśa* on TVD vs. 17.

22. *na hi māyāvādādimate śrīkṛṣṇādirvyvahārytvād brahma bhavitur-mahati / te tu sa dānandacitsvrūpamiti cāhuḥ / ataḥ svamate yathā tathā padārthasiddhyabhāvācced bhaktimārgānusārenaiva vadantīti jñātavym / tadā teṣāṁ pratitantranyāyābhyupagamasiddhānto bhavati / Prakāśa* on TVD 100.

23. *bhaktimārgānusāreṇa matāntargatā narāḥ / bhajanti bodhayan-tevamviruddhaṁ na bādhayte / naikāntikaṁ phalaṁ teṣāṁ viruddhācaraṇāt kvacit //* TVD 100.

24. *brahmānande praviṣṭānāmātmanaiva sukhapramā / saṅghātasya vilīnatvād bhaktānāṁ tu viśeṣataḥ //50// sarvendriyaistathā cāntaḥkaraṇairātmanāpi hi / brahmabhāvāttu bhaktānāṁ gṛha eva viśiṣyate //51//* TVD 50–51.

25. *bhaktimārgasyotkarṣaḥ / kriyāśakterindriyāṇāṁ ca vaiphalyaṁ jñānamārge / Prakāśa* on TVD 14c.

26. *ataḥ svarūpajñānaṁ vidhāya tasya puruṣārthatvamuktvā tadāvirbhāva eva phalaṁ siddhyatītyāvirbhāvārthaṁ premsevāṁ nirūpayantī . . . / Prakāśa* on TVD 42.

27. *yastu pūrvaṁ jñānamārge pravṛttaḥ prāptajñānaḥ kṛṣṇasevārthaṁ yatate tanniṣṭhāṁ parityajya, sa mahānityāha / Prakāśa* on TVD 14b.

28. *etadvirodhenaiva manvādīnāṁ prāmāṇyamāha aviruddhamiti / vedādinā aviruddhameva manvādikaṁ pramāṇam / kvacitsamvādaḥ, kvacid-virodha ityubhayasambhave apramāṇamevetyāha etadviruddhamiti // Prakāśa* on TVD vs. 8.

29. *yadvai kiñcana manuravadat tad bheṣajam / Prakāśa* on TVD 9, quoting *Taittirīya Saṁhīta* 2.2.10.2.

30. *codanāviṣayatvenā' vaśyakartavyatākatvenā' bhimato' rtho' tra dharmaśabdenocyate tasya dve śrutismṛtī ubhe api pare pramāpike yasya tādṛśatvāddvayaṁ / Prakāśa* on TVD 10.

31. *yathā smṛtivākyāni parasparaṁ viruddhāni smṛtivyākhyānakārairvirodhaprakāreṇa nirṇīyante, tathā nirṇyānāmapi parasparaviruddhānāṁ vaiṣṇavasmārtādibhedenāvirodha ityathaḥ // Prakāśa* on TVD 10.

32. *evaṁ pūrṇajñānodayāvadhi yadgāhyaṁ pramāṇatvena tannirūpya tadanantaraṁ yatpramāṇaṁ tadāha / Prakāśa* on TVD 9.

33. *athavā sarvarūpatvānnāmalīlāvibhedataḥ / viruddhāṁśaparityāgātpramāṇaṁ sarvameva hi //* TVD 9.

34. *yaḥ sarvatraiva saṅtiṣṭhannantaraḥ saṁspṛśenna tat / śarīraṁ taṁ na vedetthaṁ yo' nuviśya prakāśate / sarvavādānavasaraṁ nānāvādānurodhī tat //* TVD 70.

35. *yatraivaṁ parasparaviruddhā dharmā bodhyante sa eva mahān / te dharmā ubhaye satyāḥ anyathā māhāmyaṁ na siddhyet naṭavat / ato yuktyā anyatarasya na bādhaḥ // Prakāśa on* TVD 88.

36. The seven cases are: nominative, accusative, instrumental, dative, ablative, genitive, and locative.

37. *yatra yena yato yasya yasmai yadyadyathā yadā / syādidaṁ bhagavān sākṣāt pradhānapuruṣeśvaraḥ //* TVD 69, quoting *Bhāgavata Purāṇa* 10.85.4.

38. *sarveṣveva padārtheṣu kāryeṣu svayaṁ tiṣṭhaṁstānyantarayati svamadhye sthāpayatītyarthaḥ / Prakāsa* on TVD 70.

References

Betty, L. Stafford
1978 *Vādirāja's Refutation of Śaṅkara's Nondualism: Clearing the Way for Theism*. Delhi: Motilal Banarsidass.

Bijalwan, C. D.
1977 *Indian Theory of Knowledge Based upon Jayanta's Nyāyamañjarī*. New Delhi: Heritage.

Chatterjee, S. C.
1950 *The Nyāya Theory of Knowledge*. 2d ed. Calcutta: University of Calcutta.

Dasgupta, Surendranath
1975 *A History of Indian Philosophy.* 5 vols. 1922. Reprint. Delhi: Motilal Banarsidass.

Deutsch, Eliot
1969 *Advaita Vedānta: A Philosophical Reconstruction.* Honolulu: East-West Center Press.

1988 "Knowledge and the Tradition Text in Indian Philosophy." In *Interpreting across Boundaries: New Essays in Comparative Philosophy,* edited by Gerald Larson and Eliot Deutsch, 165–173. Princeton: Princeton University Press.

Gosvāmi, Śyām Manohar, ed.
1981 *Tattvārthadīpanibandhaḥ (saprakāśa).* 2d ed., 3 vols. Kolhāpur: Vaibhava Cooperative Society.

Smith, Jonathan Z.
1982 *Imagining Religion: From Babylon to Jonestown.* Chicago: University of Chicago Press.

Thibaut, George, trans.
1976 *The Vedānta-Sūtras with the Commentary of Rāmānuja.* 1904. Reprint. Delhi: Motilal Banarsidass.

Timm, Jeffrey R.
1988 "Prolegomena to Vallabha's Theology of Revelation." *Philosophy East and West* 38(2): 107–26.

1991 "The Celebration of Emotion: Vallabha's Ontology of Affective Experience." *Philosophy East and West* 41(1):59–75.

Yadav, Bhibuti S.
1980 "Vaiṣṇavism on Hans Küng: A Hindu Theology of Religious Pluralism." *Religion and Society* 27(2): 1–32.

Nine

Hermeneutics of a Kashmiri *Mahātmyā* Text in Context

Madhu Bazaz Wangu

Introduction

The previous chapters focusing on Veda and Vedānta have explored traditional hermeneutics in primarily philosophical and theological contexts. In the present chapter I would like to shift the contextual ground somewhat by examining a Kashmiri Śaiva text as it developed within its unique *sociopolitical* context. Hindu religious history of the state of Jammu and Kashmir from the 1840s to the 1920s is of paramount significance for understanding the emergence of the text under consideration. In 1846, after six centuries of Islamic rule, Hindu Maharaja Gulab Singh established the present state of Jammu and Kashmir, bringing together for the first time two distinct religious schools: Tantric Śaivism of Kashmir and the Rāma cult of Jammu. This religious intermingling fostered by political circumstances gave rise to a cultural matrix that stimulated sacred creativity. This creativity included the development of a rich religious literature in which political and socioeconomic factors played a significant role. A meaningful interpretion of any scriptural tradition requires a careful inquiry into its historical context, and that context includes both political and socioeconomic dimensions.[1] The present chapter focuses on the role these dimensions played in the emergence of one nineteenth-century Kashmiri religious tradition, and its authoratative scripture—the *mahātmyā Śrī Śrī Mahārajñī Pradhurbhāva.*[2] By considering, in some detail, the context in which the Kashmiri *mahātmyā* originated and by examining its textual meaning, this study attempts to answer some fundamental questions. Why, and under what sociopolitical conditions, was the *mahātmyā* composed? Who composed it, and by what authority? What kind of strategies were employed in creating the new religious text? What does the analysis of its contents tell us about the religio-political milieu of the second half of the nineteenth century in the state of

Jammu and Kashmir? The conclusions derived in this way unfold a unique perspective on the composition of a modern religious text and the creation of a deity, and may suggest similar factors at work in the emergence of earlier text traditions of South Asia.

The goddess Khīr Bhavānī, to whom the *mahātmyā* is devoted, is highly cherished by the local Kashmiri Hindu population. She is also known as ''Mahārajñī'' and is enshrined in the middle of a natural spring in the village Tulmul, about fourteen miles from Śrīnagar, the capital of the state of Jammu and Kashmir. The hierophany of this natural spring was recognized in the early nineteenth century when the villagers paid their homage by crossing the spring's surrounding marshes on strong reeds growing in the vicinity of the swamp (Koul 1954). Curiosity about the spring originated when the village mystic, Paṇḍit Govind Gadru, had a vision of the goddess manifested as a serpent. The devout Brahmin carried a vessel of milk, arranged a boat, rowed through the marshes of Tulmul, and, upon reaching the sacred spot to which the serpent/spring goddess had led him, slowly poured out the milk. Soon afterward, another *paṇḍit,* by the name of Krishna Taplu, envisioned a goddess who led him to the same holy spot (Koul 1954). As time passed some local legends related to the manifestation of the goddess as a spring and as a serpent (both *nāga* in the Kashmiri vernacular) were circulated throughout the valley. The holy site came to be known as Tulmul Nāga. Legends about the spot were orally circulated and conflated with other popular epic myths. It was during the reign of the early Dogri maharajas from the 1850s to the 1920s that a *mahātmyā* was composed and an island temple was created that was devoted to the goddess. From the beginning of the twentieth century onward, Khīr Bhavānī's sophisticated and complex cult expressed the local ecology and geography, the indigenous sacred beliefs and cultural values, as well as religious and sociopolitical events of Kashmiri Hindus.

Khīr Bhavānī's *mahātmyā, Śrī Śrī Mahārajñī Pradhurbhāva,* written in Devanāgarī script,[3] is considered authoritative by all Kashmiri Hindus.[4] It has an inherent religious efficacy that is carried over to its local readers. For them the *mahātmyā* is meaningful, holy, and powerful. This extraordinary sacrality is suggested by the repetition of the word *śrī* in the title, meaning ''high majesty,'' ''royalty,'' ''splendor,'' and ''glory.'' To understand how this text arrived at such an exalted status requires that we investigate not only the religious history of Kashmir, but also the region's sociopolitical history as well.

I. Hindu Religious Traditions of Kashmir

A critical survey of Hindu religious literature of Kashmir brings forth three promiment factors. First, ancient Kashmir was a stronghold of diverse, indigenous Buddhist and Brahmanical doctrines. Second, Kashmiri Tantric Śaivism has been the dominant religion of Kashmiri Hindus from the tenth century C.E. onward. Third, great emphasis has been placed on the goddess Śakti in her different manifestations, such as Umā, Bhairavī, Tripurāsundarī, and Aghoresvarī. The intermingling of various religious schools is clearly indicated in the sixth-century text *Nīlmapurāna,* in which goddess Umā is given higher status than the god Śiva. The later religious literature of Kashmir gives us further evidence of this syncretic nature of local religion and the paramount significance of the goddess in her various forms.

Abhinavagupta, the tenth-century mystic and philosopher, who expounded Kashmiri nondual Tantric Śaivism, emphasized the centrality of the goddess Kāli and her inseparable condition of being with Śiva. The eleventh-century historian Kalhana, in the historical compendium *Rājtaraṇginī,* informs us that Kashmir's ancient religious culture was highly enriched by Buddhism, Brahmanism, Tantric Śaivism, and indigenous folk cults. Kalhana also makes specific allusions to many esoteric goddesses.

Alexis Sanderson, a contemporary scholar, describes three major Śaiva traditions in Kashmir: (1) an orthodox dualistic Śaiva-Siddhānta tradition, the adherents of which worship mild, consortless Sadāśiva; (2) a heterodox nondualistic Tantric tradition in which goddess Kālī reigns supreme; and (3) a tradition that falls somewhere between these two extremes.[5]

The religious traditions of the nineteenth-century Kashmir, with which the present chapter is concerned, originated from this third kind of tradition. The people of the valley worshiped Bhairava (Svacchānanda) and his consort Bhairavi (Aghoreśvari).[6] Later in the century they were devoted to the newly emerging deities like Mahārajñī Khīr Bhavānī, Śārikā, and Jwālā who were rooted in the cult of Kālī.

Evidently the *mahātmyā, Śrī Śrī Mahārajñī Pradhurbhāva,* devoted to Khīr Bhavānī, was created within a sociopolitical milieu stimulating religious creativity and expression: new deities were emerging, and epochal religious writings were being composed. However, about a century before this period of fructification, Kashmiris had gone through a period of political, religious, and social atrocities.

II. Religious and Political Context of Kashmir: 1753–1846 C.E.

The numinosity of kingship has inspired many ideas about polity in the context of Hinduism. One such ancient view is that "a kingless country comes to ruin, and one should not settle in such a place." Such was the condition of the valley of Kashmir before the beginning of the Dogri rule in the mid-nineteenth century. It was kingless and had come to complete ruin.

From 1753 to 1819 Kashmir was ruled not by any king but by turbulent and fanatical hillmen from Afghanistan who knew how to conquer but not how to conciliate. Under their rule the Kashmiri Hindus were forced to give up Sanskrit teaching and learning; they were compelled not to wear the sacred thread. The performance of a Hindu ritual was made a criminal offense (Das Gupta 1968).

Pilgrimage centers, like Sāradā and Bheda, sustained Hindus of Kashmir during six centuries of Muslim rule.[7] However, by the eighteenth century Brahmins of Kashmir had abandoned these centers due to political conditions and geographical difficulties. Worship was thus confined to Svaccānandabhairava and Aghoreśvari Bhairavi in the seclusion of their homes. Adoration of *nāgas* and veneration of the local saints was also extremely popular (Wangu 1988a).

Under Afghan rule the daily rituals and sacred ceremonies of the Hindus were subdued. They dared not celebrate any religious festivals in broad daylight lest they be punished, tortured, or put to death.

> The peasants ceased to cultivate the land, the famous shawl weavers left their looms, merchants took to flight and even innocent citizens tried to stay confined to their homes . . . Life, in a word, was death postponed for the moment. . . . The Afghan tyranny sucked the very blood out of the Kashmiri people. (Das Gupta 1968, 29)

The sociopolitical condition of the Kashmiris was at its lowest ebb when in 1819 the Sikhs conquered the valley and took it from the Afghans.

When the Sikh ruler Rañjīt Singh annexed the valley to his empire, Kashmiris pinned great hopes on him. It was with an intense relief that they anticipated the downfall of the Afghans' evil rule. Peasants who had been cruelly fleeced by the merciless Afghani chiefs were especially glad, but their hopes were dashed. The Sikh maharaja had his heart set on becoming an undisputed master of Northwest India and, therefore, led a number of expeditions in quick succession to expand his geographic territory. Rañjīt Singh had no interest in the uplift of the inhabitants of the newly gained areas, which he could rule only *in absentia*. His appointed chiefs made no change in the system of running the state. Obviously no attempt was made to rebuild or restore the demolished temples and their mutilated images. Instead the Sikhs, who were preoccupied with military expeditions, used already dilapidated religious edifices to store military equipment and food (Bamzai 1962).

In many of the military expeditions, a Dogri Rajput chieftain from the Jammu plains, Gulab Singh, assisted Maharaja Rañjīt Singh with unprecedented valor. Impressed by Gulab Singh's achievement, the maharaja gave him the plains of Jammu "in farm," conferred on him the title of "Maharaja," and installed him on the Gadi of Jammu in 1822. Maharaja Gulab Singh thus became the hereditary ruler of the Dogri people.

Jammu plains, situated in the south of the valley of Kashmir, has been the homeland of the Dogri Rajputs for centuries. They are Vaiṣṇava in their religious belief and worship Rāma, an incarnation of Viṣṇu. The tutelary deity of Gulab Singh's family was Raghunātha, an epithet of the god Rāma. Whereas the inhabitants of Jammu were Vaiṣṇavas, the non-Muslim populace of Kashmir were largely Śaivas or Śaktas. In 1846 Maharaja Gulab Singh purchased the valley of Kashmir from the British Indian government, after the Sikhs lost it to the British in the Anglo-Sikh war, and established the present state of Jammu and Kashmir, thus bringing together politically two religiously distinct ethnogeographic areas for the first time in their history.

III. Religion and Politics under Dogri Rule: 1846–1925

Gulab Singh, 1846–56. Beginning as a petty official in the Sikh court, Gulab Singh became a powerful commander but remained an orthodox Hindu. He conquered territories and eventually established himself as a sovereign of the state of Jammu and Kashmir. Both his military and his religion were matters of deep concern to him, and he had special inclination toward the Sanskritic heritage and Hindu tradition. Under his strict orders his regiments did not copy the popular English military commands but coined new ones in Sanskrit, so that his important regiments were given the names Raghunātha, Laxaman, and Gobardhan (Pannikar 1930). His intense piety led him to many significant pilgrimage centers and also resulted in the construction of many Rāma temples at Jammu.

When Maharaja Gulab Singh added the valley of Kashmir to his territory, he found the Hindus of the valley were either Śaivas or Śaktas. He must have discovered, to his dismay, that his tutelary deity Rāma did not have even a subordinate position in the religious pantheon of the inhabitants of his newly gained territory. The Hindus of the valley were *liṇga-yonī* and Bhairava and Kālī worshipers. While following the dead body of a loved one going toward the cremation grounds, the Kashmiri Śaivas did not chant *Hey Rāma! Hey Rāma!* but *Shiv Shiv Shamboo! Shiv Shiv Shamboo!* (Wangu 1988b).[8]

Ranbir Singh, 1856–85. There was little Gulab Singh could do for the Kashmiri people within the short span of his tenure. In 1856, after ruling for a decade, the maharaja enthroned his son Ranbir Singh as the maharaja of his kingdom.

The new maharaja was not only dismayed at the religious rituals and ceremonies of Kashmiris but even disapproved of them. The German Indologist George Bühler, who visited the valley in the 1870s, writes,

> (In the valley there is) . . . a belief in the efficacy of yogini rites . . . both the Kashmirian Śaktas and Śaivas are famous for their proficiency in the Black Art (Tantric rituals?). . . . Śaivas carefully hide their art as maharaja Ranbir Singh is much opposed to them and punishes them . . . [if they are caught performing such rites]. (Bühler 1877, 23)

After centuries of mental anguish and physical deprivation, the overwhelming majority of the Kashmiris had developed a sort of philosophical detachment toward the government in general and would try their best to ignore its existence if they could. Therefore, they watched the moves of the Dogri Maharaja Ranbir Singh with deep apprehension when he began to hold regular public *durbārs* where

> grievances could be aired and redress sought . . . the ruler felt that people had complaints which could be heard and justice . . . administered. It redounds to the credit of Ranbir Singh that things started moving during his lifetime. . . . This well intentioned ruler was determined to give some relief to his oppressed people. (Das Gupta 1968, 31)

By the 1870s some progress was definitely registered. The labor classes, as a general rule, were well fed, well clothed, and fairly housed. Some progress was made in the area of cultivation and industry, trade was brought under the state monopoly, and people were taxed fairly.

Beginning with the Dogri reign, the Christian Missionary Society of London started preliminary social reform for the general uplift of the Kashmiri people. Impressed by their selfless dedication, the Maharaja granted them land for a general hospital and a women's hospital. Later this combined effort spread in the area of education, land, and juridical reform with the help of the Indian British government. These combined efforts did wonders for the inhabitants of the valley of Kashmir. The social reforms during the seventies, eighties, and nineties made Kashmiris politically, economically, and culturally somewhat self-assured. Deep apprehension was changing into recuperation. Awareness in one area led to awareness in others (Wangu 1988a).

Maharaja Ranbir Singh not only took deep interest in the physical well being of the people in general but also was personally concerned with the revival of religious awareness and education throughout his kingdom of Jammu and Kashmir (Stein 1894). His desire was to resuscitate the study of orthodox Sanskrit scriptures, which had nearly ceased to exist in Kashmir. He organized a vigorous campaign for the collection of old texts. Ancient texts were purchased from other religious centers of India, including Banaras and Bengal, and manuscripts that could not be purchased were copied by the professional scribes, the Kashmiri *bhāśa bhatta.*[9] Many Kashmiri *paṇḍits* owned manuscripts of ancient Kashmiri literature. An attempt was made to buy or copy them (Stein 1894).

Simultaneous with this revived concern with religious texts, many sacred sites were developing in the vicinity of the valley of Kashmir that were easily approachable by boat or foot. One such sacred spot was the sacred spring at Tulmul already described, which by the 1870s had become quite popular. In fact, in the 1890s the goddess who had manifested herself in the visions of the yogis as the serpent and the spring was regarded as "their favorite goddess," and her spring had become "perhaps the most sacred place in Kashmir" (Lawrence 1895). Traditionally, the sophisticated and complex deity Śiva Bhairava is the god *par excellence* in the valley; but in the *mahātmyā* of the goddess, the supreme god himself gives the goddess Khīr Bhavānī the mandate of protecting and guarding the Kashmiris.

The Sacred Complex at Jammu. In the Jammu plains the religiopolitical basis of Maharaja Ranbir Singh was well grounded. His patronage to the Vaiṣṇava god Rāma is evidenced from the construction of the large temple complex of Raghunātha *mandir* in Jammu. The foundation stone of this was laid by Maharaja Gulab Singh in 1852 C.E., and it was consecrated by Maharaja Ranbir Singh in 1857 C.E. The deities enshrined in the main temple of Raghunātha *mandir* are Rāma, Sītā, and Laxman. On the main temple doorway are imposing images of Hanumān and Ranbir Singh. This depiction equates the relationships of each devotee with lord Rāma. The parallel is obvious: the former is the divine devotee Hanumān, the latter his earthly counterpart, Maharaja Ranbir Singh.

The architectural complex of the Raghunātha *mandir* includes a Sanskrit *pustakālya* (library), a Sanskrit *pāṭhaśālā* (college), and the main temple.[10] Maharaja's enlightened interest in Sanskrit learning and orthodox Hindu religious traditions motivated him to provide rich endowments for the maintenance of the temple complex. The temple library had two kinds of texts, the ancient scriptures and the contemporary literature created and composed under the patronage of the Maharaja himself. New scriptures were composed for the newly emerging pilgrimage sites in the vicinity of the capital Srinagar. The newly developed literature that was added to the library is interesting on account of its local associations and its writing methods (Stein 1894).

Maharaja had commissioned Paṇḍit Sahibram, one of the foremost among Kashmirian Sanskrit scholars, to prepare a descriptive survey of all pilgrimage centers *(tīratha)* of Kashmir. For this purpose a staff of scholars *(paṇḍit)* and scribes *(bhāśa bhatta)* was placed at his disposal. The large work that was to be prepared on the basis of these materials was never completed, but sometime before his death Paṇḍit Sahibram had drawn up abstracts of the information he had collected under the title of *Kashmiratīrathasaṁgraha* (A collection of texts about pilgrimage centers in Kashmir) (Stein 1979 [1900]). The material collected and the abstracts made under the excellent guidance of Sahibram were probably used to develop new *mahātmyā* texts extolling the newly developed pilgrimage centers in the vicinity of Srinagar.

Stein informs us that when a new holy site was established, a shrine was built and a *mahātmyā* was prepared based on both relevant historical incidents and sacred literature. These texts praised and expanded the exploits of the presiding deity. A newly created sacred book would become popular in no time among the priests *(purohita)* of Srinagar. A new scripture would include local legends, ancient topographical names, oral myths, and extracts from the old *mahātmyās* (Stein 1979 [1900]). This quasi-antiquarianism did not seem to have any negative effect on the popularity of the new *mahātmyā*. The creation and the composition of the sacred text were, therefore, intentional and practical, and the text was given an ancient veneer. This kind of writing methodology was utilized in the composition of the *mahātmyā* of the goddess Khīr Bhavānī.

The Raghunātha *mandir* library at Jammu, which housed the rich collection of ancient scriptures and newly created sacred texts, was a brilliant jewel in the royal crown. It was not only an expression of the royal devotion toward the god Rāma but also a powerful symbol of the political and religious strength in the southern area of Jammu.

In the northern valley of Kashmir the rulers were facing a major puzzle: how could they gain the support of a Śaiva laity in the valley for the Vaiṣṇava god Rāma? Maharaja Ranbir Singh was quick to realize that such a religious mandate would eventually lead to better sociopolitical control, yet at the same time he realized that he could not force a "new religion" down the throats of his Kashmiri subjects. Ranbir Singh was aware that a Hindu king must perform a precarious balancing act between forcefully proclaiming his own writ to be *Dharma* and following unassumingly what his subjects tell him to be *Dharma,* and he was also aware the king does not derive his authority from a transcendent principle but from the community itself (Heesterman 1985).

The Dogri kings brought with them the Vaiṣṇava religious currents from Jammu, which they passionately yet patiently desired to graft over Kashmiri Śaiva traditions. It is no indictment of their personal piety that they selectively utilized the advantageous characteristics of religious nature for political purposes. Maharaja Ranbir Singh successfully did so by introducing festivals and mythology of the Rāma cult and constructing the temples of Rāma and Hanumān in the valley of Kashmir. One noteworthy religious festival introduced by Ranbir Singh into the valley at the very beginning of his reign was the *Baldev* festival. He declared a two-day national holiday for this religious festival, which was celebrated in the month of August; on these days he visited *Rāmbāgh,* a garden near the city, and worshiped Rāma. All his subjects were invited to join him for this annual occasion (Bühler 1877). Moreover, special assemblies *(darbār)* were held four times in one year, three of which were ecological, and the fourth religious, in nature. The holy festival of *Daśeherā,* the victory of Rāma over demon king Rāvaṇa, was celebrated with much pomp and show (Drew 1877). The festival of *Daśeherā* was not celebrated in Kashmir before the Dogri rule and has much subdued since then, but during the Dogri epoch this day of the triumph of Rāma, the ruler *par excellence,* was indeed celebrated with much joy. Paṇḍit Anand Kaul, who made a list of the contemporary festivals of Kashmiri Hindus during his lifetime, gives the longest description of this particular festival in his book *The Kashmiri Pandit (1924).*[11]

By celebrating religious festivals together with his people, the Maharaja not only pioneered a new tradition but also incorporated in the local calendar a time period specially devoted to his family deity Rāma, creating a novel bond between him and his Kashmiri Hindu subjects. These pleasant festivals were welcomed by the local population. Besides establishing festivals, the Maharaja also constructed many Rāma temples in which imposing images of Hanumān were installed. In the western Himalayan kingdoms, including the state of Jammu and Kashmir, wherever we find festivals, idols, and temples of Rāma, the ideal king-god, "they are set up by rajas whose main policy had been the unification and centralization of their respective state" (Goetz 1964).

A sacred site of the Kashmiri people, which was becoming increasingly popular, attracted Ranbir Singh's attention: the spring of Khīr Bhavānī. Up to that time no holy text had been written about the site, no temple constructed, nor any image created. The goddess had not yet acquired a final form. The Maharaja along with his troupe of learned Brahmins and scribes must have recognized this significant opportunity.

Under the circumstances the Dogri Maharaja and his Kashmiri Brahmins possessed the tool needed for shaping ultimate sacred value, and through that value, solidifying legitimacy and authority. They must have envisioned a way to incorporate the Vaiṣṇava god Rāma into the Śaiva cult of Mahārajñī Khīr Bhavānī by infusing Rāma mythology in a yet-to-be-composed *mahātmyā* of the popular local goddess. Furthermore, they must have recognized that the oral legends and myths of the goddess were in a stage of flux and fermentation. Right before their eyes was the opportunity for infusing the significant attributes and character of Rāma into the Kashmir valley through the cultic paraphernalia of Khīr Bhavānī.[12]

The infusion did not happen overnight. It occurred gradually, in a religiously diplomatic manner, first by introducing a religious festival in honor of Rāma; then by constructing Rāma idols and shrines; and finally, by composing, with the help of the *paṇḍits* and *bhāśa bhattas* the *mahātmyā* texts of a local goddess whose story could appropriate the Rāma mythology. It took about quarter of a century to politically utilize the rapidly increasing fame of the pilgrimage center of Khīr Bhavānī.

Pratap Singh, 1885–1926. In 1885 Ranbir Singh's son, Pratap Singh, was enthroned. Like his father and grandfather, Pratap was enthusiastic about continuing a vigorous religious campaign by using funds from the royal Dharmarth Trust of the Raghunātha temple. In addition he constructed many new temples and schools for both boys and girls.[13] The Christian Missionary Society of London suggested opening missionary schools under the reign of Pratap Singh in 1881. Within a decade the primary school was raised to the level of high school, and the number of students was in the hundreds. Eventually a girls' high school and even a college was started. Besides the establishment of educational institutions, a food control department and flood protection measures (which prevented not only floods but subsequent famine and epidemics) were adopted. In short, by the turn of the present century Pratap Singh had helped to institute several important fiscal, judicial, educational, and social reforms.

For most Kashmiris, traditional deities had lost their meaning and were intelligible to only a few elites. Among the major factor that made these deities unintelligible, and therefore meaningless, was the rapidly changing sociopolitical milieu of the valley and the esoteric nature of Kashmiri Śaivism, zealously guarded by the "insiders." The images of Bhairava and Kālī were still sacred, but under the changed circumstances Kashmiri Hindus desperately needed new deities. This is because religion, in the words of one scholar,

> is a creative language of the human spirit. Its expressions are microcosmic of the human condition. . . . People's perception of the divine often reflects the whole range of human experience: the

struggle to come to terms not only with the givens of geographical, political, economic and social reality but also with what is understood to be "more than" these. (Clothey 1982, 5)

New deities were in fact emerging from the rapidly changing socioeconomic and religiopolitical matrix of Kashmiri culture. There was an atmosphere of optimistic uncertainty. The legends and myths of deities like the goddess Khīr Bhavānī represented a hope for the present and confidence in the future. Many *ślokas* in the *mahātmyā* sing praises of the changes ushered by the rule of the Great Empress *(mahārajñī)* who arrived in the age of *kaliyuga* "in order to destroy all troubles," "the one who grants *Rāmarājya* . . . and has made Satidesa her abode." She is the one who grants all wishes: sons, daughters, money, knowledge, and salvation. Her followers always get "treasure, grain, animals, home, and fields." She eliminates "terrible famine, devastating floods, and fearful kings." "Sickness, disease, and death can be escaped if the devotee meditates upon her." The mental anguish and the physical suffering Kashmiris had gone through, the changes that had come about, and the kind of changes they expected in the future are all clearly reflected in this description of the goddess Mahārajñī Khīr Bhavānī.

Pratap Singh strengthened his sacral position not only by instituting social reforms but also by constructing a marble temple at the pilgrimage center of Khīr Bhavānī, whose mythology was already appropriated with the mythology of Rāma through her *mahātmyā*. The marble shrine was elaborated by paving its periphery with Baramulla stone and furnishing it with decorative metal railings. The surrounding area was finished with smooth grey stone and dotted with shady elm and chinar trees. By this time Khīr Bhavānī's *mahātmyā* had already been composed and the contents of the new *mahātmyā* were memorized and recited, or else read to the throngs of visiting pilgrims from copies made of the sacred book by the local *purohitas*. The composition of the *mahātmyā* crystallized the pilgrimage center and the cultural concepts of the Kashmiri people. It also captured old as well as new religious symbols of a high level of culture. In short, Khīr Bhavānī's cultic paraphanalia—*mahātmyā*, temple, visual images, and so on—originated and flourished in the context of unique sociopolitical developments. This becomes clear as we consider the text itself.

IV. Content of the Mahātmyā *Text*

The content of the *mahātmyā Śrī Śrī Mahārajñī Pradhurbhāva* not only reflects the socioeconomic changes occurring during in the nineteenth century; it also expresses political repercussions of local religious currents. Furthermore, it shows the conflation of the Rāma mythology and the legends and myths of the goddess. Myths from the ancient epic *Rāmāyana* are appropriated in the new *mahātmyā*. The epic characters are adapted creatively in a dynamic arrangement.

By the fourth quarter of the nineteenth century, and for the first time in many centuries, Kashmiri Hindus lived without famine and adversity from the ruling class. As soon as the people had enough physical and psychological strength, revolutionary change found expression unconsciously and spontaneously in several forms; one avenue of expression was the cultus of the "new" Kashmiri goddess, Khīr Bhavānī.

The esotericism of heterodox Śaiva sects, the cults of *nāgas* and *piśāchas*, the traditional goddesses, and the comparatively recent cult of the god Rāma together form the literary matrix of the *mahātmyā Śrī Śrī Mahārajñī Pradhurbhāva* of the goddess Mahārajñī Khīr Bhavānī.

The *mahātmyā* of Khīr Bhavānī has three sections. The first two sections narrate the two versions of the origin myth of the goddess, and the third section is an homage paid to her by the Great God Bhairava. The following is an English abridgement of the Sanskrit *mahātmyā Śrī Śrī Mahārajñī Pradurbhāva.*[14]

Section 1

> Long ago there lived a demon named Rāvaṇa who vigorously did penance for a hundred thousand years. Finally the great god Bhairava appeared to him and advised Rāvaṇa to worship the maiden goddess who was even greater than he; one who surpassed all *guṇas:* the great goddess Śyāmā.
>
> The great-souled Rāvaṇa prayed to the great goddess for ten thousand years. When she ultimately appeared, Rāvaṇa invited her to live in his home. The goddess agreed and from then onward lived as the goddess Śyāmā/Kālī on the island kingdom of Laṅkā, in the house of Rāvaṇa. She was worshiped by her demon devotees who used meat and alcohol as the *pūjā* ingredients. At first, the goddess in her *tāmasī* form accepted such demonic offerings. However, she eventually became disgusted with them and decided to ascend toward the northern valley of Kashmir, the abode of Śiva. Guided by Hanumān, Devī came to the valley of Kashmir with countless *nāgas* (serpents), and she decided to settle down at the sacred *nāga* (spring) in the swamps of Tulmul. Here she became known as the *sāttvika* goddess Mahārajñī Khīr Bhavānī who dwells in a state of constant Spiritual Bliss. From then on, She only accepted *sāttvika* offerings of milk, sugar, and butter.[15]

Section 2

One day the demon Rāvaṇa was crying. Śiva, seeing him weep, asked the reason for his sorrow: Rāvaṇa wanted to possess Laṅkā. Śiva said that he would receive Laṅkā only if he underwent a great penance.

Wise Rāvaṇa did penance for ten thousand long years. Pleased, Śiva granted Rāvaṇa the kingdom of Laṅkā. Rāvaṇa further asked the Great God to give him the condition of a Bhairava. Lord Śiva granted him his boon.[16]

Arrogant in his strength, Rāvaṇa decided to destroy all the seers, people, and gods; he felt concern only for the happiness of the demons. In order to protect good souls and destroy the demons, god Rāma was born. Śrī Rāma, along with his wife Sītā, went to Laṅkā in order to kill Rāvaṇa and put an end to his destruction.[17]

Rāvaṇa, however, knew that Rāma was a devotee of Kālī/Śyāmā, so he decided to invite Rāma to the sacred arena at his island home where Śyāmā was enshrined and sacrifice him to the goddess. One day Rāma, along with his wife Sītā, appeared in the middle of the worshiping area. Rāvaṇa, with a terrible look, pronounced to Rāma that if he wanted to stay alive he should leave Sītā and go home, otherwise he would be sacrificed to Śyāmā. Rāma refused to leave. He said, "I will destroy you and then take Śyāmā home." Rāvaṇa became very angry. He took out his sword and ran to attack Rāma. At this time the angry goddess Śyāmā, her voice thundering like clashing clouds, said to Rāvaṇa, "Shame on you! I am going to the valley of Kashmir in the Himalayas, and I vow to follow vegetarianism." So Rāma asked Hanumān, the foremost of his devotees, the epitome of sexual renunciation, to take the Great Goddess to Kashmir. Śyāmā rode on the back of Hanumān and reached the village of Tulmul.

Section 3

Śiva was sitting on the *śail* peak, wearing an elephant skin on his body and a half moon in his crown. His eyes looked terrible. He laughed, recited, and read over and over the *mantra* of the goddess Mahārajñī Khīr Bhavānī. His wife Umā asked him why and what he was continuously murmuring. Śiva-Bhairava replied, "I recite fifteen-worded knowledge which is esoteric, unrevealed, and supreme and belongs to the goddess Śyāmā/Kālī, who is also called Mahārajñī. She is from the family of highest Brahmins and is the kingdom-bestowing goddess of knowledge and the destroyer of the calamities and poverty."

By worshiping and meditating upon the great goddess seers obtain salvation. All the wishes of all her devotees come true. Whoever recites her *mantra* and meditates on her *yantra* can certainly achieve Śiva-hood.[18]

V. Interpretation of the Content of the Mahātmyā

How was the name of the god Rāma slowly infused into the *mahātmyā?* How is the god Rāma made significant as the reader goes through the text? How does the cult of Khīr Bhavānī play the role of popularizing the name of Rāma in the valley? In the *mahātmyā* contemporary religious history is skillfully interwoven with the local legends of the goddess. The writer priests have conflated the story of the hero of epic *Rāmayana* with the origin myth of the goddess in order to introduce the cult of Rāma into the valley.

In the first section of the *mahātmyā* no direct reference is made to the name of the god Rāma. The name *Rāmarajya* is used to refer to the peaceful and prosperous kingdom ushered into the valley by the arrival of Khīr Bhavānī. The names *Rāmaduta* and *Rāmbhakta* are used to designate Hanumān, the symbol of sexual renunciation and the supreme devotee of Rāma, who is responsible for bringing the goddess Khīr Bhavānī to the valley and, in the process, becomes her devotee. Only once is the name *Rāma* used to describe the worshiper of the goddess Khīr Bhavānī in her form as Śyāmā.

By the time a reader/devotee completes the reading of the first section, curiosity about god Rāma is evoked and devotional interest toward him stirred. The sacred persona of Rāma is reflected as an ideal king, the creator of *Rāmarājya,* a supreme devotee of the goddess, and, most important of all, the lord of Hanumān, who is the foremost devotee of the goddess. Evidently Hanumān has no status in the pantheon of Kashmiri deities; yet when he carries Khīr Bhavānī on his shoulders, bringing her from the southern capital of Jammu to the northern valley of Kashmir, he expresses supreme devotion toward his deity.[19]

Hanumān's devotion toward the goddess further suggests the newly found relationship of the Dogri kings with Khīr Bhavānī as their earthly sacred relationship to Rāma is tied and equated with the relationship of divine Hanumān. The maharajas, like Hanumān, now symbolically become the devotees of the goddess as well. Inversely, the god of the royalty, Rāma, acquires the same position as the goddess Khīr Bhavānī. Thus, Rāma's name and position is slowly but surely slipped into the *mahātmyā* through the "back door."

In the second, longer section direct references to the god Rāma are made. His name is mentioned seventeen times. The text gradually acquires interesting new overtones and makes Rāma the hero of the story. Rāma refers to the goddess as Sītā instead of Śyāmā. The superimposition of the name *Sītā* over *Śyāmā* must be deliberate. By this superimposition Rāma becomes Śyāmā's husband, which makes him, according to the tradition, stronger than the goddess and in command. His divine position is elevated. After a deliberate connection, the names *Sītā* and *Śyāmā* are clearly split again. At Rāma's authority Hanumān carries Śyāmā on his back to the valley of Kashmir where she is known as Khīr Bhavānī, while Rāma takes Sītā to Ayodhya. The Dogri Vaiṣṇava god is successfully infused into the cult of the Śaiva goddess. Having made a strong linkage between the two deities, Rāma and Khīr Bhavānī, the name *Rāma* is absorbed in the main corpus of the second section of the text but is eventually dropped in the third.

The third section of the text is exclusively devoted to the goddess Khīr Bhavānī and does not mention Rāma even once. Absence of the name *Rāma* may indicate that the influence of the Rāma cult had been satisfactorily integrated. After the writer/priest had thoroughly infused a Vaiṣṇava flavor into the pantheon of Kashmiri local deities, by asserting the name and position of Rāma in the first two sections of the *mahātmyā Śrī Śrī Mahārajñī Pradhurbhāva,* the name *Rāma* could be omitted completely.

The composers of the *mahātmyā* wrote the text with clever eloquence by interweaving the imagery of the god Rāma's cult with the imagery of the goddess's myth. The characteristics of the two deities are integrated and synthesized and thus jell together, resulting into a multifaceted goddess. Her position in the final analysis remains supreme but not before elevating the imported god Rāma to almost as significant a position as her own.

VI. Conclusion

The study and analysis of the religiopolitical context in which the *mahātmyā Śrī Śrī Mahārajñī Pradhurbhāva* was composed, and the interpretation of its contents, bring two important conclusions into focus.

First, Hindu scriptures are not exhausted, or even best expressed, by the categories of *śruti* and *smṛti*. Scriptural text traditions continue to develop and evolve in response to unique religiopolitical circumstances. The case in point is that the *mahātmyā Śrī Śrī Mahārajñī Pradhurbhāva* written by *bhāśa bhattas* in consultation with *paṇḍits* through the authority of the Dogri Maharaja Ranbir Singh. The Vaiṣṇava Dogri rulers, with religion as a high priority, deliberately and methodically infused and imported the cult of Rāma into the pantheon of Kashmiri Tantric Śaiva deities through the composition of the *mahātmyā* of the goddess Khīr Bhavānī and by the introduction of festivals and temples. Gradually the "new" god was mythologically incorporated into the local religious mainstream, thus becoming part of the ongoing tradition. Dogri rulers thus played a significant role in shaping the religious landscape of the valley of Kashmir from the middle of the nineteenth to the first quarter of the twentieth century.[20] The reason for these strategies was to influence the inhabitants of the newly acquired territory in order to gain religiopolitical sanction from them. This religiously important and politically clever act not only fused the religious festivals of the Rāma cult into the valley but also revived ancient and mostly forgotten indigenous Śaiva traditions.

Second, in the context of Hinduism new deities arise at a juncture when a cultural group undergoes drastic religious and political changes (Clothey 1982). The old deities become otiose, because they reflect certain sensibilities to which the contemporary society cannot relate. Some of their symbolic meaning is forgotten, but some is retained; this conserved symbolic meaning expresses a deep ethos upon which new deities are grafted. The new deities, pregnant with complex cultural symbols, reflect human experiences. They incorporate the microcosm and the macrocosm, the ethos and the worldview, of the community. In just this way the new goddess, Khīr Bhavānī, expresses the worldview of the Kashmiris through her *mahātmyā* and other cultic paraphernalia and, in turn, promotes their cultural values.

Notes

1. Indologists unanimously agree that scholars working in the South Asian fields of humanities and social sciences are forced to create their own individual methodology for the purposes of any textual interpretation. It is generally suggested that methods should be developed out of a particular problem and that each scholar working in an individual ethnogeographic and linguistic area must create her or his own methodology. In the present paper Wendy O'Flaherty's "toolbox approach" has been utilized in order to see what kind of contextual meaning is revealed by all the collected data. I have relied on gazetteers, library catalogues, personal commentaries, and digests, all written during the last quarter of the nineteenth century.

2. *Mahātmyās* are Hindu sacred texts that narrate myths and legends of important deities of a particular geographic area. They extol attributes and characteristics of a particular deity, eulogize the deity's pilgrimage center, and prescribe the rites to be observed by the pilgrims. These scriptures are used as the handbooks by the local priests *(purohitas)* who work as the

guides of a pilgrimage center, reciting verses from these sacred books for the benefit of the pilgrims. More importantly, *mahātmyās* reflect the ethos and the worldview of the community and are therefore highly cherished by the local population. They belong to the same genre of literature as *Purāṇas.* Like *Purāṇas, mahātmyās* incorporate in their literary maze mythology, sacred symbols, rituals, and *itihāsa*—the political history that makes these texts immensely valuable to the historian of religions as a source of history.

3. In Kashmir the *mahātmyās* written in Śāradā are older than the ones composed in Devanāgarī script. "The *Devanāgarī* MSS written in Kashmir are all very modern. . . . These characters had come into more general use during the last thirty years only (1840s?) since the annexation of Kashmir to the Jammu dominions. . . . All *Devanāgarī* MSS are written by the professional scribes, the *Bhāsa Bhattas*" (Bühler 1877, 33). The Sanskrit text of the *mahātmyā Śrī Śrī Mahārajñī Pradhurbhāva* was printed for the first time in 1981, and the printed text embellished with symbolic illustrations, iconographical images, and the *yantra* of the goddess *Mahārajñī Khīr Bhavānī.*

4. The peoples of Kashmir, mostly Muslims now, were Hindus before their conversion to Islam from the fourteenth century onward. The Hindus who did not convert to Islam were Brahmins. Kashmiri *paṇḍits,* as they are called, claim to belong to the highest order of Brahmins. They are highly educated and at present form a strong minority. In the Kashmir valley the worship of *liṇgā/yonī* and Bhairava/Kālī was prevalent from the ancient times. Rāma worship was conspicuously obscure within the religious literature of Kashmir until the nineteenth century, when the Rāma/Hanumān cult was introduced by the Dogri rulers.

5. The position of Kālī in the context of Kashmiri Tantric Śaivism is brilliantly explained by Sanderson, who writes,

> The intensification of power is expressed in the language of ritual as the gradual emergence and eventual autonomy of Sakti. In the Śiva Siddhānta this feminine essence is suppressed to the extent that in daily ritual only the male polarity is worshiped, the mild and consortless Sadāśiva. In the Bhairava teachings, represented by the cult of Svaccānada, Śiva transcends this mild form and is joined in worship by his consort in the form of Aghoreśvari. Nonetheless at this level Bhairava is still dominant. In the Trika however this relation is reversed. The three goddesses Parā, Parāparā, and Aparā are enthroned above their Bhairavas as the principal recipients of worship. Finally in the Krama, the goddess alone remains. She is no longer Śiva's consort but pure power. This unleashing of the feminine from the control of the male is also the unleashing of impurity. To move from Siddhanta to Bhairava teachings is, from the point of view

> of the former to abandon the purity of orthodox, Veda-congruent discipline. With Krama sect of Kālī this cult of impurity reaches its greatest intensity. Its Agmic literature shows the unleashed feminine presiding over a subculture contaminated by violence and death. . . . The Śaiva householder of Kashmir cannot normally have had much contact with this esoteric and extreme form of his religion but even he was drawn into contact with its goddess in the one cremation ground ritual after his own death. (Sanderson 1986, 200–1)

6. Followers of Śiva Siddhānta worship Śiva in his mild form—the consortless Sadāśiva. In the iconographical images Sadāśiva is depicted as a prostrate corpse that serves as the throne of esoteric deities like Svacchānandabhairava. In the nineteenth-century images, Bhairava is shown as riding upon the back of the Sadāśiva image. See Kramrisch 1981.

7. The pilgrimage center of Śāradā and Beda had become almost unknown to the *paṇḍits* of Kashmir by the nineteenth century. Pathan and Sikh rule had much to do with the neglect into which the worship of the shrines had fallen. Alberuni, the Arab traveler, mentions a statue of Śāradā as one of the most famous metal idols of the Hindus. For the sacred sculptures of Kashmir, see Pal 1975. Kalhana writes that during the reign of Lalityaditya (eighth century C.E.), a king of Bengal came to Kashmir under the pretense of visiting the shrine of Sarada but in reality wanted to avenge the murder of their king by Lalityaditya. Whatever the historical value of the story, it is clear that the reference to the Śāradā temple would not have been made if it was not famous far beyond its limits (Stein 1979 [1900]).

8. This information and much of the interpretation of the contents of the *mahātmyā* under discussion are based on my paper "The Sacred Name Rāma and the Goddess Khīr Bhavānī," presented at the annual meeting of the American Academy of Religion, Chicago, 1988.

9. Until the end of the nineteenth century, Kashmiri indigenous religious tradition was kept alive by three kinds of Kashmiris: the Brahmins locally known as Kashmiri *paṇḍits, bhāśa bhattas, and purohitas.* The Kashmiri *paṇḍits* were serious scholars of Sanskrit Śāstras. They "still keep up the study of Sanskrit and live on *inams* allowances from the Maharaja and on fees which they receive for officiating as *āchāryas* or superintendents of ceremonies before the domestic fire and of *śraddhās* and . . . Śaiva worship" (Bühler 1877, 20). *Bhāśa bhattas* earned their livelihoods as scribes and by performing ceremonies at homes. Of much lower ranks were *purohitas,* who worked as guides at various pilgrimage centers. Their knowledge of Sanskrit was of the "scantiest kind and their reading confined to *mahātmyās* and devotional texts learned by heart without proper comprehension" (Stein 1979 [1900], 383).

10. Only Brahmin males were admitted to the *paṭhśala* of the temple, following the tradition of Vedic *āśramas.* It was under the patronage of Maharaja Hari Singh, Maharaja Pratap Singh's nephew, that the temple complex was opened to untouchables from 1932 onward (Ganhar 1974).

11. He remarks that on this day the weapons and instruments of war are hallowed. Three immense figures stuffed with gunpowder are made to represent Rāvaṇa and his two younger brothers. These are placed in the center of a large space away from the city. To represent Rāma, Sītā, and Laxman, three little boys are splendidly dressed and carried in a palanquin to the same place. Crowds of people gather together, and the maharaja sends his troops with guns. At a certain time one of the little boys, who is dressed up as the lord Rāma, steps forth from the palanquin and fires an arrow at the large figure representing Rāvaṇa, while the other boys discharge their arrows at the other two figures, exploding all the three figures with a tremendous noise. Then the guns rattle, the cannon roars, the people shout.

12. An interesting pen drawing of the goddess created in the late nineteenth century, in which the name *Rāma* in Devanāgarī script is literally ingrained in the iconographic image of the goddess Khīr Bhavānī, is notable in this regard (Wangu 1988b).

13. Dharmarth Trust was established by Maharaja Gulab Singh for the maintenance of existing temples and for the construction of new ones. The fund was designated as the treasury of Raghunāthjī, the family deity. The fund started with a personal donation of five lakh rupees by Maharaja Gulab Singh. His son Ranbir Singh set up a council for the administration of the endowment, in addition to setting up the library and the Sanskrit college. His tradition was carried on by his sons, especially Pratap Singh (Ganhar 1974).

14. For a complete translation and interpretation of the *mahātmyā Śrī Śrī Mahārajñī Pradhurbhāva,* see my Ph.D. dissertation, *The Cult of Khīr Bhavānī: Study, Analysis, and Interpretation of a Kashmiri Goddess,* University of Pittsburg, Pennsylvania, 1988.

15. The geographic journey of the goddess Khīr Bhavānī from the south to the north symbolizes the psychological ascent of a Tantric *sādhaka* from the state of *tamas,* through the state of *rajas,* to the final state of *sattva.* In the *mahātmyā* the three *guṇas* are symbolized by Rāvaṇa, Sītā, and the Hanumān/Khīr Bhavānī pair respectively. Moreover, this geographic as well as psychological pilgrimage is congruent with the physical journey of a *sādhaka's* dormant power: the *kundālinī śakti,* from the base of the spinal cord (the south of the subtle body) to the cranium at the top of the head (the north of the subtle body).

16. Rāvaṇa, the *Piśācha* king *par excellence,* is described as a wise *yogi* in the *mahātmyā*. He is proficient in *mantra* recitation, *yantra* meditation, and breath control *(pranāyama)* but has not reached that stage of *sādhana* that demands control of the sexual drives and mind.

17. Here for the first time in the *mahātmyā* the god Rāma is introduced, whose persona and character from now onward completely envelops the rest of the section.

18. The third section is an apotheosis of the goddess Khīr Bhavānī and is of esoteric nature. Here her three essential ingredients are described: *mantra, yantra, and kundālinī yoga.*

19. The iconographical motif of carrying a deity on one's shoulders is a gesture of extreme piety as depicted in the Kashmiri sacred paintings of the nineteenth century (Parimoo 1985).

20. In 1925 Maharaja Pratap Singh enthroned his nephew Hari Singh, as he did not have a male heir.

References

Bamzai, P. N.
1962 *The History of Kashmir.* New Delhi: Metropolitan Book.

Bühler, George
1877 "Detailed Report of a Tour in Search of Sanskrit MSS made in Kashmir, Rajputana, and Central India." *Journal of the Bombay Branch of the Royal Asiatic Society of Great Britain and Ireland.* Bombay, Branch 12. Extra Number, 34A.

Clothey, Fred
1982 "Sasta-Aiyanar-Aiyappan: The God as Prism of Social History." In *Images of Man: Religion and Historical Process In South Asia,* edited by Fred Clothey. Madras: New Era.

Das Gupta, J. B.
1968 *Jammu and Kashmir.* The Hauge: Martinus Nijhoff.

Drew, Federic
1877 *The Northern Barrier of India.* London: Edward Stanford.

Ganhar, J. N.
1974 *Jammu Shrines and Pilgrimages.* New Delhi: Ganhar.

Goetz, Hermann
1969 *Studies in the History of Art of Kashmir and the Indian Himalayas.* Wiesbaden: Otto Harrawitz.

Heesterman, J. C.
1985 *The Inner Conflict of Tradition: Essays in Indian Ritual, Kingship, and Society.* Chicago: University of Chicago Press.

Kaul, Anand
1924 *The Kashmiri Paṇḍit.* Calcutta: Thacker & Spink.

Koul, S. C.
1954 *Khīr Bhavānī Spring.* Srīnāgar: Utpal.

Kramrisch, Stella
1981 *New Manifestations of Shiva.* Philadelphia: Philadelphia Museum of Art.

Lawrence, Walter
1967 *The Valley of Kashmir.* 1895. Reprint Kashmir: Kesar.

Madan, T. N.
1982 "The Ideology of the Householder among the Kashmiri Paṇḍits." In *Way of Life: King, Householder, Renouncer,* edited by T. N. Madan. New York: Advent Books.

Pal, Pratapaditya
1975 *Bronzes of Kashmir.* New York: Hacker Art Books.

Pandey, K. C.
1963 *Abhinavagupta: An Historical and Philosophical Study.* 2d enl. and rev. ed. Varanasi: Chowkhamba Sanskrit Series Office.

Pannikar, K. M.
1930 *Gulab Singh 1792–1858: Founder of Kashmir.* Srinagar: Martin Hopkinson.

Parimoo, Ratan
1985 "Naran Murtzagar: The Maker of Images." *The India Magazine,* October, 64–70.

Rastogi, Navjivan
1979 *The Krama Tantricism of Kashmir.* Vol. 1. New Delhi: Motilal Banarsidass.

Sanderson, Alexis
1985 "Purity and Power among the Brahmins of Kashmir." In *The Category of the Person.* Cambridge: Cambridge University Press.

1986 "Mandala and Agmic Identity in the Trika of Kashmir." In *Mantras et Diagrammes Rituals dans L'Hindouisme.* Paris: Centre National de la Recherche Scientifique.

Stein, Aurel
1894 *Catalogue of the Sanskrit Manuscripts in the Raghunatha Temple Library of His Highness the Maharaja of Jammu and Kashmir.* Prepared for the Kashmir State Council. Bombay: Niranaya Sagara Press.

1979 *Kalhana's Rājtaraṅgiṇī: A Chronicle of the Kings of Kashmir.* 1900. Reprint. Two volumes. Delhi: Motilal Banarsidass.

Wangu, Madhu B.
1988a *The Cult of Khīr Bhavānī: Study, Analysis, and Interpretation of a Kashmiri Goddess.* Ph.D. diss., University of Pittsburgh.

1988b "The Sacred Name Rāma and the Goddess Khīr Bhavānī." Paper read at the annual conference of the American Academy of Religion, Chicago.

Part II

Traditional Hermeneutics in Other South Asian Religions

Ten

Śvetāmbar Mūrtipūjak Jain Scripture in a Performative Context

John E. Cort

Introduction

A persistant problem for Western scholars of religion has been to perceive the ways in which participants of various religious traditions have themselves perceived and understood the texts of their traditions. Not surprisingly, many early scholars of religion searched for a text or class of texts that closely resembled the authoritative text or texts of European traditions, the Bible in its Jewish and Christian forms.[1] Possession of a sacred scripture was (and still is) oftentimes seen as a defining characteristic of a great world religion. But early scholars did more than just search for the Bibles of other traditions. Based upon an understanding of the role of canon within the Christian tradition, and the related principle of the clearly defined relative authority of different classes of texts, scholars sought for similar canons and principles of authoritativeness among other religious traditions. The deleterious effects of this application of Christian understandings of the canon to other traditions is clearly seen in the history of the Westen academic study of the Jain textual tradition. In this chapter I will briefly outline the Western academic understandings of the nature of the Śvetāmbar Jain "canon" of "scripture," and then within that framework discuss some of the ways in which the contemporary Śvetāmbar Mūrtipūjak Jains of Gujarat understand and perceive their own textual and scriptural tradition/s.

In both his 1975 Ph.D. dissertation (Folkert 1975, 40–56) and an unpublished 1979 article entitled "Scripture and Continuity in the Jaina Tradition," Folkert discussed the history behind the present academic understanding that the Śvetāmbar Mūrtipūjak Jains "possess" or "believe in'' a ''canon'' of forty-five Āgamas.[2] These forty-five texts consist of eleven Aṅgas, twelve Upāṅgas, six Chedasūtras, four Mūlasūtras, ten Prakīrṇakas, and two miscellaneous texts; the names of the texts vary in different lists. This understanding of a ''canon'' of forty-five Āgamas is found in all the standard works on the Jains, and while strictly speaking it is not incorrect, the problematic nature of this formulation has largely gone unnoticed. The problem lies in part with the status of this list of forty-five Āgamas within Jain history, and in part with the stated contents of the list.

The concept of the group of forty-five Āgamas was known to Western scholars from some of the earliest descriptions of the Jains. Both Francis Buchanan Hamilton (1827, 539) and William Miles (1835, 359, 361) wrote that the Śvetāmbars believe in forty-five Āgamas (also called ''Sūtras'' and ''Siddhāntas''), although H. H. Wilson (1862, 281) noted that the particulars of this list tended to be ''of a loose and popular character.''

A watershed in this formulation came in 1882, when Georg Bühler published a list of titles of the forty-five works in the Jain canon. Bühler received this list from Śrīpūjya Jinamuktisūri of the Kharatara Gaccha in 1871, a point noted only by A. Guérinot among subsequent authors. It became enshrined in Jain scholarship several years later in Albrecht Weber's ''Uber die heiligen Schriften der Jaina'' (1883–85). This list has been repeated by virtually every author writing on the Jains for the past century. But as Folkert points out, no one has been adequately aware of the problematic nature of Bühler's list being based on only a single source. Had this list been understood as merely one among several possible ways to characterize the Śvetāmbar Jain understanding of their own textual tradition, it would have been adequate. But over time, as it has been repeated by scholar after scholar, it has become the *only* way Jain scriptures are presented. Other ways in which the Jains, both Śvetāmbar and Digambar, have understood their textual tradition have been downplayed or even disregarded, and the fact that even Śvetāmbars have not regarded the subject in a uniform manner has been obscured. Most problematic is the way this mid-nineteenth-century list of forty-five Āgamas has been projected back into the earlier history of the Jains, as scholars have mistakenly assumed that the nineteenth-century list of forty-five texts coincides with the texts that were collected at the third Jain council at Valabhi under Devardhigaṇi Kṣamāśramaṇa in the mid-fifth century C.E. For example, Dayanand Bhargava (1968, 228) has written of the council of Valabhi, ''It was at this council that *Āgamas* assumed their present form.'' Similarly, Carlo della Casa (1971, 351) has written, ''The Śvetāmbars established their canon at the council of Valabhi''; U. P. Shah (1977, 12) has written, ''The fourth and last Jaina council, at Valabhi *c.* A.D. 454 or 467, is said to be the source of the existing Śvetāmbar Jaina canon''; Padmanabh S. Jaini (1979, 51–52) has written that at the council of Valabhi, Devardhigaṇi Kṣamāśramaṇa "compiled the final redaction of the extant canon and had it committed to writing in its entirety"; and most recently N. Shântâ (1985, 120–21) has written that the texts redacted and classified by Devardhigaṇi Kṣamāśramaṇa at Valabhi "sont ces *Âgama* que nous possédons aujourd'hui." These last four sources quoted comprise two standard encyclopedia articles on the Jains, and the two most important and authoritative scholarly books written on the Jains. So this misunderstanding occupies a central position in the academic understanding of the Jains.[3]

I. Canon-near and Canon-far

The problematic nature of both the precise contents of the list of forty-five Āgamas, and the very notion that there are forty-five Āgamas that are in some way "authoritative" or "canonical," has been ignored in subsequent scholarship. Folkert (1979, 10), citing H. R. Kapadia (1941, 30, 58), observed that the formulation of forty-five Āgamas does not show up in Jain literature until the thirteenth century, from which time it has existed side by side with another, older formulation. The older formulation, which is found in lists of texts given in the *Nandī Sūtra* and *Anuyogadvāra Sūtra*, employs a fundamental distinction between the eleven Aṅgas and sixty or more other important texts called collectively *aṅgabāhya*, or texts "external to the Aṅgas."[4] Folkert (1979, 9) noted further that the collective referent of both terms "is not specific texts or scriptures, but the class of knowledge that the Jainas term *suyanāṇa [śrutajñāna]*." The *aṅgabāhya* category is further subdivided into three broad categories: *āvassaya [āvaśyaka]*, or texts containing the rites for the six obligatory daily observances of all mendicants; *kāliya [kālika]*, texts to be studied at specific times; and *ukkāliya [utkālika]*, or texts that can be studied at any time.[5] Folkert (1979, 9) discussed two features of this older categorization:

> First, the scheme is based . . . on distinctions in types of things that one must know, and not on a distinction among texts per se. Second, the scheme shows a steady progression outward from the knowledge most directly derived from Mahāvīra (the aṅga-s), through the essentials of monastic praxis, to knowledge that may be handled incidentally.

When the various lists of texts contained in the Jain Āgamas are seen in light of this scheme, we find that whereas all lists are in agreement concerning the eleven core texts, the Aṅgas, the area of disagreement lies in the precise makeup of the texts that are *aṇgabāhya*, outside the Aṅgas.

"However," Folkert (1979, 10) observed, "when a scheme like this is one's frame of reference, the variation is not necessarily a grave problem." The variation is not among conflicting authoritative texts, but among different texts that contain essentially the same information, and so can largely replace one another.

In a later article based in large part upon his research into the Jain "canon," Folkert (1989) argued that the confusion in the academic understanding of the Jain texts resulted from a fundamental misunderstanding on the part of Bühler, Weber, and subsequent scholars concerning what kind of "canon" they were dealing with in the Jain case. Folkert developed a rough typology of canons, using the names *Canon I* and *Canon II* to designate the two different types of canons:

> Canon I denotes normative texts, oral or written, that are present in a tradition principally by the force of a vector or vectors. Canon II refers to normative texts that are more independently and distinctively present within a tradition, that is, as pieces of literature more or less as such are currently thought of, and which themselves often function as vectors . . . By "vector" is meant the means or mode by which something is carried; thus Canon I's place in a tradition is largely due to its "being carried" by some other form of religious activity; and Canon I's significance for a tradition cannot be grasped fully without reference to its carrier and to the relationship between the two. The same meaning applies to vector where Canon II may function as a "carrier" of religious activity. The most common vector of Canon I is ritual activity, but other significant carriers are also to be found. Canon II most commonly serves as a vector of religious authority, but it is also to a large degree a carrier of ritual iconolatry and/or individualist piety. (Folkert 1989, 173)

Thus, in the case of the Jain canon, the early scholars found in the largely ignored *aṅga/aṅgabāhya* distinction a principle of textual categorization understood by the tradition itself as a Canon I type, but understood by the scholars as a Canon II type. As Folkert observed, this confusion is most clearly seen when one looks at two features of the Jain canon: the commentarial traditions, and the ritual usage of the texts.[6]

> Scholars who thought (and think) of scriptures in Canon II modes are likely to do what Jaina scholars have done: they ignore or deprecate the commentaries . . . in their Canon II orientation, the early editors and translators did not wait for or insist on a full commentarial context before pushing ahead with publication and analysis of the scriptures. (Folkert 1989, 176)

I will discuss the ritual usage and understanding of part of the Śvetāmbar "canon" below. But first, in an effort to clarify Folkert's terminology, I will borrow and adapt a terminology developed by Clifford Geertz and retitle the units of Folkert's typology "Canon-near" and "Canon-far." Geertz (1983, 57–58) uses the terms *experience-near* and *experience-distant*[7] to distinguish between two different kinds of knowledge or understanding:

> An experience-near concept is, roughly, one that someone—a patient, a subject, in our case an informant—might himself naturally and effortlessly use to define what he or his fellows see, feel, think, imagine, and so on, and which he would readily understand when similarly applied by others. An experience-distant concept is one that specialists of one sort or another—an analyst, an experimenter, an ethnographer, even a priest or an ideologist—employ to forward their scientific, philosophical, or practical aims.

In a Canon-near text, primacy and authority are defined by praxis and the resultant contextualized understanding, whereas in a Canon-far text primacy and authority are located in some intrinsic ontological value of the texts themselves. Folkert (1989, 171) noted that a pervasive background problem in the comparative study of scripture/s is "the Christian, specifically Protestant, fascination with the Bible as a 'sacred book'—a fascination that is actually a dimension of Christian faith itself." A canon, however, is not necessarily sacred or in any way ontologically special. A Canon-near changes with time and place, and authority flows from the accumulated tradition into the texts; a Canon-far is (more or less) fixed and closed, and authority is conveyed, or vectored, via the texts. These are not mutually exclusive categories, and many texts exhibit both Canon-near and Canon-far characteristics. These categories are ideal types, rarely found in their pure form in practice, and as such are intended less as descriptive categories than as interpretive categories.[8]

In the remainder of this essay I will look at several instances that provide insight into contemporary Śvetāmbar Mūrtipūjak Jain understandings of their tradition's "scriptures." The first of these is an instance also cited by Folkert, that of the *Kalpa Sūtra*.

II. The Recitation of the Kalpa Sūtra

The *Kalpa Sūtra* is probably the best known of all Jain texts. As early as 1807, H. T. Colebrooke (1807, 206) described it as "a work of great authority among the *Jainas.*" It was one of the first Jain texts to be translated into English, by Rev. J. Stevenson in 1847. There have been at least three subsequent English translations, that by Hermann Jocobi in 1884 in volume 22 of the *Sacred Books of the East* being the best known.[9]

The contents of the *Kalpa Sūtra* indicate one way in which it is a central text for the Śvetāmbar Jains. The first and longest section contains detailed biographies of the twenty-fourth, twenty-third, twenty-second, and first Jinas of the current era (Vardhamāna Mahāvīra, Pārśvanātha, Neminātha, and Ṛṣabhanātha/Ādinātha), as well as brief formulaic biographical data on the other twenty Jinas. The second section, the "Sthavirāvalī," is a detailed list of the important Śvetāmbar *sādhus* from the time of Mahāvīra down to Devardhigaṇi Kṣamāśramaṇa, who probably redacted the text in the fifth century C.E. The third section, the "Sādhu Sāmācārī," gives the rules for the proper conduct of the mendicants during the rainy season retreat. Included in this section is the description of the performance of Paryuṣaṇa.[10]

As Folkert (1989, 175) noted, the placement of the *Kalpa Sūtra* within the forty-five Āgama Jain canon provided some difficulty for the early scholars. The *Kalpa Sūtra* as translated by Stevenson, Jacobi, and the others is the eighth chapter of the *Daśāśrutaskandha,* one of the Chedasūtras.[11] As such, it does not occupy a central position within the canon of the forty-five Āgamas. In fact, when Jacobi published his critical edition of the text in 1879, he thought that it was completely separate from the forty-five Āgamas, and was placed in the seemingly awkward position of having to explain the central value and popularity of a text that lay outside the perceived Canon-far scriptural core of the tradition. This misperception was corrected by Weber, and the correction was duly noted by Jacobi in the introduction to his 1884 English translation. Nonetheless, the importance of this text cannot be understood solely by reference to its somewhat marginal placement within the forty-five Āgamas; rather, as Folkert (1989, 175–76) notes, for the popularity and value of the text to be understood, one must see it in its ritual and commentarial context.

The most important annual festival of the Śvetāmbar Jains, as well as one of the oldest, is the autumnal Paryuṣaṇ.[12] As mentioned above, the history of this festival is found in the *Kalpa Sūtra,* and the recitation of the *Kalpa Sūtra* is one of the principal activities of Paryuṣaṇ. The festival lasts for eight days in the months of Śrāvaṇ and Bhādarvo (Bhādrapada). Since the festival falls during the four-month rainy season (*comāsu, cāturmāsa*), when all mendicants cease their travel (*vihār*) and reside temporarily in a mendicant rest house (*upāśray*), it is celebrated by the entire fourfold congregation of *sādhus* (male mendicants), *sādhvīs* (female mendicants), *śrāvaks* (laymen), and *śrāvikās* (laywomen) together. The principal activity for the first three days is a set of sermons by the *sādhus*, concerning the five duties for Paryuṣaṇ and the eleven annual duties enjoined on every Jain layperson.

On the fourth day the recitation of the *Kalpa Sūtra* begins. Hundreds of manuscripts of the *Kalpa Sūtra,* some written in gold ink, have been copied over the centuries for use in this recitation. On the afternoon of the third day an auction is held in the mendicant rest house among the laity for the honor of presenting the recitation copy of the *Kalpa Sūtra* the next day. The copy is taken in a small procession to the home of the person who wins the auction, where it is worshiped with devotional songs and then kept overnight (see Fischer and Jain 1977, 15 and plates 145–46; Folkert 1990, 59–60). On the morning of the fourth day the book is covered with a muslin wrapper and blessed by having *vāskep* (*vāsakṣepa:* auspicious sandalwood powder) sprinkled on it. The book is then placed on a metal plate, which in turn is covered with an embroidered cloth. This plate is carried back to the rest house on the head of a young woman in the family. She is accompanied by musicians and preceded by a man who purifies the ground by sprinkling on it water from that morning's *pūjā* in the temple.

The book is brought into the house and placed in front of the *sādhu* who will deliver the sermon. The laity who are present stand and sing devotional songs to the knowledge (*jñān*) embodied in the text. *Jñān pūjā* is then performed to the book: people wave metal plates of fruit, flowers, sweets, incense, and a lamp in front of the book, sprinkle more *vāskep* onto the book, and dab rice water onto the reflection of the book in a mirror.[13] The congregation then sings another song to the book, each person bowing in *pranām* between each verse.

The recitation of the *Kalpa Sūtra* takes four days, in daily morning and afternoon sessions of roughly two hours each. Very little of the text that is recited, however, is the Prakrit *Kalpa Sūtra* as edited and translated by scholars. Over the centuries there have been many commentaries written on the text; Vinaya Sāgar (1977, vii-xi) lists seventy-six commentaries from the sixth to twentieth centuries. The most popular of these is the Sanskrit *Subodhikā*, composed in 1640 C.E. by Vinayavijaya. The Gujarati translation of the *Subodhikā* is recited along with the Prakrit root text, and additional oral commentary is provided by the *sādhu* according to his skill and inclination. Because of the large amount of material to be covered, most *sādhus* rush through both the Prakrit and Gujarati text in a singsong manner. Unlike an academic lecture or paper presentation, the purpose of this recitation is not to communicate the contents of the text; rather, it is to ensure the recitation of every syllable of the text.

The sermon on the morning of the eight and final day of Paryuṣaṇ consists of the *sādhu* starting over and reciting the entire Prakrit root text of the *Kalpa Sūtra*. On this occasion, however, the text is not known as the

Kalpa Sūtra, but rather as the *Bārasā* (1,200) *Sūtra*, referring to the fact that the Prakrit text consists of just over 1,200 *granthas* (units of thirty-two syllables). This difference in nomenclature points up one way in which the *Kalpa Sūtra* has been understood by the Jains that has been missed by scholars. When a Jain refers to the *Kalpa Sūtra*, he or she does not refer to the same text as a scholar. The *Kalpa Sūtra* is understood by a Jain to consist of both the Prakrit root text translated by Jacobi et al. and the Sanskrit and vernacular commentary recited during the fourth through seventh days of Paryuṣaṇ. When referring to the Prakrit text alone, which is recited on the eighth day, he or she is more likely to call it the *Bārasā Sūtra*. Similarly, quotations from Aṅgas or others of the Āgamas in sermons or popular tracts will often be from what a scholar would distinguish as a later commentary on the text. But the distinction between root text and later commentary is oftentimes not felt to be all that important, as the community's understanding of the text is mediated almost solely by the commentary, and it is said that the commentary makes explicit what was implied in the root text anyway. This underlines Folkert's contention that a religious tradition's understanding of a text cannot be comprehended devoid of the commentarial tradition.

Before the recitation of the *Bārasā Sūtra* on the eighth day it is worshiped in a manner similar to that described above for the *Kalpa Sūtra*. The recitation itself is so rapid-fire as to be unintelligible, even if anyone in the audience should understand Prakrit. The *sādhu's* location within the text is therefore indicated by the public showing (*darśan*) of illustrations of the text. As one *sādhu* recites the text, another *sādhu* hands to a young layboy dressed in pure *pūjā* clothes the proper page to hold aloft. Formerly these pages were hand painted; nowadays, most congregations use modern printed reproductions (see *Kalpasūtram [Bārasāsūtram] Sacitram* 1980). As each picture is displayed, people in the congregation bow their heads to it.

These illustrations form a visual commentary to the *Kalpa Sūtra*. The earliest extant illustrated manuscript of the *Kalpa Sūtra* dates from 1278 C.E. (Singh 1977, xii), and dozens have been produced in subsequent centuries. The illustrations are of various episodes in the lives of the Jinas and a few of the more important *sādhus* of the centuries after Mahāvīra. But while the paintings are displayed to illustrate the Prakrit root text, and most illustrated manuscripts contain only the root text, a number of the paintings in fact are of events found only in the later commentaries or in other, independent works. Of the 101 separate incidents discussed by Norman Brown (1934) in his detailed study of the *Kalpa Sūtra* illustrations, only 85 are explicitly mentioned in the *Kalpa Sūtra*. For explanations of the other 16 scenes, he had to rely on medieval narrative texts such as Jinabhadragaṇi Kṣamāśramaṇa's eleventh-century *Viśeṣāvaśyakabhāṣya*, Hemacandrasūri's twelfth-century *Triṣaṣṭiśalākāpuruṣacaritra* and *Pariśiṣṭaparvan*, Devendrasūri's thirteenth-century *Uttarādhyayanasūtra Ṭīkā*, and Bhāvadevasūri's thirteenth-century *Pārśvanātha Caritra*.

We thus find within the Jain tradition multiple understandings of the nature and content of this text: (1) as the *Bārasā Sūtra* consisting of only the Prakrit root text; (2) as the *Kalpa Sūtra* consisting of the Prakrit root text, the Sanskrit commentary, and its vernacular translation; (3) and as the body of stories that are illustrated in the paintings. To these understandings we then need to add a fourth, one that has been imported into a narrow stratum of Jain society through exposure to Western Scholarship. In this understanding the *Kalpa Sūtra* is the Prakrit root text alone, standing devoid of commentary and paintings, almost like a Protestant Bible shorn of its Catholic commentarial tradition. This fourth, scholarly understanding, however, does not fully overlap with any one of the understandings found within the Jain tradition itself.

III. Contemporary Śvetāmbar Mūrtipūjak Jain Scripture Worship

I said above that the list of forty-five Āgamas published by Bühler and Weber was only one of several understandings of the Śvetāmbar Jain "canon"current in the nineteenth century. But it was certainly the dominant understanding within the tradition, and has continued to be so today. I will now turn to two related ways in which that understanding is exhibited within the Jain community. Both of these are indigenous forms of scripture worship.

In the late eighteenth and early nineteenth centuries, several reform-minded Śvetāmbar *sādhus* in Gujarat composed a number of popular *pūjās* for use by the laity. These *pūjās* are devotional rituals, based on the daily *aṣṭaprakārī pūjā*, performed by the laity under the leadership of either an experienced layman or a professional ritual expert (*vidhikār*) on the occasion of some praiseworthy event such as a mendicant initiation (*dīkṣā*), the promotion of a mendicant to a higher formal status (*padvī*), an image installation (*pratiṣṭhā*), or the completion of a long fast by a mendicant or layperson. The *pūjā* is a public expression of approval (*anumodan*) of the event at hand. The congregation gathers in the open, public part of a temple, the *gūḍh maṇḍap*. The core rite consists of offerings of water, flowers, rice, etc., onto or before a metal Jina image that is situated on a bathing stand in the *gūḍh maṇḍap* in front of the main shrine (*gabhāro, garbhagṛha*). Between each offering a number of songs are sung, some by professional musicians, most by the assembled congregation, in a sentiment of devotion to the Jina. The songs are grouped around the central concept of the *pūjā*, which may or may not be integrally linked to the event in praise of which the *pūjās* is held. There are *pūjā* to the five *kalyāṇaks* (the beneficial events of conception, birth, initiation, enlightenment, and liberation) in the lifetime of a Jina, to the nine central principles of Jain belief,[14] to the eight kinds of karma, and to the forty-five Āgamas, among other topics.

Pūjās to the forty-five Āgamas were composed by two of the most popular of the *pūjā* composers. Vīr Vijay (1773–1854) composed his *Pīstālīś Āgam Pūjā* in Ahmedabad in 1825, and Rūp Vijay (?–1849) composed his *Pīstālīś Āgam Pūjā* four years later in 1829. There is some slight discrepancy in the lists of Āgamas contained in the two *pūjās*, a discrepancy that might have troubled the earlier Western scholars on Jainism, but that was recognized by Vīr Vijay (1986b, 270) when he said of the *payaṇṇas (prakīrṇakas)*, the set of ten texts in which most discrepancies occur:

Today there are many *payaṇṇas*
  but according to all the authorities
they should be counted as ten
  of the pleasing forty-five [Āgamas].[15]

Individual verses are devoted to each of the Āgamas to form a miniature catalogue of their contents for the benefit of the laity. Of more interest to us, however, are the verses in which the authors describe the rationale behind worship of the Āgamas. Vīr Vijay (1986b, 262) says:

The sun of enlightenment has set,
  but the lamp shines in the temple;
for people in this fifth spoke of time
  the Āgams shine.

. . .

To do *bhakti* of *jñān*
  is to do *pūjā* of the Jin and the homeless [*sādhus*];
therefore *pūjā* and *bhakti*
  of the Āgam are comprehensive.

To obtain the benefit of *jñān*
  place the books in front [of the congregation]
and establish the image of the Jin on its seat
  in a beautiful manner.

. . .

Holding the Āgam in their hearts
  people do *pūjā* of Śrī Jincand [the Jina];
object and subject of meditation become one
  and the final bliss is obtained.[16]

The first verse states a fundamental assumption of Jain cosmology—the fact that enlightenment and liberation are unattainable on this earth in the current fifth spoke of time—but goes on to assert the Āgamas are still accessible as a source of ultimately salvific knowledge. Worship of this knowledge is then equated with worship of the Jina and the mendicants, those who are further along the path to liberation (*mokṣa-mārg*) than are the laity, and who for this reason are to be worshiped by the laity. Worship of the knowledge embodied in the books of the Āgama is further equated with the worship of the image of the Jina in the temple. Elsewhere, Vīr Vijay (1986b, 278) explicitly says, "Serve the Jin and the Jin-Āgam as one and the same."[17] Similarly, Rūp Vijay (1986, 341) says,

Do *pūjā* with full sentiment
  of the Jin and the Jin-Āgam;
they carry one across the ocean of rebirth
  and one attains a pure nature.[18]

Finally, the individual is advised to transcend outward worship in favor of internal worship, holding the Āgamas in the heart, so that the qualities inherent in the Āgamas become manifest in the worshiper.

This progression of acts and attitudes rests on the principle of *anumodan*, the same as that behind *pūjā* to the *mūrti* of the Jina in a temple (see Cort 1989, 398–401). This is also the logic that underlies the efficacy of *pūjās* such as that to the forty-five Āgamas for everyone involved. Jain theologians argue that just as one accrues karma by approving of a sinful act such as murder on the part of another, so by approving (*anumodan*) of a positive action, one manifests in one's soul the virtues embodied in that action. In the case of a *mūrti* in a temple, one is approving of the qualities of dispassion (*vītarāgatā*) and enlightenment (*kaivalya*) symbolized by the *mūrti* and embodied by the liberated Jina. In the case of the Āgamas, one is approving of the salvific knowledge contained in and symbolized by the Āgamas.

Such an attitude does not require that one actually read the Āgamas to benefit from the salvific knowledge contained in them. This is clear from the formula of *karvū/karāvū/anumodan*: one can gain merit and scrub off obstructing karma by performing correct deeds (*karvū*), by having someone else perform correct deeds (*karāvū*), or by approving of that performance by another (*anumodan*). Similarly, many people believe that one need not understand the recited text of the *Kalpa Sūtra* or *Bārasā Sūtra* to attain the merit of listening to the entire recitation.

The benefit to be gained from the worship of the Āgamas in these two *pūjas* also underlies the more recent phenomenon of temples to the forty-five Āgamas. These temples, known as Āgam Mandirs, are one result of the late-nineteenth- and early-twentieth-century reform movement among the Śvetāmbar Mūrtipūjak Jains. This movement, under the joint leadership of a number of charismatic *sādhus* and the Jain Śvetāmbar Conference, had a profound and little-studied impact upon the Śvetāmbar Mūrtipūjak community.[19] One major focus of the movement was the rediscovery of much Jain history through the organization, study, and, in some cases, publication of the hundreds of thousands of manuscripts in the Jain storehouses (*bhaṇḍārs*) in Patan, Cambay, Ahmedabad, Jaisalmer, Limbdi, and other places. In part as a result of this movement, and in part as a result of interaction with the first generation of European scholars, an effort was made to compile a critical edition of the eleven Aṅgas, the central texts in the Āgama. An edition was prepared by Ācārya Ānandsāgarsūri (1875–1950) and published in Surat by the Āgamoday Samiti. (This effort is still in progress. The re-editing of the Āgamoday editions was begun by Muni Puṇya Vijay [1895–1971] and has been continued by Muni Jambū Vijay, with the first volume of this re-edition released in 1978 and distributed by Motilal Banarsidass.) As a result of his efforts, Ānandsāgarsūri was given the honorific title Āgamoddhārak, "the renovator of the Āgamas."[20] In addition to the text editing, he also had his lay devotees publish a journal called *Āgam Jyot* (Lamp of the Āgama) and was the inspiration behind four Āgam Mandirs, temples devoted to worship of the Āgamas.

The first of these temples was consecrated in 1935 in Palitana at the base of Śatruñjay Hill, and the second, in Surat (where Ānandsāgarsūri spent his last years) in 1948. Two others are currently under construction, in Pune in Maharashrta, and in Shankheshvar in North Gujarat. The texts of the forty-five Āgamas are installed on the walls of the temples—in marble at Palitana, and on copper plates at Surat and Shankheshvar.[21] At Shankheshvar and Surat the central image (*mūḷ nāyak*) is of Mahāvīra, for it is his teachings that are embodied in the Āgamas. At Shankheshvar the image of Mahāvīra is flanked by images of his two chief disciples (*gaṇadharas*), Gautama Svāmī and Sudharmā Svāmī, who were responsible for the continuation of Mahāvīra's teachings following his *mokṣa*. At Palitana the main image is a four-faced (*caumukhjī*) one of the four eternal Jinas (Ṛṣabha, Candrānan, Vāriṣeṇa, and Vardhamāna), so-called because in every cycle of time "names of these four are always repeated and they flourish in any of the fifteen karmabhūmis" (Shah 1987, 86). This image indicates the eternal and universal nature of the knowledge embodied in the Āgamas. Four-faced images are also used to represent the Jina giving his or her first sermon subsequent to enlightenment while seated atop the cosmic preaching stand known as a *samavasaraṇa*, and so directly symbolize the Jina's teachings. At Palitana there are forty-five additional four-faced images to correspond to the forty-five Āgamas. The Palitana temple has seen further extensions of the *Āgama-bhakti*. The Siddhacakra Mandir has as its main image not a Jina but a three-dimensional *siddhacakra*, the *maṇḍala* containing the above-mentioned nine fundamental principles of Jainism. In subsidiary shrines are found images of each of the twenty-four Jinas, and each of the 116 *gaṇadharas*, or leaders of the *sādhu* congregations established by each Jina. The walls themselves hold the texts of the Niryuktis, the oldest strata of commentaries on the Āgamas, carved in marble. The Namaskār Mahāmantra Mandir has enshrined a painted plaque of the Namaskār Mantra, the core Jain mantra chanted daily by almost all Jains (see Jaini 1979, 162–63). The Guru Mandir has an image of Ānandsāgarsūri, and on the wall, copper plates containing the *Bārasā Sūtra*.

The core ritual performed in one of these Āgam Mandirs is the *aṣṭaprakārī pūjā* performed in any other temple. The principal focus of ritual activity is still the image of the Jina. But just as most temples have illustrations or plaques (*paṭs*) of some of the important Jain *tīrths* such as Śatruñjay, Girnār, Ābū, Aṣṭāpad, or Sammet Śikhar, to which the worshiper addresses one or more hymns of veneration (*vandan*) in the course of his or her worship, at the Āgam Mandirs the engraved Āgamas upon the walls provide the opportunity for direct worship and praise of both the Āgamas and the *jñān* they contain.

IV. Contemporary Understandings of "Śāstra"

Let me now switch directions slightly and bring in a third instance that exhibits something of the contemporary Śvetāmbar Mūrtipūjak Jain understanding of their textual/scriptural tradition and in particular addresses the question of the relative authoritativeness of texts. One of the major foci of my fieldwork was *mūrtipūjā* and the contemporary theological and historical justifications for this central ritual activity. A number of times both in conversation and in reading I came across a statement in justification of *mūrtipūjā* to the effect that, "It is said in the *śāstras*, 'In this difficult time, the Jina-image and the Jina-Āgama are the supports of the faithful.' "[22] The *śāstra* that is quoted is in fact another *pūjā* of Vīr Vijay, the *Cosaṭh Prakārī Pūjā* composed in 1818 (Vīr Vijay 1986a, 214). In other words, as one *sādhu* explained to me, *śāstra* in contemporary parlance merely refers to any printed religious book. The authoritative nature of the text cited lies not in any inherent ontological status of the text, but merely in its being relatively old or "former" (*pūrva*). *Śastra* does not coincide with the generic category of *pustak* or *copḍā; śāstra* refers only to a religious book, whereas the latter terms include secular and non-Jain religious literature.

I had begun my fieldwork with the assumption of a Canon-far concept of textual authority. I had assumed that the authoritativeness of a text was linked with its age and therefore with its greater proximity to Mahāvīra as the enlightened and therefore ultimate voice of authority. But here on an issue of central importance to the Śvetāmbar Mūrtipūjak Jain self-identity, and an issue that has been the subject of both extensive sermonizing by mendicants on the proper way to perform the ritual, and vigorous polemics concerning its appropriateness, the source I found most often quoted as authoritative was a nineteenth-century devotional *pūjā*. The authoritativeness of this text, however, lies not in its age, but rather in the fact that it is one of the most frequently performed of the many *pūjās*. The particular part of the *Cosaṭh Prakārī Pūjā* in which this verse is located is the *Antarāy Karm Pūjā*, which is commonly performed in commemoration of the virtues of a recently deceased Jain layperson. What from a Canon-far perspective is a marginal text is from a Canon-near perspective seen to be in fact a central text.

That this is not an atypical instance is demonstrated by another example. In 1986 a series of articles and letters were published in the Bombay edition of the Gujarati newspaper *Saṅdeś* concerning the appropriateness of *guru pūjan*. In the face of criticism that such a rite has no justification within the Jain tradition, but was an improper borrowing from the Vallabha *saṃpradāya*, an attempt was made to establish the *śāstrik* position on *guru pūjan*.[23] There ensued a rather vitriolic exchange of letters from Jain students, laymen, and one *paṇḍit*, in which a large number of texts were cited as either containing or not containing references to *guru pūjan*. From my Canon-far perspective I expected that the arguments would hinge upon the relative age (and therefore authoritativeness) of the texts cited, and upon an imputed superior authoritativeness of prescriptive ritual texts over descriptive narrative texts. But this was clearly not the case, and when I suggested such a hierarchy of texts to the *paṇḍit* involved in the controversy, he scoffed at the notion. Each side felt itself vindicated by the number of supporting references they had been able to muster. But with neither a Canon-far means of judging the relative authority of the texts, nor a superior Canon-near status on the part of any one of the texts, the debate was largely unresolvable on a purely textual level. In the end, it was public pressure and not scriptural authority that forced the proponents of *guru pūjan* to modify their ritual behavior.

V. Contemporary Śvetāmbar Mūrtipūjak Canons-near

I have shown in the above instances that the perceptions of "scripture" and "canon" are fluid within the contemporary Śvetāmbar Mūrtipūjak Jain tradition. I would guess that they have always been fluid, and the varying numbers and names of texts found in different lists of Ágamas or Siddhāntas at different times is a reflection of this fluidity. Western scholars in their search for a fixed, unchanging Canon-far type of scripture seized upon the concept of the forty-five Āgamas and ignored the fluidity found within this concept. The basic notion of the forty-five Āgamas is certainly not an external imposition by scholars upon the tradition. But we have also seen that in the contemporary context the concept of the forty-five Āgamas does not serve as a referent to a studied and well-known body of literature (as, for example, the Bible serves as a well-known source from which many Christians can readily supply passages in response to varying situations); rather, it serves as a focus of congregational devotional activity in which the salvific knowledge imputed to the texts is praised and worshiped. We have seen that the *Kalpa Sūtra* plays a central role in the life of both the laity and the mendicants, although this centrality is due to its ritual usage, not its placement as a chapter of one of the Āgamas.

To find the scriptures that have a living, detailed presence for the contemporary Śvetāmbar Mūrtipūjak Jain—to establish a contemporary Canon-near—we have to look in part elsewhere. The texts of the forty-five Āgamas are not as a rule studied by the laity, and one *sādhu* even went so far as to say that while the Āgam Mandirs are valuable as means to preserve effectively the texts of the *śāstras,* the real meaning of the Āgamas was never written down, but can be learnt only through a secret, verbal, guru-to-disciple transmission. Several of the forty-five Āgamas— *Daśavaikālika Sūtra, Uttarādhyayana Sūtra, Āvaśyaka Sūtra, Nandī Sūtra*—are studied by mendicants as part of their basic education, and along with other texts in the standard syllabus form the basis for the mendicants' understanding of their own tradition. The *Āvaśyaka Sūtra* in particular plays a central role in the life of mendicants, for it contains the texts that are recited daily in the mendicant praxis of the six daily necessary (*āvaśyaka*) rites. There is thus a body of texts that are known to all mendicants, in part through daily recitation, in part through the standard mendicant course of study. But the centrality—the "canonicity," if you will—of these texts would not be obvious to a scholar in a Western library; only close observation of mendicant practice will indicate the status of these texts in relation to other texts.

There is also a discernible lay Canon-near, although its boundaries are less well defined than the mendicant Canon-near. One set of texts are not so much read by the laity as they are heard by them. These are the texts from within the vast body of Jain narrative literature that live through their being used by *sādhus* as the bases for their sermons. Many of these stories have been written down time and again, so that instead of a single text, we have microgenres of closely related texts, such as those telling the stories behind the various annual festivals. These would include the many *Śripāl Rāsas,*

Jñān Pañcamī Kathās, Dīpālikā Kathās, and others (none of which have been studied by scholars, and all of which play a central role in the Jains' understanding of their own tradition). The *Kalpa Sūtra* as constituted by both the *Bārasā Sūtra* and the *Subodhikā* commentary also falls into this category.

The other lay Canon-near is composed of the many devotional hymns that are sung and recited daily by Jains all over India. Most of these are in the vernaculars such as Gujarati, Marwari, and Kacchi for the Śvetāmbars, and Hindi, Braj, Marathi, Kannada, and Tamil for the Digambars, but many are also in Prakrit and Sanskrit. A core of these, some of sufficient antiquity and popularity as to be found in both the Śvetāmbar and Digambar traditions, are those that have been gathered together into a collection known as the Nava Smaraṇa, the "Nine Remembrances" (or sometimes Sapta Smaraṇa, "Seven Remembrances").[24] Most of these are devotional texts, in which the qualities exhibited by the lives and symbolized by the images of the Jinas are praised in order that they should grow within the soul of the worshiper. These and other similar texts are known by heart—or, as is said in India, "reside in the throat" (*kaṇṭh-stha*)—by many Jains, both mendicants and laity, and a close study of these texts can provide an accurate understanding of the Jain theology as actually practiced and professed by the Jains themselves. Again, the centrality and the context of these texts is not readily apparent to the scholar in a library (and thus the early Jain scholars who studied, edited, and translated these texts did not incorporate them into their understanding of the Jains; see Jacobi 1876, 1878 and Klatt 1879), but can be fully seen only through detailed contextual observation.

VI. Conclusion

We have seen in this paper that there are multiple Śvetāmbar Mūrtipūjak Jain understandings of their own "scriptures," as well as multiple ways to present those understandings. The standard academic presentation is based upon a Canon-far notion of scripture imposed upon the tradition by the first generation of Western scholars of the Jains. The confusions resultant from this presentation have been compounded by the extensive overlap of this academic external Canon-far with one of several internal Canons-far, that of the forty-five Āgamas. As an alternative way to understand the Śvetāmbar Mūrtipūjak Jain scriptures, I have proposed that we use the concept of Canon-near to see that the Jains themselves have multiple, oftentimes loosely defined, canons. Which canon is operative in any given context will depend upon such factors as the precise form of ritual or other activity and the status (mendicant, lay) of the participants. The application of this concept to the Digambars, Sthānakvāsīs, and

Terāpanthīs will tell us which texts constitute their Canons-near.[25] Comparison of the different Canons-near can then highlight the beliefs and practices that are common to all or some of the sects, and those that are unique to just one sect. Further, this methodological tool can contibute toward a better understanding of the genesis of the Śvetāmbar division into the Mūrtipūjak, Sthānakvāsī, and Terāpanthī sects, which previous scholarship has understood to be predicated in part on canonical disputes.[26]

These are tasks that await Jain scholars, and that may well result in a very different perception of the Jains. The need for such a new understanding of the role and nature of the "canons" of "scripture" within the Jain tradition was first enunciated by Kendall Folkert. In this chapter I have provided some instances of how some people in the largest sect within the Jain tradition—the Śvetāmbar Mūrtipūjaks—perceive their own canon and scriptures. The instances I have described—the ritual use and understandings of the *Kalpa Sūtra* and the *Bārasā Sūtra*, the worship of the forty-five Āgamas in the *pūjās* and the Āgam Mandirs, and the fluid use of the term *śāstra* in contemporary practical hermeneutics—indicate that the contemporary Śvetāmbar Mūrtipūjak Jain's understanding of his or her "scriptures" is not an intellectual one based upon study and reflection, but rather a devotional one based upon praise and worship of the salvific knowledge contained within the Āgamas and the *śāstras*. These instances also indicate that, in part at least, obtaining this salvific knowledge is less an epistemological process of scholarly study, and more an ontological process of causing the qualities of knowledge to arise in one's soul through ritual devotion, veneration, and approval.

Notes

1. See Müller 1879, ix–xlvii.

2. This chapter constitutes essentially a reflection upon and an extension of Folkert's scholarship on Jain scripture and is dedicated to his memory. The fieldwork that underlies this article was conducted in Gujarat between August 1985 and May 1987, funded by a grant under the U.S. Department of Education Fulbright-Hays Research Abroad program.

3. Folkert also said that this formulation was taken up by Indian scholars and thereby reintroduced into the Jain tradition. While one does find a certain popular understanding that the texts written down at Valabhi were the forty-five Āgamas, I am not sure that on the more scholarly level this reimportation, or "pizza effect," has penetrated beyond those scholars who write in English and are in many ways dependent upon Western scholarship

for their understanding of the Jains. Tripuṭī Mahārāj (1952, 414–31), for example, in discussing the Valabhi council, say both that the eleven Aṅgas were committed to writing under the direction of Devardhigaṇi Kṣamāśramaṇa, and that eighty-four Āgamas were written down. They do not, however, say that the forty-five Āgamas were written down then.

A variant of the position that the forty-five Āgamas were redacted at Valabhi, which coincides with the internal understanding of Tripuṭī Mahārāj, is found in the works of Walther Schubring (1962, 77–78) and M. L. Mehta (1971, 17–18), who assume that it was the collection of eleven Aṅgas, the oldest strata of the canon, that was redacted at Valabhi.

4. Jaini (1979, 47) conflates these two systems of categorization, when he describes the Jain Āgama as divided into eleven Aṅgas and thirty-four Aṅgabahya texts.

5. See Folkert 1975, p.49, and 1979, p.9, for schematic outlines of this earlier way of understanding the texts.

6. Folkert elsewhere (1984, 18) noted that whereas scholars tend to focus on the root text, traditional understandings are almost always mediated by one or more layers of commentaries.

7. This latter is changed to "experience-far" by Marcus and Fischer (1986, 30–31); I follow their more felicitous wording.

8. The definition of canon here differs somewhat from that proposed by Jonathan Z. Smith (1982, 48), for whom the three necessary elements in a canon are (1) the basic list itself, (2) a hermeneute, or interpreter, and (3) a principle of closure. In the case of a Canon I or Canon-near, the hermeneute in many cases is the outside observer rather than a participant in the tradition, and closure is clearly not an operative or defining principle.

9. The other two are by Mukund Lath (see Vinaya Sāgar 1977) and K. C. Lalwani (1979).

10. In fact, Paryuṣaṇa as described in the *Kalpa Sūtra* only in part overlaps with Paryuṣaṇ as nowadays observed. See Cort 1989, 157–59.

11. Folkert uncharacteristically misspoke when he said, "As Jacobi had to admit, the *Kalpa Sūtra* that was being published as a sacred book was not in the forty-five text scripture bloc."

12. For a lengthy description and discussion of Paryuṣaṇ, see Cort 1989, 157–85. See also Folkert 1990.

13. These offerings constitute six of the eight offerings employed in the daily *aṣṭaprakārī pūjā*; see Babb 1988 and Cort 1989, 357–80.

14. These are (1) Jinas, (2) liberated souls (*siddha*), (3) mendicant leaders (*ācārya*), (4) mendicant teachers (*upādhyāya*), (5) mendicants (*sādhu*), (6) right faith (*samyagdarśan*), (7) right knowledge (*samyagjñān*), (8) right conduct (*samyakcāritra*), and (9) right asceticism (*samyaktap*).

15. *āj payannā che ghaṇā, paṇ lahī ek adhikār / daś payannā tiṇe gaṇyā, pīstāliś majhār //* Vīr Vijay, *Pistālīś Āgam Pūjā (caturth dhūp-pūjā, dohā 1)*, 270.

16. *āthamte keval ravi, maṁdir dīṁpak jyot / paṁcam āre prāṇīne, āgamno udyot //5// jñān bhakti kartā thakā, pūjyā jin aṇagār / te kāraṇ āgamtaṇī, pūjā bhakti viśāl //7// jñānopagaraṇ melīye, pustak āgaḷ sār / pīṭh racī jinabiṁbane, thāpīje manohār //8// tem āgam haiḍe dharī, pūjo śrī jinacaṁd / dhyey dhyān pad ekthī, pāmo pad mahānaṁd //10//* Vīr Vijay, *Pīstālīś Āgam Pūjā (pratham jal-pūjā,* verses 5, 7–8, 10), 262–3.

17. *jinvar jin āgam ek rūpe sevaṁtā. . . .* Vīr Vijay, *Pīstālīś Āgam Pūjā (aṣṭam phaḷ pūjā,* verse 2), 278.

18. *jinvar jin āgamtaṇī, pūjā kare dharī bhāv / te bhaviyaṇ bhavjal tarī, pāme śuddh svabhāv //* Rūp Vijay, *Pīstālīś Āgam Pūjā (pratham śrī ācārāṁgasūtra pūjā,* verse 4), 341.

19. I am unable at present to estimate the extent to which the reform movement was another of the periodic, internally generated reforms (*uddhār*) of the Jain community and practice that have punctuated Jain history, or was significantly influenced by interaction with Western ideas.

20. Similarly, Puṇya Vijay was given the honorific *Āgamaprabhākar*, "the sun of the Āgamas."

21. I have visited only the Āgam Mandirs at Palitana and Shankheshvar; information on the Āgam Mandir in Surat comes from Candroday Vijay (1971, 2).

22. *viṣam kāḷ jinabiṁb jināgam bhaviyaṇakū ādhārā //*

23. See the issues dated May 18, June 15, July 6, and December 14, 1986. For another discussion of this debate, see Cort 1989, 331–33.

24. See Nawab 1961.

25. I suspect that it would also demonstrate that one must distinguish among the Digambars of North India, Karnataka, and Tamil Nadu as having different Canons-near.

26. See also Folkert 1979, 17–18 n. 16, on a possible way to understand the relationship between these divisions and notions of canon.

References

Babb, Lawrence A.
1988 "Giving and Giving Up: The Eightfold Worship among Śvetāmbar Mūrtipūjak Jains." *Journal of Anthropological Research* 44: 67–86.

Bhargava, Dayanand
1968 *Jaina Ethics.* Delhi: Motilal Banarsidass.

Brown, W. Norman
1934 *A Descriptive and Illustrated Catalogue of Miniature Paintings of the Jaina Kalpasūtra.* Washington: Smithsonian Institution, Freer Gallery of Art.

Bühler, Georg
1882 "Ueber eine kürzlich für die Wiener Universität erworbene Sammlung von Sanskrit— und Prakrit—Handschriften." *Sitzungsberichte der Philosophisch-Historischen Classe der Kaiserlichen Akademie der Wissenschaften zu Wien* 99: 563–79.

Candroday Vijay Gaṇi, Upādhyāy
1971 *Śrī 108 Tīrth Darśanāvalī.* Surat: Śrī Desāī Poḷ Jain Peḍhī.

Colebrooke, H. T.
1807 "Observations on the Sect of Jains." *Asiatic Researches* 9: 287–322. (Reprinted in *Miscellaneous Essays,* vol. 2, 191–224. London: Wm. H. Allen and Co., 1837.)

Cort, John E.
1989 *Liberation and Well-being: A Study of the Śvetāmbar Mūrtipūjak Jains of North Gujarat.* Ph.D diss., Harvard University.

della Casa, Carlo
1971 "Jainism." In *Historia Religionum, Volume 2, Religions of the Present,* edited by C. Jouco Bleeker and Geo. Widengren, 346–71. Leiden: E. J. Brill.

Fischer, Eberhard, and Jyotindra Jain

1977 *Art and Rituals: 2500 Years of Jainism in India.* Translated by Jutta Jain-Neubauer. New Delhi: Sterling.

Folkert, Kendall W.

1975 *Two Jaina Approaches to Non-Jainas: Patterns and Implications.* Ph.D. diss., Harvard University.

1979 "Scripture and Continuity in the Jaina Tradition." Paper presented at the Center for the Study of World Religions, Harvard University. (Also in Folkert forthcoming.)

1984 "The 'Canons' of 'Scripture' " [long version]. Paper written for NEH Summer Seminar, "Scripture: Its Nature and Evolving Role." (Also in Folkert forthcoming.)

1989 "The 'Canons' of 'Scripture' " [short version]. In *Rethinking Scripture: Essays from a Comparative Perspective,* edited by Miriam Levering, 170–79. Albany: State University of New York Press.

1990 "Notes on Paryuṣaṇ in Samī and Veḍ," edited by John E. Cort, in *Bulletin of the Center for the Study of World Religions* 16:2, 54–73. (Also in Folkert forthcoming.)

forthcoming *Collected Writings on the Jains,* edited by John E. Cort. Cambridge, Mass. Center for the Study of World Religions.

Geertz, Clifford

1983 *Local Knowledge.* New York: Basic Books.

Hamilton, Dr. [F.] Buchanan

1827 "On the Srawacs or Jains." *Transactions of the Royal Asiatic Society of Great Britain and Ireland* 1: 531–40.

Jacobi, Hermann

1876 "Zwei Jaina-Stotra." *Indische Studien* 14: 359–91.

1878 "Die Çobhana stutayas des Çobhana muni." *Zeitschrift der Deutschen Morgenländischen Gesselschaft* 32: 509–34.

1879 (ed.) *The Kalpa Sūtra of Bhadrabâhu.* Leipzig: F. A. Brockhaus.

1884 (trans.) *Jaina Sūtras.* Sacred Books of the East, vol. 22. Oxford: Clarendon Press. (Reprint New York: Dover, 1968; and Delhi: Motilal Banarsidass, 1968.)

Jaina, Padmanabh S.
1979 *The Jaina Path of Purification.* Berkeley: University of California Press.

Kalpasūtram (Bārasāsūtram) Sacitram.
1980 Surat: Śrī Bārsāsūtra Prakāśan Samiti.

Kapadia, Hiralal Rasikdas
1941 *A History of the Canonical Literature of the Jainas.* Surat: Author.

Klatt, Joh.
1879 "Dhanapâla's Ṛishabhapañcâçikâ." *Zeitschrift der Deutschen Morgenländischen Gesselschaft* 33: 445–83.

Lalwani, K. C., trans.
1979 *Kalpa Sūtra.* Delhi: Motilal Banarsidass.

Marcus, George E., and Michael M. J. Fischer
1986 *Anthropology as Cultural Critique.* Chicago: University of Chicago Press.

Mehta, Mohan Lal
1971 *Jaina Philosophy.* Varanasi: P. V. Research Institute.

Miles, Lieut.-Colonel William
1835 "On the Jainas of Gujerat and Márwár." *Transactions of the Royal Asiatic Society of Great Britain and Ireland* 3: 335–71.

Müller, F. Max.
1879 "Preface to the Sacred Books of the East." In *The Upaniṣads,* translated by F. Max Muller. Part I, ix-xlvii. Sacred Books of the East, Vol. 1. Oxford: Clarendon Press.

Nawab, Sarabhai Manilal, ed.
1961 *Mahāprābhāvika Navasmaraṇa*. Ahmedabad: Published by the editor.

Rūp Vijay, Paṇḍit
1986 [1829] *Pīstāliś Āgam Pūjā*. In *Vividh Pūjā Saṅgrah*, edited by Paṅnyās Jinendra Vijay Gaṇi, 341–97. Sivana: Tapāgacch Jain Saṅgh.

Schubring, Walther
1962 *The Doctrine of the Jainas*. Translated by Wolfgang Beurlen. Delhi: Motilal Banarsidass.

Shah, U. P.
1977 "Jainism." In *Encyclopædia Brittanica, Macropædia*, 15th ed., vol. 10, 8–14.

1987 *Jaina-Rūpa-Maṇḍana*. New Delhi: Abhinav.

Shântâ, N.
1985 *La voie jaina*. Paris: O.E.I.L.

Singh, Chandramani
1977 "Paintings of Kalpasūtra." In *Kalpasūtra*. See Vinaya Sāgar 1977, xi–xx.

Smith, Jonathan Z.
1982 "Sacred Persistence: Toward a Redescription of Canon." In *Imagining Religion*, 36–52. Chicago: University of Chicago Press.

Stevenson, Rev. J., trans.
1972 *The Kalpa Sūtra, and Nava Tatva* [sic]. 1847. Reprint. Varanasi: Bharat-Bharati.

Tripuṭī Mahārāj [Munis Darśan Vijay, Jñān Vijay, Nyāy Vijay.]
1952 *Jain Paramparā no Itihās*. Ahmedabad: Śrī Cāritra Smārak Granthmālā.

Vinaya Sāgar, Mahopādhyāy, ed. and Hindi trans.
1977 *Kalpasūtra*. English translation by Mukund Lath. Jaipur: Prakrit Bharati.

Vīr Vijay, Paṇḍit
1986a [1818] *Cosaṭh Prakārī Pūjā*. In *Vividh Pūjā Saṅgrah*, edited by Paṅnyās Jinendra Vijay Gaṇi, 110–219. Sivana: Tapāgacch Jain Sangh.

1986b [1825] *Pīstālīś Āgam Pūjā*. In *Vividh Pūjā Saṅgrah*. See Vir Vijay 1986a, 261–80.

Weber, Albrecht
1883–85 "Über die heiligen Schriften der Jaina." *Indien Studien* 16–17: 211–479, 1–90. (English translation: H. Weir Smyth, *Weber's Sacred Literature of the Jains*. Bombay: Education Society's Steam Press, 1893. Reprinted from *Indian Antiquary* 17–21 [1888–92].)

Wilson, H. H.
1862 *Essays and Lectures Chiefly on the Religion of the Hindus*. 2 vols. Edited by Reinhold Rost. London: Trübner & Co.

Eleven

Evam Me Sutaṁ

Oral Tradition in Nikāya Buddhism

Frank J. Hoffman

Introduction

The importance of texts (whether called "scriptures," "holy books," or just "texts") is basic to the study of religion, especially when such study is done with an interest in philosophical questions. But in this chapter I intend to direct philosophical attention not to Buddhist texts themselves, but to the importance of the spoken, rather than the written, word. Even those of us who work primarily on the philosophical implications of written texts ought to realize the considerable importance traditionally attached to the spoken word in Buddhism. Indeed, the phrase *evam me sutaṁ* (thus have I heard) begins many a Pali text in the *Nikāyas.* As John Brough has argued, however, *evam me sutaṁ* is not to be construed as indicating that Buddhism rests upon hearsay, but instead as indicating personal testimony (Brough 1949–50, 424). Although there have been scattered references here and there to oral tradition in Buddhological writing, Western scholarship has paid little attention to the oral tradition in *Nikāya* Buddhism.[1]

To begin with some preliminary observations on the contemporary hermeneutical scene in Buddhist studies, one notices a de-emphasis (if not an outright rejection) of the possibility or desirability of fathoming the intentions of Sakyamuni Buddha in interpreting a specific passage. This trend follows one in aesthetics set by Wimsatt and Beardsley in their classic article "The Internationalist Fallacy," in which intention is regarded as neither available nor desirable as a standard in evaluating a work of art (Wimsatt and Beardsley 1946, 468–88). As Donald Lopez states in *Buddhist Hermeneutics* (1988), the task of Buddhist exegetes is not simply "the modest, and in the old-fashioned sense, philological effort to find out what the author meant'' (p. 50). In the same place, however, Lopez goes on to assert that they were incapable of understanding that they must eventually enter the Mahāyāna, a point that may seem presumptuous to Pali exegetes.

My suggestion is that there are lines of development other than the study of written texts that may broaden, and at the same time deepen, religious studies by providing additional foci to written texts. Two such foci are (1) visual art as ''text'' and (2) the spoken word as ''text'' (later to be discussed herein as ''dicts'' in Beardsley's sense). In both sorts of case there are intriguing hermeneutical possibilities. Possibility (1) is suggested by a passage in Jonathan Z. Smith's *Imagining Religion* (1982): ''One possibility is to examine the widespread evidence for the use of a totalistic and complete system of signs or icons which serve as functional equivalents to a written canon'' (p. 49).

Since my intention is to concentrate on (2) herein, I shall only briefly illustrate (1). In the Great Stupa at Sanchi are several *toraṇas* (''gateways'') on which are depicted scenes from the life of Buddha (Rowland 1967, 59, plate 21). No words are graven in stone, and yet one finds visual material easily interpretable to the circumambulating monk or pilgrim. Whether highly literate or not, the Buddhist faithful find meaning conveyed by the system of signs. Benjamin Rowland suggests that the *toraṇa* of the east gate at Sanchi represents a scroll. ''It is possible that these long horizontal panels terminating in tightly wound spiral volutes are a transference to stone of popular picture scrolls partly unrolled for exhibition'' (Rowland 1967, 59). In Victor Mair's detailed study of picture recitation around the world, the first textual reference in Indian tradition is Patañjali's *Mahābhāṣya* (ca. 160–140 B.C.E. (Mair 1988, 17). Rowland dates the *toraṇa* on the east gate at Sanchi to the ''early decades of the first century C.E.'' (Rowland 1967, 59). Consequently, the written textual evidence for the supposition that the ends on the *toraṇa* are the east gate of Sanchi represent a scroll is inconclusive as it stands. However, as Mair points out, F. W. Thomas's study of the Mauryas (325–184 B.C.E.) mentions ''spectacles with displays of pictured objects of curiosity—*no doubt the private showman with his pictures of Hades, etc., was also active.*'' (Mair 1988, 17). In view of the existence of a tradition of picture recitation going back to ancient India (Mair 1988, 17–37; Teiser 1988, 87, 14, 26, 31, 107, 213, 224) it is quite possible that this *toraṇa* functioned as a pictorial stimulus for the *bhāṇakas* (reciters, chanters) to whom I shall now turn.[2]

Masatoshi Nagatomi has called attention to the importance of oral tradition in his presentation ''Thus Have I Heard'' for NEH participants in the summer institute at Harvard during 1988, and in so doing has stimulated some participants to examine a range of literature with a similar emphasis.[3] To take a few examples of such literature, Eliot Deutsch (citing Karl Potter) points out how the tradition of commentary and subcommentary reflects the importance of oral tradition (Deutsch 1988, 167–68). Miriam Levering asserts the power and truth of the performance of words independently of whether hearer or reciter understands them (Levering 1989, 7). William A. Graham points out the great esteem given to those who "know by heart," and in this connection one could mention the *bhāṇakas* (Graham 1987a, 138). In the present volume, the importance of the oral tradition is emphasized by Narayana (chapter 6) and Cort (chapter 10).

I. Orality in the Pali Tradition

Reciters. A line of development for Buddhist hermeneutics focusing on (2), the spoken word as text, is another possibility. It should be kept in mind that recitation is a bodily act involving a group ritual. As William LaFleur (1983) observes of ritual in the Japanese context:

> That ritual is done with the body rather than with the mind alone is not only fully harmonious with Buddhism's traditional discomfort with mind/body dichotomies but is also harmonious with what is increasingly recognized to be a salient feature of the Japanese *intellectual* tradition, going at least as far back as the insistence by Kukai (774–835) that enlightenment for a Buddhist occurs "with this very body" ("sokushin jobutsu"). Even the Kamakura figures, although they are sometimes compared to the Protestant reformers, did not denigrate ritual or propose a dualism between mind and body. (pp. 16–17)

As for the Indian context, I doubt whether there is any dualism of mind and body in early Buddhism.[4] Even before Buddhism arose in India, *mantras* had great importance in the South Asian context and were regarded as powerful and the practice of their recitation virtuous (Alper 1989). In *Nikāya* Buddhism the existence of the *bhāṇakas* is well-established by the Bharhut inscriptions. As B. C. Law (1933) points out:

> The tradition says that previous to the reign of Vaṭṭagāmanṇi the texts were handed down by an oral tradition *(mukhapāṭhavasena)* from teacher to teacher *(ācariya-paramparāya),* the process of transmission being compared to the carrying of earth in baskets from head to head. Buddhaghosa says (*Sumaṅgalavilāsinī,* pt. I, pp. 12 foll.) that immediately after the demise of the Buddha and after the session of the First Buddhist Council, the task of transmitting and preserving each of the five nikāyas was entrusted to an

> individual thera and his followers, which ultimately gave rise to some schools of *bhāṇakas* or chanters. The existence of the distinct schools of reciters of the five nikāyas is clearly proved (as shown by Dr. B. M. Barua) by the Milinda Panha where we have mention of the Jātakabhāṇaka (the repeaters of the Jātakas), in addition to the Dīghabhāṇaka, the Majjhimabhāṇaka, the Śamyuttabhāṇaka, the Anguttarabhāṇaka, and the Khuddakabhāṇaka. The terms 'pañcanekāyika' (one well-versed in the five nikāyas) and bhāṇaka, as well, occur as distinctive epithets of some of the Buddhist donors in the Sanchi and Barhut inscriptions which may be dated in the lump in the middle of the second century B.C. The inference from the evidence of these inscriptions has already been drawn by Prof. Rhys Davids to the effect that before the use of Pañcanekāyika (one who knows the five nikāyas by heart), Suttantika (a man who known a suttanta by heart), Suttantakinī (a feminine form of Suttantika) and Peṭaki (one who knows the piṭaka by heart) as distinctive epithets, the piṭaka and five nikāya divisions of the Pali Canon must have been well known and well established. (pp. 27–28)

Law is careful to point out that this does not imply that all five *Nikāyas* were composed at that time, but that the first four were closed while the *Khuddaka* remained open. For some time after the *parinibbāna* of Sakyamuni Buddha, the sound was the "text," and the spoken word became the handed-down property of custodial *bhāṇakas.* As time passed these schools of reciters, or chanters, developed into "distinct schools of opinion and interpretation" (Law 1933, 28).

The monks who specialized in recitation (that is, "*bhāṇaka, bhānaka,* or *bhanaka,*" Lamotte 1988, 150) played important roles in preserving, transmitting, and proselytizing. *Bhāṇaka* was a specialism listed in the Bharhut inscriptions (Lamotte 1988, 414). In his monumental magnum opus on Buddhism, Lamotte is sometimes skeptical that there was a Rajagrha council at which *bhāṇakas* recited the canon:

> We studied at length in Chapter Two (pp. 124–140) the Buddhist works concerning the specialty of the reciters *(bhāṇaka)* and the supposed compilation of the writings at the council of Rajagrha. We reached the conclusion that the facts given about the extent and content of that compilation are contradictory and hence apocryphal. (Lamotte 1988, 573)

Earlier in the same work, however, he says that it would be imprudent to commit oneself "*for or against*" (my italics) the historicity of the councils (p. 140). Prima facie this general claim about the councils as a whole does not square with the specific claim above that the Rajagrha compilation is "apocryphal" in the stronger sense. One should notice an ambiguity in the claim that the compilation at Rajagrha is "apocryphal": in a strong sense of (a) being inauthentic, fictitious, false, fabulous, or mythical; in a weaker sense of (b) being of uncertain or doubtful origin. It appears that Lamotte holds that the council compilations in general are apocryphal in sense (b), and that the compilation at Rajagrha in particular is apocryphal in sense (a). For Lamotte says first that it would be imprudent to commit oneself for or against the historicity of the councils (from which the same follows about Rajagrha, one of the councils). This implies that Rajagrha is apocryphal in sense (b). Later he says that the supposition of a compilation of Rajagrha contains contradictions and is hence apocryphal. This implies that Rajagrha is apocryphal in sense (a). This point of his exposition could have been more clearly stated if the distinction between these two senses of "apocryphal" was utilized.

Yet Lamotte skillfully points out how the tradition of the councils has served the diverse purposes of proving the authenticity of the texts, the continuity of Buddhist tradition through many depositories, and explaining how schisms and schools arose. Even if the existence and dates of the councils cannot be ascertained beyond reasonable doubt, Lamotte concedes that one or more groups of specialists (whether assembles in councils or not) did codify the *dhamma* and *vinaya* (p. 140).

In view of the existence of the *bhāṇakas,* the temporal primacy of orality in Pali Buddhist tradition is clear. In discussing the pre-Islamic Avesta, Wilfred Cantwell Smith (1989) observes:

> As has been true elsewhere at times, at first writing was perceived as simply a mnemonic device, to facilitate or to ensure that the oral rendering be accurate. The oral form was clearly primary, and for many centuries it had been unsupplemented. (p.35)

What Smith says about Avesta is also true in the early Buddhist context.

In order to accurately describe what occurs in oral tradition, it is useful to have some technical terminology. One term from philosophical aesthetics that may prove useful in this connection is coined by Monroe Beardsley against the background of the type/token distinction in philosophy, that is, *dict.* Beardsley (1977) observes:

> We need a way of speaking of two performances as performances of the same work in the absence of a script. . . . A script is connected by rules of pronunciation with sequences of verbal sounds. The production of such a sequence of sounds in accordance with a script is a sounding or oral performance of that script. And just as

> we distinguish between scripts as characters and their individual inscriptions, so we can form the concept of *dicts* as spoken characters which may have as instances innumerable individual utterances. Each time a correct inscription of "Invictus" is correctly read aloud and recited, we have an utterance; the class of all such utterances is the oral composition, the dict, that corresponds to the script. (pp. 521–22)

The following diagram may be useful in understanding Beardsley's view:

Types:	Characters (classes of inscriptions, scripts, texts)	Dicts (oral compositions, classes of utterances)
Tokens:	Inscriptions	Utterances

By using Beardsley's concept of a dict, it becomes easier to think of there being "oral literature" in preliterate Buddhist tradition (as well as in the continuing oral tradition of the not-so-literate contemporary Buddhists and their proverbs). One benefit of this approach is that it militates against an oversharp distinction between "elite" and "popular" Buddhism (for both have literature, on this view). But it might be argued that "oral literature" is simply a contradiction in terms, since literature is "by definition" written. In deciding whether to adopt Beardsley's sympathetic stance to oral literature, one is not on noncontroversial ground. So too with the extension of "scripture" to include orality championed by W. C. Smith, Graham, and Levering. Do the benefits of these extensions of "scripture" and "literature" outweigh the liabilities of departure from what some might regard as "standard usage"?

I think so. Indeed, the utterances of the *bhāṇakas* may thus be described as comprising dicts (rather than written texts) in those days before the canon was committed to writing. And in contexts where the texts have already been written down, such as contemporary Buddhist proverbs, Beardsley's concept of a dict may provide a common reference point for various utterances of a particular spoken proverb. For examples, one might consult the compilation of contemporary Thai Pali Buddhist proverbs edited by Vajirananavarorasa and Kittidharo (1955).

Text in Context. I would like to distance myself from (what I regard as) a caricature in Pali Buddhist studies, in order to be rightly able to reaffirm the value of such studies. The danger is one of simplistic "Buddhist fundamentalism." Walter Clark (1930) provides a good example of this caricature as follows:

> Most students of Pali, under the enthusiasm of working with a definite canon in a single language and a comparatively homogenous block of texts, have tended to exaggerate the value of the Pali tradition, have tended to claim that the Pali canon represents the main trunk of Buddhist tradition, that the Pali texts are to be treated practically as a unit both as texts and as doctrine, and that all non-pali texts can safely be ignored, at least in so far as Buddhism down through the third century B.C.E. is concerned. They conceive that all it is necessary to do is to sift out some later accretions (largely on the basis of some subjective element, the intuition of each individual author), and that what is left will be the oldest form of canonical Buddhism. This is then confidently identified with primitive Buddhism, and this with the Buddhism of the Buddha himself. (p. 122)

Especially in the last two sentences, the gaps in the reasoning Clark so perceptively caricatures are wide. It is not necessary, however, for scholars of Pali Buddhism to succumb to the temptation of "Buddhist fundamentalism." Elsewhere I have described an approach to Pali Buddhism that avoids such pitfalls, and I will not repeat all the details of that discussion here (see Hoffman 1987, 5). Suffice it to say that the term "early Buddhism" may be used to indicate that five *Nikāyas*, a set of texts. As such, in my usage the term is not primarily a chronological one;[5] *Nikāya* Buddhism would do as well. There are multiple "understandings" of Buddhism possible depending on which (and as I argue herein, whether) written texts are selected for study, and there is no privileged point of view from which to confidently assert what is "the real Buddhism." Having said so is double-edged: it allows one to cut through the simplistic belief that non-*Nikāya* Buddhist texts and doctrines are necessarily "heretical" (and to expurgate presumptuous locutions like "Mahāyāna heresy"); it also allows the option of focusing on the Pali *Nikāyas* without the *Abhidhamma* commentaries for the specific purpose of gaining a certain sort of understanding of Buddhism. (It would be gratuitous to assert that other sorts of understandings are inferior.)

Clark published the paper from which the above quotation was taken in 1930. But in our time, when sociopolitical focus on Tibet, Japan, and China is so great that Pali studies are often ignored and sometimes belittled, it is instructive to see that even Clark must concede that the Pali canon "represents on the whole the earliest preserved form of Buddhist literature" (Clark 1930, 142). However, if one is inclined to think that the *bhāṇakas* provided a sufficient check on pristine doctrinal orthodoxy, then K. R. Norman's words stand as a useful reminder: "Different schools of *bhāṇakas* might remember different versions of the verses, and the independence of the schools prevented one version being 'corrected' in the light of another version" (Norman 1983, 74). There being no such thing as "copyright," the same verse could even be attributed to different Theras.

Although there have been many studies of oral tradition, the importance of oral tradition in its relationship to scripture has just begun to be understood in the West. In South Asia, Buddhists themselves have long recognized the importance or orality in their tradition. As K. R. Norman (1983) observes: "It was the realization that canonical texts could easily disappear if the oral tradition died out which precipitated the writing down of the canon during the reign of Vattagamani" (p. 87).

The Importance of Right Speech. The recent emphasis on orality is more than scholarly fashion: it is built into the earliest doctrines, as is evident in the inclusion of "right speech" *(sammavācā)* in the eightfold noble path. It is also evident even in contemporary times in the oral tradition of Buddhist proverbs.

In a book chapter called "Right Speech" Piyadassi Thera (1964) calls attention to the importance of right speech for laymen and monks alike (pp. 131, 134, 137–41). He points out that although the "four abstentions" concerning "right speech" (that is, abstention from falsehood, slander, harsh speech, and idle chatter) appear to be negative prohibitions, the idea of "right speech" is actually positive, since these abstentions encourage purity. Why so much attention to right speech in Buddhism? Because, as Geoffrey H. Hartman (1981) has recently emphasized, the possibilities of words that wound are very great (pp. 118–57).

The continuing tradition of Buddhist proverbs also attests to the importance of right speech. Some of these very proverbs show the importance of oral tradition and the power of the spoken word. Some examples from Vajirananavarorasa and Kittidharo (1955) are[6]

I, 215. Negligence of reciting blots out the memory of a lesson.

I, 265. Wisdom can be known in discussion.

II, 172. A thousand useless words are not worth one by which the mind can be calmed after listening to it.

A considerable range of other proverbs exist, some based on Pali canonical sources, others expressive of Buddhist ideas but popularized by twentieth-century figures (such as Prince Vajirananavarorasa). Some of these are clever and memorable, and I offer four additional examples:[7]

II, 72. Great is the power of the moon, the sun, the hermit and the seashore. But greater still is that of a woman.

II, 87. A careless person talking the Buddha's words without putting any of them to practice himself, is like a hired cowboy counting the cows for others (never tasting their milk or having a part of the sale).

II, 162. Just as clay-pots made by potters are to be broken at last, so are the lives of sentient beings.

II, 196. Just as a leaf smells sweet when it wraps up a perfumed herb, so does a man gain reputation when he is befriended by the wise.

II. How Oral Tradition Affects What Counts as "Scripture" in Pali Buddhism

Evam Me Sutaṁ and Janata Passata. There is an interesting juxtaposition in Buddhism of two ideas—*evam me sutaṁ* and *janata passata*—that are prima facie incompatible but are actually harmonized. First, there is to be no reliance on "report, tradition, or hearsay" for the Buddhist adept, who must know and see *(janata passata)* for him- or herself. Secondly, what is heard is of great importance, so much so that the phrase *evam me sutaṁ* (thus have I heard) begins many a text. The harmony between hearing and seeing is affected by each having its proper place: in Buddhism, reports of Buddha's life are important, not in themselves, but in order to set the stage for one's own enlightenment.

Oral Transmission and Folk Tradition. William Graham (1987b) points to an important contrast between, on the one hand, oral transmission of scripture and, on the other, folk oral tradition in which verbatim accuracy is not an aspiration:

> Oral use and even oral transmission of scripture should not be confused with folk oral tradition in which verbatim accuracy is not aspired to (i.e., in which "formulaic composition" predominates: see, for examples, Albert B. Lord, *The Singer of Tales,* Cambridge, Mass., 1960). The technical mnemonic methods of oral transmission have sometimes been so highly developed for sacred texts as to render the oral text more reliable than the manuscript tradition—notably in the Islamic and Hindu cases. In any event, few if any scriptural books have the verbatim uniformity popularly associated with the written and especially the printed word. Even

> the "fixation" of a sacred canon in writing has rarely meant that one definitive documentary text is universally recognized or that variant texts disappear. (pp. 13, 38)

The last sentence certainly applies to Pali Buddhism, for any given Pali language volume in the standard Pali Text Society edition of the canon is itself based upon recensions of texts in several different languages. As to the question whether the oral tradition is "more reliable" than the Pali texts, however, it is helpful to recall K. R. Norman's comment above to the effect that the *bhāṇakas* were independent groups (there were *Majjhima bhāṇakas, Samyutta bhāṇakas,* etc.) such that one group did not check the others for accuracy.

The Importance of Myths, Actions, and Symbols. Miriam Levering (1989) calls attention to an important tendency in religious studies:

> Phenomenologists of religion and other later groups proposed that attention should be focused on myths, actions and symbols that expressed religious meanings rather than on texts and beliefs. Much has been gained thereby. An important advance is the realization that the cultures of oral peoples are as profound and sophisticated as the cultures of literate peoples. (p. 4)

In the same passage Levering goes on to notice the scholarly predilection for the textual ("elite") versus the oral ("popular"), and comments that reflection on the religious expressions of early or oral cultures results in "insights into all human religiousness" (p. 4). For Levering, these insights have to do with the power of the word.

Clearly the Pali Buddhist *Nikāyas* are not only texts with philosophical implications; they are also religious texts formulated by reciters for whom the power of the spoken word was a participatory reality. Clearly, too, the texts are certainly not put forth in the spirit of the *takki* or rationalist logicians of Buddhist antiquity. It is also evident that if one imposes a basically alien Western "ism" onto the texts in a wholesale manner, distortion of the religiosity of the Pali texts will result. But as Hajime Nakamura (1988) quite rightly points out: "If we insist on being too strict in emphasizing either philosophy or religion, eliminating the other from the scope of investigation, we fail to grasp many important problems" (pp. 150–51).

The question of whether Buddhism is a philosophy, a religion, both, or neither (to apply the early Buddhist fourfold logic) is a separate question from whether philosophical attention to Pali materials is possible without distortion. On the first question, I tend to think that early Buddhism is a religion with philosophical implications (rather than a philosophy with marginal religious accretions).[8] In my view, this position accommodates the importance of both philosophy and religion.

Nakamura makes the significant point that the basis for the problem is a split between philosophy and religion that arose in the Western context due to an antagonism between philosophy and religion unlike in Japan, where Amane Nishi had to coin the new word *tetsugaku* in his 1874 work *Hyakuichi Shinron*. In universities in the United States in which there are separate departments of philosophy and religion, at best members of each camp eye each other suspiciously over the wall, and at worst the situation may be positively acrimonious. In the case of Buddhist studies such divisions can be particularly unhelpful, since Buddhism has elements of interest to both groups (and to theologians inter alia as well). What is necessary is not that scholars abandon their disciplinary commitments, but that they internalize the fact that Buddhism can be usefully approached from other disciplinary perspectives than their own.[9]

On the second question, I have no doubt that sensitive, sympathetic, philosophical attention to Buddhism can elucidate it without engaging in wholesale reductionism to a specific school of Western philosophy. Ninian Smart's idea of ''cross-cultural world view construction'' is one element in my program, but not the whole of it (1988, 182). (An example of this sort of sympathetic philosophical attention is contained in chapter six of my word, *Rationality and Mind in Early Buddhism* [Hoffman 1987].) Another role that philosophy can play in relation to Buddhism is calling attention to conceptual difficulties the resolution of which are difficult if not impossible from within the Buddhist frame of reference (as exemplified in chapter four of the same work). Both roles are important in order to arrive at a sympathetic but critically aware perspective on early Buddhism.

What I find refreshing in the recent attempt by scholars to think again about the meaning of scripture is that it allows one to do textual exegesis with an understanding of the role of oral tradition in shaping what counts as a text or canon.[10] It is not necessary to abandon the enterprise of traditional textual interpretation. Continuing to interpret texts but with the realization of the importance of preliterate and oral phenomena makes for a renewed understanding of both the basis of, and the limits to, the traditional approach of Western scholars.

Nonpropositional aspects of Buddhism such as myths, actions, and symbols (Levering 1989, 4; see also pp. 88, 100 n. 64) are indeed important if one is to understand the religiosity of Buddhism and not misconstrue it as only an abstract system of ideas. What Jonathan Z. Smith (1982, 49) indicates about the possible use of a system of signs or icons as functional equivalents to a written canon is what philosophically inclined art historians (such as Prithwish Neogy at University of Hawaii) have been moving toward for a number of years.

The upshot of this section of our discussion is that there is more to understanding Buddhism than one finds when analyzing texts, but that does not imply that analyzing texts is unimportant. In concluding his introduction to the *Buddhist Hermeneutics* anthology, Donald Lopez (1988) writes of residual questions:

> Among the questions left unexplored in this volume is that of the hermeneutical enterprise not of the ancient Buddhist exegete but of the modern western Buddhologist. Although it is impossible in light of the work of Gadamer to separate the study of Buddhist hermeneutics from the question of the hermeneutics—the principles and presuppositions of interpretation—of the modern scholars who today interpret Buddhist texts, such a separation is attempted here (perhaps naively), with the essays devoted to an evaluation of the dynamic relationship that existed between Buddhist scriptures and their traditional exegetes. An attempt to become aware of the prejudices and preunderstandings that the modern Buddhologist, alienated from his subject by both time and culture, brings to the study of Buddhist texts remains a desideratum. (p. 9)

Lopez's desideratum cannot be definitively achieved in this paper and, in any case, is likely to require sustained effort of a group of self-reflective Buddhologists if any progress is to be made. However, I would like to make a start. It is perhaps odd that Lopez should leave untouched precisely the most interesting and relevant question, that of the nature of "the hermeneutical enterprise not of the ancient Buddhist exegete but of the modern western Buddhologist." What is required is an understanding of *one's own role qua interpreter,* not just the role of an ancient exegete (such as Buddhaghosa). In "Towards a Philosophy of Buddhist Religion" (Hoffman 1991) I have outlined a methodology for textual exegesis of Buddhist texts through philosophy of religion that moves more in the direction of Lopez's desideratum than the present paper.

III. How What Counts as Scripture in the Pali Tradition Holds a General Philosophical Lesson for the Very Concept of Scripture

The concept of scripture is a complex one. Although literally scripture is that which is written down, as Wilfred Cantwell Smith (1989) points out, scripture has also been *heard and seen* (Levering 1989). Think, for example, of the reciters *(bhāṇakas)* or bas-relief sculptures of *Jātaka* tales. In

Buddhism, scripture was recited before it was written down as a canon, and it was heard by people regardless of their literacy level. Thus, the concept of scripture itself may be broadened from its usual construal as "written text" by attending to visual and auditory manifestations of scripture that can be found in the Pali Buddhist tradition.

Recent work by William Graham and others has emphasized the *relational* quality of scripture. Graham writes:

> No text, written, oral, or both, is sacred or authoritative in isolation from a community. A text is only "scripture" insofar as a group of persons perceives it to be sacred of holy, powerful and meaningful, possessed of an exalted authority, and in some fashion transcendent of, and hence distinct from, other speech and writing. What is scripture for one group may be a meaningless, nonsensical, or even perversely false text for another. (Graham 1987b, 134)

This point is structurally analogous to the point I made about blasphemy, namely, that what counts as blasphemy depends on what is taken as the focal point. A corollary is that one cannot say what is and is not blasphemy *simpliciter* apart from all contexts (Hoffman 1983). One does not need to carry any particular brief for relativism as a general position in order to see and agree that scripture, like blasphemy, is a "relational concept" in Graham's sense. (The same might be said about "superstition.")

IV. How Narrow and Broad Construals of the Nikāyas *Affect What Counts as Commentary*

Some scholars of Buddhism speak of the "five *Nikāyas,*" others of the "four *Nikāyas.*"[11] The decision as to whether to include the *Khuddaka Nikāya* as the fifth one along with the *Aṅguttara-, Dīgha-, Majjhima-, and Saṃyutta Nikāyas* holds important implications for how "early Buddhism" is construed.

First, if the *Khuddaka* is included in early Buddhism, then the *Jātaka* (as part of the *Khuddaka*) must also be included in early Buddhism. And, if that is the case, then elements usually considered as "folk elements" (for example, the miraculous birth of the Buddha)—far from being popular accretions sullying the purity of abstract doctrine—are part of the parcel of even early Buddhism.

Secondly, depending on whether or not the *Khuddaka* is taken as part of early Buddhism, the distinction between canonical scripture and traditional embellishment is drawn in a different place. Consequently, the question may even arise as to whether on the "four *Nikāyas*" usage the *Khuddaka* is a sort of commentary on the canon of four *Nikāyas*? I mention this possibility not to suggest that it is definitely so, but instead to indicate the fluid relationship between the concept of "canon" and that of "commentary."

Donald Lopez (1988) argues that Buddhist hermeneutics involves neither the "old-fashioned," "philological" effort to find out what the author meant, nor a Schleiermachian attempt on the part of the interpreter to fathom the "unconscious intentions of the Buddha," thereby transforming himself into the author by knowing the text better than the author (pp. 50–51). The positive suggestion that Lopez offers is that one might rely on "instructions provided by the Buddha." Relying on the *Saṃdhinirmocana* Sūtra (glossed as the "what I was thinking of" sutra), Lopez argues: "This, then, is the sutra in which the Buddha's intention, his underlying meaning, is freed from the illusory knots of contradiction that appear when all his statements are read literally" (p. 59). As Lopez observes for his own purposes: "Here the interpreter becomes the arbiter of meaning, the interpreter becomes the author as the author sits in silence" (p. 67). Yet in the same place Lopez concludes by cautioning against *hubris* with an amusing anecdote in which retribution befalls the poet who creates the palace with too much verisimilitude for the king's taste: "You have robbed me of my palace!" says the king before the sword falls. But there is more to it than *hubris*. For on Lopez's view the commentator's job is to replicate the experience of the Buddha's enlightenment, but, paradoxically, if one succeeds in this replication one also fails, in that the effective commentary would be tantamount to the original text.

In the recognition of the fact that the distinction between text and commentary is fluid and not absolute, and that philosophical interpretation of the texts is itself a form of commentary, one should not be so awed by commentaries as not to do a fresh examination of the texts themselves from contemporary philosophical vantage points. One does not have to be so naive or so arrogant as to assume that in so doing one is revealing "the one true interpretation." It is enough if one's interpretation speaks to a contemporary audience. But is this not giving up the search for what the Pali texts "really mean," a critic might ask? I submit that the exact, pristine, presectarian meaning of Siddhartha Gotama Buddha Sakyamuni is beyond determination of the fine points of doctrine that are philosophically interesting. If so, then there is nothing to give up that might possible be had. Of course, in particular cases one will tend to think that one interpretation of a passage is more defensible than an alternative interpretation and may beg to differ in a conversation with a colleague. But notice that such disagreements are about what is the more natural reading of the text. The disagreement is not about "the real *Buddhavacana*." Since the powerful spoken words of the Buddha are not at our disposal, the main focus of attention for those contemporary persons who can neither hear *bhāṇakas* recite nor see Indian art as "text" is the written text. (Herein the phrase *written text* is not redundant.) The very *Buddhavacana* needs pluralizing: what a Zen Buddhist takes as *Buddhavacana* may be different from what a Theravadin monk takes as *Buddhavacana.*[12] "Which *'Buddhavacana'*?" is therefore not an absurd question for hermeneutically sophisticated exegetes. As Mark Taylor (1982) observes: "We must move from reflection to reflexion, from criticism to metacriticism by interpreting interpretation" (p. 81).

In Sri Lanka, for instance, Buddhaghosa the commentator is revered to a great extent. It is my contention, however, that Pali scholars who would address a philosophical audience must "become their own Buddhaghosas."

V. The Importance of Judgment in Demarcating What Counts as Scripture and What Counts as Commentary

How can we demarcate the boundary between (1) scripture and commentary and that between (2) commentary and philosophical interpretation? And how can we demarcate the boundary between (3) *Buddhavacana* and what is non-Buddhist?

1. In Eliot Deutsch's paper, "Knowledge and the Tradition Text in Indian Philosophy" (1988), some points are made that I would like to discuss and selectively apply to this discussion of oral tradition. First, there is no sharp cleavage between scripture *(sutra)* and commentary *(kārikā).* Instead, text and exegesis move together in a joint revealing (Deutsch 1988, 169). Secondly, as a corollary of the first point, the attempt of the philosopher-commentator is "to remain faithful to his or her authoritative sources, but in his own creative terms" (Deutsch 1988, 170). One is not then remarking on a finished product, the meaning of which is entirely "given" in the text itself, but is involved in a process of creative appropriation.

Deutsch denies that there is any "opposition" between "legitimate explication" and "creative innovation" in Indian thought (*contra* Larson 1988), and denies that the *sutra* (or *kārikā*) "is in fact a carefully structured argument that has a unity and coherence, at least once we have the map, as it were, to traverse its passageways. I do not think we have to go that far" (1988, 168–69). Deutsch does not follow Larson in thinking that *sutra* (or *Kārikā*) is a carefully structured argument to which one can find the map. Perhaps not. (We need to go case by case.) But one can find "*a* map." Maps are not always drawn to scale, nor need they be, for some purposes.

There can be alternative maps without one being the "best" in all contexts (Wittgenstein: a blurry picture will sometimes do as well as a sharp one). So, in a way, Larson's *sort* of position can be right, as long as one does not become narrow-minded and think that one has got the conceptual map of a text once and for all ("*the* map"). Deutsch, too, has an important point in emphasizing that text and commentary are, as Buddhists may put it, "dependently co-arising."

2. As a case in point, consider the importance of Buddhaghosa's commentaries to the contemporary Sinhalese understanding of the Pali *Nikāyas.* From that point of view it may be difficult (I do not say always impossible) to separate the "legitimate explanation" of the Pali *Nikāyas* from the "creative innovation" of Buddhaghosa to explain them. This does not mean that no distinction could be made between "creative innovation" and perverting, distorting, or misrepresenting the text.

3. My point is that *judgment* plays a crucial role in demarcating the line between innovation and distortion and between *Buddhavacana* and whatever is non-Buddhist. There is no absolute right or wrong about this sort of judgment, but neither does just anything go. There is a *range* of acceptable options within which judgment may operate. Akin to aesthetic evaluation, where reasons or considerations play a role without dictating a particular aesthetic judgment, critical philosophical judgment about *Nikāya* Buddhism requires philosophical ability, textual finesse, and the courage of one's convictions. Effective aesthetic reasoning requires that one become a "connoisseur" (a *sahrdaya,* "one of similar heart") who is one with the work of art in recognizing its "aesthetic rightness." In both cases reasoning plays a role without being by itself determinative to the outcome. As Deutsch observes, where knowledge involves appropriation, there is "a creative retaining and shaping of a content that is made one's own" (1988, 172). So this judgment is not a matter of "fathoming the intentions of the Buddha" (whatever exactly that would be like!), but involves a creative rethinking of the texts.

The sort of judgment being recommended has an element of "understanding" emphasized by Wendell V. Harris (1988) as against post-structuralist criticism:

> Interpretation can never rise from probability to certainty; but then certainty is appropriate only to the realm of Plato's ideas. One of E. D. Hirsch's most cogent comments on the business of criticism is that "It is a logical mistake to confuse the impossibility of certainty in understanding with the impossibility of understanding." (VI17). We may also say that it is an error to confuse the impossibility of demonstrating the relation of every sentence to the author's total intentions with the impossibility of there being an

> interpretable intent. . . . Much post-structuralist criticism relies on the impossibility of a stable centre, or first principle, or ground of judgement. But it is once again essential to hold to the difference between that which can be proved true and that which can be understood. (pp. 160–61)

Harris's distinction is a useful one in the present context. Although in the case of the Pali Canon there is no "author" except the Sangha; the Buddha did not "authorize" what came to be known as the canon. Nevertheless, one can understand the Sangha's intentions in the *Nikāya* Buddhist texts quite independently of whatever were the intentions of Sakyamuni Buddha.

Perhaps there has been too much emphasis placed on *Buddhavacana* (often naively, as if the words of Gotama Buddha were easily and exactly recoverable with reference to the Pali Canon): after all, it was the *Sangha* who canonized the *Dhamma* taught by the Buddha. (Recall also that Gotama Buddha is not regarded as "the Founder" by Buddhists.) Even if one's interpretations are uncertain, one's interpretations nevertheless offer an understanding of the texts, which texts are communal products. We can understand the Sangha's intentions through the texts of the Pali Canon, even if we would not care to describe our enterprise as fathoming the Buddha's intentions.

How does such interpretive judgment operate? I have already called attention to a basic principle of Buddhist hermeneutics where the text is the spoken word: "speech" *(vaca),* rather than abstract proposition, is the focus of the heuristic principle of noncontradiction (Hoffman 1982, 324). Although it would also apply to written statements, it is clear that the early Buddhist construal of the principle is in reference to speech. It is this basic principle that guarantees the possibility of cross-cultural philosophy. However, the principle of noncontradiction supplies only heuristic guidance; it tells us nothing about the specific range of acceptable content a judgment must have to be plausible.

In formulating a judgment about what counts as *Buddhavacana,* one cannot altogether escape presuppositions about philosophy of Buddhist history. Indeed, many of the papers in the *Buddhist Hermeneutics* anthology derive their inspiration from a remark by Etienne Lamotte cited by Lopez: "We are of the opinion that the Buddhist doctrine evolved along the lines which its discoverer had unconsciously traced for it" (Lamotte 1988, 47). Can we who engage the Theravada in philosophical dialogue accept such a preunderstanding of the texts? Or shall we, alternatively, adopt the posture of a Buddhist fundamentalism and the quest for the historical Buddha? Indeed, the contemporary interpreter of Theravada appears caught between a rock and a hard place.

An option open to Theravada exegetes (in contrast to those who would, with Lopez, be happy to describe the Theravadins as unaware that they must eventually enter the Mahāyāna) is to reject both the preunderstandings of those for whom the history of Buddhism is all downhill after *Abhidhamma* (''Buddhist fundamentalism?'') as well as the preunderstandings of those for whom the history of Buddhism is a continual development of an ongoing truth (''making a virtue of necessity?''). The middle way between these extremes for the Theravada exegete may well be in understanding the ''written text'' (in contrast to both auditory and visual ''texts'') as *one* sort of text the intentions of which are worth both pondering and pursuing in innovative directions.

Perhaps contemporary aesthetics and text theory can, in part, point the way. Lars Aagaard-Mogensen concludes his article, ''Has Beardsley Disproved the Identity Thesis?'': ''There's no reason why we can't admit some meanings to be author's and others readers' and critics', whatever their respective ages, they don't have all to be texts' '' (Aagaard-Mogensen 1986, 173). As applied to the problem at hand, this sort of move amounts to a pluralizing of *Buddhavacana*, admitting many different sorts of understanding as possible ones. This does not mean that we who seek to unpack the philosophical implications of Buddhist texts must do something else (become specialists in art history or linguistics, say). It means that all parties concerned with the study of Buddhism would profit from an increased awareness of the importance of preunderstandings in all attempts to understand Buddhism through any particular disciplinary filter.

The two philosophy-of-Buddhist-history assumptions are equally problematic: the one would hold that the *early* work is *eo ipso* more true; the other that truth is an ongoing development such that the *latest* Buddhist viewpoint is more true because more trendy. But for any such enlightened beings as may exist (from *paramartha*), both assumptions are only conventionally true (that is, are *samvṛtti*). For those for whom ''mountains are again mountains and rivers are again rivers,'' there is no turning back: still working on Buddhist texts, but with awareness of the provisional nature of one's own understanding and the insight that there are other possible hermeneutical foci for those who choose art as ''text'' or spoken word as ''text''(or more precisely, ''dict'' in Beardsley's sense). The disinterested *pursuit* of truth may be granted to such a philosophical exegete in Sisyphian perpetuity.[13] As for Buddhist experience, at the end of the day the important thing is the ability to (in the words of Fujiwara no Teika)[14]

Gaze out far enough,
Beyond all cherry blossoms
and scarlet maples,
to those huts by the harbor
fading in the autumn dusk.

Notes

1. Brough (1949–50) on oral tradition and Pali Buddhism is an exception. George Bond (1982) is also noteworthy in this connection as is Lance Cousins (1987) and Richard Gombrich (1990). Peter Masefield (1986) attempts to call attention to oral tradition, but, as Paul Harrison points out, does so in such a way as to be poorly received by Buddhist monks, Buddhist laity, and philosophers alike (*Numen* 34(2):263–64). But why have scholars of Pali Buddhism usually *not* emphasized the importance of orality in shaping written texts? I suspect that issues of power, class, and gender underlie this "blindspot" in addition to cultural factors. Whalen Lai (1989) points out that despite the fact that narrative literature runs through the entire Buddhist tradition from the *Jātakas* onward, for the most part only the Japanese scholars have paid it much attention.

2. *Apropos* of the issues raised by Mair, it is interesting to notice that Franklin Edgerton (*Buddhist Hybrid Sanskrit Dictionary* vol. 2, 408) has: "*bhāṇaka,* reciter (a kind of entertainer) . . . Cf. Pali *bhāṇaka* f. ika (only of one who recites religious texts?)." Edgerton is thus uncertain. Were there two distinct types of reciters, entertainers *(bhāṇakas 1)* and Buddhist reciters *(bhāṇakas 2),* or were both entertainment and Buddhist text recitation done by the same people? Some *bhāṇakas* were clearly monks, but were all? Further, were monk *bhāṇakas* admitted as reciters only if enlightened? Since "*bhāṇaka*" was an epithet of Buddhist *donors* (presumably householders) mentioned in the inscriptions at Barhut and Sanchi, perhaps their inclinations contributed to the inclusion of *yakshis* (voluptuous tree spirits), *mithunas* (loving couples), and other architectural elements with an appeal more popular than monastic. If so, then another type of explanation for the fusion of spirituality and sexuality in Indian art may be available than vague appeal to "the Indian mind" in contrast to the "American mentality of work ethic and sexual denial or sublimation." For a discussion of later Tantric influence on thought and sculpture, see Coomaraswamy 1985.

3. This paper was written during the William LaFleur/Steven Teiser 1989 NEH Summer Seminar, "Buddhism and Culture: China and Japan." I am grateful to NEH and the co-directors and participants for this stimulating opportunity. My initial interest in the topic began with the John Carman/William Graham 1988 Harvard NEH Summer Institute, "Teaching Comparative Courses." Lecturers Nagatomi, Carman, Graham, and Levering deserve special thanks, as do scripture subgroup participants Jeffrey Timm and José Cabezon. Paul Griffiths, William Graham and Charles Hallisey have written helpful comments on a version of this paper.

4. Paul Griffiths traces "the mind body problem" all the way back to early Buddhism, but I cannot follow him in this. See Hoffman 1989b.

5. Pace A. K. Warder, who calls attention to the importance of historical studies (1985, 115–16). Without denying the great importance of work such as Warder's *Indian Buddhism*, historical and philological approaches to the texts are not the only ones. To emphasize the importance of philosophical approaches to Buddhism is not, of course, to agree with those chastised by Warder who think that Mahāyāna is earlier than Theravada!

6. Vol. 1, no. 215, *Asajjhāyamalā mantā;* vol. 1, no. 265, *Sākacchāya pañña veditabbā;* vol. 2, no. 172, *Sahassamapi ce vācā anatthapadasañhita ekaṃ atthapadam seyyo yaṃ sutvā upasammati.* [Volumes contain number verses but no pagination.]

7. Vajirañāṇavarorasa and Kittidharo (1955). 2:72 *Balaṃ cando balaṃ suriyo balam samanabrāhmanā balaṃ velā samuddassa bhalātibalamitthiyo;* 2:87 *Bahumpi ce sahitaṃ bhāsamāno na takkaro hoti naro pamatto gopova gāvo gaṇayaṃ paresaṃ na bhāgavā sāmaññassa hoti;* 2:162 *Yathāpi kumbhakārassa katā mattikabhajanā sabbe bhedapariyantā evam maccāna jīvitaṃ;* 2:196 *Tagaraṃ va palāsena yo naro upanayhati pattāpi surabhī vāyanti evaṃ dhīrupasevanā.*

8. As LaFleur (1988, 8) observes, " 'Taking refuge in the dharma' corresponds to the content of Buddhist belief and Buddhist philosophy; it is the intellectual component of Buddhism, although many Buddhists will wish to insist that its content is richer and deeper than those things we usually discover by our intellect alone."

9. The 1989 NEH UCLA Summer Seminar "Buddhism and Culture: China and Japan" exemplified well how the initially problematic situation of discussing Buddhism without a common (disciplinary) language can be transformed into a beneficial cross-disciplinary learning situation for those involved.

10. Readers interested in the idea of the Pali Canon may consult Steven Collins's (1990) important contribution on this topic.

11. There is something to be said for the "five *Nikayas*" usage, but see, for example, Richard Gombrich (1988) speaking of the "four *Nikayas.*"

12. Here a pertinent philosophical question arises: Is the underlying *experience* of enlightenment the same in the different Buddhist traditions? For an attempt to find "the same nondual experience" in Buddhism and much else besides, see *Nonduality* (Loy 1988, 184).

13. Among the residual questions for this paper are: Can the recognition of the importance of orality be a continuing part of a research program that concentrates primarily upon written texts? Is orality destined to be an issue important in, but marginal to, mainstream scholarship on written texts? If not, then how can it make a continuing impact as a topic to be investigated? If so, what does this say about our culture—is it really a "culture of the book" (as William Graham and others suggest)?

14. Cited in LaFleur (1983, 101–2) along with the following gloss: "Perhaps the speaker wants to see not only beyond conventional notions of beauty and transience but also beyond all impermanent things. . . . Although not conventional images of mujo, the huts are no less characterized by the radical impermanence of all existent things."

References

Aagaard-Mogensen, Lars, ed.
1986 *Text, Literature, and Aesthetics.* Amsterdam: Rodopi.

Alper, Harvey
1989 *Understanding Mantra.* Albany: State University of New York Press.

Beardsley, Monroe
1977 "Aspects of Orality: A Short Commentary." *New Literary History* 8(3): 521–30.

Bond, George
1982 *The Word of the Buddha.* Colombo: M. D. Gunasena & Co.

Brough, John
1949–50 " 'Thus Have I Heard.' " *Bulletin of the School of Oriental and African Studies, University of London* 13(2): 416–26.

Clark, Walter E.
1930 "Some Problems in the Criticism of the Sources for Early Buddhist History." *Harvard Theological Review* 23(2): 121–47.

Collins, Steven
1990 ''On the Very Idea of a Pali Canon.'' *Journal of the Pali Text Society* 15: 89–126.

Coomaraswamy, A. K.
1985 ''Sahaja.'' In *The Dance of Shiva.* New York: Dover.

Cousins, Lance
1987 ''Pali Oral Literature.'' In *Buddhist Studies* edited by Philip Denwood and Alexander Piatigorsky, 1–11. London: Curzon Press.

Deutsch, Eliot
1988 ''Knowledge and the Tradition Text in Indian Philosophy.'' In *Interpreting across Boundaries,* 165–73. Princeton: Princeton University Press.

Gombrich, Richard
1988 *Theravada Buddhism.* London: Routledge.

1990 ''How the Mahāyāna Began.'' In *The Buddhist Forum* edited by Tadeusz Skorupski, 21–30. London: School of Oriental and African Studies.

Graham, William A.
1987a *Beyond the Written Word.* Cambridge: Cambridge University Press.

1987b ''Scripture.'' In *Encyclopedia of Religion,* edited by Mircea Eliade, 133–45, New York: Macmillan.

Griffiths, Paul
1986 *On Being Mindless: Buddhist Meditation and the Mind-Body Problem.* LaSalle, Ill.: Open Court.

Harris, Wendell V.
1988 *Interpretive Acts.* Oxford: Clarendon.

Hartman, Geoffrey
1981 *Saving the Text.* Baltimore and London: Johns Hopkins University Press.

Hoffman, Frank J.

1982 "Early Buddhist Four Fold Logic." *Journal of Indian Philosophy* 10(4): 309–37.

1983 "Remarks on Blasphemy." *Scottish Journal of Religious Studies* 4(2): 138–51.

1987 *Rationality and Mind in Early Buddhism.* Delhi: Motilal Banarsidass.

1989a "More on Blasphemy." *Sophia.* Australia: Deakin University. 28(2): 26–34.

1989b Review of Griffiths 1986. *Journal of the International Association of Buddhist Studies* 11(2).

1991 "Towards a Philosophy of Buddhist Religion." *Asian Philosophy* (University of Nottingham) 1(1).

LaFleur, William R.

1983 *The Karma of Words.* Berkeley and Los Angeles: University of California Press.

1988 *Buddhism.* Englewood Cliffs, N.J.: Prentice-Hall.

Lai, Whalen

1989 "Avadana-vada and the Pure Land Faith." *Pacific World* (Berkeley, Calif.), 1–7.

Lamotte, Etienne

1988 *History of Indian Buddhism.* Louvain: Peeters Press.

Larson, Gerald James

1988 "Introduction: The Age-old Distinction Between the Same and the Other." In *Interpreting across Boundaries,* 3–18. Princeton: Princeton University Press.

Law, Bimala Churn

1933 *A History of Pali Literature,* Vol. 1. Varanasi: Bhartiya.

Levering, Miriam, ed.

1989 *Rethinking Scripture.* Albany: State University of New York Press.

Lopez, Donald, ed.
1988 *Buddhist Hermeneutics.* Kuroda Institute Studies in East Asian Buddhism. Honolulu: University of Hawaii Press.

Loy, David
1988 *Nonduality.* New Haven: Yale University Press.

Mair, Victor H.
1988 *Painting and Performance.* Honolulu: University of Hawaii Press.

Masefield, Peter
1986 *Divine Revelation in Pali Buddhism.* London: Allen & Unwin.

Nakamura, Hajime
1988 "The Meaning of the Terms 'Philosophy' and 'Religion' in Various Traditions." In *Interpreting across Boundaries,* edited by Gerald Larson and Eliot Deutsch, 137–51. Princeton: Princeton University Press.

Norman, K. R.
1983 *Pali Literature.* In *A History of Indian Literature,* Vol. 7, edited by Jan Gonda. Wiesbaden: Otto Harrasowitz.

Piyadasi, (Thera)
1964 *The Buddha's Ancient Path.* London: Rider & Co.

Rowland, Benjamin
1967 *The Art and Architecture of Ancient India.* London: Penguin Books.

Smart, Ninian
1988 "The Analogy of Meaning and the Tasks of Comparative Philosophy." In *Interpreting across Boundaries,* edited by Gerald Larson and Eliot Deutsch, 174–83. Princeton: Princeton University Press.

Smith, Jonathan Z.
1982 *Imagining Religion.* Chicago and London: University of Chicago Press.

Smith, Wilfred C.
1989 "Scripture as Form and Concept." In *Rethinking Scripture,* edited by Miriam Levering, 29–57. Albany: State University of New York Press.

Taylor, Mark C.
1982 *Deconstructing Theology.* AAR Studies in Religion, no. 28. New York and Chico: Crossroad and Scholars Press.

Teiser, Stephen
1988 *The Ghost Festival in Medieval China.* Princeton: Princeton University Press.

Vajirananavarorasa, Prince H. R. H, and Kittidharo, Phra Maha Prayong, eds.
1955 *Buddhasasanasubhasita Buddhist Proverbs.* Vols. 1–3. Bangkok: Mahamakut Educational Council, Buddhist University of Thailand.

Warder, A. K.
1985 *New Paths in Buddhist Research.* Durham: Acorn Press.

Wimsatt, W. K., and Beardsley, M. C.
1946 "*The Intentionalist Fallacy.*" *Sewanee Review* 54: 468–88.

Twelve

VASUBANDHU'S *VYĀKHYĀYUKTI* ON THE AUTHENTICITY OF THE MAHĀYĀNA *SŪTRAS*[1]

José Ignacio Cabezón

Introduction

What is a canon, and what does it mean to be authentic scripture? Scholars in the field of scripture studies have often overlooked the views of traditional scholars in their attempts to provide answers to these questions. The reasons for this perceived need to distance oneself from traditional exegesis, from the way traditional scholars read their own texts, are, it seems to me, various. In some cases the tradition's readings of its own texts are perceived as naive and unsophisticated, especially when compared to the principles set forth in contemporary philosophical hermeneutics and literary theory. The frequently consistent and univocal nature of a tradition's interpretive principles in this regard are seen as signs of simplicity and naiveté, again, especially when compared to the debates over methodology that rage in the corresponding Western fields. In other instances, "overlooking" traditional hermeneutics provides modern scholarship with the necessary space to develop "exegesis" (*lege* agenda) of their own, and there is certainly nothing wrong with this as long as it is acknowledged as such and not portrayed either as *the* unique reading or as the views of the tradition. But sadly, this is too often the case. In its most offensive form, this attitude toward traditional hermeneutics has manifested itself as a speculative enterprise, often based on reductionist ideologies that use native exegesis selectively in an attempt to create a formal system unknown to, and frequently in conflict with, the tradition's self-understanding. Oftentimes, however, the views of traditional scholars are set aside neither because of a perceived naiveté nor for the purpose of axe grinding but because the traditional answers to such questions are couched in a nexus of overt religious presuppositions, with respect to which the "objective" scholar must, by convention, remain neutral. But as we have seen already in the preceding chapters, it is in these very presuppositions, in the very expression of such religious claims as set forth by the traditional exegete, that tremendous insight and originality manifests itself.

Consonant with the thrust of this book, the goal of the present chapter is to present the views of one such traditional Buddhist scholar, Vasubandhu, on the question of the nature of the canon and of the authenticity of scripture. The *Vyākhyāyukti,* Vasubandhu's text, is a clearly apologetic work that presupposes a variety of overtly religious claims, and yet it will emerge that the *Vyākyāyukti's* treatment of the question of the canon and its authenticity is both imaginative and sophisticated. Its repudiation of both historical and linguistic/philological criteria as determinants of authenticity, as we shall see, speaks as much to the modern as to the Buddhist scholastics of Vasubandhu's day.

In an influential and provocative essay, "Sacred Persistence: Toward a Redescription of Canon," Jonathan Z. Smith (1982) reflects on the way religious traditions define and limit their identity through a fixed set of elements—texts in the case of literate cultures—and the concomitant process of transcending these limits through the rule-governed exegetical enterprise.[2] Smith argues that the examination of this process of limitation and extrication, of canon formation and exegesis, ought to be one of the chief concerns of comparative religions.[3] He states that

> this has a number of consequences. It would mean that students of religion might find as their most congenial colleagues those concerned with biblical and legal studies rather than their present romantic preoccupation with the "primitive" and "archaic"—terms which have largely meant simple or primordial in the sense of uninterpreted, and which have given the historians of religion license for ultimate acts of imperialism, the removal of all rights to interpretation from the native, and the arrogation of all such rights to themselves. (p. 43)

This exegetical imperialism, as we have seen, has found a number of expressions. Eschewing such exegetical imperialism, this chapter proposes a description of some of the interpretive techniques found in early Mahāyāna Buddhist scholasticism. Whereas Smith's article focuses on exegesis as the medium through which a tradition "ingeniously" extricates itself from the limiting predicament that is the canon, the present work seeks to show the role that exegesis plays in the very process of canon formation. In other words, Smith demonstrates how interpretation is the vehicle for the influx of creativity in a tradition with a well-established canonical corpus. This chapter, taking this insight a step further, will argue that interpretation is itself an essential part of the process of establishing the canonical status of disputed texts. Specifically, the present chapter will examine the role of systematic exegesis in early scholastic polemics regarding the authenticity of the Mahāyāna scriptures, a corpus of Buddhist texts that began to emerge in the first few centuries of the first millennium C.E., texts perceived as apocryphal (*gzhung du byas ba*) by earlier Buddhist sects.[4]

The goal of the Mahāyāna scholastics who take up the question is, of course, to refute the arguments of the "Śrāvaka sects," who wish to demonstrate that "the Mahāyāna is not the Buddha's word." By so doing, the Mahāyānists seek to establish the authenticity of their *sūtras.* A variety of early sources indicate that the Mahāyāna scriptures were disputed texts whose authenticity was often questioned. The *Lotus Sūtra,* itself an early Mahāyāna scripture, condemns to dire consequences those who would question its authenticity,[5] something hardly necessary if aspersions had not already begun to be cast on the authenticity of texts of this genre. The question is taken up a number of times by the Indian scholastics themselves. The earliest instance is the brief polemic found in Nāgārjuna's *Ratnāvalī* (second century C.E.).[6] Bhāvaviveka (sixth century C.E.) spends a considerable portion of the fourth chapter of the *Madhyamakahṛdaya*[7] and its autocommentary, the *Tarkajvālā,*[8] discussing this very issue, though it is clear that many of his arguments are borrowed from an earlier text, the *Vyākhyāyukti,* of which we shall have more to say below. The question is also taken up by Śāntideva (ca. 650–750 C.E.) in his *Bodhicaryāvatāra.*[9] Barring Nāgārjuna's treatment of the subject, which is brief, the earliest full account of the question of the authenticity of the Mahāyāna scriptures is to be found in the *Vyākhyāyukti* [The Science of Exegesis] a work of the fourth-century Indian Buddhist scholar, Vasubandhu.[10]

I. The Vyākhyāyukti[11]

The *Vyākhyāyukti* is a work of the Mahāyāna scholastic tradition.[12] It is a fascinating text for a number of reasons, not least of which is the fact that it sets forth in a lucid and systematic manner the theoretical foundation for the entire scholastic enterprise, something that depends so heavily on the exegetical act. Given the richness, breadth, and importance of the text, it is amazing that it has received so little attention on the part of Buddhologists.[13] This is due, in part, to the inherent complexity of the work and in part to the fact that the only extant version of the text is the Tibetan one.

The *Vyākhyāyukti* (tib. *rNam bshad rigs pa*) is a work of slightly over one hundred folios in five chapters found in the *sems tsam* (*cittamātra*) section of the Tibetan *bsTan 'gyur.*[14] As the name implies, it is a treatise on the art of proper (*yukti*) commentary (*vyākhyā*), providing not only practical examples of how one is to go about the process of "explaining the *sūtras*,"[15] but also elucidating certain theoretical concerns that arise in the process of determining what constitutes (both structurally and ideologically) a proper commentary.

Ancillary to the *Vyākhyāyukti* are two texts that, at least for the modern scholar, serve functions more text critical than explanatory. The first is the *Vyākhyāyuktisūtrakhaṇḍaśata,*[16] a collection of 105 *sūtra* passages that serve as Vasubandhu's source material, both in his task of demonstrating commentarial technique and in his exposition of theoretical issues. The second ancillary work is the *Vyākhyāyuktiṭīkā*[17] of Guṇamati (fifth century C.E.).

In the *Vyākhyāyukti* Vasubandhu examines in detail not only the question of what it means to explain the purport of the text, but also the *object* of the exegetical enterprise, to wit, the Buddha's word. In this context, and more specifically in the context of replying to objections (*brgal lan*) concerning *buddhavacana,* he examines the question of the authenticity of the Mahāyāna *sūtras,* the subject to which we now turn.

II. The Mahāyāna as the Buddha's Word

A variety of textual sources are witness to the fact that the Mahāyāna scriptures were considered apocryphal by a significant sector of the Indian Buddhist philosophical community for a considerable period of time. Indeed, for more than six hundred years we find Mahāyāna scholars engaged in what they considered to be a refutation of the arguments of their opponents, the followers of the Śrāvakayāna.[18] As with a great deal of scholastic polemic, it must be granted that, especially in the later scholastic literature, the controversy must have been purely theoretical. Certainly by the time of Śāntideva in the eighth century (and probably much earlier) the vast majority of Mahāyāna *sūtras* were already accepted as the Buddha's word by anyone who was going to do so. Despite the fact that the later tradition's treatment of the subject might have been a mere theoretical exercise, a vestige of past concerns, there is no reason to doubt that for the early Mahāyāna scholastics the issue of whether or not the Mahāyāna *sūtras* were the Buddha's word was a viable one, reflecting an ongoing controversy that threatened the very foundations of the Mahāyāna scholastic enterprise. If the Great Vehicle was not the Buddha's word, then needless to say, the scholastic edifice based on them would be seriously compromised.

Perusing the arguments in their most elaborate form (i.e., as presented in the *Vyākhyāyukti* and in the *Tarkajvālā*) reveals first of all the highly polemical nature of the rhetoric. Most of Vasubandhu's treatment of the subject, for example, is in an opponent/reply format, where different followers of the "Śrāvakayāna" (*nyan thos theg pa*) give reasons for why the Mahāyāna cannot be considered the Buddha's word, followed by Vasubandhu's rebuttals. In the *Vyākhyāyukti,* as in the *Tarkajvālā,* the burden of proof rests with the Śrāvaka sectarians (*nyan thos sde pa*). Hence, the focus of both texts is on refuting the position of opponents and, at least in the fourth chapter of the *Vyākhyāyukti,* Vasubandhu never argues in a positive fashion for the authenticity of the Mahāyāna *sūtras.* This is hardly surprising; indeed, even imagining the form that such an argument might take is not easy.[19]

III. The Nature of the Arguments

Morphologically, the arguments in the *Vyākhyāyukti* may be categorized into three specific types.[20] This is to say that the arguments put forth by the followers of the Śrāvakayāna in their attempts to call into question the authenticity of the Mahāyāna *sūtras* are of three basic kinds. The first type can be characterized as arguments from form; the second, arguments from content; and the third, arguments based on intercanonical criteria for authenticity. The arguments from form, or structural arguments, assume a certain normative structure to the collection of Buddhist texts as a whole; that is, they assume a distinctive notion of a canon, and attempt to show how the Mahāyāna texts cannot be considered the Buddha's word by demonstrating some incompatibility with what had come to be accepted (*'grags pa*) as the canon. The second type of argument, that from content, assumes certain *doctrinal* norms and, similarly, seeks to establish the apocryphal nature of the Mahāyāna *sūtras* by urging that their doctrinal content does not conform to what is doctrinally normative. In the third type of argument we find the Śrāvakas citing scriptural passages in which the Buddha is portrayed as setting forth criteria for what is to be considered his word, this with a view toward demonstrating that the Mahāyāna fails to meet these criteria. Vasubandhu sees his main task in the fourth chapter of the *Vyākhyāyukti* as the refutation of these arguments.

It seems that the earliest notion of a Buddhist canon is that of the *tripiṭaka,* or three baskets, consisting of the Buddha's discourses (*sūtra, mdo sde*), those concerned with the discipline of the monks and nuns (*vinaya, 'dul ba*) and the treatises on speculative metaphysics (*abhidharma, chos mngon*). There were other methods of subdividing the canon, however.

A late Mahāyāna *abhidharma* text, the *Saṃskṛtāsaṃskṛtāviniścaya* of Daśabalaśrīmitra, describes a fivefold division (*rnam pa lnga*) that includes stanzas (*gathas, tshigs su bcad pa*) and proto-*abhidarma* texts called *matṛkas* (*ma mo*). In addition Daśabalaśrīmitra goes into considerable detail concerning one ninefold and another twelvefold division (*aṅga*) of the scriptures,[21] demonstrating how these more elaborate structures can be subsumed within the tripartite formulation of the three baskets. Although interesting in its own right, especially to those of us enamored of what one contemporary scholar has termed *listenwissenchaften,* the relevance of this topic to the present discussion lies in the fact that it was particularly within the twelvefold schema that Mahāyānists sought to locate their *sūtras.* Hence, Daśabalaśrīmitra states: "The *Vaipulya* (*shin tu rgyas pa*) and *Adbhuta* (*rmad du byung ba*) sections are the *Bodhisattvapiṭaka.*"

Throughout the *Vyākhyāyukti* Vasubandhu argues not merely for the authenticity of the Mahāyāna *sūtras* but for the equivalency of the Mahāyāna and *Vaipulya* portion of the twelvefold division as well.[22] In short, he argues not only for the authenticity of the Mahāyāna *sūtras* but for their canonicity as well. Through his defense of the authenticity of the Mahāyāna *sūtras,* he is seeking to give these texts a canonical home.

The Structural Arguments. The structural arguments, as we have mentioned, presume a distinctive form for the Buddhist canon and urge the incompatibility of the Mahāyāna with this form. For the most part, Mahāyāna scholastics such as Vasubandhu criticize these arguments by showing that they are based on faulty or naive notions of the canon. For example, in the first argument in the *Vyākhyāyukti* the follower of the Śrāvakayāna is portrayed as challenging the authenticity of the Mahāyāna scriptures on the basis of the fact that "they contradict what has come to be recognized as the Buddha's word" (Vasubandhu, n.d., P.113b, D.97a).[23] Vasubandhu's rebuttal is primarily aimed at demonstrating the naiveté of the opponent's conception of the Buddha's word. Instead of contesting the fact that the Mahāyāna contradicts the corpus of religious literature recognized as canonical by earlier Buddhists, he shows how that earlier canon (a) suffers from the same apparent contradiction that the Mahāyāna is being accused of and (b) is incomplete.

Citing a series of passages from a variety of acknowledged canonical sources, including the controversial "Killing one's father and mother," he concludes that *if taken at face value* even the Śrāvaka canon would have to be accepted as being rife with contradictions. The solution, he states, is not to question the authenticity of what has for centuries come to be regarded as the Buddha's word, but instead to show some sophistication in its manipulation. It is at this juncture that he introduces his Śrāvaka opponent to the doctrines of definitive meaning (*nītārtha, nges don*) and provincial meaning (*neyārtha, drang don*).[24] Citing yet other passages from the early canon, he goes on to show how the apparent inconsistencies can be reconciled through interpretation. Those passages that cannot be taken literally must be considered to be of ulterior purport (*ābhiprāyika, dgongs pa can*) and must be interpreted. It is clear from his rhetoric that Vasubandhu perceives himself as having turned the tables on his Śrāvaka critic. When challenged concerning the fact that the Mahāyāna contradicts the doctrines of the established canon, Vasubandhu demonstrates that that very canon, naively thought by the Śrāvaka to lack inconsistency, actually suffers from the same fault. What is more, by introducing the doctrines of definitive meaning and ulterior purport, he is in a sense playing a form of one-upmanship with his opponent by showing that the Mahāyāna has a method of coping with scriptural inconsistency that the Śrāvakayāna does not, hence the relative hermeneutical sophistication of the Mahāyāna.

Again, in an attempt to expose the naiveté of his opponent in regard to the notion of canon, Vasubandhu goes to great lengths to demonstrate that the Śrāvaka canon by comparison to which the authenticity of the Mahāyāna is being challenged is itself incomplete.[25] Citing over a dozen *sūtra* passages, he proves without a doubt that there are texts mentioned in the Śrāvaka's own canon that no longer exist historically, that is, *sūtras* whose oral recitation lineages have been lost.[26] Not only are we missing *sūtras* and portions of *sūtras*, but we cannot even be sure of the editions of the texts that we do have. He states:

> *sūtras* such as the *Mahāparinirvāṇa Sūtra* are recited differently. Hence . . . it is clear that even in the Śrāvakayāna the word of the Buddha is incomplete. Even the authorized editions (*yang dag par bsdus pa'i gzhi bo*) which are composed by the four arhants such as Mahākaśyapa, etc. have degenerated, for the various sects (*sde pa*) have disparate ways of setting forth the scriptures, of dividing them into chapters, and so forth. . . . What is more, even in one sect, one and the same *sūtra* will oftentimes have different passages and chapters. . . . Hence, when the authorized versions have degenerated how can we know that the word of the Buddha exists in its entirety? (P.116b, D.99b)

Another form of structural argument attributed to the Śrāvakas is more crass. Here we find attempts to bring into question the canonical status of the Mahāyāna by offering definitions of *buddhavacana* that clearly cannot include the Mahāyāna *sūtras*. Among them we find the claim that the Buddha's word "is anything held in common by the eighteen (Śrāvaka) subsects" (P.124a, D.106b). To this Vasubandhu retorts that even among the eighteen Śrāvaka subsects there is considerable disagreement as to what is canonical work,[27] making this criterion an unacceptable one on which to base the definition of the Buddha's word.

Realizing that consensus among all of the eighteen subsects as a criterion for authenticity excludes a vast amount of literature from the canon, another opponent urges that only those works that are upheld (as authentic) by certain lineages of masters (*acārya, slob dpon*) should be considered the Buddha's word (P.124b, D.106b).[28] Although allowing for canonicity of a wider range of textual material, this definition in a sense begs the question, for it must offer reasons for accepting certain "lineages of certain masters" while repudiating others, which it fails to do. As Vasubandhu states, "How can *all* of those mutually inconsistent expositions be considered the Buddha's word?" (P.124a, D.106b). Moreover, given the fact that "not all of the Buddha's word exists nowadays," any definition of the Buddha's word that seeks to characterize *buddhavacana* in terms of what exists at any point in time is bound to fail in that it is unable to account for the canonicity of lost works. Hence, from Vasubandhu's viewpoint, neither history nor philology can serve as the basis for the criterion of authenticity or canonicity.

Arguments from Content. The arguments that challenge the authenticity of the Mahāyāna *sūtras* on the basis of their content are, by comparison to the structural arguments, far more prevalent, not only in the *Vyākhyāyukti* but in other texts such as the *Tarkajvālā* as well. Here the Śrāvakas are characterized as claiming that the *sútras* of the Great Vehicle cannot be considered the Buddha's word because uniquely Mahāyāna doctrines such as the selflessness of phenomena and the fact that the historical Buddha was an illusory manifestation (*nirmāṇa, sprul pa*) cannot be considered Buddhist doctrine. Vasubandhu, of course, never questions the uniqueness of certain Mahāyāna doctrinal tenets, nor does he attempt to reduce the Mahāyāna to the Śrāvakayāna, for, as he states, these tenets "were not meant to be taught to [the Śrāvakas] . . . for it would depress them" (P.125b, D.107b). When a Śrāvaka opponent then asks him whether the Buddha was deceptive, whether he "taught to the Śrāvakas [a doctrine] that was half true and half false" (P.125b, D.108a), Vasubandhu answers with a question:

> [Reply:] Is the Blessed One being deceptive when he teaches that sentient beings are manifest and existent?
>
> [Opponent:] (But he does not mean this literally). When the Blessed One explains things by means of an ulterior purport he is not being deceptive.

> [Reply:] Then when the Blessed One explains (to you, the Śrāvaka) that phenomena exist by means of an ulterior purport (when they are actually empty) he is not being deceptive.

In short, Vasubandhu uses the uniqueness of certain Mahāyāna doctrines as a way of entering into a discussion of the notion of *upāya* (*thabs*), or skillful means. Again his tack is to demonstrate that this notion cannot be repudiated by the Śrāvakas because it is an implicit, though perhaps unacknowledged, element in the reading of their own canon, as the above passage clearly demonstrates.

The notion of skillful means comes into play, however, only after the doctrine in question has been shown to be a viable one. Obviously it would be absurd to claim that the Buddha had taught an untenable doctrine as supreme. Before invoking the *upāya* principle to explain the different levels of tenets, it is necessary to prove their viability *as* tenets. Thus, one of the principal tasks of the *Vyākhyāyukti* is to demonstrate that these uniquely Mahāyāna tenets are reasonable. Anticipating the objection that the *Prajñāpāramitā Sūtras*, perhaps the most important genre of Mahāyāna scripture, teach nihilism when they quite pointedly state that nothing exists, Vasubandhu explains that these claims cannot be taken literally and that the *Sūtras* themselves are of ulterior purport. This does not, however, prevent the opponent from raising the objection that within the *Prajñāpāramitā* lies the danger of nihilism:

> Hence, because this will destroy those of feeble intellect, how can one accept them to be scriptures at all? Even if you claim, as you do, (that they are not to be taken literally), there will always be someone who will be attracted to the view that nothing exists. (P.118a, D.101a)

Vasubandhu's reply is a reasonable one. He states that if these works lead to the degeneration of certain individuals, it is no fault of the texts themselves but either of the "faulty wisdom" of the adepts or of their *karma*. Ultimately, he claims, it is obstinacy in one's refusal to admit that there are nonliteral passages, passages that require exegesis, that is the cause of being lead astray:

> If one *does* accept (that there are non-literal passages) then how could the Mahāyāna scriptures be regarded as apocryphal, as works that lead to the destruction (of those who follow them)? (P.118b, D.101b)

Vasubandhu then cites a variety of Mahāyāna scriptures to prove that these are the works that repudiate false views such as nihilism, that they advocate the conventional doctrines of Buddhism such as charity, moral conduct, love, and compassion. More importantly, however, he actively demonstrates how the apparently nihilistic claims of the *Prajñāpāramitā* are to be correctly interpreted. In this he relies heavily on the *Saṃdhinirmocana Sūtra,* the text that forms the basis of the hermeneutic of the Mind-only school to which Vasubandhu and his brother, Asaṅga, belong.[29]

We must remember that Vasubandhu is engaged not only in establishing the validity of the Mahāyāna but in upholding the tenets of a particular philosophical subschool of the Mahāyāna, the Cittamātra, or Mind-only, school. Here the great nemesis is not the Śrāvakayāna but a rival Mahāyāna school known as the Madhyamaka. The Madhyamaka, of course, does not dispute the authenticity of Mahāyāna scriptures such as the *Prajñāpāramitā Sūtras,* but it does offer explanations of these works that contrast markedly with the Cittamātra's. By interpreting these *sūtras* literally, the followers of the Cittamātra claim that the Mādhyamikas fall into the extreme of nihilism. Hence we find that Vasubandhu on several occasions[30] faults the Mādhyamikas for failing to properly interpret the message of the *Prajñāpāramitā Sūtras.* In this sense it is clear that he views the Madhyamaka and the Śrāvakayāna as two sides of the same coin in that both fail to realize the importance of interpretation. The Śrāvakayāna, on the one hand, because of its naive notion of canon and its fixation on completeness and consistency, fails to appreciate the need for exegesis. The Mādhyamikas, on the other hand, attracted as they are to doctrinal nihilism, are portrayed as lacking the will to repudiate, through proper exegesis, the *Prajñāparamitā's* claims that nothing exists. In both cases the lack of proper interpretation of the scriptures (either through naiveté or through obstinacy) condemns these two schools to logical fault.

Intercanonical Criteria for Authenticity. One of the most interesting arguments ascribed to the Śrāvakas in the *Vyākhyāyukti* is based on canonical passages that themselves give criteria for what is to be considered the Buddha's word. As we have pointed out above with reference to the *Lotus Sūtra,* the fact that there exists intercanonical speculation concerning the question of authenticity is clear indication of the fact that this must have been an issue prior to the discussions we find in the scholastic literature. Be that as it may, the Śrāvakas are here portrayed as relying on these intercanonical criteria as a way of bringing into question the authenticity of the Mahāyāna *sūtras.* The argument, as we shall see, is in part an argument from form and in part one from content. In so far as it presumes a normative notion of canon (here specifically *sūtra* and *vinayapiṭakas*) and urges commensurability with these as necessary conditions for authenticity, it shares obvious similarities to the structural arguments described above. In so far as the final of the three criterial is "noncontradiction with reality" (*dharmatā, chos nyid*), it hearkens back to the arguments from content.

The actual statement of the position in the *Vyākhyāyukti* reads as follows:

> Let us say that what is commensurate with the *sūtrānta,* what appears in the *vinaya* and what does not contradict reality is the Buddha's word, for these are the reliable teachings of the Great One. (P.124b, D.106b)

Although the *sūtra* that is the basis of this paraphrase is not identified in Vasubandhu's text, it is cited in the *Ṭīkā*:

> That is the valid teaching of the Great One. It is not the teaching of the Dark One. Simply because a monk says that he directly heard something, that he directly apprehended it from the Blessed One, one should not rejoice in his explanation, one should not be dazzled by it. One should neither rejoice nor should one be dazzled by it. It should be commensurate with the *sūtrānta,* it should appear in the *vinaya,* it should be consistent with reality. If it is *made* to exists in the *sūtrānta* and *made* to appear in the *vinaya* but is not (actually) in the *sūtrānta,* does not actually appear in the *vinaya* and is not consistent with reality, then you should address the monk as follows. "Venerable One, without a doubt, those doctrines are not the workds of the Blessed One (D.270b); the Venerable One has incurred a fault. Those doctrines have been made to exist in the *sūtrānta,* have been made to appear in the *vinaya*, whereas they do not exist in the *sūtrānta*, they do not exist in the *vinaya* and they are inconsistent with reality. Hence, they are not the Dharma, they are not the *vinaya,* they are not the teachings of the teacher. Knowing this, you should give them up!" (P.153a–b, D.270a–b)

Vasubandhu's response to such an argument is straightforward. Consider the following exchange:

> [Reply:] But what *are* the *sūtrānta* and the *vinaya,* and what *is* reality?
>
> [Opponent:] The *sūtrānta* and the *vinaya* are what have been properly collected by the redactors; and reality is the characteristic of phenomena as it has come to be known through those (two sets of texts).
>
> [Reply:] Haven't I demonstrated that the basis of the collections has deteriorated?

> [Opponent:] Well, let reality be (that doctrine) that has been set forth in whatever has been collected in any sect.
>
> [Reply:] Haven't I already refuted that by saying, "How can all of these mutually contradictory (doctrinal positions) be considered the Buddha's word?" (P.124b, D.107a)

Hence, as in the previous arguments, the historical incompleteness and philologically problematic nature of the various editions of the canon vitiate against it being the standard of authenticity. At this point, however, the Śrāvaka changes tactics, and the argument shifts from a structural one to one based on content *qua* doctrine:

> [Opponent:] Well then, let us say that (the Buddha's word) is that which is *not discordant* with what exists in the *sūtrānta* that teach the four noble truths, with (a notion of *vinaya*) as the disciplining of the afflictions and with a notion of reality as dependent origination. (P.124b, D.107a)

Vasubandhu makes it clear that he is quite willing to live with such a definition of the Buddha's word but hastens to add that the Mahāyāna is quite compatible with such a definition.

This same argument we find duplicated in *Bodhicaryāvatāra* (IX,43) and its commentarial literature. Śāntideva's conclusion being, "Whatever reasons you (the opponent) give for your belief (that your own scriptures are the Buddha's word) similarly (apply to validate) the Mahāyāna." Hence, from Śāntideva's viewpoint, any criterion that is general enough to account for the textual and doctrinal diversity of the Śrāvaka *piṭaka,* would also serve to validate the authenticity of the Mahāyāna *sūtras.* After citing the Śrāvaka's argument, that concordance with *sūtra, vinaya,* and reality is the criterion for authenticity, and after maintaining that the Mahāyāna qualifies as being *buddhavacana* according to this criterion, Prajñākaramati's rebuttal takes a slightly different direction. Arguing that in the Mahāyāna there also exist scriptural (i.e., intercanonical) sources for determining what is to be considered the Buddha's word, he cites the *Sūtra Eliciting the Superior Thought* (*Lhag pa'i bsam pa bskul ba'i mdo*) as providing *the* correct definition of the Buddha's word.[31] A work, states the *Sūtra,* is authentic if it (1) is meaningful, (2) possesses the Dharma, (3) eliminates the afflictions, and (4) teaches the benefits and qualities of *nirvāṇa.* What is most interesting about this passage, however, are the lines that follow:

> Maitreya, whatever monk or nun or layman or laywoman has had, will have or has confidence in those four reasons should be regarded by the son or daughter of good family as a buddha. Regarding them as the teacher, they should listen to the holy Dharma

> from them. Why? Maitreya, it is because whatever is spoken correctly (*legs par*) is the Buddha's word . . . the fact that it does not contradict reality is the proper definition (of the Buddha's word). (P.246a–b)

Vasubandhu himself never goes so far as to suggest that anything that is true, anything that is spoken correctly, is the Buddha's word, but it is clear that later scholastics who base themselves on his arguments do not hesitate to do so. The *Vyākhyāyukti's* claim, as well as the claim of the root text of the *Bodhicaryāvatāra,* is more modest; namely, that any intercanonical definition of the Buddha's word having a chance of success is bound to be general enough to allow for the authenticity of the Mahāyāna *sūtras.*

IV. Conclusion

Against the onslaught of Śrāvaka arguments that question the authenticity of the Mahāyāna *sūtras,* Vasubandhu's chief weapon seems to be what he characterizes as "proper exegesis," the literal title of his work. Against the structural arguments he argues for a more sophisticated notion of canon. In the process he rejects the Śrāvaka presupposition that the Buddhist canon, even the less complex version known to them, is complete and consistent. The lack of completeness, he implies, is a fact that we must live with, but the lack of consistency is something that is in the scholar's power to rectify. Through "correct exegesis," that is, through interpretation based on the distinction between principles of definitive meaning and ulterior purport, the apparent inconsistency disappears. The implication is, of course, that this same hermeneutical strategy can be applied to the *Mahāyāna* scriptures, thereby reconciling *them* to the existing canon. Though perhaps not guaranteeing their authenticity through positive arguments, Vasubandhu repudiates the claim that they are apocryphal.

Just as "proper exegesis" is Vasubandhu's response to the structural arguments, so too is it his solution to the doctrinal ones. If properly interpreted, he claims, even the apparently nihilistic claims of the *Prajñāpāramitā Sūtras* can be understood to be cogent. Hence, in the process of arguing for his particular interpretation of the doctrine of emptiness, that of the Cittamātra school, he argues for the need to properly interpret the *Prajñāpāramitā Sūtras,* perhaps the principal source of this doctrine. This silences the Śrāvaka opponent, whose principle objection to these texts lies in the fact that their doctrines, if taken literally, are tantamount to nihilism. "Proper exegesis," says Vasubandhu, is the corrective to this misunderstanding. He claims that these scriptures were never meant to be taken literally, that their meaning must be elucidated through exegesis. Ironically, the same argument applies to the Mādhyamikas. If the Śrāvakas can be characterized as attempting to fault the Mahāyāna for its nihilism, from Vasubandhu's viewpoint, the Mādhyamikas are evidenty seen as having already fallen into the trap by willingly accepting the literal, and therefore in his eyes the naive, interpretation of these works. The solution to both problems is therefore identical: it is proper exegesis that insures the legitimacy of the doctrines espoused by the Mahāyāna *sūtras.*

Of the arguments that rely on certain scriptural citations (i.e., canonical sources) for the determination of criteria of authenticity, we can recognize two types. The more crude forms of these arguments are shown to either beg the question or to be reducible to the arguments from form or content already discussed. If, however, these passages, and others from the Mahāyāna's own corpus, are "properly interpreted," and if the Mahāyāna *sūtras* in question are themselves "properly interpreted," these criteria will also be seen to imply the authenticity of the Mahāyāna scriptures.

In a recent article, Matthew Kapstein (1989) has argued that the definitions of *buddhavacana,* the Buddha's word, that depend on "concepts of consensus, doctrinal content, accord with manifest reality, and so forth, all involve a weakening of the view suggested by strict historical realism," (P.222) the view that the Buddha's word is "the actual speech sounds produced at given places by the Śākyamuni himself" (P.221). Hence he concludes that the Tibetan tradition, the heirs to the form of Indian scholasticism that gave rise to these ahistorical characterizations of the Buddha's word, "was never successful in its attempt to elaborate from the standpoint of historical realism a satisfactory set of criteria for scriptural authenticity" (P.224), with the result that it was "incapable of giving rise to a wholly critical method of textual research" (P.237).

The question raised implicitly in Kapstein's article is one of the most fascinating in the field of comparative hermeneutics. When it comes to the question of the authenticity of texts, there seem to be two major avenues of approach: the first, a path admired by elements of the Śrāvaka community and many members of our own, looks to history and to philology as the answer to questions of authenticity; the second, espoused by early Mahāyāna scholastics such as Vasubandhu, looks only to ahistorical elements, where accordance with reality is the ultimate and final criterion, as the relevant factors in the determination of authenticity. It is tempting at this point to suggest the naiveté of this latter approach, either attributing the ahistorical nature of the analysis to a form of religious dogmatism that refuses to subject its tenets to spaciotemporal scrutiny or, worse, attributing it to a historical naiveté that seems to many to be endemic to India. I would suggest, however, that when Vasubandhu rejects historical and philological criteria as irrelevant in the discussion of the authenticity of texts, he does not do so naively, that is, unaware of historical or philological methods. Even a cursory reading of the fourth chapter of the *Vyākhyāyukti* reveals Vasubandhu's critical examination of historical and philological methodology. Far from rejecting these in an *ad hoc* or naive way, he does so *consciously* and only after considerable reflection. In his critique of the completeness of the canon Vasubandhu demonstrates the futility of applying philological or text-critical methods (e.g., the comparison of different lineages of recitation) toward the goal of producing an historically accurate and complete corpus of texts giving us access to the Buddha's word. Hence, the Mahāyāna scholastic rejection of history (or what Kapstein calls "historical realism") in favor of a doctrinal or philosophical principle ("accordance with reality") as the ultimate criterion of authenticity is far from being an instance of hermeneutical naiveté. It is, in fact, the result of a considerable critical reflection.[32] That reality was the guiding principle of Mahāyāna scholastic hermeneutics, and that exegesis was the road to it, will not surprise those familiar with this literature. That scholars like Vasubandhu were aware of the myriad obstacles involved in advocating such a theory, that they defended it rigorously in a manner critically sophisticated even by today's standards, may come as a surprise. In such insights, I believe, lies the unique value of exploring comparative traditional hermeneutics.

Notes

1. This article was written during tenure of a Fulbright Senior Research Fellowship in India in 1989. I take this opportunity to express my thanks to the staff of the United States Educational Foundation in India and to Professor Ramshankar Tripathi of the Sraman Vidya Sankay, Sampurnananda Sanskrit University, for their hospitality as my hosts during my pleasant stay in India.

2. I have discussed some of the limitations of Smith's article, specifically his notion that the process of canonization is arbitrary, in a recent article, "The Canonization of Philosophy and the Rhetoric of *Siddhānta* in Tibetan Buddhism," forthcoming in the Minoru Kiyota *festschrift* volume.

3. "The task of application as well as the judgment of the relative adequacy of particular applications to a community's life situation remains the indigenous theologian's task, but the study of the process, particularly the study of comparative systematics and exegesis, ought to become a major preoccupation of the history of religions" (Smith 1982, 43) And also,

"I look forward to the day when courses and monographs will exist in both comparative exegesis and comparative theology, comparing not so much conclusions as strategies through which the exegete seeks to interpret and translate his received tradition to his contemporaries" (Smith 1982, 52)

4. It will become evident from my remarks below that I disagree with Matthew Kapstein (1989) when he states that "a text is called 'aprocryphal' not so much in virtue of its being so regarded within the tradition in whose scripture it is found but, rather, in virtue of the scholar's judgement" (P.219), as when he claims that there is no sufficient basis "for the regular use of the phrase 'Buddhist apocrypha' except in the sense first defined, that which refers to texts whose origins, when scrutinized from a philological standpoint, are deemed suspect" (P.220). The notion of "apocrypha" found in polemics concerning the authenticity of the Mahāyāna *sūtras* of the sort I describe below, a notion found within the tradition itself, seems to me to be perfectly understandable. Of course, such a notion must be recognized to be relative in the sense that what is apocryphal for one segment of a tradition might very well be canonical for another, a point that Professor Kapstein himself makes but one page earlier in his essay. Nonetheless, that there is an identifiable and meaningful notion of an apocryphal text in the Buddhist tradition seems to me to be indisputable. By this passing remark I do not mean to question the overall importance of Professor Kapstein's excellent essay, which I consider to be one of the most lucid, sophisticated and provocative articles on the question of canonicity in Buddhist Studies to date. It seems that Dr. Ronald M. Davidson has also devoted an article on this subject, to appear in Robert Buswell, ed., *Buddhist Apocrypha*, a work that I have yet to see.

5. Gāthās 113–36; see also Dutt (1976, vi).

6. sDe dge edition (D) of the Tibetan Tripitaka, Toh. no. 4158, Peking edition (P) no. 5658, dBu ma *dza*. The relevant passage is to be found at the end of the fourth chapter, P folio 147a. See also the very brief comments in the *Ṭīkā* attributed to Ajitamitra, P no. 5659, dBu ma *dza* folios 194a–b. For a partial bibliography of work that has been done on *Ratnāvalī* see Nakamura (1987, 241); see also Hahn 1982, and an unpublished article by the same author, "Das alteste Manuskript von Nāgārjunas Ratnāvalī," as well as the forthcoming study of the text by Ngawang Samten.

7. D Toh. no. 3855; P no. 5255, dBu ma *dza*. The fourth chapter is to be found on folios 19a–22b. Most of the text has been studied by the Japanese but has received little attention on the part of Western scholars. See Nakamura (1987, 284) and the following note.

8. D Toh. no. 3856; P no. 5256, dBu ma *dza*. The commentary on the fourth chapter is to be found on folios 157b–218b. See also Nakamura (1987, 284); also Iida 1980 and Gokhale and Bahulkar 1985.

9. D Toh. no. 3871; P no. 5272, dBu ma *la*. The relevant portion is to be found on folios 36b–37a. See also Nakamura (1987, 287–88).

10. On the dates of Vasubandhu, see Frauwallner 1951 and Jaini's 1958 response to Frauwallner; for bibliographical references to the work of Japanese scholars who contest Frauwallner's thesis, see Nakamura (1987, 268).

11. This section is for the most part a synopsis of a recent paper that is to appear shortly in the Jagannath Upadhyaya *festschrift* (Cabezón, "Some Notes on the *Vyākhyāyukti,*" *forthcoming).*

12. I discuss the tradition of Buddhist scholasticism in a forthcoming book, *Buddhism and Language: A Study of Indo-Tibetan Scholasticism.*

13. Aside from passing references in a variety of works, to my knowledge there exist only the two articles of Susumu Yamaguchi on the *Vyākhyāyukti,* viz. *Nippon Bukkyō Gakukai Nenpō* 25 (1959) pp. 35–68, and *Tōhō Gakukai Sōritsu Jūgoshūnen Kinen Tōhōgaku Ronshū* (1962) pp. 369–91, and the one of Matsuda (1985).

14. D Toh. no. 4061, Sems tsam *si,* folios 29a–134b; P no. 5562, Sems stam *si,* folios 31b–156a. As with the other two works we shall mention below, the *Vyākhyāyukti* was translated into Tibetan from the Sanskrit by a team consisting of two Indian scholars, Viśuddhasiṁha and Śākyasiṁha, and one Tibetan scholar, Devendrarakṣita.

15. D 29a: *mdo rnams 'chad 'dod de dag la / de la phen par bya ba'i phyir/ man ngag cung zad bstan par bya.* "I will now give a little advice that may be of help to those who wish to comment on the *sūtras.*"

16. D Toh. no. 4060, Sems stam si, folios 17b–29a; P no. 5561, Sems tsam *si,* folios 19a–31b. The *Vyākhyāyuktisūtrakhaṇḍaśata* does not identify the scriptural sources of the passages it collects, nor are they identified in the *Vyākhyāyukti* itself. Of the 105 passages in the *Sūtrakhaṇḍaśata,* the first chapter of the *Vyākhyāyukti* is devoted to the explanation of the first, taking it as the "excuse" for setting forth a general theory of commentarial science, not an unknown strategy of the scholastics. The theory is set forth in a verse, the *Vyākhyāyukti* stanza most frequently quoted by Tibetan exegetes:

> Those who relate the meaning of *sutras,*
> Must state their purpose (*prayojana, dgos pa*), their concise meaning
> (*piṇḍārtha, bsdus pa'i don*),

The meaning of the words (*padārtha, tshig don*), the boundaries (of their different sections) (*anusaṃdhi, mtshams sbyar*),
And the contradictions (urged by opponents) with their rebuttals (*codyaparihāra, brgal lan*).

mdo don smra ba dag gis ni
dgos pa bsdus pa'i don bcas dang
tshig don bcas dang mtshams sbyor bcas
brgal lan bcas par bsnyad par bya. (D.30b, P.33b)

This is one of the few verses of the *Vyākhyāyukti* available in Sanskrit:

prayojanaṃ sapiṇḍārthaṃ padārthaḥ sānusaṃdhikaḥ /
sacodyaparihāraśca vācyaḥ sūtrārtha vādibhiḥ // (Haribhadra 1934, 15)

The second chapter, by far the longest, comprising as it does almost half of the entire work, then comments on the remaining 104 passages. Special attention is given in the second chapter to passages 2 through 5, which set forth the qualities of the Buddha. The third chapter begins with a general explanation of the four aspects of the "meaning of the words," namely, synonyms (*paryāya, rnam grangs*), definition (*lakṣaṇa, mtshan nyid*), etymology (*nirukti, nges pa'i tshig*), and the subdivisions (*prabheda, rub tu dbye ba*). Using this model, then, Vasubandhu goes on to consider several passages from the *sūtras* that lead him to discussion of topics as diverse as the theory of dependent arising (*pratītyasamutpāda*), causality, the two truths, and the moral status of getting drunk. In the fourth chapter, our focus in this paper, he defends the authenticity of the Mahāyāna *sūtras* and gives a detailed exposition of the doctrines of provisional (*neyārtha*) and definitive (*nītārtha*) strategies involved in the exposition of the *sūtras,* demonstrating how one should take into account the mental abilities of one's audience.

17. D Toh. no. 4069, Sems tsam *si,* folios 139b–301a; P no. 5570. Sems tsam *si,* folios 1–194a. Guṇamati is attributed with commentaries on the *Abhidharmakośa,* the *Mūlamadhyamakākarikās* of Nāgārjuna, a work entitled *Lakṣaṇanusāraśāstra,* which is an *abhidharma* work whose purpose is to refute the soul theories of the non-Buddhists, as well as with a subcommentary on Vasubandhu's commentary on the *Pratītyasamutpādādivibhaṅganirdeśa-sūtra.* On Guṇamati, see Taranatha (1970 trans.: 10, 212), who states that he was a contemporary of the King Pañcamasiṃha, and also a contemporary of "Saṃpradutaḥ, a disciple of Bhavya." See also Takakasu (1966, lviii, lix, 181); and especially Watters (1961, I, 324; II, 108, 165, 246) where he is variously identified as the "teacher of Vasumitra," a contemporary of Sthiramati, and as having lived earlier than 600 C.E.

18. In this regard, some Tibetan sources make a distinction between the Śrāvakas and the followers of the Śrāvakayāna. We find, for example, in mKhas grub dGe legs dpal bzang's *sTong thun chen mo* (1972, 19) the claim that a Śrāvaka arhant, for example, could not possibly dispute the authenticity of the Mahāyāna *sūtras* because "it would follow, absurdly, that though the arhant had eliminated all of the afflictions, he/she could nonetheless accumulate the karma of disparaging the doctrine (*chos spong gi las*), as if they were still ridden with the ignorance of the afflictions." Hence, from mKhas grub rje's viewpoint, though such a challenge may come from individuals who are Śrāvakas philosophically, it cannot come from the Śrāvakas who have actually obtained the end result of their path.

19. Such arguments were attempted by some early modern Japanese Buddhist scholars; for a summary of some of these arguments, see Mizuno (1982, 125–33).

20. It will become clear that the three types of arguments described here are not always mutually exclusive and at times tend to overlap. Despite this, it seems to me to be a valid and helpful distinction to make in the analysis of these polemics.

21. Nakamura (1987, 28) proposes a theory for the development of the canon based on the diachronic development of the *aṅgas.*

22. The fourth chapter ends with the following lines: "Hence, there is no contradiction in claiming that the Mahāyāna is the word of the Buddha; and therefore there is no contradiction in maintaining that the Vaipulya is the Mahāyāna" (P.133a, D.114a).

23. All references to the *Vyākhyāyukti* are given in terms of the folio numbers of the Peking and sDe dge editions of the Tibetan *tripiṭaka.* For the full references to these texts, see note 14.

24. It is interesting to note that throughout Vasubandhu's arguments he does not actually use the term "provisional meaning," instead pitting the concept of *sūtras* of definitive meaning against that of *sūtras* of ulterior purport. At one point, however, he does use the expression "meaning that is to be interpreted" (*bkri ba'i don*) (P.116b, D.99b).

25. This discussion occurs as a response to an objection concerning the doctrine of definitive meaning raised by the Śrāvaka, one that is not altogether clear. The opponent's question reads as follows: "Why is it that in the Mahāyāna there is absolutely no definitive meaning that allows one to ascertain the lack of contradictions (among scriptures)?" (*theg pa chen po la ni gang gis na 'gal ba med par nges par bzung ba'i nges pa'i don cung*

zad kyang med do zhe na) (P.114b, D.97b) From one viewpoint, the question makes sense, because up to this point Vasubandhu has cited only from the Śrāvakas' own canon in support of the fact that contradictions can be reconciled through reference to other scriptures and through interpretation. One would think, however, that in reply to the Śrāvakas' objection Vasubandhu would simply have stated that such Mahāyāna scriptures, texts that arbitrate between disparate claims such as the *Saṃdhinirmocana Sūtra,* do exist (something that he in any case does do subsequently). Instead he uses the opponent's remark as a springboard to an excursus on the incompleteness of both canons, so that the first statement of his rebuttal is, "Have you been told or shown the entire Mahāyāna by the grace of the gods?" from which he goes on to demonstrate that the canon is incomplete and that the editions of texts that we do have are untrustworthy. From this it seems that this is a subject that Vasubandhu felt was important to treat in its own right right, so that despite the fact that he had a much easier rebuttal to the Śrāvaka objection available at this point, he chose a more circuitous approach with the aim of bringing up the question of the incompleteness of the canons.

26. On the question of the oral transmission and preservation of the Buddhist *sūtras,* see Graham (1987, 68).

27. Here he cites the example of two works that, though accepted by some, are contested by other subsects, to wit, the *Sūtra of Ultimate Emptiness (Don dam pa stong pa nyid kyi mdo)* and the *Sūtra of the Seven Existences (Srid pa bdun gi mdo).* He goes on to state that this same disagreement exists concerning the *vinaya* and *adhidharma* as well as the *sūtrānta.*

28. This argument is repeated with a slight variation in Śāntideva's *Bodhicaryāvatāra* (IX, 43). For the most extensive discussion in the Indian commentarial literature, see Prajñākaramati's remarks in his *Pañjikā,* P no. 5273, dBu ma *la,* folios 247ab.

29. The principles of this hermeneutical method have been discussed extensively in Tsong kha pa's *Legs bshad snying po,* translated by Thurman (1985, 191–208). See also mKhas grub rje (1972, 20–67).

30. See, for example, P.128a, D.109b passim.

31. Vasubandhu (P.125b, D.107b) also cites a different unidentified Mahāyāna *sūtra* as providing five reasons that determine whether or not something can be considered a *sūtra:* (1) because it is in complete accord with the correct usage of terminology, (2) because it is in accordance with the method of various intentions, (3) because it accords with the fact that those who hold to it with great force understand reality, (4) because it is in

accordance with the fact that from the understanding of its meaning one comes to abide in the happiness that is distinguished by bliss and (5) because, since it sets forth a coherent narrative (*'bel ba'i gtam nyid*), it accords with the way in which wisdom analyzes things.

32. Of course, whether or not such reflection is valid is a different question altogether. It will itself have to be subjected to the same type of scrutiny as any other form of critical self-reflection.

References

Bu ston Rin chen grub
1986 — *The History of Buddhism in India and Tibet.* 1932. Reprint. Translated by E. Obermiller. Delhi: Sri Satguru.

Cabezón, José Ignacio
forthcoming — "The Canonization of Philosophy and the Rhetoric of *Siddhānta* in Tibetan Buddhism." M. Kiyota *festschrift.* Edited by J. Keenan and P. Griffiths. San Francisco: Buddhist Books International.

forthcoming — "Some notes on the *Vyākhyāyukti* of Vasubandhu and Its Ancillary Literature." To appear in the Jagannath Upadhyaya *festschrift.*

forthcoming — *Buddhism and Language: A Study of Indo-Tibetan Scholasticism.* Albany: SUNY Press.

Davidson, Ronald M.
in press — "Appendix" to *Buddhist Apocrypha,* edited by Robert Buswell. Honolulu: University of Hawaii Press.

Dutt, Nalinaksha
1976 — *Mahāyāna Buddhism.* Calcutta: Firma KLM. (Corrected reprint of the 1973 edition)

Frauwallner, E.
1951 — *On the Date of the Buddhist Master of the Law Vasubandhu.* Serie Orientale Roma 3. Rome: IsMeo.

Gokhale, V. V., and Bahulkar, S. S.
1985 "Madhyamakahṛdayakārikā Tarkajvālā, Chapter I." In *Miscellenea Buddhica*, Indiske Studier 5, edited by Chr. Lindtner. Copenhagen: Akademisk Forlag.

Graham, William
1987 *Beyond the Written Word: Oral Aspects of Written Scriptures*. Cambridge: Cambridge University Press.

Hahn, Michael
1982 *Nāgārjuna's Ratnāvalī*. Vol. 1. Bonn: Indica et Tibetica Verlag.

Haribhadra
1934 *Abhisamayālaṁkārāloka Prajñāpāramitāvyākhyā. Edited by U. Wogihara. Tokyo: Toyo Bunko.*

Iida, Shotaro
1980 *Reason and Emptiness: A Study in Logic and Mysticism*. Tokyo: Hokuseido Press.

Jaini, P.
1958 Review of E. Frauwallner's *On the Dates of the Buddhist Master of the Law Vasubandhu. Bulletin of the School of Oriental and African Studies* 21: 48–53.

Kapstein, Matthew
1989 "The Purifactory Gem and Its Cleansing: A Late Tibetan Polemical Discussion of Apocryphal Texts." *History of Religions* 28 (3): 217–44.

mKhas grub dge legs dpal bzang
1972 *sTong thun chen mo*. In Madhyamaka Text Series, vol. 1, edited by Lha mkhar yongs 'dzin bstan pa rgyal mtshan. New Delhi: Editor.

Matsuda, Kazunobu
1985 "The Two Truths Discussed in the Vyākhyāyukti: Notes of Vasubandhu (2)" [in Japanese]. *Indogaku Bukkōyagaku Kenkyū* 33(2): 750–56.

Mizuno, Kogen
1982 *Buddhist Sūtras: Origin, Development, Transmission*. Tokyo: Kosei.

Nakamura, Hajime
1987 *Indian Buddhism: A Survey with Bibliographical Notes*. Delhi: Motilal Banarsidass.

Smith, Jonathan Z.
1982 "Sacred Persistence: Toward a Redescription of Canon." In *Imagining Religion: Babylon to Jonestown*. Chicago: University of Chicago Press.

Takakasu, J.
1966 *A Record of the Buddhist Religion as Practiced in India and the Malay Archipelago by I-tsing*. New Delhi: Munshiram Manoharlal.

Taranatha
1970 *History of Buddhism in India*. Translated by Lala Chimpa and A. Chattopadhyaya, and edited by D. Chattopadhyaya. Simla: Indian Institute of Advanced Studies.

Thurman, Robert A. F.
1987 *Tsong kha pa's Speech of Gold in the Essence of True Eloquence*. Princeton: Princeton University Press.

Vasubandhu
n.d. *Vyākhyāyukti*. Tibetan translation in the Tibetan Tripitaka, Peking edition no. 5562, sDe dge edition (Toh. no. 4061), Sems tsam *si*.

Watters, T.
1961 *On Yuan Chwang's Travels in India (A.D. 629–645)*. New Delhi: Munshiram Manoharlal.

Thirteen

Poetics as a Hermeneutic Technique in Sikhism

Nikky-Guninder Kaur Singh

> In the process of understanding there takes place a real fusing of horizons, which means that as the historical horizon is projected, it is simultaneously removed.
>
> —(Gadamer 1986, 273)

Introduction

The foregoing chapters have considered, in great detail, a variety of hermeneutical moments from among the religious histories of South Asia. Conspicuous by its absence from this array of hermeneutical strategies and approaches is the consideration of poetics as a hermeneutical technique. The composition and recitation of poetry is not an uncommon form of religious expression, but it may not be immediately thought of as a hermeneutic technique. In the present chapter I propose to examine how poetics was employed as a means of encountering scripture by the Sikh hermeneute Bhāī Vīr Singh. Born on December 5, 1872, in a devout Sikh family, with traditions of learning on both the paternal and the maternal side, Bhāī Vīr Singh from a very early age engaged his intellectual energies in the process of understanding and interpreting Sikh scripture, the Gurū Granth. Between the interpreter and his text was a gap of approximately three centuries that not merely contained the given linear progressions' alterations and developments but also played host to a dynamic encounter between East and West on Indian soil.

With the fall of the Sikh kingdom in 1849, Punjab became the last major territory in India to become part of the British empire and, with the shattering of cultural barriers, found itself within the orbit of a new consciousness. Christian missions, English schools and colleges, while inviting attention to their unique ideologies and independent denominational world-views, fostered—ironically—the development of indigenous cultural traditions and the vernacular Punjabi language and literature. The Presbyterian mission that preached the Gospel, ran an English school with a rather innovative curriculum, and set up a printing press—a pioneering enterprise for Punjabi publications—extended its work from Ludhiana to Lahore. The press initiated a number of translations into Punjabi of sections of the Bible and English classics such as *The Pilgrim's Progress.* Indeed, the first book to be printed in the Gurmukhī script was the Bible itself. Amritsar, the city where Bhāī Vīr Singh came of age and where he spent most of his adult life, also became an important seat of Christian missionary activity. The evangelists read in the Sikhs' rejection of caste and idolatry an openness to "scriptural truth." Their optimism regarding the potential of finding converts from the Sikh faith is apparent in the valedictory instructions given T. H. Fitzpatrick and Robert Clark, the first missionaries of the Church of England appointed to the Punjab:

> Though the Brahman religion still sways the minds of a large proportion of the population of the Punjab, and the Mohammedan of another, the dominant religion and power for the last century has been the *Sikh religion,* a species of pure theism, formed in the first instance by a dissenting sect from Hinduism. A few hopeful instances lead us to believe that the Sikhs may prove more accessible to scriptural truth than the Hindus and Mohammedans. (*Historical Sketches of the Indian Missions,* 27)

The evangelizing efforts in the region of Punjab were immensely successful, and several Sikhs embraced Christianity. With the advent of Western learning, there was also a loosening of the hold of Brahmanical wisdom: Sikhs saw alternative models for apprehending their scriptural inheritance. Overall, the atmosphere was one in which tradition and modernity, East and West, combined to either create a rich synthesis or erode the self-esteem and identity of the natives. Bhāī Vīr Singh seized the moment and the mechanisms to signal a return to the sacred Sikh text and recapture the original message of the Gurūs in order to reestablish Sikh identity. While he looked to the past to revive the original purity of Sikh belief, he also looked to the future with a view to leading the community into the modern age. Bhāī Vīr Singh possessed the wide, superior vision that allowed him to extend "beyond what was close at hand—not in order to look away from it, but to see it better within a larger whole and truer proportion" (Gadamer 1986, 272). While projecting the Sikh historical perspective, Bhāī Vīr Singh succeeded in simultaneously blending the past with the present; the origins of Sikh faith were infused with the thought processes of the twentieth century.

This fusion, it may be stated, was a combination of three elements: understanding the Sikh scriptural writ, interpreting it in the context of the prevalent *zeitgeist*, and applying it to obtaining conditions. Although this tripartite preoccupation can be construed as identifying three distinctions made within the tradition of hermeneutics (namely, that of *subtilitas intelligendi, subtilitas explicandi*, and *subtilitas applicandi*), in Bhāī Vīr Singh's outlook they comprise a unified process.

Prior to Bhāī Vīr Singh's advent on the Punjabi literary scene, the emphasis was on *subtilitas intelligendi*. Sikh scriptural commentators assiduously cultivated a highly complicated and metaphysical conceptual framework. Rather than simple interpretation, an esoteric textual meaning was profferred. Scholars within the two early schools of Sikh scriptural interpretation (Udāsī and Nirmalā), being essentially reared in classical Indian exegesis, amplified Sikh thought through classical Hindu texts. The works of Anandghana and Bhāī Santokh Singh—representatives of the Udāsī and Nirmalā schools, respectively—have been carefully researched by Nripinder Singh (Nripinder Singh 1985, chapter 5). His study shows that the Udāsī and Nirmalā exegesis of Sikh scripture was saturated with Upaniṣadic and Purāṇic learning, and the style and content of their speculations brought about a reincubation of Hindu ideology in Sikh thinking (579–946). The *Farīdkot Tīkā*, a project entrusted to a team of scholars by Mahārājā Bikram Singh, ruler of the principality of Farīdkot (hence the name *Farīdkot Tīkā*), was in many ways a turning point in Sikh hermeneutics, but it too had its limitations: its Sikh authors used the stylized vernacular reminiscent of Sanskrit scholars and emulated the devices prevalent in learned Hindu discourse.

In contrast, the thrust of Bhāī Vīr Singh's interpretation was to render the Sikh message clearly and simply—and independent of the Hindu *zeitgeist*. In this, his aim was to elicit the attention of the common person, the average Sikh, and bring about a fresh consciousness of and a new commitment to Sikh values. Simple Punjabi became the medium of his writing. His interpretations took on varied forms: poetry, novel, exegesis, and tract. His literary production is voluminous. His writings include eight collections of poetry, four novels, a play, five biographies, and nine texts that he meticulously annotated and commented upon, all along keeping up with journalism and tractarian writing. The formal commentary on the Gurū Granth was started late in his career, and he devoted several years unsparingly to the project. Unfortunately, it was not completed during his lifetime and was published posthumously in seven large volumes. Bhāī Vīr Singh's exegesis of the *Japujī* in 178 pages is a telling illustration of his erudite scholarship.

The verses have been analyzed in great length and depth; allusions, symbols, and a glossary of terms have been provided; individual words have been etymologically traced; references to preceding commentators have been extensively made *(Japujī Sāhib Saṅthyā)*. He is also the reviser of *Gurū Granth Kosh*, a dictionary of the Gurū Granth, which again explains important terms and allusions in great detail. It provides extensive information on the musical notation adopted for the Gurū Granth as well (Talib and Singh 1973, 15).

Bhāī Vīr Singh's most significant contribution is also a radical one: in interpreting the Gurū Granth he was singularly successful in using poetics as a methodological principle of interpretation and exploration. Since the source of Bhāī Vīr Singh's inspiration was the Sikh faith, and since the resurrection of the message of the Gurū Granth was the preeminent principle governing his literary activity, he is, to use Emerson's analogy from *The Poet*, a glass through which later generations can see the Gurū Granth in all its philosophical, spiritual, ethical, and aesthetic richness. Not through the deployment of traditional modes of commentary but through poetry alone is the poetry of the Gurū Granth to be understood. The present chapter endeavors to show how Bhāī Vīr Singh made the poetic technique an integral part of Sikh hermeneutics. We will look into the Gurū Granth as the poetic matrix; focus on Bhāī Vīr Singh's anthology of poems called *Mere Sāiān Jīo* as the hermeneutic text; and explore the uniqueness of the Sikh poetic syntax.

I. Gurū Granth: The Poetic Matrix

The genesis of the Sikh religion can be traced to Gurū Nānak's drinking of the cup of Name-adoration. As recorded in the *Purātan Janamsākhī*, the young Nānak was ushered into the Divine Presence and blessed: "I have bestowed upon thee the gift of My Name. Let this be your calling"[1] (Bhāī Vīr Singh 1948, 16–17). Nānak celebrated the favor through a song of praise; and song was to be the medium of his divine inspiration ever after. He reveled in calling himself a poet: "To you belong my breath, to you my flesh; says the poet Nānak, you the True One are my Beloved"[2] (Gurū Granth, 660). In *Gurū Nānak and Origins of the Sikh Faith*, Harbans Singh distinctly affirms the significance of the first Sikh mentor-prophet's poetic technique:

> All of Gurū Nānak's teaching is set forth in verse. His genius was best expressed in the poetical attitude. No other way would have been adequate to the range and depth of his mood—his fervent

> longing for the Infinite, his joy and wonder at the beauty and vastness of His creation, his tender love for his fellowmen, his moral speculation and his concern at the suppression and exaction to which the people in his day were subject. His compositions reveal an abounding imagination and a subtle aesthetic sensitivity. (pp. 215–16)

The source of Gurū Nānak's artistic outpourings was the Transcendent One: "As comes to me the Lord's Word, that is how I deliver it, O'Lālo,"[3] said the Gurū (Gurū Granth, 722). The Gurū Granth evolved from the sacred songs of Gurū Nānak.

Although Gurū Arjan, Nānak V, compiled the Granth, the overall involvement with a book proclaiming the Word of divine truth had started with Gurū Nānak himself. We hear from Bhāī Gurdās that Gurū Nānak carried a book (a manuscript of his poetic utterances) under his arm (Bhāī Gurdās, Vārāṅ I.32). It has also been recorded in the *Purātan Janamsākhī* that before Gurū Nānak passed away, he bequeathed his Word recorded in book form *(pothī)* to his successor, Gurū Angad. "It was Gurū Nānak who celebrated and consecrated the item by making his *pothī* the oil and mantle for the anointing of a successor who, in turn, composed more hymns, commissioned more *pothīs* for a growing body of disciples already attuned to the words of their First prophet-mentor" (Nripinder Singh 1985, 436–37). Soon afterward there arose schismatic groups that started composing hymns and making them current under the name of Nānak. The problem of the "counterfeit" writings became acute during Gurū Arjan's time. Since Gurū Rām Dās had bypassed his two older sons and appointed the third—Arjan—to Gurūship, Pirthī Chaṅd, the eldest, was estranged from him. He and his gifted son, Miharbān, began to compose poetry under the name of "Nānak." It was with a view to affixing the seal on the sacred poetry and preserving it for posterity that Gurū Arjan codified the sayings of the Gurūs into an authorized volume. And in any case, as Nripinder Singh writes, "the Gurū-s' word, cherished and venerated from the very beginning as the medium of divine revelation and comprising a significant factor in the reflection of the faith, had one day to receive form" (Nripinder Singh 1985, 437). Gurū Arjan worked on the sacred text on the outskirts of Amritsar; Bhāī Gurdās was the calligrapher. Poetry of several Hindu Bhaktas and Sufis was also included in the volume. Gurmukhī was the script used for transcription. The completion of the Granth was celebrated with much jubilation. The completed volume was placed in a palanquin bedecked with precious stones and carried by Gurū Arjan, his son Hargobind, Bhāī Gurdās, and Bhāī Buddha, and installed at the Harimandir on August 16, 1604. On October 6, 1708, Gurū Gobind Singh, Nānak X, apotheosized the Granth as Gurū: the poetic text was to become the Gurū eternal for the Sikhs.

The 1,430 pages of the Gurū Granth are but an exposition of the opening statement: ੧ ਓ ⌒ "One Reality Is."[4] Numerical, alphabetical, and geometrical forms have been used to signify and celebrate the existence of the Singular One. Although ੧ and ਓ are the beginning of the mathematical and verbal languages, the arch rising above the syllable ਓ is at once without beginning or end. Here, then, is succinctly presented the Sikh ontological framework: the "One" is the beginning of all, and yet no one can comprehend the commencement or cessation of Its condition. The Transcendent Reality that it represents is thus "One," beyond gender and causality; it is spaceless and timeless. The theme running throughout the Sikh Holy Writ is the human being's longing for this Singular Being, which is molded into poetic symbolism of great aesthetic delicacy and charm. The central image is that of the bride, with whom the Gurūs and Bhaktas identified themselves; the ardor of the heart is expressed through her voice. Throughout the scripture, the bride remains a very potent figure, intensely devoted to her Transcendent Groom and ever seeking for It. The Gurū Granth contains no dogma. There is no societal code prescribed in it. There are no obligatory acts enumerated. The text carries only intimations. Sikh thought has felt itself at home in poetry. The "*Muṅdāvanī,*" the seal to the Granth put by Gurū Arjan, states that the word be partaken of, that it be savored:

> On the platter lie arranged three delicacies:
> Truth, contentment, and contemplation.
> S/he who eats them, s/he who savours them
> Obtains liberation.[5]

No conceptual formulations are offered; a full and rich relishing of the sacred poetry is the response demanded. The aesthetic experience of the Granthian poetry is reinforced by the fact that the entire text (with the exception of the *Japu*) was arranged in *rāgas,* or musical measures, by Gurū Arjan himself. The poetry of love and devotion is to be approached with reverent wonder; it cannot be pried into with mere intellect. The Granthian poetry empowered by the *rāgas* in turn becomes the conduit to stimulating the senses and mind into intuiting the Transcendent One.

From the day of its compilation, the Gurū Granth has exerted a profound power in Sikh life. "Acknowledge the Gurū Granth as body visible of the Gurūs"[6] is recited by the Sikhs daily in their morning and evening supplications. The poetic text for the Sikhs is the continuing authority, spiritual as well as historical. Through this sacred poetry they have been able to observe their faith more fully, more vividly. From the Gurū Granth the community's ideals, institutions, and rituals have derived their meaning. Ceremonies relating to birth, initiation, marriage, and death take place in the sound and sight of this text. The antithesis put forth by Victor Zuckerkandl (1956) that one "attains the inwardness of life by hearing and its outwardness by seeing" (p. 2) is resolved in the Holy Book of the Sikhs, for they cherish not only hearing but also seeing it. It is the sole—aural and visual—icon of the Sikh religion. In times of uncertainty, difficulty, or of joy and auspiciousness, *saptāh* (seven-day), *akhanḍ* (nonstop for forty-eight hours), *sampat* (one particular hymn repeated after each hymn), and *khullā* (not limited in time or manner) recitations of the Gurū Granth are prescribed modes for religious observance. For the Sikhs, the physical presence of the Gurū Granth and its sublime poetry have constituted the twin regulative principles of their psyche and conduct (Harbans Singh 1985, 47–48).

II. Mere Sāinān Jīo*: The Hermeneutic Text*

In the late nineteenth century, when the message of the Gurū Granth began to get blurry, Bhāī Vīr Singh realized the acute need for recovering the value and ideal of Sikhism from within the Sikh scripture. With the establishment of Mahārājā Rañjīt Singh's rule in the Punjab and the splurge of stately power, formal ritual and ceremonial had been ushered into the Sikh faith. Brahmanic rituals discarded by the Gurūs had entered into the Sikh way of life. The loss of political power following the annexation of the Sikh kingdom to British India encouraged conversion to the faith of the new rulers and, oftentimes as a response to that phenomenon, reversion to ceremonial Hinduism. Conversions by Christian missionaries particularly added to the gravity of the identity crisis. In this situation arose Singh Sabhā, a reform movement in Sikhism, corresponding to the Aryā Samāj in Hinduism and the Aligarh awakening in Islam. The Singh Sabhā issued from the deliberations of leading Sikhs of the time such as Thākur Singh Sandhānwāliā, Bābā Sir Khem Singh Bedī, and Kañwar Bikrama Singh of Kapurthalā meeting in Amritsar in 1873. Less than a year old at that time, Bhāī Vīr Singh eventually became its most ardent exponent and eloquent spokesman. According to Harbans Singh, Bhāī Vīr Singh's central aim was the furtherance of the Singh Sabhā enlightenment: "He was able to comprehend the significance of the Sikh traditions so accurately and interpreted them to his generation so powerfully that Sikhism experienced a much-needed revival" (Harbans Singh 1972, 26).

Poetry was Bhāī Vīr Singh's most natural way of self-expression. His epic poem, *Rāṇā Sūrat Singh* (which went the length of twelve thousand lines of verse), was published in 1905. Several collections of shorter poems appeared thereafter. The form of these poems was an innovation in Punjabi literature, and they became instantly popular. While ushering new and quicker lyric tunes and measures into Punjabi prosody, the short poem introduced new words and images as well. *Trel Tupke* was the first collection of poems, to be followed at quick intervals by *Lehrān de Hār, Bijlīān de Hār, Preet Veenā, Kaṅt Mahelī.* An anthology of songs in praise of the Sikh Gurūs was published in 1933 under the title of *Kaṁbdī Kalāī* (The Trembling Wrist). At the age of 81, Bhāī Vīr Singh published his last collection of verse—*Mere Sāiān Jīo.*[7] The dominant strand underlying this prodigious output was his use of poetic strategy to evoke, elucidate, and expand the Sikh scriptural message. Poetically Bhāī Vīr Singh grasped the Gurū Granth, making it diaphanous and alive for his readers. For example, the final stanzas of Gurū Nānak's *Japu* are most artistically and comprehensively explained in *Rāṇā Sūrat Singh* by the protagonist Rāṇī Rāj Kaur, when she describes her journey through light and radiance, a journey in which she is guided by a divine companion to get a sight of her husband in Realm Celestial. For our purposes here, however, we shall concentrate on Bhāī Vīr Singh's last specimen of poetry as a hermeneutic text of the Gurū Granth for the simple reason that that marked the final and culminating point in his poetical career.

The basic Sikh theological concept is elaborated by the heroine of *Mere Sāiān Jīo.* In ardently addressing her Beloved, she is but substantiating the opening statement of the Gurū Granth: *Ikk Oan Kār.* The existence, the being of the Beloved, is affirmed in her very salutation:

My songs,
My Beloved!
Songs sung for you . . .
The waves rise like wind from the ocean,
My silent voice has now burst forth like the nightingale singing,
Like from a child's throat
May the tremors reach forth.
To your presence,
O, my Beloved![8]

These are the opening verses of the poem and provide a personal witness to the is-ness *(Kār)* of the Beloved. The expression is imaginative. The woman's silent voice *(cup galā)* has burst forth like the nightingale's song. The vibrations gushing forth from her heart have been compared to the gusty wind from the ocean on the one hand and to the tiny tremors in a baby's throat on the other. But where are these sound waves heading toward? *"Tusān—mere sāiān jīo—dī hazūrī vic"* is the answer. The presence of the Beloved is thus acknowledged and celebrated. The destination may be far—the gusty wind indicates that—but it certainly exists. The woman needs no ontological, cosmological, moral, or teleological proofs: she knows, she feels, and therefore she yearns for, the presence *(hazūrī)* of her Beloved. She lyrically asserts the Scriptural view that the One is present everywhere. Says Gurū Nānak: ''In whichever direction I turn my eyes, I see You (Gurū Granth, 1343)[9] and Gurū Arjan: ''Visibly present everywhere is the lord of Nānak'' (Gurū Granth, 397).[10]

The origin of her longing for the Beloved, she traces to him: ''You are the One who implanted this sapling.''[11] In this short poem, the woman states that his single glance of benevolence[12] breathes new life into her; his single beautiful gesture[13] fills her with fragrance. Further on she says,

> An aroma struck the mind again,
> Intoxication overtook consciousness. (Bhāī Vīr Singh 1948, 199)[14]

The Beloved thus is the one who created her, sustained her, and awakened her. The aroma, a hint from him—the yonder, formless, intangible, yet powerful and aesthetically pleasing—touches her, and she becomes inebriated with the longing for him. Interestingly, the sense of fragrance intoxicates her mentally, linking up the usual dichotomy of body and mind. Clearly, her desire is not only material in nature but also spiritual. It comes from the depth of her very being. This combination of materiality and spirituality underscores the message of the Gurū Granth: it is the physically attractive woman dressed up in all her finery—with perfumes and jewels—who has the longing for the Divine Groom.

With the vista of the garden as the backdrop, she also makes the philosophical point that the entire universe is dependent upon its singular gardener, her Beloved. In the Gurū Granth, the totally abstract and metaphysical One has been metaphorically addressed as the gardener: ''The world is the garden; my lord is its gardener; ever he guards it, leaving none without protection'' (Gurū Granth, 118).[15] Through his twentieth-century protagonist, Bhāī Vīr Singh is paraphrasing the creating and nurturing functions belonging to the gardener. Through the course of the brief poem, we hear her repeat several times that he is the one who had implanted the sapling *(būtī)*. For their origin and sustenance, the individual shrub and the garden as a whole depend upon him: ''If you forget us even for a moment how will we remain in bloom or be fragrant?'' she asks. The fragrance that the gardener bestows upon the *būtī* is both her elemental energy and the desire for him; the identity between her élan vital and the longing for the gardener, the beloved, constitutes the core of the thematic burden of the poem.

Also to be noted is the fact that Bhāī Vīr Singh is simultaneously highlighting another element from the Sikh worldview: the feminine dimension of the Transcendent One. The One beyond *(Ikk)* is a Gardener—ever caring for and nurturing the world. A harmonious and loving relationship between the Creator and creation has been postulated.[16]

The Beloved[17] is transcendent beyond reach and beyond all categorizations. Nowhere are any contours drawn sketching his form or personality. The metaphor of the Beloved is quickly and skillfully moved into the second person.[18] Although in our references (and in translation as well) the specification of gender occurs, in Bhāī Vīr Singh's composition itself there is scarcely any. *Sāiān Jīo* is constantly beckoned in the second person as *tūṅ* (the neuter form of "you"). The Beloved thus is encountered informally, intimately, but without the emphasis upon "his" form. Therewith, the utter unicity and singularity—the *ikk*-ness of the Sikh ultimate reality is also projected. In one passage she rhythmically repeats "you, you, you,"[19] which but echoes the Granthian style of saluting the *Ikk Oan*. Gurū Arjan's words "you are my father, you my mother, you my friend, you my brother"[20] (Gurū Granth, 118), while shattering the monopoly of male symbols in the depiction of the unicity of the Ultimate Being, expresses the intimate relationship between one and the One. The "I-Thou" encounter put forth by Buber resembles the Sikh communion between the individual and the Divine.

Instead of creating or employing male images, we hear and see the singer of *Mere Sāiān Jīo* trying to visualize the One, the totally abstract and metaphysical Being, in aesthetic terms. A prominent "form" for the Infinite Beloved comes from the aural sphere. It is rendered through the term *rasa* and its variations—as, for instance, in the poem entitled "Rasa, Rasīā Rasāl," which ends with the following lines:

> *vāh vāh coj tere, mere sāiān*
> *tere geetān dīān tainū vadhāiān*
> *tuhon geet, saṅgeet, te suād*
> *rasa, rasīā te āp rasāl.* (Bhāī Vīr Singh 1948, 193)

In the opening line, the maiden expresses her amazement at the marvelous aspect of the Beloved. In the second line, she celebrates the richness and beauty of his songs *(geetān)*. In line three she directly states, "You yourself are the song *(geet)*, you the music *(saṅgeet)*, and you the essential taste *(suād)*." In the final line she addresses him as the aesthetic delight itself *(rasa)*, as the relisher of aesthetic delight *(rasīā)*, and as the provider of aesthetic delight *(rasāl)*. The Beloved therefore is all-encompassing: he is not only the aesthetic joy but its savorer and bestower as well. He is the primal cause and ultimate end of joy. His One-ness is repeated over and over again. Again, Bhāī Vīr Singh is expanding upon scriptural ideas and vocabulary. Song, music, and tasting were, as we saw, very important factors in the creation of the Gurū Granth itself. The songs that Nānak sang, around which the Holy Book was compiled, had their genesis in the Divine Beloved. The image of the Transcendent as possessor of *rasa* also has its archetype in the Gurū Granth. For Gurū Nānak says, "compassionate, beneficent, beloved, enticer of the hearts, full of flavours *(ati rasa),* ever sparkling like the *lala* flower . . ." (Gurū Granth, 1331).[21] In fact, the passage quoted above from *Mere Sāiān Jīo* echoes much of Gurū Nānak's terminology and is evocative of the Gurū's verse in the Gurū Granth: "It itself is the relisher of *rasa,* it itself is the essence, it itself is the bestower" (Gurū Granth, 23).[22]

In her perception of the Beloved, Bhāī Vīr Singh's heroine also avails herself of the symbol of light. For instance, she exclaims that one ray of the Beloved from his luminous form *(nūrī rūp)* so enchanted her. The Arabic/Persian term *(nūr)* for light is also used in two other instances to qualify the Transcendent: "Your light pervades the earth and skies;" "I am desirous of the vision of your luminous form." In another verse she implores her transcendent Beloved:

> Bestow your vision upon me,
> Oh radiance of radiance(s). (Bhāī Vīr Singh 1948, 199)

Here she alludes to him as light of lights or radiance of radiances,[23] which recalls the perception of ultimate reality as *Jyotisam jyoti* and *Nūr al-anwar* from the Hindu and Islamic traditions, respectively. In the Gurū Granth as well, "light" in its Sanskrit and Arabic equivalents has been extensively used as a symbol for the Absolute. For instance, Gurū Nānak in the Gurū Granth states,

> Wheresoever I turn, I see your light,
> what a wondrous form you have! (Gurū Granth, 596)[24]

The concept of light and wonderment at the brilliance of this form is reiterated in *Mere Sāiān Jīo.*

The distance from him—underscoring his transcendence—constitutes the core of an intense experience for Bhāī Vīr Singh's heroine. He remains an enchanting paradox: he is infinite; he is infinitesimal! In either fashion, he is totally beyond her grasp. In the poem entitled "Nikkī God Vic" (In the Tiny Lap), she marvels at the all-pervasive Beloved playing in the tiny lap of a rose:

> At the touch of light *(nūr)* today
> When the morning was beginning to stir . . .
> In the silky lap of a blossomed rose,
> You were playing my Beloved.
> How, yes, how
> Did you enter that tiny lap?
> My great and vast Beloved! (Bhāī Vīr Singh 1948, 195)[25]

The reader is not to infer that her Beloved was literally playing *in* the silky rose; the Beloved was not encapsulated in the rose. That would constitute a misunderstanding of the poet's intent and message. The maiden is struck with the sight of the rose in full bloom during the glory of the morning. So overpowering is the scene that she imagines the infinite Beloved playing in the little rose. The transcendent is never enclosed, never in the rose as such. That Its infinity and formlessness can never be confined in a finite frame has been categorically affirmed in the Gurū Granth: "It cannot be molded; it cannot be shaped,"[26] says Gurū Nānak in the *Japu* (Gurū Granth, 2).

Similarly, in "Sadke Terī Jādūgarī De" (Homage to Your Wondrous Feats), she states that he is within her:

> In me, deep inside, deep inside somewhere
> is hidden my Beloved!
> Yes,
> You strike me with your melodious tunes,
> Touching
> My inner strings.
> They sing songs—
> Songs of separation form you, songs of the anticipation,
> of union with you.
> These do cast magic upon me.
> I gaze all around.
> Trembling, quivering.
>
> Oh Beloved!
> Behind sight hidden Beloved!
> Very near *(kol kol),* but far far *(dūr dūr)*
> Far far *(dūr dūr),* but near, very near *(kol kol)*
> Homage to your miracle! (Bhāī Vīr Singh 1948, 191–92)[27]

Paradoxically, closeness to and distance from the Beloved, as well as his infinitesimalness and infinity, are felt deeply by the woman. He is "close close, but farther than the farthest."[28] He is so close and so small that he abides in her innermost being. But he is hidden *(ohle)* somewhere. Thus, even though he may be very close, very near, he remains inaccessible, totally transcendent. Again, it is clear that he is not enclosed in her; his form is not present within her. Formless, he remains hidden somewhere in her being. Simultaneously, he is infinite and far, far away, and the categories of time and space do not delimit him. In "Dil Saddhar," she says,

> Unfathomable amongst the most unfathomable are you, my Love.
> (Bhāī Vīr Singh 1948, 205)[29]

Finally she accepts the utter ineffability: "Tongue be silent! Trembling and quivering tongue, be silent! Friends! Nothing can here be uttered." The paradox therefore cannot be verbalized. Silence alone can be the only indicator. Having him so close and yet so far, experiencing its infinitesimalness and infinity together is totally overwhelming and defies the articles of speech.

What we have here is a poetic exposition of the scriptural dialectic of the transcendence and proximity of the One *(Ikk).* While maintaining the utter unfathomability and infinity of the Ultimate Reality, the Gurū Granth posits Its presence within everyone:

> You the Primal Being, you are the Infinite Creator
> None can fathom you.
> But within each and every being you are
> Equally, constantly ever.[30](Gurū Granth, 448)

These words of Gurū Rām Dās (Nānak IV) are reiterated by his successor Gurū Arjan (Nānak V): "You are present within all"[31] (Gurū Granth, 1095). In the Āratī the Gurū exclaims: "Within all is the light and the light is That One"[32] (Gurū Granth, 13). The symbol of the insubstantial and nonmaterial light is used extensively in the Gurū Granth to portray the Transcendent One remaining within all of Its manifestations. In another passage, "unfathomable, ineffable, truth is my Lord"[33] (Gurū Granth, 743). The Gurū Granth moreover contains passages expressing the marvel of the dialectic: "Formless and yet archetypal, it takes on substances that enchant all"[34] (Gurū Granth, 287). This enchantment felt by the Fifth Gurū finds a precedent in the thought of Gurū Nānak: "You have a thousand eyes but without eyes you are; you have a thousand forms, but without form you are . . . you have a thousand noses but without nose you are; I am left thoroughly enchanted"[35] (Gurū Granth, 13). Through the expression "thousand," Gurū Nānak is describing the One in terms of the entire gamut of comprehension. Additionally, he juxtaposes Its immensity and infinity, and thus delineates It as beyond all expression and thought. In line with the concept of the *Ikk Oan Kār* as expounded in the Gurū Granth, the woman's vision renders a very positive and joyous image of the Transcendent. Yet it is no image, for the aesthetic delight is devoid of all materiality and substantiality; its intangibility and transcendence can never be formalized into a figure. Pure form is the Beloved, but form realized only in experience. Thus, the marvel of the paradoxical nature of the Metaphysical One encountered in the Gurū Granth is recreated with a sense of wonder and joy.

In presenting Sikh theological concepts enshrined in the Gurū Granth, through his poetry, Bhāī Vīr Singh has succeeded remarkably in emulating the style and idiom of the Sikh scripture. The anthology of poems *Mere*

Sāiān Jīo is saturated with the personal pronoun *"tūn"* encountered in the Gurū Granth. The vocabulary and metaphors and symbols of that text, *"agam," "mālī," "rasa," "nūr,"* occur frequently in his own poems. The very title, *Mere Sāiān Jīo,* furthermore, seems to be both based upon and in turn unfolding the Granthian passage *"kar kirpā mere sāin."*

Besides interpreting the fundamental theological concept, Bhāī Vīr Singh's *Mere Sāiān Jīo* also unfolds the essential epistemological ideal enshrined in the Sikh holy text. The basis of Sikh epistemology is that the *Ikk Oan Kār* is not intellectually apprehended or made the object of reasoning, but felt. The One cannot be objectively proved, it cannot be tested out in mathematical equations; rather, it is subjectively recognized. The *Ikk Oan Kār* is not posited as an impossible goal; rather, it becomes an object of ardent quest, or ardent longing to be undertaken by the self to attain supreme knowledge.

In "Sāiān Jīo dī Siāṇ" (Recognition of the Beloved), Bhāī Vīr Singh's protagonist actually refutes those who think that the Metaphysical One is impossible to know. The opening verse contains the question:

> Who are they who say:
> "Your Beloved cannot be known"? (Bhāī Vīr Singh 1948, 195)[36]

After posing this question, she directly addresses her Beloved, saying that those who see, hear, smell, touch, and taste discern him. Again, it is a short poem but of great artistic and philosophical import. The maiden asserts that those who have eyes discern him from his overflowing beauty *(ḍulh ḍulh pai rahī suṅdartā ton),* which is reflected from the scenes around *(nazārian ton)* and upon the eyesight *(nāzarian te).* She continues in the same lyric style: "Those who have ears know him from his melodious word which reverberates everywhere . . . those who drop away their fears, know him from his sensation-creating touch." His brimming ambrosial drops drop into the mouths of those who, like the *papīhā,* longingly sing for him. At some auspicious moment these ambrosial drops provide the taste of his existence *(hond).* It is thus a clear announcement about the certain possibility of the apprehension of the Beloved, of the *Ikk Oan Kār,* the Ultimate Reality.

Her emphasis is upon *siaṇ,* or recognition, an immediate and exhaustive recovery, reseeing. The Beloved is here, there, everywhere. The vast and magnificent panoramas, the dulcet symphony echoing throughout the universe; these are hints of its ontological presence. But it is the human being who has to apprehend that through all five senses. The physical senses are thus a crucial channel. The process is not an arduous one; it does not call for asceticism; it does not call for the stifling of the senses. Knowledge, too, is not of any new subject-matter, nor is it a garnering of new abstract or scientific facts. On the contrary, the physical senses have to be sharpened and heightened in order for them to recognize the spaceless and timeless Beloved. It is as if Bhāī Vīr Singh were illuminating for readers and hearers the third stage of the *Japu*, the *Saram Khaṇḍ*, wherein "consciousness, perception, mind, and wisdom are sharpened"[37] (Gurū Granth, 7–8). The heightening of the senses means sharpening the perception so that instead of dull and ordinary sensations one experiences deeply the extraordinary. Says Bhāī Vīr Singh's heroine: "Those who transcend the ordinary seeing, hearing, smelling, touching, and tasting, yes, you yourself reveal yourself unto them."[38]

The process of recognition *(siaṇ)* that underlies the Sikh envisioning of the Transcendent is further elaborated in the poem entitled "Andarle Nain" (Inner Eyes). Herein the maiden throws light upon the phenomenon of insight that combines the physical seeing with knowledge and intelligence; *siaṇ* (recognition) by the individual with *lakhānā* (revelation or showing) from the Beloved. The poem in its entirety:

> Eye—the human eye
> Could not see you,
> My Beloved!
> Darkness has overtaken
> Knowledge *(ilmu)* and intelligence *('aql)*.
> Yes, the strong light of intellect,
> It still cannot see you,
> The brilliance is too dazzling.
> Do cast a favourable glance *(nazar)*,
> Do please open the inner eyes,
> Which would see thee
> Whether it be light, dark or bedazzling,
> You, my Beloved! Beloved!
> In every place *(har jā)* in every colour *(har rang)*
> in every direction *(har su)*
> Playing *(kardā khelān)*, yet remaining apart *(rahindā asang)*.
> Handsome, you are the acme of splendour. (Bhāī Vīr Singh 1972, 196)

It is reiterated that the Beloved is all-pervading. The One is in all space, in every color,[39] and in all directions. That he is not only in light but also in darkness is perceived by the maiden. And he pervades everything. Yet paradoxically, he always remains apart *(rahindā asang)* from everything. Again, he is not in anything; he plays within all and everything, maintaining constantly his distance. The Transcendent therefore always remains transcendent.

It is, then, the inner eye that perceives the omnipresent Being. Human knowledge and intelligence are deficient; the physical eye is precluded from discerning It. But a favorable glance *(nazar)* from the Other would open the inner eye and thus provide insight into the Divine Reality. This is the fourth stage of spiritual ascension as delineated by Gurū Nānak in the *Japu Karam Khaṇḍ,* the Realm of Grace. Grace *(nadari),* that is, his glance *(nazar)* of favor, is what the maiden seeks. Touched by his grace, her inner eye would encounter the bedazzling brilliance. The merging of eyesight with insight makes the juncture where human effort is touched by divine grace. It is also the moment of revelation.

Central to Sikh epistemology is the vision of the *Ikk Oan* as a perennial movement. As originally experienced by Gurū Nānak and as illustrated by the heroine of *Mere Sāiān Jīo,* it remains the objective, the goal for every man and woman. The longing for the vision of the Beloved, a mystic consummation between one and the One, is the dominant motif of this anthology of poems; yet the longing remains sheer longing. The finale of *Mere Sāiān Jīo,* ''Nām Piālā'' (The Cup of Nām):

> The cup of the beautiful Word
> Is overflowing O friends.
> Who will have a sip of it?
> Keep watching, O friends.
> She whose own cup of longing is brimming,
> She alone will receive the cup of nectar. (Bhāī Vīr Singh 1948, 212)

The poem recalls the historical moment portrayed in the *Purātan Janamsākhī,* the moment of Gurū Nānak's mystic experience some five hundred years earlier (Bhāī Vīr Singh 1948, 17). That is when he received the ambrosial cup of Divine Name and was launched on his mission. Bhāī Vīr Singh's interpretation of that event through the medium of twentieth-century Punjabi poetry acknowledges that primal moment in Sikh history and projects its application toward the present and future. In the ''Nām Piālā'' segment, the heroine is addressing her female friends. The future of society depends upon them and their male counterparts. Their mission will get launched with the drinking of the ambrosial Word. But who gets to have a sip of it? Who savors it? Paradoxically, it is the individual whose cup brims *(ḍulh ḍulh pai rihā hovai)* with longing *(saddhar)* who stands to gain! For the emptier the inside, the stronger the urge; and, hence, greater the chance of receiving the divine nectar.

Thus, while fusing the horizons and while fusing the processes of understanding, interpretation, and application, Bhāī Vīr Singh's poetry further fuses polarities such as proximity and distance, infinitesimal and infinite, human and divine, male and female, past and future, empty and full. The heroine of *Mere Sāiān Jīo* weaves garlands of songs for her Beloved, who, though close by, remains constantly far away. The *Ikk Oan* is felt intimately by her, within her very self. Yet That One, Transcendent, ever transcendent remains. Through the maiden's songs one realizes that polarities in the Sikh tradition do not violate each other and, instead of being mutually exclusive, enhance each other. First, distance and proximity are fused together. Second, the Unfathomable Infinite Beloved is "seen" by her in the dewdrop shimmering on the silky lap of a rose at the break of dawn. How could the shimmering, miniscule droplet present the indescribable vastness? Third, human language explodes and participates in the communication with the divine. For how else would there be garlands of waves? Fearlessly, the maiden expresses the emotion of love delineated in the Gurū Granth and weaves together the chasm between the human and divine realms. Fourth, Bhāī Vīr Singh's heroine, like the bride figure in the Gurū Granth, restates the primacy of the feminine consciousness in the search for the Transcendent One. Fifth, the crucial moment in Sikh history, the experience of the "primal paradox" by Gurū Nānak, is thrust into the future. And the emptier the cup of longing for a vision of the *Ikk Oan,* the fuller will be the experience of union.

III. Sikhism: The Poetic Syntax

In the above two sections we came face to face with the poetic matrix of the Gurū Granth as the quintessence of Sikh thought and practice, through a sampling of Bhāī Vīr Singh's poetic exegesis. In this final section we will consider two primary questions: What is the relationship between the text and the hermeneute? Why is the poetic syntax so central to the Sikh enterprise? As we consider these questions, what is also disclosed is the criterion for the hermeneute in the Sikh tradition and the unique attributes that inhere in the Sikh poetic syntax.

To repeat, Bhāī Vīr Singh was born in a devout Sikh family with members on both sides deeply imbued in the scholarly study of the Sikh tradition. The relationship between the text and its hermeneute? Indeed, it is a familial and organic one: from childhood on, Bhāī Vīr Singh must have heard the text; he must have grown up with it, absorbed it so fully that its format and expression became a part of his own style. Certainly at times during our analysis of *Mere Sāiān Jīo* it appeared as if he were quoting the Gurū Granth without quotation marks!

This intimate connection between the text and the commentator brings us inevitably to the hermeneutic circle and the problem of prejudice raised by Heidegger and restated by Gadamer. According to Heidegger,

> It is not to be reduced to the level of a vicious circle, or even of a circle which is merely tolerated. In the circle is hidden a positive

> possibility of the most primordial kind of knowing. To be sure, we genuinely take hold of this possibility only when, in our interpretation, we have understood that our first, last and constant task is never to allow our fore-having, fore-sight, and fore-conception to be presented to us by fancies and popular conceptions, but rather to make the scientific theme secure by working out these fore-structures in terms of the things themselves (quoted by Gadamer 1986, 235–36).

Bhāī Vīr Singh's entire being, we maintain, was formed by the Sikh scripture; his "having," his "sight," and his "conception" were indeed constituted by the text itself. How could he go to the text, bracketing out himself? Can one bracket out one's matrix? Can one annihilate (or, in the least, circumvent) one's past? Can the historical horizon ever be shattered? Bhāī Vīr Singh certainly possessed the "pre" or "fore" to all the mentioned dimensions, having, sight, and conception. But when he returned to the text, hermeneutically oriented as he was, he used his preconceptions, his preunderstanding—"a positive possibility of the most primordial kind of knowing hidden in the circle"—in such a way as to charge and ignite the impulse forward. It was not an arbitrary or fanciful usage of his so-called prejudices. The Gurū Granth, to begin with, is, to use Barthe's expression, a "radically symbolic" text (Barthes 1979, 76). Its integrally symbolic nature was conceived, perceived, and received by our hermeneute living in a milieu where Western literature and philosophy were also making their entry. There was then an authentic assimilation of tradition and modernity in the poet's person, the quotation marks being unnecessary. The act of "appropriation" suggested by Eliot Deutsch in "Knowledge and the Tradition Text in Indian Philosophy" is helpful in comprehending the role of the "poet-commentator" in our case (Larson and Deutsch 1988, 172). "Appropriation," Deutsch explains, "is a creative retaining and shaping of a content that is made one's own. It is not a passive receptivity, but a dynamic engagement" (p. 172). When the poetry of the Gurū Granth flowed in Bhāī Vīr Singh's veins, how could his exegesis be otherwise? Then again, his is not a simple reciting of the text that gave him breath but an inventive enterprise forged in the smithy of his very own vision. Bhāī Vīr Singh engaged himself with the text artistically, imaginatively, responding to the inspired utterance through a profoundly grasped perception. He experienced and reimagined in an act of consciousness that, as our analysis of *Mere Sāiān Jīo* showed, linked at once the literary heritage and newness. The reciprocal interplay between the text and the interpreter can be seen as a re-fusion, creating a power and dynamism of its own. In conclusion, Bhāī Vīr Singh's poetic commentary on the Gurū Granth proves Gadamer's point that the Heideggerian hermeneutical circle "possesses an ontologically positive significance" (Gadamer 1986, 236).

It was a return to the poetic syntax that impelled the thrust forward. The Gurū Granth is in the poetic form; Bhāī Vīr Singh's interpretation is in the poetic form. The eminent Sikh theologian Bhāī Gurdās also used the poetic form to interpret and conceptualize aspects of the developing faith.[40] (His ballads, for example, are an imaginative recreation of penetrating intellectual insights.) Our question then is: Why the poetic syntax? Poetry is essential to the basic character of human existence. Here again Heidegger's understanding of poetry is helpful in grasping the importance of the poetic mode in Sikhism. Heidegger makes the point that human existence rests and builds upon poetry. "Language itself is poetry in the essential sense" (Heidegger 1971, 74).[41] For Heidegger,

> Poetry . . . is not an aimless imagining of whimsicalities and not a flight of mere notions and fancies into the realm of the unreal. What poetry, as illuminating projection, unfolds of unconcealedness and projects ahead into the design of the figure, is the Open which poetry lets happen, and indeed in such a way that only now, in the midst of beings the Open brings beings to shine and ring out. (Heidegger 1971, 72)

Vivid visual and aural images have been used to describe the nature of poetry: it is the disclosure of truth, a disclosure that clearly shines and rings, a disclosure that takes place here and now, but that is only a beginning, a leap forward! What is illuminated by Heidegger for us is that the very arch in the configuration of the *Ikk Oaṅ Kār* at the outset of the Gurū Granth projects one here and now into the Open, into a nonending beginning. . . .

The inquiry—Why the poetic syntax?—in the context of Sikhism leads us further into discerning the importance of direct and unmediated religious experience within the tradition. Between the One there and the one here, there are no material barriers: there being no priests, no commentators, no rituals, no philosophical doctrines, no societal or gender hierarchies in Sikhism. Authority—that of the *paṇḍit* in Hinduism, of the *'ulama* in Islam, of the rabbi in Judaism—that would interpret for the person his or her duty, has no place in this direct encounter. Only the veil of ignorance or ego stands in the way. The poetry of the Gurū Granth, then, is the dynamism that tears the veil and thrusts one forward into recognizing That One. Gurū Arjan in his *Sukhmanī* has said, "Singing the divine praises, all pollution disappears, the poison of ego is bid riddance"[42] (Gurū Granth, 289). The poetic syntax provides stability for the flickering psyche, enabling the flight from the conscious to the unconscious and into the transcendent. The words of the Gurū Granth come with their own speedy meter and cadence. Full and sensuous to begin with, they were further energized by Gurū Arjan when he put them into musical measures. The poetic dynamism of the Sikh sacred literature comes from the presence of alliteration, assonance, consonance, the constant repetition, symmetry, and rhythm that create a momentum so that the reader, the hearer, the singer go beyond themselves and are launched on to intuiting the Unintuitable One. The direct experience that forms the core of Sikhism is induced solely by the poetic mode.

The only way to understand the Gurū Granth is to be launched on the quest for the Infinite Beloved. However paradoxical it may sound, the Universal One has to be experienced fully by each particular human being. "The experience has a definite immediacy which eludes every opinion about its meaning. Everything that is experienced is experienced by oneself" (Gadamer 1986, 60). The commentary on the Gurū Granth cannot then but be in the poetic mode. The exegesis cannot be a process that would halt the mind into deciphering and unfolding complexities philosophical, linguistic, or whatever; there can be no mediations in the way. In other words, the Sikh hermeneutic act cannot be a prosaic exegesis belonging to the side of a passage, underneath a line, on the bottom of a page, in a footnote, a passive act. It must of necessity be engendered by the poetic spirit itself. As we marked in the second section, *Mere Sāiān Jīo* has the lyric of movement that generates a momentum in the reader's or hearer's consciousness that is synchronous with the Gurū Granth itself. Poetically, our Sikh Hermes injected an invigorating spirit into his people, bringing about a renovation of sensitivity.

The poetic syntax unfolds Sikhism as a religion of aesthetics. By aesthetics is meant the heightening of the senses and mind. It is the route to the Transcendent One; and route it remains. "Religion is a means and not the end. If we make it the end in itself we become idolatrous," wrote Rādhākrishnan (1969, 2). The poetry of the Gurū Granth Sāhib is a channel toward that Infinite One; the more it stirs, the closer becomes the destination. The basis of the Sikh community, then, is the poetic sensation received through the medium of the Gurū Granth. From the time of Gurū Nānak, *sangats* (Sikh congregations) met on the banks of the River Rāvī and recited the sacred songs. The hearing or reciting of the Gurū Granth, being stirred by its rhythm, is shared by the *sangats* of the past, present (and, perhaps, also) future and across the continents. That shared experience constitutes the Sikh Panth or community. A joyous view of life, as brought out by the female protagonist in *Mere Sāiān Jīo,* pervades the entire Sikh tradition. The Gurūs themselves have declared, "Singing the divine songs day and night is my joy"[43] (Gurū Granth, 762). A cheerful attitude is prized in the Sikh way. Life, then, is not to be shunned. One cannot retreat and become a recluse. The joyous savoring of each moment and every space is accomplished through the poetic syntax. According to the Gurū Granth, "Where there is the recitation and hearing of the divine word, that indeed is paradise."[44] In this religion of aesthetics, the goal of the hermeneute, then, would be to recreate the joyous mode and thereby incite in his or her fellow human beings an urge for an intuition of the Unfathomable *Ikk Oaṅ*. The Tolstoyan criterion for the artist, that he be able to infect the recipient, seems to be the criterion for the Sikh hermeneute as well. In Bhāī Vīr Singh's case, he was first himself impressed by the poetry of the Gurū Granth, a feeling that he then transmitted within Punjabi society via his poetic output. The deeper or more sincere the artist's or hermeneute's experience, the clearer will be the expression, and stronger will be the infection!

Through the poetic syntax is verbalized the Sikh acknowledgment of the equality of humanity. In the instance of the protagonist in *Mere Sāiān Jīo,* she is not assigned any social or religious position. We do not know her name or identity. She is perceived as a human individual, the category valued most in Sikhism. Like the bride figure in the Gurū Granth, she spells out that all are equally equipped in the search for the Transcendent One: there is no hierarchy between the reciter and the listener, the musician and the hearer, the interpreter and the reader. Mind and senses, matter and spirit, are together impelled onward. Dualisms and antitheses seen by many feminist scholars to be at the heart of the patriarchal vision of reality are overtaken by the holistic and direct aesthetic experience of Sikhism.[45]

In fact, Sikh poetics is replete with feminine imagery and symbolism. Descriptions of woman's physical attraction, mental tenacity, and spiritual radiance pervade the Gurū Granth. Through *her* we get to see who we are and what we might hope to become. As in *Mere Sāiān Jīo* also, the quest is verbalized in her tone and through her sentiment; she is the paradigmatic figure who opens the way toward the *Ikk Oan*. The identification of Bhāī Vīr Singh with the female, and the creation of female protagonists as the archetypes of morality, courage, spirituality, and philosophical search, manifest not only the tenderness of his poetic perception but also the Sikh worldview in which woman is a profoundly valued human being. Unfortunately, that is where our hermeneute is misunderstood. A quotation from a renowned scholar illustrates this sad tendency:

> It is in his diction bearing the perfume of Punjab's sacred literature and the expression of sensibility that Bhāī Vīr Singh achieves the poetic quality. Very often his sensibility declines to sentimentality and the feminine small-change of feeling—but rises with recurring spurts to the true emotional level. (Talib 1973, 7)

The assessment that Bhāī Vīr Singh's "sensibility declines to sentimentality and the feminine small-change" only indicates the critic's glossing over the delicacy, the refinement, the multivalency attributed the female person and psyche in both the poetry of the Gurū Granth itself and in the poetry of its exegete, Bhāī Vīr Singh.

Returning to Gadamer's rich and complex image of fusion, with which we opened our essay, we may concede that Bhāī Vīr Singh has fused many horizons. His writings were the vehicle for the Sikhs' self-understanding through which Sikh men and women were stirred to a new awareness not only of their tradition but also of their destiny. We end by saying that his hermeneutic act in *Mere Sāiān Jīo* is ultimately a fusion of the earth and sky. These two metaphors can be found in Heidegger's essay on "The Origin of the Work of Art," wherein he traces the origin of a work of art to the strife between the grounding earth and the flamboyant sky. Bhāī Vīr Singh's hermeneutic process was grounded, based, founded on the earthlike Gurū Granth, which in turn was impinged upon by the twentieth-century poet's skylike imagination and inspiration, thrusting it toward a rich experience—"opening it out, making it go"—for his contemporary society.

Notes

1. *main tere tāin nām dīā hai*
   tūn ehā kirati kari

2. *sāsu māsu sabhu jīo tumārā tū mai kharā piārā*
   nānaku sāiru ev kahatu hai sāce parvadgārā

3. *jaisī main āveh khasm kī bāṇī*
   taisaṛā karī giān ve lālo

4. *Ikk Oan Kār*

5. *thāl vici tini vastū paio*
   sat santokh vicāro . . .
   je ko khāvai je ko bhuncai
   tis kā hoi udhāro

6. *Gurū granth jī mānio pargat gurān kī deh*

7. *Bhāī Vīr Singh Racnāvalī: Volume I:* Poetry (Patiala; Punjabi Bhasha Vibhag, 1972). This will be the primary text.

8. *mere geet*
   mere sāiān!
   tusān lai gāe gae geet . . .
   uṭhan tarangān sāgaron āe paun vāngūn,

chhir paea merā cup galā, boldī bulbul vāngūn,
hān bāl-gale diān thibakdiān thibakdiān
tusān mere sāiān jio dī
hazuri vic.

9. *jah jah dekhā tah tah soi*

10. *nānak kā pātisahu disai jāhara*

11. *tuhon būtī e laī sī*

12. *ikk nadari*

13. *ikk nāz de gamze*

14. *musk ikk phir macī*
magan surati hu ai sī . . .

15. *ihu jagu vaṛī merā prabhu mālī sadā samāle ko nahī khālī*

16. A relationship that is much desired by Western feminists. See, for example, Sallie McFague 1989.

17. *Oan*

18. *tūn*

19. *tūhin, tūhin, tūhin,*

20. *tūn merā pitā tun hai merā mātā tun merā bandhapu tūn merā bhrātā*

21. *dīn dayāl prītam manmohan ati rasa lāl sagūṛau*

22. *āpe rasīā āpu rasu āpe rāvanhār*

23. *ujjalān de ujjal*

24. *jahi jahi dekhan tahu jyoti tumhārī*
terā rūp kanehā

25. *aj nūr de tarke*
jadon lai rahī sī saver angṛāiān . . .
ikk khiṛe gulāb dī kūlī god vic
tusīn khed rahe sao mere sāiān
kinjh, hān kinjh! a gae sao
os nikkī god vic?
mere aidhe vadhe visāl sāiān?

26. *thāpiā na jāe, kītā na hoi*

27. *mere andar, dhur andar, dhur andar de*
kise ohle luke mere prītam!

hān,
tumbane o apnīān sangeetak tumbān nāl
jagā dene o tarbān tārān
andarle dīān
gaondīan han uh geet
tusān jī de birhe, tusān jī de milan de tarāne
jo karde han jadūgarī mere hī utte
mere main bir bir takkadī
rahi jānī e kambdī te tharrandī
āh prītam
dissan de ohle luke prītam
kol kol par dūr dūr,
dūr dūr par kol kol
sadke terī jadūgarī de

28. *ure ure pai agamo agam*

29. *agamo agam agam he mere tūn pyārnā*

30. *tūn ādi purakhu apranparu kartā*
terā pāru na pāiā jāi jīu
tūn ghat ghat antari sarab nirantari
sabh mahi rahiā samāi jīu

31. *tū sabh mahi vartahi āpi*

32. *sabh mahi jyoti, jyoti hai soi*

33. *agam agocaru sacu sāhibu merā*

34. *nirgunu āpi sargunu bhī ohi kalā dhāri jini sagalī mohi*

35. *sahas tav nain nan nain hahi tohi kau sahas tav mūrati nanā ek tohi . . .*
sahas tav gandh iv calat mohī

36. *kaun han jo ākhde han: "tere sāiān jī siān nahin hunde?"*

37. *tithai ghaṛiai surati mati mani budhi*

38. *panjān de rasiān ton ras ucian nūn, hān, lakhā dene ho tusin āp*

39. Probably denotes that It is in every material object, for according to the Samkhya theory everything is constituted of the three strands, *sattva, rajas,* and *tamas,* signifiying white, red, and black.

40. See Bhāī Vīr Singh, *Vāraṅ Bhāī Gurdās.*

41. In Shelley's "A Defense of Poetry" an identical statement is found: "language itself is poetry."

42. *gun gāvat terī utrasi mailu binasi jāe haumai bikhu phailu*

43. *gun gāvan dinu rāti nānak cāu ehu*

44. *tahān baikunṭh jahān kīrtan terā*

45. See Rosemary Radford Ruether 1989.

References

Barthes, Roland
1979 "From Work to Text." In *Textual Strategies,* edited by J. V. Harari. Ithaca: Cornell University Press.

Gadamer, Hans-Georg
1986 *Truth and Method.* New York: Crossroad.

Heidegger, Martin
1971 *Poetry, Language, Thought.* Translated by Albert Hofstadter. New York: Harper & Row.

Historical Sketches of the Indian Missions.
1886 Allahabad: n.p.

Larson, Gerald James and Eliot Deutsch, eds.
1988 *Interpreting across Boundaries.* Princeton: Princeton University Press.

McFague, Sallie
1989 "God As Mother." In *Weaving the Visions: New Patterns in Feminist Spirituality,* edited by Judith Plaskow and Carol Christ, 139–150. New York: Harper & Row.

Rādhākrishnan, Sarvepalli
1969 "Gurū Nānak: An Introduction." In *Gurū Nānak: His Life, Time and Teachings,* edited by Gurmukh Nihal Singh. New Delhi: Gurū Nānak Foundation.

Ruether, Rosemary Radford
1989 "Sexism and God-Language." In *Weaving the Visions: Patterns in Feminist Spirituality,* edited by Judith Plaskow and Carol Christ, 151–162. New York: Harper the Row.

Singh, Bhāī Vīr, ed.
1948 *Purātan Janamsākhī*. Amritsar: Khalsa Samachar.

1972 *Bhāī Vīr Singh Racnāvalī: Volume I: Poetry*. Patiala: Punjabi Bhasha Vibhag.

1977 *Vāraṅ Bhāī Gurdās*. Amritsar: Khalsa Samachar.

1981 *Japujī Sāhib Saṅthyā*. Amritsar: Khalsa Samachar.

Singh, Harbans
1969 *Gurū Nānak and Origins of the Sikh Faith*. Bombay: Asia Publishing House.

1972 Bhāī Vīr *Singh*. New Delhi: Sahitya Academy.

1985 *The Heritage of the Sikhs*. New Delhi: Manohar.

Singh, Nripinder
1985 "Ethical Perceptions of the Sikh Community of the Late Nineteenth/Early Twentieth Century: An Essay in Sikh Moral Tradition." Ph.D. diss., Harvard University.

Talib, G. S., and Attar Singh, eds.
1973 Bhāī Vīr *Singh: Life, Times, and Works*. Chandigarh: Publication Bureau, Punjab University.

Zuckerkandl, Victor
1956 *Sound and Symbol: Music and the Eternal World*. Princeton: Princeton University Press.

Fourteen

The Textual Formation of Oral Teachings in Early Chishtī Sufism[1]

Carl W. Ernst

Introduction

The historical formation of mystical Islam in India is a process that has taken centuries, and the origins of Indian Sufism are available to us only through a series of later literary reconstructions. Although the Persian texts that became central to Sufi teaching transmitted an Islamic tradition rather than a Vedic or Vedantic one, an analysis of their canonical status should take account of some of the same factors used to assess the other Indian texts discussed in this volume. In this analysis, the transition from oral teaching to written text is the factor that best explains how Indian Sufism acquired its own canon of authoritative texts.

From the time of Hujwīrī (d. 1074 C.E.), the northwestern cities of India were home to a number of Sufis, though Hujwīrī is one of the few whose writings have come down to us. Later tradition records that in the late twelfth century, when most of the great Sufi orders began to crystallize in different parts of the Islamic world, the Chishtī order first became established in India. Probably the most popular order in the subcontinent, the Chishtiyya originated in the town of Chisht in Afghanistan. Although later authors such as Jāmī (d. 1492) tell stories of the early Sufis of Chisht, the first Chishtīs themselves wrote nothing, and contemporary witnesses do not tell us anything of their lives (Jāmī 1959, 323–31). Even in the case of Mu'īn al-Dīn Chishtī (d. ca. 1233), whom tradition identifies as the founder of the Indian Chishtiyya, in order to find any connected written account of him we must wait until the fourteenth century, when the Chishtī order suddenly reveals itself in a full-blown literary tradition written in Persian

(Lawrence 1978). The oral teachings of the Chishtīs, as revealed in the "oral discourses (*malfūẓāt*)" literature, took on a canonical textual form that soon became authoritative and normative both for members of the order and for their lay followers. The transition from oral to written form was reflected in diverse literary styles adapted to different audiences. Modern critical debates about the authenticity of some of the Chishtī *malfūẓāt* have put into prominence the question of the Chishtī canon, yet the imposition of Western models of literary criticism needs to be supplemented by attention to internal critical categories that help explain the textual mediation of mystical Islam in India.

I. From Oral Teaching to Written Text in Sufism

The explosion of Sufi literary activity in India in the thirteenth and fourteenth centuries had a powerful formative effect on Indian Sufism. The widespread Suhrawardī order, which came from Baghdad, boasted outstanding mystical writers in its Indian branch, such as Qāżī Ḥamīd al-Dīn Nāgawrī (d. 1244), who wrote sophisticated meditations on the ninety-nine names of God and on mystical love (Lawrence 1975; Lawrence 1978, 60ff.). While the Chishtīs did not at first express themselves in writing, they eventually produced a broader and more sustained literary tradition than any other Indian Sufi order. According to well-attested early traditions, neither Mu'īn al-Dīn Chishtī nor his two main successors, Quṭb al-Dīn Bakhtiyār Kākī (d. 1232) and Farīd al-Dīn "Ganj-i Shakkar" (d. 1265), wrote any books (the discourses attributed to them are discussed below); the first generations of Indian Chishtīs continued to emphasize oral instruction, although masters such as Farīd al-Dīn also taught standard Arabic works on religion and mysticism, such as the *'Awārif al-ma'ārif* of Shahāb al-Dīn Suhrawardī. Yet in the next generation, the Chishtī master Niẓām al-Dīn Awliyā' (d. 1325) made such a profound effect on his contemporaries that a new genre of literature, the *malfūẓāt*, emerged to embody his teachings.

In theory, the *malfūẓāt* was as close as one could get in words to the actual presence of the Sufi master. Although the authors of the *malfūẓāt* texts did not actually take dictation at the time when the master was speaking, they typically tried to write out his talks from memory as soon as a daily session ended, and in some cases they had the good fortune to have their work corrected by the master. Nonetheless, in the act of rewriting the master's words, the writer inevitably exercised some kind of selection and interpretation, and so produced a narrative structure depicting the Sufi teaching from a particular point of view. This combination of oral transmission and narrative recasting naturally had precedents in Sufi tradition. By the tenth century, the collecting of Sufi biographical dictionaries, with emphasis on sayings, had become an established category in Arabic religious literature; Sufi hagiography, insofar as it stressed sayings, was basically an outgrowth of the *ḥadīth* literature, which collected the sayings of the Prophet Muḥammad (Ernst 1985). Oral traditions from several outstanding personalities in the early Sufi movement, such as Abū Yazīd al-Bisṭāmī (d. 874) and al-Ḥallāj (d. 922), were collected in Arabic in monograph form; typically these traditions were related as disconnected episodes, often introduced (as in *ḥadīth*) by the chain of transmitters (*isnād*) (Sahlajī 1949; Massignon and Kraus 1957). In Persian the first monographic Sufi biographies concern Abū Sa'īd ibn Abū al-Khayr (d. 1049). His two biographies, written by his descendants some 100 to 150 years after his death, narrate a long series of incidents that reveal his actions and sayings as a Sufi teacher (Meier 1976, 19–21). Other works, no longer extant, recorded the sayings of Abū Sa'īd from two hundred different "sessions" (*majālis*), and Abū Sa'īd's contemporary al-Qushayrī is said to have recorded the sessions of his teacher Abū 'Alī al-Daqqāq (Meier 1976, 22 n. 9). Disciples also preserved the oral discourses of some other early Sufis, such as Jalāl al-Dīn Rūmī (d. 1273) (Rūmī 1959; Arberry 1961). In India, however, the *malfūẓāt* quickly became a dominant literary form for the transmission of Sufi teaching, so that later generations of Indian Sufis found it almost indispensable to commit their discourses into this textual mold.

How accurate is the *malfūẓāt* literature as a written record of oral teaching, and what criteria should be used to analyze it? The early Iranian Sufi biographies illustrate the same problem that occurs in the Indian *malfūẓāt* texts. In the case of the sayings of Abū Sa'īd, the modern Iranian literary critic Bahār believes that, on linguistic grounds alone, these sayings as recorded in his biographies must be considered a fairly accurate record of the actual words of the shaykh:

> The Sufis preserved the words of their saints, as the *ḥadīth* reports have to be preserved, word by word and letter by letter, and they permitted little change or interpolation in them. The credibility of some of the sentences and terms and their chain of transmission and correctness is such that no room remains for doubt or denial. The style of *Asrār al-tawḥīd* in its totality, i.e., from the viewpoint of grammar and syntax, is without the slightest discrepancy equivalent to the style of the Samanids. (Bahār 1959, 2:198).

This general observation on style of language is valuable and doubtless accurate as far as it goes, but it unfortunately does not shed any light on the process of literary composition that gave the text its form. To say that the compilers of hagiographical texts used the method of *ḥadīth* reporting glosses over two separate problems. First, the *ḥadīth* literature has its own historiography and redactions, raising questions concerning the transition from oral to written form and canon formation. Regrettably, most discussions of *ḥadīth* tend toward extremes, as traditionalists assert its absolute authority while modernists and some Western scholars reject it altogether on hypercritical grounds. Second, the interval of three to four generations between Abū Sa'īd's death and the writing of his biographies raises the question of how his sayings were chosen and preserved, and to what end. We may legitimately ask, too, about the political background of the biographies of Abū Sa'īd, since the *Asrār al-tawḥīd* was the first Sufi biography dedicated to a ruling monarch, in this case the Ghurid sultan Muḥammad ibn Sām (d. 1203) (Meier 1976, 21). The question of reliability, which tends to dominate critical discussions, should yield to the analysis of oral and written styles, canonical function, literary composition, and audience, as the basis for study of *malfūẓāt* texts.

II. The Foundation of the Chishtī Malfūẓāt *Literature: Niẓām al-Dīn*

The development of Chishtī *malfūẓāt* literature may be sketched in two stages. First it is necessary to describe the discourses of Niẓām al-Dīn Awliyā' and compare them with those of his two disciples Naṣīr al-Dīn Maḥmūd Chiragh-i Dihlī (d. 1356) and Burhān al-Dīn Gharīb (d. 1338). Of these, only the first two have been published in modern critical editions, and only Niẓām al-Dīn's has been translated into English.[2] Next, these "original" texts, all written by literate and courtly disciples, may be juxtaposed with a series of *malfūẓāt* purporting to be dictated by the principal Chishtī shaykhs to their successors, illustrating the main line of initiatic authority in the order. These "retrospective" texts, the authenticity of which has been challenged, stressed the hagiographic mode of personal charisma and authority, while the others focused on the teaching element consisting of practice and speculation, but all of the *malfūẓāt* texts made the person of the Sufi master an essential part of the teaching.

The recording of the oral teachings of Niẓām al-Dīn Awliyā' was evidently the spontaneous decision of his disciple, the poet Amīr Ḥasan Sijzī Dihlawī (1253–1336). Beginning in 1307, until 1322, Ḥasan recorded as much as he could of his teacher's conversations, whenever leisure from his official duties as court poet permitted him leave in Delhi. The resulting book is called *Fawā'id al-fu'ād* (Morals of the Heart) (Dihlawī 1966). Ḥasan was a skilled and eloquent poet in Persian; his poetic output includes several hundred lyric poems (*ghazals*) as well as panegyric odes (*qaṣīdas*) addressed to the sultans of Delhi (Borah 1941; Dihlawī 1933). Although much of his poetry was of the standard erotic type popular at court, Ḥasan also injected the symbolism of Sufism into his verse; the Chishtī hagiographer Mir Khwurd called him "Amīr Ḥasan 'Alā' Sijzī, whose burning lyrics brought forth the fire of love from the flint of lovers' hearts, whose pleasing verses conveyed solace to the hearts of the eloquent, and whose invigorating subtleties are the sustenance of the discerning."[3]

Fawā'id al-fu'ād is a beautifully written account of the Sufi teaching of Niẓām al-Dīn, and it is certainly one of the most popular Sufi works in India. It was some time before Ḥasan revealed to Niẓām al-Dīn that he was recording the conversations in the shaykh's circle:

> It is more than a year that I have been connected to my master, and every time that I have had the happiness of kissing your feet, I have heard useful morals (*fawā'id*) from your pearl-bearing speech: sometimes preaching, advice, and encouragement of virtue, and sometimes stories of the shaykhs and their states; on every subject your inspiring words have reached the writer's hearing. I have wanted that to be the model for this helpless one's state, or rather the guide of the path for this wretch. I have written it down to the best of my understanding, inasmuch as your blessed speech has frequently mentioned that one ought to keep before one's eyes the books of the masters and the indications that they have made about the spiritual path. Since no collection can be superior to the refreshing sayings of my master, for this reason I have collected whatever I have heard from your blessed speech. Until this time I have not revealed it, and I [now] await your command.[4]

On hearing this declaration, Niẓām al-Dīn replied that, when he had attended upon his own master Shaykh Farīd al-Dīn, he too had formed the resolve to write down his teacher's sayings; he still vividly recalled the Persian verse with which Farīd al-Dīn had first greeted him: "The fire of separation from you has burnt up hearts, / the flood of longing for you has laid souls waste!"[5] Ḥasan, greatly affected, was momentarily overcome by the attempt to express his own feelings. But then Niẓām al-Dīn requested him to show some samples of his notes, which fortunately Ḥasan had brought along. The shaykh complimented Ḥasan on his writing, but was puzzled by several blank spots in the manuscript. Ḥasan explained that those were places where he did not know the rest of the words—that is, his memory was not clear about those points. Niẓām al-Dīn then graciously told him what was missing, so that the account became complete (Dihlawī 1966, 50–51). This tender exchange between master and disciple illustrates Ḥasan's purpose in writing *Fawā'id al-fu'ād*: just as Niẓām al-Dīn had previously urged reading the classical writings of the Sufi shaykhs along with religious ritual and worship (Dihlawī 1966, 39), so now Ḥasan wrote his diary as an evocation of his master's presence as well as his teaching.

Several years later, another conversation took place between Ḥasan Sijzī and Niẓām al-Dīn that underlined the role of the *malfūẓāt* as a nearly sacred text that served as a religious standard. When Ḥasan brought out the completed first volume of *Fawā'id al-fu'ād,* Niẓām al-Dīn read it over with approval, saying, "You have written well, you have written like a dervish, and you have also given it a good name."[6] The shaykh "in connection with this state"[7] went on to make lengthy comments about the sayings of the Prophet Muḥammad as recorded by his associates, implicitly suggesting a comparison between Ḥasan's rendering of his own conversations and the collection of the prophetic *ḥadīth* literature. Such was the devotion of Abū Hurayra toward the Prophet, he noted, that Abū Hurayra, despite knowing the Prophet only three years, managed to transmit more *ḥadīth* than all the other companions put together; it was his concentration on the person of the Prophet that enabled Abū Hurayra to extend the skirt of his garment whenever the Prophet spoke, slowly gather in the garment when the words were finished, and place his hand upon his breast; this routine would enable him to memorize Muḥammad's words (Dihlawī 1966, 198–99). As the *ḥadīth* conveys ethical and ritual norms to the Muslim community, so the *malfūẓāt* establish the principles of mysticism; in both cases the focus upon the personal source of the teaching is an essential part of the disciple's ability to remember the teacher's words, to preserve them for himself and others. In this way the Sufi *malfūẓāt* function as a parallel to the primary canon of Islam, the Qur'ān and *ḥadīth*.

The success of *Fawā'id al-fu'ād* as an exposition of Chishtī Sufism was tremendous. The court historian Baranī, in an oft-quoted passage, has recorded the popularity of *Fawā'id al-fu'ād* as an instance of the great influence that Niẓām al-Dīn exerted over the whole population of Delhi:

> Owing to the influence of the Shaikh, most of the Mussalmans of his country developed interest in mysticism, prayers and aloofness from the world, and came to have a faith in the Shaikh. The hearts of men having become virtuous by good deeds, the very name of wine, gambling and other forbidden things never came to anyone's lips. Most of the scholars and learned men, who frequented the Shaikh's company, applied themselves to books on devotion and mysticism. The books *Qut-u' l-Qulub, Ihya-u' l-'Ulum*, [etc.] . . . found many purchasers, as also did the *Fawā'id al-fu'ād* of Amīr Ḥasan owing to the sayings of the Shaikh which it contains. (Baranī, *Tārīkh-i Firūz Shāhī*, 347, as quoted by Nizami 1978, 198)

While Baranī's account of the mystical and religious inclinations of the Muslim populace is perhaps exaggerated, it does testify to the extraordinary respect that Niẓām al-Dīn commanded among the people.

What were the reasons for the popularity of *Fawā'id al-fu'ād*? The book's popularity was doubtless a measure of Ḥasan Dihlawī's success in evoking the presence of Niẓām al-Dīn. The skilled pen of this poet, combined with the close relationship between master and disciple, made *Fawā'id al-fu'ād* an effective presentation of the teaching relationship in the Chishtī order. While *Fawā'id al-fu'ād* inspired a host of imitations, few of these survive. Four other disciples of Niẓām al-Dīn compiled his *malfūẓāt*, but only one of these texts, "an inferior work," can still be found in manuscript (Lawrence 1978, 45; Nizami, "Introduction," in Qalandar 1959, 1). In addition, the contents of Niẓām al-Dīn's teachings were in this way made available to a wide public, so that the book in reality became "the guide of the path" for many, as Ḥasan had hoped. A recent Urdu biography of Ḥasan stresses the significance of *Fawā'id al-fu'ād* for its original audience in terms of explaining Islamic religious duties in detail, clarifying problems of mystical practice, and rejecting and correcting ethically dubious customs and traditions (Ṣiddīqī 1979, 218–71). In modern times, scholars have, in contrast, valued this important *malfūẓāt* text less for its religious contents than for its historical value, as a corrective to the exclusively dynastic focus of the court historians. As K. A. Nizami observed,

> Through these records of conversations we can have a glimpse of the medieval society, in all its fullness, if not in all its perfection—the moods and tensions of the common man, the inner yearnings of his soul, the religious thought at its higher and lower levels, the popular customs and manners and above [all] the problems of the people. There is no other type of literature through which we can feel the pulse of the medieval public. (Nizami 1978, 374)

The *malfūẓāt* texts certainly do throw light on aspects of social history that are ignored in dynastic chronicles, but the main reason for their popularity is the success with which they have expounded and evoked the Sufi teaching.

III. The Elaboration of the Malfūẓāt *Tradition: Chirāgh-i Dihlī*

With Niẓām al-Dīn's successor in Delhi, Naṣīr al-Dīn Maḥmūd "Chirāgh-i Dihlī" ("the lamp of Delhi," d. 1356), the *malfūẓāt* took on a self-consciously literary and imitative character using *Fawā'id al-fu'ād* as the authoritative canonical model. The compiler, an unconventional wandering mystic named Ḥamīd Qalandar, has given an elaborate description of how the collection of *Khayr al-majālis* (The Best of Assemblies) began, in 1353. After taking it upon himself to record five sessions in the circle of Chirāgh-i Dihlī, Ḥamīd brought his compilation and showed it to the master. Much to Ḥamīd's delight, Chirāgh-i Dihlī approved of it, and related a long story about the value of memorizing the words of the saints; typical of Chirāgh-i Dihlī's concern with the study of Islamic law, his example was drawn from the life of a legal scholar. The story concerned Mawlānā Ḥamīd al-Dīn Żarīr of Bukhara, who had memorized the Qur'ān and a text on ritual prayer before becoming a disciple of Mawlānā Shams al-Dīn Gardīzī. Moving from the elementary classes to the advanced ones, Ḥamīd al-Dīn Żarīr would sit before the master with his skirt (*dāman*) extended, and at the conclusion of the lesson would gather up his skirt to his chest, as if he carried in it the literal fruit of the teacher's discourses (precisely recapitulating the technique that Niẓām al-Dīn had described to Ḥasan Dihlawī, which Abū Hurayra had used when memorizing the *ḥadīth* of the Prophet Muḥammad). Ḥamīd al-Dīn Żarīr eventually succeeded to his master's place and wrote famous commentaries on works of Islamic law. On hearing this story, Ḥamīd Qalandar took the example to heart:

> I extended my skirt before the revered master, who is my teacher and instructor and leader, and asked him for a *Fātiḥa* [Qur'ānic prayer] for the sake of memory. I formed the intention that I would not love anyone who was not a lover and adherent of the master, nor go to such a one's place, nay, as far as possible I would not look upon his face.[8]

Ḥamīd enthusiastically equated his own personal devotion to Chirāgi-i Dihlī with the years of scholarly apprenticeship described in the story.

We cannot be so confident, however, regarding the scholarly pretensions of Ḥamīd Qalandar. Ḥamīd has indicated that at times Chirāgh-i Dihlī took pains to correct the manuscript of *Khayr al-majālis*, even in matters of Arabic vocabulary (Qalandar 1959, 218). Other disciples of Chirāgh-i Dihlī reported that when shown sections of Ḥamīd's compilation, the shaykh remarked that they were inaccurate, and threw them away, having no time to correct them (Muḥammad Gīsū Darāz, *Jawāmi' al-Kilam*, 134, cited by Nizami, "Introduction," in Qalandar 1959, 5 n. 2). Ḥamīd himself reflected that at times he did not understand the shaykh's words, but "if I do not comprehend, let me write down once what I do understand, so that it is a memorial."[9] When Chirāgh-i Dihlī discussed topics such as fasting, Ḥamīd would confess his own inability to fast, and admitted his preference for composing mediocre Persian verse instead of meditating (Lawrence 1978,

28–30, translating Qalandar 1959, 69–70). From the "telegraphic" manner in which Chirāgh-i Dihlī's theological and moral teachings are summarized in *Khayr al-majālis*, and on the basis of the apparent shortcomings of its compiler, Paul Jackson has admitted to having "very serious reservations" about the accuracy of this text as a record of the teachings of Chirāgh-i Dihlī (Jackson 1985). The editor of *Khayr al-majālis*, K. A. Nizami, remarked that Ḥamīd Qalandar "had no real and genuine aptitude for mysticism" (Nizami, "Introduction," in Qalandar 1959, 6). For his own part, Ḥamīd Qalandar confidently compared his own compilation to *Fawā'id al-fu'ād*, and called *Khayr al-majālis* his auspicious "religious child" (*farzand-i dīnī*) that would bring him great reward (Qalandar 1959, 279). Despite these strictures on his accuracy, Ḥamīd Qalandar's compilation is nonetheless an important link in the recording of Chishtī teachings. Some of the stories of Chirāgi-i Dihlī that he records, such as the tale of Moses and the idolater in the thirty-sixth session, demonstrate how Sufis adapted traditional materials to portray contemporary situations; in this case, the idolater addresses his deity in Hindi, making the situation much more vivid for Chirāgh-i Dihlī's listeners (Qalandar 1959, 123–24).[10]

More importantly from the perspective of this study, Ḥamīd Qalandar's work reflects from the beginning a certain tension with the *malfūẓāt* texts of Burhān al-Dīn Gharīb as rivals for canonical status. The *malfūẓāt* texts had begun to take on the function of what Kendall A. Folkert called "Canon II" (or "Canon-far," as John Cort has put it in chapter 20 of this volume), acting as a normative text that serves as vector for religious authority as well as individualist piety (Folkert 1989, 173). The flattering tone of Ḥamīd Qalandar's first conversations with Chirāgh-i Dihlī suggests that one of his motives was to establish the supremacy of Chirāgh-i Dihlī within the Chishtī succession. When Ḥamīd Qalandar first came into the assembly of Chirāgh-i Dihlī, it happened to be the day when the latter was celebrating the death-anniversary (*'urs*) of his old friend and fellow disciple Burhān al-Dīn Gharīb; this would have taken place on 11 Ṣafar 755/7 March 1354, seventeen lunar years after the death of Burhān al-Dīn Gharīb. Ḥamīd Qalandar immediately introduced himself to Chirāgh-i Dihlī and informed the shaykh that he had associated with Burhān al-Dīn Gharīb in Deogīr, and that he had in fact recorded the conversations of Burhān al-Dīn Gharīb in a *malfūẓāt* (no longer extant) containing twenty sessions (Qalandar 1959, 8–9). This remark reveals how the genre of *malfūẓāt* had already been established as a model among the Deccan Chishtīs. The very example that Ḥamīd Qalandar then related from memory was Burhān al-Dīn Gharīb's account of how he had sought and received spiritual advice from Chirāgh-i Dihlī when he had lost a hat given to him by Niẓām al-Din Awliyā'; Chirāgh-i Dihlī had emerged from a trance, and correctly predicted that

Burhān al-Dīn Gharīb would receive even greater gifts from Niẓām al-Dīn (Qalandar 1959, 9–10). After hearing Ḥamīd Qalandar's story, Chirāgh-i Dihlī confirmed its truth, and was very happy to be reminded of this incident with his old friend after so many years (Ḥamīd would retell this story in more high-flown and dramatic language in the biography of Chirāgh-i Dihlī attached as a supplement to *Khayr al-majālis*, where he specifically called this event a miracle) (Qalandar 1959, 284–85). Ḥamīd Qalandar further observed that Burhān al-Dīn Gharīb had great faith in Chirāgh-i Dihlī, so Ḥamīd as an admirer of Burhān al-Dīn Gharīb was especially eager to see a man who was even greater. Chirāgh-i Dihlī's response to this flattery was to change the subject (Qalandar 1959, 10). Ḥamīd Qalandar at their next meeting continued in the same vein, though, saying, "Lord! Mawlānā Burhān al-Dīn was a darwish who attained union, but the revered master [Chirāgh-i Dihlī] is an Abū Ḥanīfa in learning, and in asceticism and mastery is the Shaykh Niẓām al-Dīn of the age. God willing, I shall record the master's sessions."[11] Nonetheless, the figure of Burhān al-Dīn Gharīb looms over the composition of *Khayr al-majālis* at the end as well as at the beginning. In the one hundredth and final session, Ḥamīd Qalandar reports that Chirāgh-i Dihlī told a story that Ḥamīd had previously heard from the lips of Burhān al-Dīn Gharīb. That very night he had a dream in which Burhān al-Dīn Gharīb appeared and announced that the book of *Khayr al-majālis* was now complete, handing a luminous copy of the book to Ḥamīd Qalandar (Qalandar 1959, 279).

Curiously, neither Ḥamīd Qalandar himself nor the incident of the hat is even mentioned in any of the genuine *malfūẓāt* of Burhān al-Dīn Gharīb. In fact, one of the Burhān al-Dīn Gharīb's disciples pictured his relationship to Chirāgh-i Dihlī in quite the opposite fashion. Majd al-Dīn 'Imād Kāshānī, one of the four Kāshānī brothers, took up the task of recording Burhān al-Dīn Gharīb's miracles and revelations in a work called *Gharā'ib al-karāmāt* (The Rare Miracles) (Majd al-Dīn 1340). In this account, which predates Ḥamīd Qalandar's book by over a decade, Majd al-Dīn maintains that at their first meeting, Burhān al-Dīn Gharīb at once perceived the great spiritual potential of the youthful Chirāgh-i Dihlī, and warned him to be heedful and take advantage of the guidance of Niẓām al-Dīn, in this way acting as a preceptor rather than as a suppliant (Majd al-Dīn 1340, 14). This incident, which occurs as the first *mukāshafat*, or revelation, in the book, has a certain prominence mirroring that given to the contrary story, which Ḥamīd Qalandar likewise put at the beginning of his book. Majd al-Dīn also tells a story in which Chirāgh-i Dihlī states that he learned the ability to perceive the states of souls after death from Burhān al-Dīn Gharīb (Majd al-Dīn 1340, 31). Ḥamīd Qalandar's remarks betray the competition that must have come into existence between the centers established by various disciples of Niẓām al-Dīn Awliyā'. Regardless of the historicity of the incident of the hat, the unusual prominence of that story and Hamīd Qalandar's obsequious praise of Chirāgh-i Dhilī suggest a deliberate design to elevate the latter to a central position in the Chishtī order, at the expense of Burhān al-Dīn Gharīb. Other disciples of Chirāgh-i Dihlī made similarly deprecatory remarks about Burhān al-Dīn Gharīb.[12] Stressing the primacy of one co-disciple over another was perhaps an inevitable result of the canonical focus on the centrality of the Sufi master.

IV. The Elaboration of the Malfūẓāt *Tradition: Burhān al-Dīn Gharīb*

The existing accounts of the early *malfūẓāt* literature have generally ignored the largely unpublished texts produced in the circle of Burhān al-Dīn Gharīb (d. 1338), another major disciple of Niẓām al-Dīn, who led the Sufis who participated in the enforced migration of the Muslim elite of Delhi to the Deccan capital of Daulatabad in 1329. As we have seen, Ḥamīd Qalandar's account of his compilation of *Khayr al-majālis* presupposed the existence of a developed *malfūẓāt* tradition among the Deccan Chishtīs. Without appreciating the wide scope of the *malfūẓāt* texts written in the Deccan by Burhān al-Dīn Gharīb's disciples, it is impossible to form a complete understanding of the origin of this genre of Sufi writing among the Chishtīs.[13]

The first and perhaps most important of the *malfūẓāt* texts emanating from the circle of Burhān al-Dīn Gharīb also followed the model of *Fawā'id al-fu'ād*. This was *Nafā'is al-anfās wa laṭā'if al-alfāẓ* (Choice Sayings and Elegant Words), compiled by Rukn al-Dīn Dabīr Kāshānī in forty-eight sessions between Muḥarram 732/October 1331 and 4 Ṣafar 738/1 September 1337. Rukn al-Dīn, as his title *dabīr* indicates, was a secretary in the service of Sultan Muḥammad ibn Tughluq's administration at Daulatabad. In his preface, Rukn al-Dīn remarks that in hearing the oral teachings of Burhān al-dīn Gharīb, he had found that "no wayfarer has seen written in the writings of bygone shaykhs any of those subtleties and cyphers, nor has any seeker of truth read a word of those subjects and rarities."[14] Just as the admired Ḥasan Dihlawī (himself an emigré to Khuldabad) had collected and arranged the discourses of Niẓām al-Dīn Awliyā', now Rukn al-Dīn had determined to do the same with the words of Burhān al-Dīn Gharīb, whom he addresses by the loftiest of epithets. In a style considerably more prolix than that of Ḥasan, Rukn al-Dīn states that the purpose of his book is to see that

> speakers with the brides of the meanings of the path by this means attain the throne-place of union with the real beloved, and seekers of the maidens of the subtleties of wayfaring by reading it may gaze on and contemplate the world-adorning beauty of the essential goal of desire.[15]

He therefore at the first session he recorded proposed this project to Burhān al-Dīn Gharīb, who approved wholeheartedly, saying, "For a long time, this idea has been established in my mind,"[16] and he thanked God that it had been preordained that this book should be written by Rukn al-Dīn. Burhān al Dīn Gharīb further encouraged Rukn al-Dīn by quoting from the poet Niẓāmī: "Freshen me with the heart of David, and make my psalms cry aloud."[17] In terms invoking the authority of scripture, Rukn al-Dīn was to proclaim like David the psalm-like words that would constitute his book (Dihlawī 1966, 4). Toward the end of the session, the shaykh turned to Rukn al-Dīn and said, "Amīr Ḥasan, who has written the *Fawā'id*, [acted] in this way: whatever tale the shaykh [Niẓām al-Dīn] told, he turned toward Amīr Ḥasan. He [Ḥasan] wrote down whatever words were spoken in the session."[18] Rukn al-Dīn understood from this that he would have the great fortune to play the same role for Burhān al-Dīn Gharīb as Ḥasan had for Niẓām al-Dīn (Rukn al-Dīn 1338, 10).

As in the case of Ḥasan Dihlawī, Rukn al-Dīn Kāshānī was intent on accurately communicating the teachings of his master. *Nafā'is al-anfās* contains discussions, questions directed at Burhān al-Dīn Gharīb, stories both personal and legendary, and the explanation and performance of religious duties with an emphasis on Sufi rituals and their interpretation. While a number of famous early Sufis are mentioned, the greatest stress lies on the Chishtīs, in particular Burhān al-Dīn Gharīb's teacher Niẓām al-Dīn, who is mentioned on every other page; the next most prominent figure in Burhān al-Dīn Gharīb's conversations is "the great shaykh," Farīd al-Dīn Ganj-i Shakkar. *Fawā'id al-fu'ād* clearly exerted a profound influence on Burhān al-Dīn Gharīb, as it had on Niẓām al-Din's other disciples, and it suggested itself as a model that was eagerly followed in the recording of Burhān al-Dīn Gharīb's own teachings, even in the selection of the diary format and the preservation of its oral character.

Later texts from the circle of Burhān al-Dīn Gharīb have a much more literary character, and while they retain oral elements, they abandon the diary *malfūẓāt* structure for other genres. A more systematic approach characterizes the *malfūẓāt* compiled by Rukn al-Dīn's brother Ḥammād al-Dīn Kāshānī (d. 1360), entitled *Aḥsan al-aqwāl* (The Best of Sayings) (Ḥammād al-Dīn, 1338). This book is divided up into twenty-nine chapters, each called a *qawl*, or saying, covering all aspects of Sufi practice (Nizami

1955). As a handbook, it presents under each heading a series of principles and practices (*rawish*) in the words of Burhān al-Dīn Gharīb, usually followed by a concrete example, drawn from the experience of the Chishtī masters, that will serve as a proof (*burhān*, a play on the name of the Shaykh). Some of the sayings preserve distinct characteristics of speech rather than written composition, so the words of Burhān al-Dīn Gharīb have a decidedly spoken flavor.[19] At the beginning of most chapters, Burhān al-Dīn Gharīb is introduced by a distinct set of lofty epithets in accordance with the topic of that chapter. The title of the book is drawn from two passages from the Qur'ān (39.18 and 41.33) that stress both hearing and following good advice. This text, which was completed in the year of Burhān al-Dīn Gharīb's death (1338), is fortunately also available in a scholarly Urdu translation (Ḥammād al-Dīn 1987).

Although the emphasis of *Aḥsan al-aqwāl* is again on Sufi teaching, it imitates Rukn al-Dīn's *Nafā'is al-anfās* as a *malfūẓāt* text and claims a similar authority. The focus of the book is on social, ethical, psychological, and ritual practices (by far the longest chapter is the twenty-fifth, on prayers), but only the last three chapters are devoted to the miracles and experiences of Burhān al-Dīn Gharīb and his disciples. The structured format of this work does not reveal as much of the personality of the author as do the works written in diary form, although at the end he reveals that Burhān al-Dīn Gharīb prayed that Ḥammād al-Dīn should become a living saint (the implication is that the prayer of Burhān al-Dīn Gharīb would be answered) (Ḥammād al-Dīn 1338, 147). It seems that the author may have reedited the book later on, perhaps in the writing of the last three chapters, whose biographical content does not fit well with the very practical subject matter of the first twenty-six chapters; in chapter twenty-seven, Ḥammād al-Dīn quotes from his brother Majd al-Dīn's *Gharā'ib al-karāmāt*, a work that was certainly begun much later than the original edition of *Aḥsan al-aqwāl* (Ḥammād al-Dīn 1338, 141). The language of the preface to *Aḥsan al-aqwāl* is closely modeled on the preface to Rukn al-Dīn's *Nafā'is al-anfās*, quoting some phrases nearly verbatim. Ḥammād al-Dīn follows Rukn al-Dīn's language particularly closely, but with greater rhetorical luxuriance, when he insists that no written source has ever indicated the profound depths of knowledge to be found in the present treatise (Ḥammād al-Dīn, 1338, 4). Although the topical organization of this work seems on the surface to be a departure from the diary format of *Fawā'id al-fu'ād*, *Aḥsan al-aqwāl*, through the concrete examples that it gives for each practice, retains the essential focus on the person of the master as the embodiment of the teaching.

The third *malfūẓāt* text to be written by a member of this remarkable family was Majd al-Dīn Kāshānī's *Gharā'ib al-karāmāt wa 'ajā'ib al-*

mukāshafāt (Rare Miracles and Wondrous Unveilings), a work that falls more nearly into the category of narrative hagiography (Majd al-Dīn 1340). Although the date of its composition is not known, the benedictory formulas addressed to Burhān al-Dīn Gharīb indicate that is was begun after the latter's death. Majd al-Dīn in his preface observed that for some time the idea for this book had been on his mind, that he "should make a book of the influential words of the Shaykh al-Islam."[20] His friends urged him to follow the example of his two brothers, whose works have been described above; since they all have been constantly praising and remembering Burhān al-Dīn Gharīb, no gift could provide them more joy and ecstasy than a book chronicling the miracles (*karāmāt*) and unveilings (*mukāshafāt*) of the shaykh. The preface continues with an extended narration of the severe discipline (*riyāżat*) that enabled Burhān al-Dīn Gharīb to attain the powers and knowledge that occupy the bulk of this book (Majd al-Dīn 1340, 6–12). The focus of this work is much more on the man than on his teachings. The way in which Majd al-Dīn was persuaded to write the book suggests that its purpose was primarily devotional. Yet Burhān al-Dīn Gharīb's miracles are modest enough. There are no accounts of teleportation or nightly visits to Mecca. Of the fourteen events described as miracles, nearly all concern the saint's foreknowledge of the future (Majd al-Dīn 1340, 17–18, 22, 39, 43, 45, 46, 49, 74, 75), while the nineteen "unveilings" are mostly occasions when he reads the thoughts or unspoken questions of others (Majd al-Dīn 1340, 13–16, 18, 23, 25, 26, 28, 30, 33–35, 37, 39, 42, 44, 47). In effect, these were teaching miracles, evidences of the saint's transmission of Sufi teaching. The disciples of Burhān al-Dīn Gharīb evidently had a great desire for material of this kind, for Majd al-Dīn later authored a supplementary collection of narratives entitled *Bāqiyat al-karāmāt* (The Rest of the Miracles); this work is apparently no longer extant.[21] In any case, this work is primarily aimed at the devotee, and testifies to the spiritual authority of the Sufi master Burhān al-Dīn Gharīb:

> His disciples reached from the level of discipleship to the rank of mastery, and those accepted by him transformed the world; because they saw his blessed face, their sins were forgiven. [Verse:] I also have become his servant / so that the sins of this fool are forgiven. He is an intercessor with God / so that he may bestow the cloak of acceptance.[22]

As in the more narrowly construed hagiographies, this book reveals the shaykh as the one who has the power to read the disciple's heart and intercede with God on the disciple's behalf.

The fourth *malfūẓāt* work oriented toward Burhān al-Dīn Gharīb also came from the pen of Rukn al-Dīn Kāshānī, but its encyclopedic literary scope makes it only in part a record of the sayings of the shaykh. This monumental treatise is entitled *Shamā'il al-atqiyā' wa dalā'il al-anqiyā'* (Virtues of the Devout and Proofs of the Pure), the only one of the Khuldabad texts to be published in Persian (Rukn al-Dīn 1928). *Shamā'il al-atqiyā'* is an enormous collection (455 pages, in the rare lithographed edition) of excerpts from Sufi writings and oral traditions, covering a full range of topics related to mystical thought and practice. In his preface, Rukn al-Dīn has presented a list of over 250 classical authorities on Sufism and religion that he consulted, which are scrupulously cited as sources on every page of the book. This bibliography, including both Arabic and Persian sources, comprises about seventy-five works on the standard Islamic religious sciences (Qur'ānic exegesis, *ḥadīth*, theology, and law), about 125 books on Sufism, and another fifty sources of oral traditions.[23] A number of these titles are evidently no longer extant, aside from the quotations in this work. *Shamā'il al-atqiyā'* also includes excerpts from several other lost treatises on Sufism written by the Kāshānī brothers. Rukn al-Dīn's bibliography thus constitutes what Jonathan Z. Smith would call an ordered catalogue of texts rather than a closed canon (Smith 1978, 45). Its inclusion of oral sources makes it essentially open-ended. The Chishtī *malfūẓāt*, which straddle the boundary between text and speech, are prominently featured in this catalogue.

Rukn al-Dīn began writing *Shamā'il al-atqiyā'* during the lifetime of Burhān al-Dīn Gharīb, who approved the first few sections and bestowed upon Rukn al-Dīn the title "the spiritual secretary" (*dabīr-i ma'nawī*). The book was not completed, however, until some unspecified time after the shaykh's death (Rukn al-Dīn 1928, 3). The subjects that Rukn al-Dīn included in *Shamā'il al-atqiyā'* address a select audience of educated Sufis. The two principal sections are, first, a discussion in fifty-two chapters of Islamic rituals and the interior stations (*maqāmāt*) of Sufism, and second, an analysis of mystical states (*aḥwāl*). The third and fourth sections, on theology and anthropology, are miniscule in comparison and function only as appendices. As is common in Sufi manuals, each chapter begins with quotations from the Qur'ān and *ḥadīth*, followed by excerpts from works of exegesis, Islamic law, and theology, and from a multitude of Sufi sources. The popularity of *Shamā'il al-atqiyā'* can be gauged from its translation into Dakhani Urdu in the seventeenth century (Qādirī 1967, 118–19; Ja'far 1983, 104–20). The special interest of this text for the development of *malfūẓāt* is due to its incorporation of many of Burhān al-Dīn Gharīb's oral teachings.[24] Rukn al-Dīn did not intend merely to make a compilation based on written sources, but viewed the preceding Sufi tradition as a heritage alongside the oral teaching received from Burhān al-Dīn Gharīb. He formed the resolve that

> in this book should be written and recorded the different sayings and virtues of the devout and the saints, and the kinds of spiritual states and customs of the virtuous and the pure, which have issued from these treatises and writings, [and] from the conceptual wonders and esoteric rarities that have been heard from the jewel-bearing tongue and pearl-scattering discourse of that unveiler of scriptural difficulties and clarifier of intricate proof, that is, my master and patron, my elder and teacher.[25]

Unlike the *malfūẓāt* written in diary form, which strive to recreate the living presence of the master, this scholarly production places the master's oral teaching in the context of a vast historical tradition. The ordered catalogue of texts that forms its bibliography, while not a closed canon, confers canonical authority on the Chishtī *malfūẓāt* texts while still recognizing the importance of oral sources.

V. The Problem of Inauthentic Malfūẓāt

It was probably the impact of Niẓām al-Dīn Awliyā' through the teachings of *Fawā'id al-fu'ād* that led to the reconstruction of earlier Chishtī tradition along similar lines, through the fabrication of *malfūẓāt* texts. As Baranī observed, one of the effects of Niẓām al-Dīn's popularity was to arouse people's curiosity about the teachings and practices of the earlier Chishtī masters, such as Farīd al-Dīn and Quṭb al-Dīn (Baranī, in Nizami 1978, 197). It was in this spirit that the grandson of Shaykh Ḥamīd al-Dīn Suwāli Nāgawrī (d. 1276) compiled the latter's sayings, in a large and rambling *malfūẓāt* composed around 1350 (Lawrence 1978, 21, 97; Nizami 1950, 167–69). As shown above, the purpose of the *malfūẓāt* was to evoke the personal presence of the Sufi master as well as to record the shaykh's teachings. Niẓām al-Dīn had also attempted to record some of the conversations of his master Farīd al-Dīn to this end, though no trace of this survives. But somehow a series of books, attributed to the earlier Chishtī shaykhs, began to appear. By a kind of principle of plenitude, every great teacher in the Chishtī succession was credited with a book of teachings. Even before the completion of the first part of *Fawā'id al-fu'ād*, a book falsely ascribed to Niẓām al-Dīn was in circulation in Awadh; Niẓām al-Dīn, who firmly denied having written that or any other book, reflected that problems of plagiarism and inauthentic books had also plagued Indian Sufi authors even in the time of 'Ali Hujwīrī (Dihlawī 1966, 76). Perhaps the most telling piece of evidence against the false *malfūẓāt* occurs in the conversations of Naṣīr al-Dīn Maḥmūd Chirāgh-i Dihlī; when a disciple asked about one of these writings, Naṣīr al-Dīn rejected it as unworthy of the Chishtī masters, emphatically stating that none of them had ever written a book.

In a brilliant critical article, Mohammad Habib called attention to these *malfūẓāt*, demonstrating their variance from accepted Chishtī teachings, their historical anachronisms, and their lack of authenticity according to the testimony of the Chishtī masters themselves. Habib concentrated on six unauthentic works, listed here according to their ostensible chronological order:

1. *Anīs al-arwāḥ,* the conversations of 'Usmān Hārwanī allegedly collected by Mu'īn al-Dīn Chishtī;
2. *Dalīl al-'ārifīn*, the conversations of Mu'īn al-Dīn Chishtī collected by Quṭb al-Dīn Bakhtiyār Kākī;
3. *Fawā'id al-sālikīn*, the conversations of Quṭb al-Dīn Bakhtiyār Kākī collected by Farīd al-Dīn Ganj-i Shakkar;
4. *Asrār al-awliyā'*, the conversations of Farīd al-Dīn Ganj-i Shakkar collected by Badr al-Dīn Isḥāq;
5. *Rāḥat al-qulūb*, the conversations of Farīd al-Dīn Ganj-i Shakkar as collected by Niẓām al-Dīn; and
6. *Afẓal al-fawā'id,* and its continuation *Rāḥat al-muḥibbīn*, the conversations of Niẓām al-Dīn as recorded by the poet Amīr Khusraw (Habib 1971, 1:401–25).

These books, according to Habib, lack the personal touch that made *Fawā'id al-fu'ād* such an effective presentation of Niẓām al-Dīn's teaching. The false *malfūẓāt* focus on establishing the authority of the Chishtī masters at all costs, describing, for instance, the Prophet's miraculous recognition of the Chishtī saints during their pilgrimages to Mecca, although reliable Chishtī tradition firmly records that none of these masters ever made the *ḥajj* pilgrimage. While the genuine *malfūẓāt* contain lively conversations, the audiences in the fabricated works are silent witnesses to the monologues of saints. The spurious *malfūẓāt* are characterized by a profusion of exaggerated miracles designed to enhanced the saint's prestige, and by an extreme fascination with chants (*awrād*) and their benefits. Although the unauthentic works are not devoid of merit, they betray their secondary status by plagiarizing on occasion from *Fawā'id al-fu'ād*. The reconstruction they offer of the early Chishtī order tends toward the simplistic, dwelling on charisma and miraculous power rather than evoking a guiding presence. The stress on presenting the unbroken initiatic line of the early Chishtīs may have been due to anxiety about the dispersal of the Chishtī order after the death of Niẓām al-Dīn in 1325 (Nizami 1973, 118–20; Lawrence 1976, 124). The primary concern of these texts is to establish the mere fact of spiritual authority rather than to convey the teachings upon which that authority rested. At a loss for an explanation for the popularity of these works, Habib finally suggested that they were forgeries commissioned by booksellers in order to drum up trade (Habib 1971, 1:430).

Despite the criticisms of Habib, it must be acknowledged that traditional Chishtī circles from an early date generally accepted these documents as genuine, and they are still very popular in Urdu translation. The authenticity of these *malfūẓāt* has been defended by a number of traditional-minded scholars (Ṣabāḥ al-Dīn 1949). Today, most followers of the Chishtī order in fact rely primarily on the inauthentic *malfūẓāt* for their understanding of the early Chishtī masters; the only exception to this rule is *Fawā'id al-fu'ād*, which has continued to be universally popular up to the present day. The discourses of Chirāgh-i Dihlī and Burhān al-Dīn Gharīb can only be found in a few rare Persian manuscripts preserved in private libraries and Sufi shrines, and on the rare occasion when they have been translated into Urdu, these publications remain extremely hard to get. Nizami, finding only three manuscripts of *Khayr al-majālis*, attributed their rarity to the rigor of Chirāgh-i Dihlī's teachings, since the shaykh insisted on observance of Islamic law, criticized hereditary succession in Sufi lineages, and rejected the inauthentic *malfūẓāt*. This strict approach necessarily lacked the popular appeal of the inauthentic *malfūẓāt* (Nizami, ''Introduction,'' in Qalandar 1959, 7). At shrines such as the tomb of the Farīd al-Dīn Ganj-i Shakkar in Pakistan, the most commonly available text today consists of the Urdu translations of eight *malfūẓat* texts in a single volume entitled *Hasht bihisht* (Eight Heavens), which contains *Anīs al-arwāh, Dalīl al-'ārifīn, Fawā'id al-sālikīn, Rāḥat al-qulūb, Miftāh al-'āshiqīn* (discourses attributed to Naṣīr al-Dīn Maḥmūd), *Fawā'id al-fu'ād, Rāḥat al-muḥibbin,* and *Asrār al-awliyā' (Hasht bihisht).* The eclipse of the early *malfūẓāt* texts by other writings believed to be inauthentic constitutes a problem for critical scholarship. The problem is that Habib's critical approach, while partly framed in terms of traditional standards, draws primarily upon modern Western categories of analysis that are foreign to the material under consideration. His distaste for miracle stories might even be said to reveal a positivistic bias.

The theoretical distinction we have attempted to make between the genuine and spurious *malfūẓāt* is compromised by the appearance of some of the inauthentic works in *Shamā'il al-atqiyā'*. In his bibliography, Rukn al-Dīn Kāshānī lists the apocryphal *malfūẓāt* of the early Chishtī shaykhs right along with Ḥasan Dihlawī's *Fawā'id al-fu'ād* and his own *Nafā' is al-anfās*.[26] The citations of Chishtī apocrypha in *Shamā'il al-atqiyā'* appear to be the earliest literary reference to the spurious *malfūẓāt*. Only seven citations from these works appear in *Shamā'il al-atqiya'*.[27] The subjects covered in these quotations are for the most part concerned with Sufi practice, although one anecdote refers to the power of the master to discern the thoughts of prospective disciples (a prominent hagiographic theme in *Gharā'-ib al-karāmāt*). The distinction between the genuine and false *malfūẓāt* is not absolute; it must be admitted that this distinction is significant primarily from the academic point of view. Both kinds of texts contain extracts from Sufi teaching, and both illustrate the charisma of the Sufi teacher; the difference is primarily in emphasis. Rukn al-Dīn, by including these texts in his catalogue, was attempting to represent the breadth of the Sufi tradition in the widest possible way. His concern was not to establish rigid standards of textual authenticity but to summarize the range and depth of Sufi teaching available to the Chishtī masters in his day, and in his experience the literary tradition was closely tied to the oral one. He cites over thirty authorities simply as "The Treatise of So-and-so," refers to over fifty oral sources as "The Saying of So-and-so," and reserves an extra catchall category for anonymous sayings. In compiling *Shamā'il al-atqiyā'*, Rukn al-Dīn was probably happy to include some references to the spurious Chishtī *malfūẓāt*, insofar as they contributed to his overall presentation of Sufi teaching. The anachronisms and contradictions that they contain would not have presented a problem for him, since he only extracted materials that were relevant to his purpose. Since Rukn al-Dīn felt free to give excerpts from these apocryphal works in his Sufi encyclopedia, we can only conclude that even at this early date the hagiographic interest in the early Chishtī order had already reached a fairly high level; in other words, the inauthentic *malfūẓāt* were very popular manifestations of religious sentiment among Indian Muslims.

VI. Conclusions

If we set aside the problem of authenticity and turn to other axes of comparison, we can nevertheless distinguish between the two classes of texts in terms of the previously mentioned categories of oral or written character, canonicity, and audience. Let us refer to the discourses of Niẓām al-Dīn, Chirāgh-i Dihlī, and Burhān al-Dīn Gharīb as the "original" *malfūẓāt* texts for purposes of discussion. These works preserve many unmistakable features of oral style. Here, the Sufi masters in their conversations frequently use the typically oral mnemonic devices of clustering related items into groups of three, four, or five. Questions, exclamations, impromptu quotations of poetry, and occasional dramatic interactions with interlocutors dominate these early texts. What may be called the "retrospective" *malfūẓāt* texts in contrast show them delivering monotonous sermons and narrative pericopes that betray a purely literary hand at work (Lawrence

1976, 120, 122). This increasingly literary quality of *malfūẓāt*, and the loss of oral character, is characteristic of the later proliferation of *malfūẓāt* texts that emerged from subsequent generations of Chishtī masters (in most of these cases there is no question about the authenticity of these works). By the fifteenth century, the oral element in *malfūẓāt* is in many cases entirely eliminated.

As far as indigenous categories are concerned, while both types of text function canonically (as Canon-far), they can be distinguished in terms of their relative emphasis on normative teaching or religious authority. Following the model of *ḥadīth* reports, the original *malfūẓāt* as described above stress the contents of Sufi teaching, particularly with regard to practice. The retrospective works, on the other hand, move largely in the direction of hagiography in emphasizing personal charisma and authority over teaching. Of course, hagiographic elements of authority do appear in the original *malfūẓāt*, and the retrospective works pay attention to practices such as the efficacy of chants, but the main tendencies of Canon-far tend to break along these lines. This distinction is further demonstrated in the authorship of the texts. The compilers of the original *malfūẓāt* were disciples trying to preserve and convey their masters' teachings: Ḥasan Dihlawī was a court poet, the Kāshānī brothers of Khuldabad were all court officials, and Ḥamīd Qalandar was a marginal Sufi hanger-on and poet. The retrospective texts, on the other hand, form an extended literary elaboration of the initiatic genealogy, unambiguously guaranteeing and concretizing the authority of the order. Even miracle stories tend to break down in the same fashion, with the original *malfūẓāt* stressing miracles as part of the teaching and the retrospective texts using them to demonstrate authority.

The original *malfūẓāt*, finally, differ from the retrospective works in terms of their audience. The recorders of the original *malfūẓāt* were addressing elite members of the Turkish nobility and military class that ruled northern India in the thirteenth and fourteenth centuries. These were people who could put themselves in the place of a Ḥasan Dihlawī, imagining themselves to be the disciple of the Sufi shaykh, and using the text as what Ḥasan Dihlawī called "the guide of the path." The audience of the retrospective *malfūẓāt*, on the other hand, was less concerned with Sufi practice and Islamic law, but much more interested in the powers of the saints as intercessors with God. For them, the value of the *malfūẓāt* was relational rather than informational; the *malfūẓāt* functioned scripturally to put them in touch with the heart of the Chishtī lineage, and therefore in close relationship with God's representatives on earth. Because of the pseudonymous character of the retrospective works, it is difficult to identify their "popular" audience with much more precision than this on purely internal grounds. Yet *Fawā'id al-fu'ād*, the foundational text of the genre, was not limited by these restrictions and appealed to both audiences.

The Sufi teaching is essentially a personal mediation of a complex teaching tradition. In its normative aspect, it follows the model of *ḥadīth* by transmitting religious guidelines through a chain of reliable witnesses. Hagiographical writing in its most extreme form disregards the teaching aspect of Sufism and concentrates instead on authority. In the Chishtī Sufi order, the original *malfūẓāt* by their dialogical format used the *ḥadīth* method of oral transmission to embody the teaching process in a written form. The process of textualization of oral teaching led to the formation of a kind of secondary canon of Indian Sufi literature, in which the retrospective elaboration of the discourses of the early Chishtī masters supplemented the original texts, proceeding along purely literary lines. The modern debate about the authenticity of the *malfūẓāt* literature has been conducted in terms of Western critical standards that are sometimes quite removed from the self-understanding of the tradition. Wilfred Cantwell Smith has observed that "we have tended to derive our concept of scripture from the Bible; I am suggesting that we are now in a position where our understanding of the Bible, and of much else across the world, may begin to be derived from a larger concept of scripture" (Smith 1989, 45). In trying to understand the emergence of the canon of Chishtī *malfūẓāt* texts, or any other non-Western religious texts, it may be tempting to apply the same standard techniques of literary criticism that were developed in Biblical studies, in terms of a scriptural model that was basically Protestant. But the limitations of this kind of approach become apparent when the interpreter ends up dismissing as "inauthentic" and "apocryphal" a literature that continues to have a demonstrably canonical function for its community. By observing how this tradition has interpreted its own canonical texts, we can not only enlarge our comprehension of this particular phenomenon, but also we can expand our categories of analysis so that they may more adequately reflect the global scope of the study of religion.

Notes

1. Portions of the research for this chapter were supported by a Senior Research Fellowship from the American Institute of Indian Studies in 1981 and a Fulbright Islamic Civilization Research Fellowship in 1986. An earlier version was delivered at the Conference on Modes of Transmission of Religious Thought in Islam, held at Princeton University in April 1989.

2. Faruqi 1982–85; a complete English translation of *Fawā'id al-fu'ād* has been promised by Bruce B. Lawrence.

3. *kih ghazaliyyāt-i jigar-sūz-i ū az chaqmaq-i dil-hā-yi 'āshiqān ātish-i maḥabbat bīrūn mī-āward . . . wa laṭā'if-i rūḥ-afzā-yi ū māya-i ahl-i zawq-ast.* (Kirmani 1978, 318; Borah 1941, 52)

4. *az sālī ziyādat bāshad kih dar bandagī-yi makhdūm payvasta am wa har bār kih sa'ādat-i pāy-būs ḥāṣil shuda ast az lafẓ-i durar-bār fawā'id shunida am chi va'ẓ wa naṣiḥat u targhīb dar ṭā'at wa chih ḥikāyāt-i mashā'ikh wa aḥwāl-i īshān az har bāb kalimāt-i rūh-afzāy ba-sam'-i kātib rasīda ast wa khwāsta am kih ān dastūr-i ḥāl-i īn bī-chāra bāshad balkih dalīl-i rāh-i īn shikasta, ba-qadr-i fahm-i khwud dar qalam āwarda am, ham banābarān kih bārhā bar lafẓ-i mubārak rafta ast kih kitāb-i mashā'ikh wa ishārāt-i īshān kih dar sulūk rānda and dar naẓar mī-bāyad dāsht pas hīch majmū'a warāy anfās-i jān-bakhsh-i makhdūmī na-tavānad būd, bar ḥukm-i īn muqaddama banda ān chih az lafẓ-i mubārak shunida ast jam' karda ast wa tā īn zamān iẓhār na-karda ast muntaẓir-i farmān ast.* (Dihlawī 1966, 49)

5. *ay ātish-i firāqat dilhā kabāb karda / saylāb-i ishtiyāqat jānhā kharāb karda.*

6. *nīkū nibishta-ī wa darvīshāna nibishta-ī wa nām ham nīkū karda-ī.*

7. *az nisbat-i īn ḥāl.*

8. *banda nīz pīsh-i khidmat-i khwāja kih ustād u murabbī u makhdūm-i man ast, dāman farāz kard wa ba-jihat-i ḥifẓ fātiḥa dar khwāst wa niyyat kard kih har kih muḥibb u mu'taqad-i khwaja na-bāshad bā ū maḥabbat na-kunam wa dar kū-yi ū na-gardam balkih tā mumkin bāshad rū-yi ū na bīnam.* (Qalandar 1959, 31)

9. *agar ḥawī na-tavānam shud, amā ānchih dar fahm-i man mī man mī-gunjad bārī dar qalam āram, tā Yādgārī bāshad.* (Qalandar 1959, 47)

10. Jackson (1985, 35) too hastily dismissed this type of anecdote in his analysis of the text.

11. *khudāwand! mawlānā Burhān al-Dīn darvīsh-i wāṣil būd, amā khidmat-i khwāja dar 'ilm Abū Ḥanifa and wa dar zuhd wa shaykhī Shaykh Niẓām al-Dīn-i waqt inshā' allāh majālis-i khwāja ba-nivīsam.* (Qalandar 1959, 12)

12. Discussion of the attitudes of Mīr Khwurd and Gīsū Darāz toward Burhān al-Dīn Gharīb would take up too much space at this point.

13. I would like to express my profound thanks to Mr. Fariduddin Saleem, president, Committee Dargahjat Hadd-e Kalan, Khuldabad, India, for making available to me the manuscripts of Burhān al-Dīn Gharīb's circle, without which this study would not have been possible.

14. *hīch sālikī dar taṣānīf-i shuyūkh-i salaf daqīqa az ān daqā'iq u rumūz masṭūr dīda wa na hīch muḥaqqiqī dar kutub-i sulūk-i sābiq ḥarfī az ān ba-ḥaqq u gharā'ib khwānda.* (Rukn al-Dīn 1338, 3)

15. *tā khāṭibān-i 'arā'is-i ma'ānī-i ṭarīqat ba-dīn wāsiṭa ba-takhtgāh-i wiṣāl-i maḥbūb-i ḥaqīqī rasand wa ṭālibān-i abkār-i daqā'iq-i sulūk ba-muṭāla'a-i ān jamāl-i jahān-ārā-yi maṭlūb-i aṣlī mu'āyana u mushāhada kunand.* (Rukn al-Dīn 1338, 3)

16. *muddatī-yi madīd īn-ma'nī dar żamīr mutamakkin ast.*

17. *ba-dā'ūdī dil-am-rā tāza gardān / zabūr-am-rā buland āvāza gardān.*

18. *Amīr Ḥasan raḥmat allah 'alayhi kih fawā'id nibishta ast īnchunīn būd shaykh har ḥikāyatī kih guftī rūy sū-yi Amīr Ḥasan kardī chih dar majlis sukhan raftī ba-nivishtī.*

19. For example, the use of the word *khayr* (good) instead of *na* (not) as a negative (cf. modern Persian *nakhayr*, "no") to ward off ill omen (Ḥammād al-Dīn 1338, 14, 44, 68). This habit of speech can still be observed in Punjabi today.

20. *kih az āsār-i anfās-i ḥazrat-i shaykh al-islām risāla sāzad.* (Majd al-Dīn 1340, 3)

21. I am not aware of the existence of any copies of this text, but some quotations are given in Rawnaq 'Alī (1931) and in the notes to Āzād Bilgrāmī (1926–7, 13, 19, 25, 31–32, 41, 45, 86, 135).

22. *murīdān-ash az daraja-i irādat ba-martaba-i shaykhī rasīdand maqbūlān-ish muqabbilān-i jahān shudand az ān kih rū-yi mubārak-ish dīdand gunāhān-ishān bakhshīdand. naẓm: Man nīz az ān shudam ghulām-ish / tā jurm-i man-i fużūl bakhshand // dar ḥazrat-i ḥaqq shafī' bāshand / tā khil'atī az qabūl bakhshand.* (Majd al-Dīn 1340, 12)

23. An annotated translation of this "Sufi bookshelf" will form an appendix to my forthcoming monograph on Khuldabad.

24. Burhān al-Dīn Gharīb is quoted in *Shamā'il al-atqiya'* by name sixteen times (Rukn al-Dīn 1928, 21, 47, 53, 68, 69, 98, 137, 151, 201, 232–33, 238, 316, 382, 383, 384, 381), and as "the revered master" (*khidmat-i hkwāja*) another sixteen times (Rukn al-Dīn 1928, 52, 53, 68, 137, 149, 168, 207, 210, 213, 217, 222, 252, 261, 276, 281, 418).

25. *aqwāl u shamā'il-i mukhtalifa-i atqiyā' u awliyā' wa aḥwāl u khaṣā'il-i naw'a-i azkiyā' u aṣfiyā' khārij-i ta'līfāt u taṣnīfāt-i muzkūra az 'ajā'ib-i zihnī u ghara'ib-i baṭnī kih az zabān-i guhar-bār u taqrīr-i durar-nisār-i ān kāshif-i mushkilāt-i furqān wa mubayyin-i mu'zilāt-i burhān a'nī pīr u murabbī shaykh u mubannī-yi khwud samā' shud.* (Rukn al-Dīn 1938, 4)

26. *Anīs al-arwāḥ*, *Dalīl al-'ārifīn*, *Fawā'id al-sālikīn*, *Rāḥat al-qulūb*, and *Asrār al-mutaḥayyarīn* (a previously unmentioned compilation of Farīd

al-Dīn Ganj-i Shakkar's sayings) occupy nos. 102 to 106 in the bibliography, and Amīr Khusraw's *Rāḥat al-muḥibbīn* is no. 149. *Fawā'id al-fu'ād* is no. 107, and *Nafā'is al-anfās* is no. 108.

27. *Fawā'id al-sālikīn*, cited in Rukn al-Dīn (1938, 31, 46); *Rāḥat al-muḥibbīn*, in Rukn al-Dīn (1928, 58, 65, 67, 93); *Asrār al-mutaḥayyarīn*, in Rukn al-Dīn (1928, 403).

References

Arberry, A. J., trans.
1961 *Discourses of Rūmī*. London: John Murray.

Āzād Bilgrāmī, Ghulām 'Ali
1926–7 *Rawżat al-awliyā' al-ma'rūf bi-nafaḥāt al-aṣfiyā'*. Urdu translation by Muḥammad 'Abd al-Majīd. Hyderabad: Maṭba'-i Karīmī.

Bahār, Muḥammad Taqī
1959 [1337] *Sabk-shināsī yā tārīkh-i taṭawwur-i nasr-i Fārsī*. 2d ed., 3 vols. Tehran: Mu'assasa-i Chāp wa Intishārāt-i Amīr-i Kabīr.

Borah, M. I.
1941 "The Life and Works of Amīr Ḥasan Dihlavi." *Journal of the Royal Asiatic Society of Bengal*, Letters, 7: 1–59.

Dihlawī, Amīr Ḥasan 'Alā' Sijzī
1933 *Dīwān*. Edited by Mas'ūd 'Alī Maḥwī. Hyderabad: Ibrahimiyah Steam Press.

1966 *Fawā'id al-Fu'ād*. Edited by Muḥammad Laṭīf Malik. Lahore: Malik Sirāj al-Dīn & Sons.

Ernst, Carl W.
1985 "From Hagiography to Martyrology: Conflicting Testimonies to a Sufi Martyr of the Delhi Sultanate." *History of Religions* 14 (4): 308–27.

Faruqi, Ziya-ul-Hasan, trans.
1982–85 "Fawa'id-ul-Fu'ad of Khwajah Ḥasan Dehlawi." *Islam and the Modern Age* 13: 33–44, 126–41, 169–80, 210–28; 14: 195–213; 15: 25–36, 167–92; 16: 231–42, etc.

Folkert, Kendall A.
1989 "The 'Canons' of 'Scripture'." In *Rethinking Scripture: Essays from a Comparative Perspective*, edited by Miriam Levering, Albany, 170–79. Albany: State University of New York Press.

Habib, Mohammad
1974 "Chishtī Mystics Records of the Sultanate Period." In *Politics and Society During the Early Medieval Period, Collected Works of Professor Mohammad Habib*, vol. 1, edited by K. A. Nizami, 385–433. New Delhi: People's Publishing House.

Ḥammād al-Dīn Kāshānī Chishtī
ca. 1338 *Aḥsan al-aqwāl*. MS in collection of Fariduddin Saleem, Khuldabad.

1987 *Aḥsan al-aqwāl Urdū al-ma'rūf bi-afżal al-maqāl*. Translated by Muḥammad 'Abd al-Majīd. Hyderabad, 1342. Reprint. Miraj: Ganj Bakhsh.

Hasht bihisht
n.d. Lahore: Allāh Wāle ki Qawmī Dukān.

Jackson, Paul
1985 "Khair Al-Majalis: An Examination." In *Islam in India: Studies and Commentaries*, vol. 2, *Religion and Religious Education*, edited by Christian W. Troll, 34–57. Delhi: Vikas.

Ja'far, Sayyida
1983 *Dakanī nasr kā intikhāb*. New Delhi: Taraqqi Urdu Bureau.

Jāmī, 'Abd al-Raḥmān ibn Aḥmad
1959 *Nafaḥāt al-uns min ḥażarāt al-quds*. Edited by Mahdī Tawḥīdīpūr. Tehran: Kitābfurūshī Maḥmūdī.

Kirmānī, Sayyid Muḥammad Mubārak al-'Alawī al-, "Mīr Khwurd"
1978 *Siyar al-Awliyā'*. Delhi: Maṭba'-i Muḥibb-i Hind, 1302. Reprint. Islamabad: Markaz-i Taḥqīqāt-i Fārsī-i Irān u Pākistān.

Lawrence, Bruce B.
1975 "The Lawā'iḥ of Qāḍī Ḥamīd ad-dīn Nāgaurī." *Indo-Iranica* 20: 34–53.

1976 "Afzal-ul-fawa'id—a reassessment." In *Life, Times, and Works of Amīr Khusrau Dehlavi, Seventh Centenary*, edited by Z. Ansari, 119–31. New Delhi: National Amīr Khusrau Society.

1978 *Notes from a Distant Flute: The Extant Literature of Pre-Mughal Indian Sufism*. Tehran: Imperial Iranian Academy of Philosophy.

Majd al-Dīn Kāshānī
ca. 1340 *Gharā'ib al-karāmāt*. MS in collection of Fariduddin Saleem, Khuldabad.

Massignon, Paul, and Kraus, Paul, eds. and trans.
1957 *Akhbār al-Ḥallāj, Recueil d'oraisons et d'exhortations du martyr mystique de l'Islam*. Études Musulmanes 4, 3d ed. Paris: Librairie Philosophique J. Vrin.

Meier, Fritz
1976 *Abū Sa'īd-i Abū l-Ḫayr (357–440/967–1049), Wirklichkeit und Legende*. Acta Iranica 11. Leiden: E. J. Brill.

Nizami, Khaliq Ahmad
1950 "The Sarur-u's-Sudur." In *Proceedings of the Indian History Congress, Nagpur Session*, 167–69.

1955 "A Note on Ahsan-al-Aqwal." *Journal of the Pakistan Historical Society* 3: 40–44.

1973 *The Life and Times of Shaikh Farid-u'd-Din Ganj-i-Shakar*. IAD Religio-Philosophy Series, no. 1. 1955. Reprint. Delhi: Idarah-i Adabiyat-i Delli.

1978 *Some Aspects of Religion and Politics in India During the Thirteenth Century*. IAD Religio-Philosophy Series, no. 2., 2d ed. Delhi: Idarah-i Adabiyat-i Delli.

Qādirī, Shams Allāh
1967 *Urdū-i qadīm*. Lucknow: Tej Kumar.

Qalandar, Ḥamīd comp.
1959 *Khayr al-Majālis*. Edited by Khaliq Ahmad Nizami. Aligarh: Department of History, Muslim University.

Rawnaq'Ali
1931 *Rawzat al-aqṭāb al-ma'rūf bi-maẓhar-i āṣafiyya*. Lucknow: Dilgudaz Press.

Rukn al-Dīn Dabīr Kāshānī
ca. 1338 *Nafā'is al-anfās*. MS in collection of Fariduddin Saleem, Khuldabad.

1928 *Shamā'il al-atqiyā'*. Edited by Sayyid 'Aṭā' Ḥusayn, Silsila-i Ishā'at al-'Ulūm, no. 85. Hyderabad: Maṭbū'a Ashraf Press.

Rūmī, Jalāl al-Dīn
1959 *Fīhi mā fīhi*. Edited by Badī' al-Zamān Furūzānfar. Tehran: Shirkat-i Sihāmī-i Nāshirīn-i Kutub-i Irān.

Ṣabāḥ al-Dīn 'Abdal-Raḥmān
1949 *Bazm-i Ṣūfiyya*. A'ẓamgaṛh: Dar al-Musannifīn.

Sahlajī, al-
1949 *Kitāb al-nūr min kalimāt Abī Ṭayfūr*. In *Shaṭaḥātal-Sūfiyya, part 1, Abū Yazīd al-Bisṭāmī*, Darasāt Islāmiyya, no. 9, edited by 'Abd al-Raḥmān Badawī. Cairo: Maktabat an-Naḥda al-Miṣriyya.

Ṣiddīqī, Muḥammad Shakīl Aḥmad
1979 *Amīr Ḥasan Sijzī Dihlawī, ḥayāt awr adabī khidmāt*. Lucknow: Muḥammad Shakīl Aḥmad Ṣiddīqī.

Smith, Jonathan Z.
1982 "Sacred Persistence: Toward a Redescription of Canon." In *Imagining Religion: From Babylon to Jonestown*, 36–52. Chicago: University of Chicago Press.

Smith, Wilfred Cantwell
1989 "Scripture as Form and Concept." In *Rethinking Scripture: Essays from a Comparative Perspective*, edited by Miriam Levering, 29–57. Albany: State University of New York Press.

Fifteen

CONCLUSION

Traditional Hermeneutics in South Asia

Jeffrey R. Timm

Typically, in a multiauthored book of this sort, it is the duty of the editor to provide a framework, typology, or definition of the subject under examination, drawing together the individual contributions. The study of traditional hermeneutics, however, does not dispose itself to making universal claims, or synthesizing a plurality of perspectives to a conclusive typology or a generic definition. Understood as a cultivated sensitivity to the hermeneutical strategies developed by native exegetes, who themselves interpreted the form and the content of their own sacred text traditions, the study of traditional hermeneutics suggests guidelines that are more ethical than they are methodological. The Other deserves to be encountered through its own categories of understanding, instead of forced into a culturally foreign framework. If we agree to avoid, insofar as possible, the arrogance of cultural imperialism in our scholarship, if we agree that the interpretive efforts of the native hermeneute deserve to be approached with a desire to understand the "otherness" of traditional hermeneutics *in its own terms*, then we are left with a problem. Can any *appropriate* generalization be made about the pluralism of incommensurable theologies, ideologies, and worldviews reflected through a multitude of traditional interpretive understandings? Is anything shared by all of the traditional encounters with sacred texts we have considered? Do any common features emerge from the diverse instances of hermeneutical probing examined in this book? If the answer to any one of these questions is yes, then have we discovered a basis for an extracultural, generic definition of sacred text and its interpretation?

The search for generic definitions is a positive development in the study of non-Western religious traditions, insofar as it represents a desire to get beyond unexamined presuppositions favoring Western cultural forms and categories. Today, however, it is no great revelation to recognize that the form and content of the Protestant scriptures is not an adequate model for encountering the sacred texts of South Asian religious traditions. But is it any improvement to replace such a model with a culturally neutral, generic definition? Even granting the tenuous possibility of such neutrality, a generic definition, because its reductionism would be couched in the guise of scholarly objectivity, may be more problematic than the earlier Protestant Christian bias.

One of the ways out of this problem is to challenge static definitions or lists of fixed characteristics by representing "scripture" and its interpretation as a dynamic and relational phenomenon. In the recent volume *Rethinking Scripture: Essays from a Comparative Perspective* edited by Miriam Levering, the term *scripture* literally gives way to a new coinage that aims at approximating this dynamic, relational character: "scripturalizing," i.e., "the human propensity to produce scriptures" (p. 5). But isn't there some inappropriate reductionism even here? Many of the traditions we have examined assert the divine origin of their sacred texts or even the beginninglessness of these words. Wouldn't such traditions take strong exception to the suggestion (at least in the case of their primary scriptural corpus) of *human productivity*? The present volume has attempted to express scriptural dynamism in a different way by examining, in the context of South Asian religions, some of the traditional attempts to encounter, understand, define, limit, and expand the words identified by a given community as possessing a special normative, salvific, or transformative power. This is the study of "traditional hermeneutics."

As we have seen, the presentation of this subject requires a familiarity not only with texts and commentaries, but also with other dimensions of religious expression—that is, with the rituals, the languages and the histories of the traditions in question. And, perhaps even more important, the scholarly study of traditional hermeneutics requires a genuine sensitivity (may I even say affection?) for the tradition being explored. Efforts to meld the individuality of these traditions by synthesizing their diversity into a generic definition would lead away from, rather than toward, the goal of an authentic, nonreductionist understanding of the Other. This is not to advocate a debilitating relativism; far from it. Common threads do connect the individual hermeneutical moments presented in this volume (and beyond, although I'll not hazard beyond the South Asian context here). The problem is how to identify these "harmonic resonances" across traditions without distorting, in the process, the very traditions we wish to understand. Levering has proposed one solution to this problem by suggesting six basic polarities designed to illuminate the dynamism of scripture in the world's religions. These six polarities are form/fluidity, orality/writtenness, boundedness/openness, vectoring/being vectored, cosmic status/contingency, and normativity/selection and reinterpretation. In the few pages that remain I would like to consider to what degree these polarities can help to bring into focus the multidimensional character of the traditional encounter with sacred texts in South Asia.

The interplay of form and fluidity can help us to recognize that the dominant forms and contents of sacred texts and their interpretations are never static. If we have not done so already, this recognition will lead us to challenge the misleading presuppositions that Western scholars have sometimes carried to the study of non-Western religions, presumptions about the form and the content of scripture and its interpretation based on a familiarity with Western traditions (Levering 1989, 11). Although the existence of specific scriptural forms and interpretive strategies found in a religious tradition, at any given moment of its life, may seem to suggest a rigid set of characterizing features, arriving at such a set of features independent of a specific cultural and historical context will inevitably and falsely value one scheme over all others and will ultimately obscure the dynamic and persistent pluralism of changing forms and contents. The diverse interpretive strategies and understandings of sacred text employed by native exegetes in the traditions of South Asia dramatically illustrates the amazing fluidity of the sacred text category.

The work of historians like Wilfred Cantwell Smith has shown that Western definitions of scripture and judgments about appropriate interpretive modes, which have sometimes restricted Western thinking about non-Western text traditions, are themselves the products of dynamic historical processes. By recognizing the historicity of Western views, we can break with the tendency to unconsciously valorize Western views as normative. This may be a liberating insight, but does it go far enough? From the standpoint of the study of traditional hermeneutics in South Asia, the very notion of history being employed here may be understood as a Western construction. As we have seen in the contribution of Daniel Sheridan on Madhva, and in Carl Ernst's work on Chishtī Sufism, a Western view of history may itself be misleading when applied in the South Asian religious context if it is employed, for example, to isolate the "dispensable mythic overlay" or to exclude the "apocryphal add-ons" when such a "scholarly and objective" move flies in the face of the tradition's self-understanding. Our modern, commonsense distinction between historical-secular experience and mythic-religious experience is not shared by Madhva's biographer, Nārāyaṇa Paṇḍitācārya, when he describes Madhva's pilgrimage to his guru, Vyāsa. This raises a crucial question. How much of our own worldview can or should we suspend in our quest for an authentic understanding of the Other? Ernst's analysis of the so-called inauthentic *malfūẓāt* gives some idea of how such incommensurability might be handled without burking the tradition's self-understanding. By shifting the language of analysis from an evaluative mode, where one speaks of true and false *malfūẓāt*, to a descriptive mode, where one speaks instead of original and retrospective texts in the *malfūẓāt* genre, a valuable scholarly distinction is made without riding roughshod over the tradition's self-understanding. Clearly we must recognize that our invocation of "history" and "the historical" does not put us in touch with an unchanging, absolute normative ground.

The relationship between orality and writtenness touches on an aspect of the Western study of sacred texts that has received much attention in recent scholarship. In the present volume contributions by Carl Ernst, Vasudha Narayanan, and Frank Hoffman reveal in different ways the dynamic interplay between the oral and the written text. But does this interplay suggest that the experience of oral culture is not merely temporally prior to written culture, but foundational, even essential, to religious life? Ernst, for example, describes the creation of a new text-tradition, illustrating a transition from orality to writtenness. Narayanan, in her study of the *Tiruvāymoḻi* commentary tradition, points out that "despite the conscious decision to *write* commentaries, the Śrīvaiṣṇava tradition has a strong oral base and believes that oral interpretation is the only way of communicating a commentary if the purpose is to obtain salvific knowledge" (p. 93). Hoffman's examination of orality in Pali Buddhism goes even further in exposing the limitations of the modern Western bias favoring the written text. He asserts not only the temporal primacy of orality in Pali Buddhism, but also its ongoing importance, by pointing to the prescription of "right speech," one of the injunctions of the eightfold path. In all of these instances we are treated to some insight into a traditional understanding of the transformative potency characterizing the oral text. Yet before we conflate these hermeneutical moments and push the traditions of South Asia to the orality side of this distinction, some words of caution may be in order.

Consider, for a moment, David Carpenter's contention that Bhartṛhari would dismiss any characterization of *Veda* as a written text subject to interpretations. The cosmic reality of *Veda* as a "sonic manifestation of the ultimate ground of reality within the world of time and space" (p. 19), an eternal, verbal reality that underlies and supports the phenomenal word, reveals that the written text called "*Veda*" is but a pale approximation of the true *Veda*. At first glance such a view seems to support the valorization of orality, yet Carpenter himself alludes to the problem of overemphasizing the orality of the *Veda* (p. 29). Bhartṛhari's concern is with the fundamental "linguisticality" of reality, not with a distinction between orality and writtenness that, in fact, may carry implications conflicting with the grammarian's own view.

What, then, is implied by contrasting orality and writtenness? Harold Coward (1990) suggests that this distinction often implies "logocentricism," a view of language as an *a priori* experience of divine presence in which spoken language is the first conventional symbolization of this experience. In this view, written language is understood as twice removed from the originary, divine presence. While logocentricism may correspond well to the Śrīvaiṣṇava valorization of oral commentary over written, it may in fact obscure the worldview of thinkers like Bhartṛhari who assert the beginninglessness of language. To clarify the grammarian's worldview, Coward invokes Derrida's notion of "writing"; that is, writing as both exterior and *interior*, situated in the very core of language as the principle of differentiation, instead of twice removed. As Coward points out, "The shift from originary presence to originless difference has significant implications for the privileging of speech over writing . . . " (1990, 7). Such privileging, as a corrective to a modern Western prejudice favoring the written text, may have the happy result of bringing into clearer focus those South Asian religious traditions that have elevated the oral over the written in a logocentric fashion. But as Bhartṛhari's understanding of the *Veda* makes clear, the logocentric elevation of orality over writtenness cannot be presented as a universal feature of South Asian traditions.

The third polarity, boundedness/openness, cautions that we must not expect to find scriptural traditions always neatly circumscribed. The boundedness of a formal canon helps to define the community. It may provide self-definition, identifying the present community as a link in a tradition enduring through time, capable of transmitting itself from one generation to the next. But when the limits of boundedness, necessary for the perpetuation of a tradition, are not counterbalanced by the pole of openness, tradition becomes moribund and passes away.

Several authors in the present volume provide compelling evidence for the dynamic interplay of this polarity. Consider, for example, the openness of the "accordance with reality" principle described by José Cabezón, part of Vasubandhu's program of defining the Mahāyāna canon that is picked up by later thinkers to argue that *anything* spoken correctly is the Buddha's word. Or to take an example from Vedānta, consider Vallabha's assertion of a delimited, fourfold canon, along with his claim that, if properly understood, all words are the words of *bhagavan*. The simultaneity of boundedness and openness in such instances is nothing short of remarkable. This polarity plays out in other ways as well. In Islam, the Chishtī Sufi development of a new sacred text genre in the form of the *malfūẓāt* could be seen as a response to the boundedness of the *Qur'ān*.

The fourth polarity is "vectoring/being vectored." This terminology originates in Kendall Folkert's work on Jainism picked up by John Cort in his contribution to the present volume. Cort clarifies Folkert's Canon I/ Canon II distinction, by speaking instead of ''Canon-far'' (i.e., texts that are understood as possessing principle, ontological authority that ''vectors'' or carries other aspects of the tradition) and ''Canon-near'' (i.e., texts that are ''vectored'' or carried by other aspects of the tradition, for example the ritual use of the *Kalpa Sūtra* in the annual autumnal festival of Paryuṣaṇ described by Cort). There is no reason to suppose that a given scripture cannot possess both Canon-near and Canon-far characteristics. In many cases, in fact, a single text plays both roles. Nikky Singh illustrates this when she points out that the sacred text of Sikhism, the *Gurū Granth*, is the primary carrier of power and meaning, as well as the ''sole—aural and visual—icon of the Sikh religion'' (p. 251). Recognizing the textual multivalence suggested by this polarity is clearly not possible until the performative context of the text is brought into focus. Thus, the Canon-near/Canon-far distinction brings into sharp relief the intimate relationship between sacred text and the ''nontextual'' (i.e., contextual) dimensions of a tradition, a relationship at the very center of the study of traditional hermeneutics.

A fifth polarity involves the relationship between cosmic status and contingency. Here ''cosmic status'' refers to the ontological quality of the text that makes it efficacious and elevates it above other sorts of verbal constellations. To one degree or another all traditions valorize special collections of words, isolating them from the mundane uses of language by asserting their special origins. In the spectrum of South Asian traditions, the wide range of this polarity is well illustrated. At one extreme we find Pali Buddhism, a religious worldview that could be said to valorize contingency in its doctrine of momentariness. It accords status to its scriptures by elevating certain words through identification as *buddhavacana*, the speech of the Buddha. At the other end of the spectrum, Bhartṛhari accords the *Veda* the ultimate cosmic status by pronouncing it uncreated and eternal, the sonic foundation of time and space. As the treatments of Francis Clooney and Anantanand Rambachan make clear, Śaṅkara viewed sacred texts as the preeminent avenue through which the extratextual reality of *brahman* is communicated to a humanity trapped in ignorance. For Advaita Vedānta the sacred texts are crucial, yet they are ultimately contingent, to the degree that they are in, and of, the world. But such a view of scripture was rejected as both heretical and logically self-contradictory in the Vedānta theologies promulgated by thinkers like Vallabha and Madhva.

The sixth and final polarity is ''normativity/selection and reinterpretation.'' This, of course, is *the* crucial polarity for appreciating the interpretive strategies developed by native exegetes, the raison d'être of the study of traditional hermeneutics. The entire dynamic of the hermeneutical enterprise could be understood as an interplay between these two poles. Despite the independent, ontological status awarded specific sacred texts and collections of texts by individual communities, sacred texts are sacred also because they are received as such by living communities of faith. Some sort of normativity is required for self-identity, but selection and reinterpretation are crucial if a tradition is to respond creatively to the changes that affect its life. This ability to change and yet stay the same insures that a tradition will endure. A good illustration of this ability is given by Madhu Wangu as she describes the emergence of a novel *mahātmya* text that integrated Vaiṣṇava and Śaiva motifs in response to new political realities. The process of selection and reinterpretation can be identified in all hermeneutical moments and at all levels of interaction with a text tradition. Patricia Mumme reveals how the selection and reinterpretation of a single *pāda* from the *Bhagavad Gītā* had a momentous effect on the theological self-understanding of the Śrīvaiṣṇava community. José Cabezón examines Vasubandhu's rationale for a Mahāyāna version of this process at work in the establishment of a multi-textual canon.

The process of establishing and then challenging normativity by selection and reinterpretation of sacred texts, the movement between boundedness and openness, the interplay of form and fluidity—each of these polarities similarly evokes multiple examples from our study of traditional hermeneutics. The chapters of this volume provide compelling evidence that sacred text-traditions in South Asia may be understood as both philosophical and poetic, oral and written, transcendent and political, eternal and of recent vintage, injunctive and kataphatic, performative and iconological. This remarkable range of understandings issuing from the religious pluralism of South Asia should not lead us to the erroneous conclusion that these traditions represent a loose amalgam of inchoate views, or that this diversity can by synthesized as an "identity-in-difference" absorbing pluralism into some sort of "spiritual oneness." Both of these conclusions damage the very thing we are trying to understand, and, as we have seen through our study, such conclusions fall away as soon as serious attention is given to the details of historical and religious context. When Bhartṛhari describes ultimate reality as *śabdatattva*, or when Vedānta Deśika interprets the *Bhagavad Gītā*, or when Vasubandhu argues for a Mahāyāna understanding of canon, we are presented with compelling efforts to assert a *particular* view, which its promoter deems as true and then rigorously defends in the face of opposing points of view. Although the religious diversity we have examined, when it is viewed from a cultural and historical distance, may suggest an overall context of almost fantastic scriptural fluidity and openness, this perception of openness must be balanced by the reality of form, boundedness and normativity, often asserted by the native hermeneute quite rigidly, in the context of the individual hermeneutical moment.

This book, then, has sought to illuminate a dynamic and creative interplay of sacred texts and their interpretations in the religions of South Asia. It confounds efforts to arrive at a generic definition of sacred text. A typology of polarities may help to focus attention on the dynamic and relational quality of traditional hermeneutics, but such a typology is merely a heuristic device to be employed so long as it serves the movement toward a deeper understanding of how these texts were understood by the native exegete. Only after we have made the genuine effort to authentically understand—an understanding that we may or may not ultimately achieve—can we ask these traditional thinkers to address our criticisms, and to respond to our concerns about the nature of scripture and its interpretation.

References

Coward, Harold
1990 ''Derrida and Bhartṛhari's Vākyapadīya on the Origin of Language.'' *Philosophy East and West*, 40 (1): 3–16.

Levering, Miriam
1989 *Rethinking Scripture: Essays from a Comparative Perspective*. Albany: SUNY Press.

Contributors

José Ignacio Cabezón is Assistant Professor at the Iliff School of Theology, Denver, Colorado. He has served as an official translator for the Dalai Lama. In addition to articles in the *Journal of Indian Philosophy* and the *Journal of the International Association of Buddhist Studies*, he has published *One Hundred and Eight Verses in Praise of Great Compassion* (1985) and *A Dose of Emptiness* (forthcoming from SUNY Press), both translations from Tibetan texts. He has edited *H.H. The Dalai Lama, The Bodhgaya Interview: 1980–1985* (1988) and *Buddhism, Sexuality, and Gender* (also forthcoming from SUNY Press).

David Carpenter is Assistant Professor of Theology at Saint Joseph's University, Philadelphia, Pennsylvania. He recently completed his Ph.D. with a thesis titled "The Light of the Word: A Comparative Study of the Phenomenon of Revelation." His writings appear in *The Encyclopedia of Religion*, the *Journal of the American Academy of Religion*, as well as in *Wiener Zeitschrift für die Kunde Südasiens*.

Francis X. Clooney, S.J., is Associate Professor of Comparative Religion at Boston College, Boston, Massachusetts. His published articles appear in *History of Religions, Harvard Theological Review, Theological Studies, Journal of the American Academy of Religion, Journal of Indian Philosophy,* and *Numen*. His book *Thinking Ritually: Rediscovering the Pūrva Mīmāṁs of Jaimini* is scheduled for publication in the De Nobili Research Series this year.

John E. Cort is Lecturer at Harvard University, Cambridge, Massachusetts. He recently completed his Ph.D with a thesis titled "Liberation and Well-being: A Study of the Śvetāmbar Mūrtipūjak Jains of North Gujarat." In addition to articles in the *Journal of South Asian Literature* and *Numen* and in edited anthologies, he has published *Bhartrhari: An Old Tree Living by the River* (1983).

CARL W. ERNST is Associate Professor of Religion at Pomona College, Claremont, California. He is a recent recipient of an NEH translation grant. His articles have appeared in *History of Religions, Islamic Culture*, and *The Journal of Religious Studies*, as well as in numerous edited anthologies. He is the author of *Words of Ecstasy in Sufism* (1984).

FRANK J. HOFFMAN is Assistant Professor of Philosophy at West Chester University, West Chester, Pennsylvania. His articles appear in *Religious Studies, Journal of Indian Philosophy, Scottish Journal of Religious Studies, Asian Philosophy,* and *Comprehensive Harmony*. He is the author of *Rationality and Mind in Early Buddhism* (1987).

PATRICIA Y. MUMME is Assistant Professor of Religion at Denison University, Granville, Ohio. In addition to numerous articles in journals and in edited collections, she has published *The Mumukṣuppaṭi of Piḷḷai Lokācārya with Maṇavāḷamāmuni's Commentary* (1987) and *The Śrīvaiṣṇava Theological Dispute: Maṇavāḷamāmuni and Vedānta Deśika* (1988).

VASUDHA NARAYANAN is Associate Professor of Religion at the University of Florida at Gainesville. In addition to numerous articles, she has published *Gods of Flesh, Gods of Stone: The Embodiment of Divinity in India* (1985), *The Way and the Goal: Expressions of Devotion in the Early Śrī Vaīṣṇava Tradition* (1987), and *The Tamil Veda: Piḷḷāṉ's Interpretation of the Tiruvāymoḻi* (1989).

ANANTANAND RAMBACHAN is Assistant Professor at St. Olaf College, Northfield, Minnesota. His writings have appeared in various journals including *Philosophy East and West, Religious Studies, Religion, World Faiths Insight, Theology,* and *Current Dialogue*.

NIKKY-GUNINDER KAUR SINGH is Assistant Professor at Colby College, Waterville, Maine. She is the author of many scholarly articles in the *Journal of Religious Studies, Journal of Medieval Indian Literature,* and *The Journal of Sikh Studies*, as well as in edited collections. She has also published *The Gurū Granth Sāhib: Its Physics and Metaphysics* (1981).

DANIEL P. SHERIDAN is Associate Professor of Religion at Loyola University, New Orleans, Louisiana. His numerous articles have appeared in the *Journal of Dharma, Anima, Horizons, Indian Philosophical Annual, Purana, Journal of Religion, Cross Currents,* and others. He is the author of *The Vedāntic Theism of the Bhāgavata Purāṇa* (1986).

JEFFREY R. TIMM is Associate Professor of Religion at Wheaton College, Norton, Massachusetts. His writings appear in *Philosophy East and West*, *Journal of Ecumenical Studies*, *The Pacific World: Journal of the Institute of Buddhist Studies*, and *The Journal of Dharma*.

MADHU BAZAZ WANGU is a recent recipient of the Ph.D. degree in Religious Studies from the University of Pittsburgh. Her dissertation is titled "The Cult of Khīr Bhavānī: Study, Analysis, and Interpretation of a Kashmiri Goddess."

Index

A

Aagaard-Mogensen, Lars, 212
Abhidhamma, 201, 212
abhidharma, 226
Abhidharmakośa, 238 n.17
Abhinavagupta, 149
abhyāsa, 41
Abū 'Alī al-Daqqāq, 273
Abū Hurayra, 276
Abū Sa'īd ibn Abū al-Khayr, 273, 274
Abū Yazīd al-Bisṭāmī, 273
ācārya(s), 70, 73, 74, 89, 109, 164 n.9
action: path of, 75. See also *karmayoga*
Acyutaprekṣa, 112, 113, 117; becomes Madhva's disciple, 114
adhikaraṇa(s), 23, 50
adhikārī, 42
adhyayana utsava (Festival of Recitation), 87
Advaita Vedānta, 33–43 passim, 47–63 passim, 79, 111, 115, 128, 129; interpretation of the *Veda,* 20; Vallabha's assessment of, 134–136, 137, 138, 141
Advaita Vedānta: A Philosophical Reconstruction, 127
Āgamas, 172, 187; as source of salvific knowledge, 181; concept of 45, 172, 173, 185, 187 n.3; temples devoted to, 182–183; worship of, 180–181
Āgam Jyot [Lamp of the Āgama], 182
Āgam Mandirs, 181
Āgamoday Samiti, 182
Aghoreśvari Bhairavi, 149, 150
Aḥsan al-aqwāl [The Best of Sayings], 282–283
Akapporuḷ, 100 n.10
Āḷavantār (Yāmuna), 97
al-Ḥallāj, 273
Aligarh, 251
al-Qushayrī, 273
ālvār(s), 90, 96, 97
Amalānanda, 60, 64 n.2
Amīr Ḥasan Sijzī Dihlawī, 9, 274, 275, 276, 277, 290
Amritsar, 246, 251
Ānandagiri, 57, 64 n.2
Ānandatīrtha, 111; *See also* Madhva
Anandghana, 247
Ānandsāgarsūri, 182, 183
aṅga/aṅgabāhya distinction, 174
aṅgabāhya, 173
Aṅgas, 172, 173
Antarāy Karm Pūjā, 184
anuvāda, 78
Anuvyākhyāna, 116, 119
Anuyogadvāra Sūtra, 173
apādāna, 23
apauruṣeyatva, 56
apocryphal texts, 223, 224, 233, 288, 291, 236 n.4
apologetics, 52
Appaya Dīkṣita, 64 n.2, 64 n.12
apūrva, 41

Mehta, M. L., 188 n.3
Mere Sāiān Jīo, 248–266 passim
metaphysics, 69–70
Miharbān, 249
Miles, William, 172
Mīmāṁsā, 21, 33, 39, 47, 53, 56, 58, 70, 78; definition of *Veda,* 25; exegesis of the *Veda,* 34; on *mantras* 30 n.10; view of the *Upaniṣads,* 33
Mīmāṁsā-Vedānta, 63
Mir Khwurd, 275
Modi, P. M., 48
mokṣa, 45 n.13, 76, 77, 79, 182
Morals of the Heart, 9. See also *Fawā' id al-fu' ād*
mother-of-pearl/silver analogy, 76, 82 n.15
Muḥammad, 273, 276, 277
Mu'īn al-Dīn Chishtī, 271, 272
mukāshafat, 280
Mūlamadhyamakākarikās, 238
Mūlasūtras, 172
Müller, F. Max, 2
Mumukṣuppaṭi, 75, 82 n.12
Muni Jambū Vijay, 182
Muni Puṇya Vijay, 182
mūrti, 181
mūrtipūjā, 183
Murty, S., 48
music, 87, 250, 264
mysticism, 279, 285

N

Nafā' is al-anfās wa laṭā' if al-alfāẓ [Choice Sayings and Elegant Words], 281–282, 283, 288
Nāgārjuna, 223
nāgas, 148, 150
nāgas and *piśāchas:* cults of, 158
Nagatomi, Masatoshi, 196
Nakamura, Hajime, 204, 205, 239 n.21
Nakkīrar, 100 n.10
Namaskār Mahāmantra Mandir, 183
Namaskār Mantra, 183
Nammāḻvār, 7, 86, 97, 98; as ideal devotee, 89
Nampiḷḷai, 91–93, 97, 100, n.7, 102 n.20
Nānak, *see* Gurū Nānak
Nanda sword, 115
Nandī Sūtra, 173, 185
Nañjīyar, 91–92, 100 n.7, 102 n.20
Nappiṉṉai, 98
Nārāyaṇa, 114, 115, 119, 121
Nārāyaṇa Paṇḍitācārya, 111–117, 119, 301; condemnation of Śaṅkara, 111
Nārāyaṇa/Viṣṇu, 111, 113, 119, 120
Nāthamuni, 86–87, 94
natural theology, 134
Nava Smaraṇa, 186
Neogy, Prithwish, 205
nihilism, 234
Nikāya Buddhism, 195–212 passim
Nīlmapurāna, 149
nirguṇa brahman, 62, 129
nirguṇa/saguṇa distinction, 51, 52, 55
Nirīśvara Sāṃkhya, 115
Nirmalā, 247
Nishi, Amane, 205
niyamas, 26
Niẓām al-Dīn Awliyā', 272, 274–277, 279, 286
Nizami, Khakiq Ahmad, 277, 279, 288
Norman, K. R., 202, 204
Nyāya, 53, 130, 131, 134, 141
nyāyas, 61

O

Oberhammer, G., 30 n.15
O'Flaherty, Wendy Doniger, 3, 162 n.1
oṃ, 20, 21
Ong, Walter, 85, 102 n.19
ontology, 22, 129, 130, 133, 142; Sikh, 250
oral: commentary, 93; recitation, 87; sources, 286
orality, 271, 272–274, 285, 291; and writtenness, 302–303; in Hinduism, 4, 102 n.19

P

Q

W

Y

Z